Prose Models

FOURTH EDITION

FOURTH EDITION

Prose
Models

GERALD LEVIN
The University of Akron

HARCOURT BRACE JOVANOVICH, INC.
New York   San Diego   Chicago   San Francisco   Atlanta

ISBN: 0-15-572278-6

Library of Congress Catalog Card Number: 77-83616

Printed in the United States of America

Preface

The purpose of the Fourth Edition is the same as that of the first three editions: to introduce the elements of rhetoric and logic in prose composition through the analysis of prose models. The selections are both models of good writing and interesting discussions of important ideas. New to this edition are the following sections: Addition and Modification (of the sentence), Analysis (including definition, division, comparison and contrast, example, and cause and effect), and Controversy.

The book progresses from part to whole. The first half considers such topics as emphasis and the coordination and subordination of ideas in the paragraph and the sentence; the second half considers their use in the whole essay. Throughout, the sections are developed cumulatively, building on earlier definitions and discussions and providing a continuity for class use that is difficult with a random collection of illustrative selections. In this way students are encouraged to think about the rhetoric and logic of the essay through close analysis of models followed by the writing of paragraphs, sentences, and essays. Each section is self-contained, however, and can be taught in a different order whenever that seems desirable.

A discussion of each rhetorical or logical topic follows the first selection in each section. For this edition, many of the discussions have been simplified, including those dealing with the principles of logical analysis. Wherever possible, the questions and writing assignments that follow each selection are based on the rhetorical or logical topic of that selection as well as on its content. For the first time, an Instructor's Manual is available for *Prose Models*. It provides suggestions for teaching each selection, alternative rhetorical topics for many of the selections, and answers to all the questions.

Of the 112 selections, 52 are new to this edition and 43 are complete essays or sections of books complete in themselves. In the first part of the book, the selections by Peter Fleming, Dereck Williamson, George Orwell, and Thomas Middleton, and "Central Park" by John Updike are complete essays. In the second part, only the selections by Jacques Maritain, Edward Jay Epstein, and Bernard Shaw are excerpts from sections of books. Writers new to this edition include Eudora Welty, Paul Fussell, May Sarton, Annie Dillard, Robert Coles, Joyce Maynard, Robert Benchley, Art Buchwald, Shirley Jackson, L. E. Sissman, and Barry Commoner. The book contains new essays on ecology, the media, the problems of growing up in America, and capital punishment. Some of the essays have been paired to provide contrasts in point of view and ideas; examples of such pairings are the essays by Bernard Shaw, George F. Will, and Anthony Lewis, which offer contrasting views on capital punishment; and the essays by Barbara Ward and Jonathan Swift, which offer contrasting discussions of hunger.

Ideas introduced in the shorter selections that open the book are often developed at greater length or from other points of view in the essays in Part Two. A thematic table of contents groups the selections for quick reference and illustrates this continuity of ideas. The final essay by Walter Houghton is an example of a documented paper.

Again I wish to thank Forrest Read for suggestions and corrections in the original manuscript. Alan Hart, The University of Akron, read the first draft of the logic discussions, and made valuable suggestions for the revision of these sections. I also wish to thank the following people, all of The University of Akron, for their helpful suggestions: Mary Alice DeHaven, William A. Francis, Bruce Holland, Julia A. Hull, David L. Jones, Alice J. MacDonald, Ruth Messenger, Arthur L. Palacas, D'Orsay Pearson, Sally K. Slocum, Frederik N. Smith, James Switzer, Cathryn Taliaferro, and Arlene A. Toth.

Many other helpful suggestions came from instructors across the country who have taught from the Third Edition. These include Mildred R. Bensmiller, Iowa Wesleyan College; Ralph H. Bierce, College of San Mateo; Simone J. Billings, San Francisco State University; Dolores L. Bowyer, Phoenix College; Wilsonia E. D. Cherry, University of North Carolina, Chapel Hill; Peter Chetta, Iona College; Martha E. Cook, Longwood College; John Fleming, West Valley Community College; Donna Givens, Iowa State University; Daniel J. Harper, Cabrillo College; Douglas Kilday, University of Wisconsin, Oshkosh; Aarona Kohlman, Graceland College;

Colleen J. McElroy, University of Washington; Rex A. McGuinn and William M. Ramsey, both of the University of North Carolina, Chapel Hill; Grant C. Roti, Housatonic Regional Community College; Robert B. Siegle, University of North Carolina, Chapel Hill; Ellen Solomon, New York Institute of Technology, Old Westbury; Delija J. Valiukenas, Bridgewater State College; T. C. Ware, University of Tennessee, Chattanooga; Steven Weisenburger, University of Washington; and Joseph H. Wessling, Xavier University.

My wife, Lillian Levin, and Elizabeth and Sylvia Levin helped me in preparing the manuscript. Natalie Bowen and Eben W. Ludlow, both of Harcourt Brace Jovanovich, gave me valuable advice and assistance at each stage of the revision, and I am grateful for their encouragement.

GERALD LEVIN

Contents

PART ONE
The Elements of the Essay

PART TWO
The Whole Essay

EXPOSITION   207

PART ONE

The Elements of the Essay

The Paragraph

TOPIC SENTENCE

EDWIN WAY TEALE

Country Superstitions

[1] In the folklore of the country, numerous superstitions relate to winter weather. [2] Back-country farmers examine their corn husks—the thicker the husk, the colder the winter. [3] They watch the acorn crop—the more acorns, the more severe the season. [4] They observe where white-faced hornets place their paper nests—the higher they are, the deeper will be the snow. [5] They examine the size and shape and color of the spleens of butchered hogs for clues to the severity of the season. [6] They keep track of the blooming of dogwood in the spring—the more abundant the blooms, the more bitter the cold in January. [7] When chipmunks carry their tails high and squirrels have heavier fur and mice come into country houses early in the fall, the superstitious gird themselves for a long, hard winter. [8] Without any scientific basis, a wider-than-usual black band on a woolly-bear caterpillar is accepted as a sign that winter will arrive early and stay late. [9] Even the way a cat sits beside the stove carries its message to the credulous. [10] According to a belief once widely held in the Ozarks, a cat sitting with its tail to the fire indicates very cold weather is on the way.

COUNTRY SUPERSTITIONS: In *Wandering Through Winter* by Edwin Way Teale (New York: Dodd, Mead and Company, 1966). Reprinted by permission of the publisher. Selection title by editor.

DISCUSSION: TOPIC SENTENCE

The topic sentence is exactly what the term suggests: a statement of subject, or topic, of the paragraph, usually presented at the beginning. The topic sentence may be reduced to a single word, as in these opening sentences of a Dickens novel:

> London. Michaelmas Term lately over, and the Lord Chancellor sitting in Lincoln's Inn Hall. Implacable November weather. As much mud in the streets, as if the waters had but newly retired from the face of the earth. . . .—*Bleak House*

Usually the topic sentence is a complete statement of the central or topic idea. This topic idea may be repeated in the course of the paragraph, or restated at the end through the details of the discussion:

> There is something depressing about French eighteenth-century literature, especially that of the latter half of the century [*topic sentence*]. All those sprightly memoirs and risky stories and sentimental effusions constitute, perhaps, the dreariest body of literature we know, once we do know it. The French are essentially critics of life, rather than creators of life. And when the life itself runs rather thin, as it did in the eighteenth century, and the criticism rattles all the faster, it just leaves one feeling wretched [*topic sentence restated*].—D. H. Lawrence, "The Good Man"

In short, the topic sentence introduces an impression, an idea, a consideration, or a question—to be developed in specific detail, examined, or answered in the paragraph.

Occasionally a paragraph will open with a transitional sentence linking it to the previous paragraph or serving as a lead-in to the topic sentence:

> At the outset we run into a difficulty that can be no more than acknowledged. The Middle Ages regarded both the knight and the saint as complementary facets of a single ideal, the Christian; both were needed servants of God and of His order on earth.—Crane Brinton, *A History of Western Morals*

Occasionally the topic sentence appears toward the middle or at the end of the paragraph, a series of details building to it. The topic sentence is said to be *implied* when the details make the point without a statement of the topic idea.

QUESTIONS

1. The topic sentence of Teale's paragraph—sentence 1—states the main idea; sentences 2–10 illustrate it. What do the illustrations tell us about country life?
2. Where later in the paragraph does Teale remind the reader of his topic idea?

WRITING ASSIGNMENTS

Describe a series of superstitions relating to another season of the year or to a particular activity. Build your paragraph to a conclusion about these superstitions.

Write your own definition of *superstition,* basing it on various superstitions you hold. Describe each of them briefly but informatively. Your topic sentence might state your definition, or it might introduce your example, your definition coming at the end of the paragraph.

PETER FLEMING
The End of the World

¹The other day a great many people in Rome became suddenly and inexplicably convinced that the world was going to end at midnight on Monday; the Vatican had to issue a statement saying "there is nothing to warrant the present panic." ²When I read about this I began to wonder how, if the British nation knew for a fact that the world was going to end in twenty-four hours' time, it would spend those hours. ³I suppose that most people, including many who had not done such a thing for years, would go to church. ⁴What else would happen? ⁵Except for midwives, stockmen, B.B.C. announcers, the crews of ships at sea and keepers in zoological gardens, hardly anybody would have any reason to do any work. ⁶If the Government recommended a "business as usual" policy, would it work? ⁷There wouldn't be much point in the shops

THE END OF THE WORLD: In *My Aunt's Rhinoceros* by Peter Fleming. © 1956 by Peter Fleming. Reprinted by permission of Simon and Schuster, Inc., and Rupert Hart-Davis Ltd.

or the banks staying open, since money and goods would be value-less; and the schools (which in Rome were poorly attended on Monday) might just as well be closed. [8] It would, on the other hand, be a pity to cancel cricket fixtures. [9] Cricket is one of the few forms of human activity which would not be robbed, both for players and spectators, of all meaning and all interest by the fact that the world was about to end; it would still be worth hitting a six or holding a catch, when designing a cathedral or assassinating a tyrant had become completely pointless acts. [10] But I suspect that most people would spend an anxious, frustrated and probably rather boring day, irked by remembrance of all the things they had always wanted to do and by the realization that, if it was not too late, it was either impossible or useless to do them now.

QUESTIONS

1. Fleming's paragraph is a short essay, complete in itself. Which of the first two sentences states the topic idea? How are these open-ing sentences related to each other?
2. Does Fleming reach a specific conclusion or thesis about people, or does he instead present a series of random observations about how people would spend their last hours?
3. Fleming is writing for a British audience. If he had been writing for an American audience, what similar examples might he have cho-sen?

WRITING ASSIGNMENT

Write a paragraph on another form of human activity that, in your opinion, would be robbed of all meaning if the end of the world were imminent. Use your topic sentence to introduce your main idea—or, if you prefer, to state it fully.

ANTHONY BAILEY

The Qualities of the Dutch

1. "Little" is a term much used in Holland. It comes not so much as a separate word, *klein,* but as the suffix *-je,* attached to the end of almost any word, like *straatje,* little street, or *huisje,* little house. A *dubbeltje* is a small coin worth ten Dutch cents and *meisje* is a young miss; if she is a very little girl she might be called a *klein meisje.* The diminutive bespeaks deprecation (*kippetjes* are not only little chickens but ladies of little virtue) and affection (*poffertjes* are scrumptious miniature pancakes). "Come on, Pietje," one says to one's friend Piet, who is pie-eyed drunk and needs to be helped homeward lest he fall and knock his head against the *kinderhoofdjes,* tiny heads of little children, the nickname for the cobblestones still used together with bricks for hand-paving the streets and sidewalks of this always sinking and settling land. The Dutch like small things. They cherish objects, knickknacks, mementoes, like dried flowers, seashells, pieces of wood or porcelain, all talismans and touchstones. In Scheveningen one day I met a hydraulic engineer who had on his desk three small bricks he couldn't refrain from caressing; they were from a house that was being built for him, one red-brown, one grey, and one glazed black, each brick not only with its own color and texture but its own response to the light and climate of the moment. The Dutch often insist that big things are not for them; for example, Rotterdam and The Hague have never been properly incorporated as cities; they are villages; and if Amsterdam is a city, at least it is a relatively small and cozy city. What is small has value. One can cope with it, look after it, find its proper place, and properly maintain it. It was a Dutchman, Anton van Leeuwenhoek (1632–1723) who perfected the microscope; he was the first man to see a microbe.

· · ·

2. This turning in, this traveling in the interior, is something the Dutch have learned to do even in unpropitious circumstances. One

THE QUALITIES OF THE DUTCH: In *The Light in Holland* by Anthony Bailey. Copyright © 1970 by Anthony Bailey. Most of the material originally appeared in *The New Yorker* in slightly different form. Reprinted by permission of Alfred A. Knopf, Inc. Selection title by editor.

feels that in the most public of worlds, they have discovered how to get wrapped up in themselves. I have passed houses at night and looked in, as one is encouraged to look in through those uncurtained windows, to see the head of the household seated in a self-created pool of privacy, sometimes not reading the paper or book before him, not smoking the pipe in his hand or sipping the gin on the table, cut off as if with the thickest of curtains from his wife sewing or his children reading—simply sitting with his head on one hand, staring and thinking. If you could get round in front and look into his eyes, you might see that look, fixed on a point halfway between you and himself, which Rembrandt painted in his great self-portraits, the look of a man staring at himself in a mirror or in the mirror of his own mind, the look of someone trying to find an answer to the question of how to balance the two demands of life— the demand of possessions, of the need to acquire and then look after *things;* and the demand of ideas, of the spirit, of all the insubstantial daydreams one needs to give time to, even if it is but as a never-ending brooding on the question: What am I doing here?

3.   To me, being by myself means being in a room alone. The Dutch, like children from big families, can be by themselves in a room with six other people or on a canal bank lined with people fishing, almost shoulder to shoulder. Stand on any street corner in Amsterdam at 5:30 in the evening and watch the phalanxes of bicycles go by—a sight not quite what it used to be, but still impressive enough. If you pick at random one serenely pedaling individual from the thick, staggered formation, you see that he isn't really looking at the city, the street, or the other bicyclists around him. He seems aware only of a small portion of space, a bubble within which he and his bike exist with a few spare inches outside his knuckles on the handlebars, his twirling feet, his steady shoulders. He is secure within this space which encloses him and moves with him, the way energy moves through water, giving an appearance of fast forward motion to a wave. Then the traffic light has changed, he is gone, and others have whirled up to the junction, jousting with each other in a remote, impersonal way, ignoring an interloping car or a sputtering *bromfiets.* On each face—the face of a girl, the face of a dignified gentleman wearing a hat—you may glimpse the most private of smiles. Pedaling homeward, they have their own thoughts as their wheels revolve and cars and trams and *brommers* assail them from four or even six directions, the man on the right, whatever his vehicle, having the right of way

which he—sometimes with courage rather than sense—always takes, their reflexes operating splendidly though their minds are elsewhere. These Amsterdam rush-hour bicycles always move me. They are a wonder, like salmon going upstream, demonstrating as they do that in the most crowded places a human being can go on being himself—can become even more himself—and that, in such a place, if you pause for a moment, you can't help but be aware of it.

QUESTIONS

1. These paragraphs are taken from a chapter of Bailey's book describing the people of Holland. What sort of illustrations does Bailey provide in paragraph 1?
2. Paragraph 2 introduces a later passage of the chapter. What is the topic sentence, and what is its purpose?
3. How is the opening sentence of paragraph 3 related to the topic idea of paragraph 2?
4. What is the topic idea of paragraph 3—what it means to be alone generally, or what it means to be alone in Holland? Which of these ideas do the details of the paragraph develop?
5. Does sentence 11 of paragraph 3 merely restate the first sentence, or does it introduce a new idea—based on details of the Dutch cyclists?

WRITING ASSIGNMENTS

In a single paragraph illustrate a quality of the people in your neighborhood, town, or city. Draw your examples from different areas of experience, as Bailey does. Write for an audience that has not seen the place you are describing.

In a single paragraph develop an idea concerning people your age—perhaps their attitude toward privacy—and support it with a series of examples. State your idea early in the paragraph and restate it at the end.

Drawing on your experience, discuss in one or two paragraphs the obstacles that a teenager finds in seeking privacy. Build your discussion to a conclusion about the special problems of teenagers.

MAIN AND SUBORDINATE IDEAS

SALLY CARRIGHAR
The Blast Furnace

1.   We were a father and his first-born, a four-year-old girl, setting out every Sunday afternoon to see the industrial marvels of Cleveland, Ohio. The young man had grown up in a smaller Canadian town and he was delighted with Cleveland, which hummed and clanged with the vast new developments steel had made possible. In temperament he was anything but an engineer; here however he was excited to feel that he had jumped into the very heart of the torrent of progress.

2.   Most often we walked on the banks of the Cuyahoga River to see the drawbridge come apart and rise up, like giant black jaws taking a bite of the sky, so that boats could go through: the long freighters that brought iron ore from Lake Superior, other large and small freighters, fishing boats, passenger steamers. My father's eyes never tired of watching them make their smooth way up and down the river. His father, born in Amsterdam of a seagoing family, had been a skipper on the Great Lakes. Perhaps my father too should have been a sailor, but he was something nearly as satisfying—he worked for a railroad.

3.   And so we went to the roundhouse where the steam engines stood when they were not pulling trains. They had all entered through the same door but inside their tracks spread apart, as gracefully as the ribs of a lady's fan. My father knew a great deal about engines, he knew the names of some of these and he walked among them with pride.

4.   On our way to the roundhouse we passed through the freight yards where long trains of boxcars lay on their sidings. My father said that the cars belonged to different railroads and came from various parts of the country, being coupled together here because

all those in one train were bound for the same destination. This was getting too complicated but there was nothing complicated about my father's emotion when he said, "Working for a railroad is like living everywhere in the country at once!" A characteristic enchantment came into his eyes and voice, a contagious exhilaration which meant that anything it attached to was good. Living everywhere was something that even a child could grasp vaguely and pleasantly.

5.   My father and I made other trips and best were the ones to the blast furnaces. He explained how the iron ore from the boats was mixed with coal and carried in little cars to the top of the chimney above the furnace. It was dumped in, and as it fell down "a special kind of very hot air" was blown into it. The coal and iron ore caught fire, and below they fell into great tubs as melting metal, a pinkish gold liquid, incandescent as the sun is when it is starting to set. The man and child were allowed to go rather near the vats, to feel the scorching heat and to drown their gaze in the glowing boil. All the rest of the building was dark; the silhouettes of the men who worked at the vats were black shadows. Wearing long leather aprons, they moved about the vats ladling off the slag. That was very skilled work, my father said; the men had to know just how much of the worthless slag to remove. For years afterwards, when we could no longer spend Sunday afternoons on these expeditions, we used to go out of our house at night to see the pink reflections from the blast furnaces on the clouds over Cleveland. We could remember that we had watched the vatfuls of heavily moving gold, and those events from the past were an unspoken bond between us.

6.   Someone once said, "Your father must have been trying to turn you into a boy. He'd probably wanted his first child to be a son." Perhaps; but it was not strange to him to show a girl the achievements of men. He thought of women as human beings and assumed that they, even one very young, would be interested in anything that was interesting to him. He had absorbed that attitude from the women he'd grown up with, his mother and her four sisters, all of whom led adventurous lives. His favorite Aunt Chris had married a clipper captain and sailed with him all her life. When they retired, having seen the entire world, they chose to settle in Burma. Another aunt married one of the Morgan family, who established the famous breed of Morgan horses, and took up a homestead in Manitoba. Aunt Mary, a physician's wife, went with

him out to San Francisco during the Gold Rush and stayed there. The fourth aunt had married the inspector of ships' chronometers at Quebec; and my father's mother, of course, had married her skipper from Holland. In the winter when he was not on his ship he ran a factory for making barrel staves that he had established in western Kentucky—all this and the fathering of five children by the time he was twenty-eight, when he lost his life in a notorious Lake Erie storm. His wife, a musician, brought up her five without complaint, just as her mother, also an early widow, had reared her five gallant girls. With his memories of women like these it was not surprising that my father would wish, even somewhat prematurely, to show his daughter the things that were thrilling to him. I did not comprehend all his family history at four but I did absorb the impression that girls and women reached out for life eagerly and that it was natural for them to be interested in absolutely everything.

DISCUSSION: MAIN AND SUBORDINATE IDEAS

The main idea of a paragraph may be developed through a series of subordinate ideas that illustrate or develop it. Each of these ideas in turn may be illustrated or developed:

> Although the forest looks peaceful it supports incessant warfare, most of which is hidden and silent. [*topic sentence: main idea of paragraph*]
>> [1] For thirty-five years the strong have been subduing the weak. [*subordinate idea: specific detail about the forest*]
>>> [2] The blueberries that once flourished on the mountain have been destroyed. [*subordinate idea: a more specific detail—blueberries*]
>>> [3] All the trees are individuals, as all human beings are individuals; and every tree poses a threat to every other tree. [*subordinate idea: another more specific detail—trees*]
>>>> [4] The competition is so fierce that you can hardly penetrate some of the thickets where the lower branches of neighboring trees are interlocked in a blind competition for survival. [*subordinate idea: development of sentence 3*]—Brooks Atkinson, "The Warfare in the Forest Is Not Wanton"

In longer paragraphs, the main idea may be distinguished by repeating or restating it, by opening the paragraph with it as Atkinson does, or by building the paragraph to a statement of it. When you organize a paragraph, keep in mind that the beginning and ending are usually the most emphatic parts because of their prominence.

QUESTIONS

1. In paragraph 1 Carrighar develops her opening sentence—the main idea of the paragraph—with specific detail about her father. What is the main idea of paragraph 2, and how does she use the detail of the paragraph to develop it?
2. Paragraph 4 moves from specific detail to the main idea. What is that idea, and how does the author give it prominence?
3. Which of the subordinate ideas in paragraph 5 are in turn illustrated or developed?
4. Paragraphs 1–5 are subordinate to paragraph 6, which draws a conclusion from the experiences described, and develops this conclusion through details of a different sort. What is this conclusion, and what new details develop it? How is this conclusion—the main idea of the paragraph—restated later in the paragraph and made prominent?

WRITING ASSIGNMENTS

Write several paragraphs describing childhood experiences with a parent or relative that taught you something about the adult world and about yourself. Begin with these truths, or build the paragraphs to them, as Carrighar does.

Write several paragraphs about the impressions you received as a child about girls and women, from information you received or impressions you developed about women in your family. If you wish, contrast these impressions with those you received about boys and men.

Discuss how particular childhood experiences with friends led you to discoveries about yourself and the world that conflicted with values and ideas held by your parents and teachers. Use this discussion to draw a conclusion about growing up.

UNITY

EUDORA WELTY

The Corner Store

1.   Our Little Store rose right up from the sidewalk; standing in a street of family houses, it alone hadn't any yard in front, any tree or flower bed. It was a plain frame building covered over with brick. Above the door, a little railed porch ran across on an upstairs level and four windows with shades were looking out. But I didn't catch on to those.

2.   Running in out of the sun, you met what seemed total obscurity inside. There were almost tangible smells—licorice recently sucked in a child's cheek, dill pickle brine that had leaked through a paper sack in a fresh trail across the wooden floor, ammonia-loaded ice that had been hoisted from wet croker sacks and slammed into the icebox with its sweet butter at the door, and perhaps the smell of still untrapped mice.

3.   Then through the motes of cracker dust, cornmeal dust, the Gold Dust of the Gold Dust Twins that the floor had been swept out with, the realities emerged. Shelves climbed to high reach all the way around, set out with not too much of any one thing but a lot of things—lard, molasses, vinegar, starch, matches, kerosine, Octagon soap (about a year's worth of octagon-shaped coupons cut out and saved brought a signet ring addressed to you in the mail). It was up to you to remember what you came for, while your eye traveled from cans of sardines to tin whistles to ice cream salt to harmonicas to flypaper (over your head, batting around on a thread beneath the blades of the ceiling fan, stuck with its testimonial catch).

4.   Its confusion may have been in the eye of its beholder. Enchantment is cast upon you by all those things you weren't supposed to have need for, to lure you close to wooden tops you'd outgrown, boy's marbles and agates in little net pouches, small rubber balls that wouldn't bounce straight, frail, frazzly kite string, clay bubble pipes that would snap off in your teeth, the stiffest

THE CORNER STORE: Reprinted by permission of Russell & Volkening, Inc., as agents for the author. Copyright © 1975 by Eudora Welty.

scissors. You could contemplate those long narrow boxes of sparklers gathering dust while you waited for it to be the Fourth of July or Christmas, and noisemakers in the shape of tin frogs for somebody's birthday party you hadn't been invited to yet, and see that they were all marvelous.

5.   You might not have even looked for Mr. Sessions when he came around his store cheese (as big as a doll's house) and in front of the counter looking for you. When you'd finally asked him for, and received from him in its paper bag, whatever single thing it was that you had been sent for, the nickel that was left over was yours to spend.

6.   Down at a child's eye level, inside those glass jars with mouths in their sides through which the grocer could run his scoop or a child's hand might be invited to reach for a choice, were wineballs, all-day suckers, gumdrops, peppermints. Making a row under the glass of a counter were the Tootsie Rolls, Hershey bars, Goo Goo Clusters, Baby Ruths. And whatever was the name of those pastilles that came stacked in a cardboard cylinder with a cardboard lid? They were thin and dry, about the size of tiddledy-winks, and in the shape of twisted rosettes. A kind of chocolate dust came out with them when you shook them out in your hand. Were they chocolate? I'd say, rather, they were brown. They didn't taste of anything at all, unless it was wood. Their attraction was the number you got for a nickel.

7.   Making up your mind, you circled the store around and around, around the pickle barrel, around the tower of Crackerjack boxes; Mr. Sessions had built it for us himself on top of a packing case like a house of cards.

8.   If it seemed too hot for Crackerjacks, I might get a cold drink. Mr. Sessions might have already stationed himself by the cold-drinks barrel, like a mind reader. Deep in ice water that looked black as ink, murky shapes—that would come up as Coca-Colas, Orange Crushes, and various flavors of pop—were all swimming around together. When you gave the word, Mr. Sessions plunged his bare arm in to the elbow and fished out your choice, first try. I favored a locally bottled concoction called Lake's Celery. (What else could it be called? It was made by a Mr. Lake out of celery. It was a popular drink here for years but was not known universally, as I found out when I arrived in New York and ordered one in the Astor bar.) You drank on the premises, with feet set wide apart to miss the drip, and gave him back his bottle and your nickel.

9.   But he didn't hurry you off. A standing scales was by the door, with a stack of iron weights and a brass slide on the balance arm, that would weigh you up to three hundred pounds. Mr. Sessions, whose hands were gentle and smelled of carbolic, would lift you up and set your feet on the platform, hold your loaf of bread for you, and, taking his time while you stood still for him, he would make certain of what you weighed today. He could even remember what you weighed the last time, so you could subtract and announce how much you'd gained. That was good-bye.

DISCUSSION: UNITY

A paragraph or essay will be unified if its writer deals with one idea at a time, without shifting abruptly from one to another. Writers must have clearly in mind their reason for proceeding from one idea to the next—what we will call in this book the *principle of order*. In a unified paragraph each sentence is related to a central, controlling idea. More than this, the relation of main to subordinate ideas is clarified for the reader, sometimes through transitional words and phrases, and sometimes, as in the following passage, through parallel phrases, clauses, or sentences:

> Though we like to tell ourselves that our purpose is to solve the social problem by ministering to men's needs, in practice we have a conception of human nature, and derived from it an educational system and a commercial and political propaganda, which treat all needs as unlimited. [*topic sentence: central, controlling idea*] *No income can therefore be sufficient to satisfy men's needs.* For the appetite merely grows from feeding it. *No standard of living is a standard.* For there is always a more luxurious standard. *No prosperity is rich enough.* For the statistical curves on the charts might always go higher. *No nation can be big enough and no state can be powerful enough.* For until someone has conquered the whole world, it is always possible to be bigger and greater than you are.—Walter Lippmann, "An Image of Man for Liberal Democracy" (italics added)

Paragraph unity demands that we consider the audience we are writing for. One kind of organization may be suited to one audience but not to another: schoolchildren need the details of a process like boiling water before the reason why bubbles form can be explained to them; scientists can be given the principles or theory of a newly discovered process before being given the details. The choices open to the writer are sometimes restricted by the subject matter; for example, an account of how the planet Neptune was discovered must be mainly chronological. However the writer may combine this chronological account with subordinate ideas presented in a different order. The principles of order possible in the paragraph are many: the writer may proceed from the least to the most interesting or important idea; or from the general to the specific—from the theory of combustion to the details of that process; or from the specific details of how oxygen combines with the substance being burned to the general theory that explains this process; or from the simple to the complex—from simple effects of gravity like falling to complex effects, like the collapse of giant stars into "black holes" through their internal gravity.

Practiced writers often make these choices in organization without giving much if any thought to them. They may favor some particular organization of ideas—a manner shaped by their own way of looking at experience or by their own habits of thought, perhaps a habit of beginning with specific details and experiences and proceeding to general principles and ideas. We sometimes refer to a particular manner or habit as a "style of thought," a matter we will discuss later.

QUESTIONS

1. The principles of order in Welty's paragraphs, taken from a longer essay on the corner store, are chronological and spatial. What parts of the description are presented chronologically, and what parts are presented spatially?
2. What is the main idea of paragraph 8? How are subordinate ideas distinguished from the main idea?
3. What overall impression does Welty convey of the store? Does she state the impression directly, or does she let it emerge from the details of her description? What details most contribute to this impression?
4. Does Welty present each feature of the store and her experience one at a time without repetition, or does she return to earlier features and details?

WRITING ASSIGNMENTS

Describe some store or shop you remember from childhood. Decide on a dominant impression and make your details contribute to that impression. Organize each paragraph through one or more principles of order. Remember that your reader probably has not seen the store.

Welty states in paragraph 4: "Its confusion may have been in the eye of its beholder." Write a description of another kind of store or institution—a public library, a government office, a schoolroom or cafeteria—and show how a sense of confusion may arise from the feelings and attitude of the viewer.

MARY McCARTHY
Uncle Myers

[1] And here was another strange thing about Myers. [2] He not only did nothing for a living but he appeared to have no history. [3] He came from Elkhart, Indiana, but beyond this fact nobody seemed to know anything about him—not even how he had met my aunt Margaret. [4] Reconstructed from his conversation, a picture of Elkhart emerged for us that showed it as a flat place consisting chiefly of ball parks, poolrooms, and hardware stores. [5] Aunt Margaret came from Chicago, which consisted of the Loop, Marshall Field's, assorted priests and monsignors, and the black-and-white problem. [6] How had these two worlds impinged? [7] Where our family spoke freely of its relations, real and imaginary, Myers spoke of no one, not even a parent. [8] At the very beginning, when my father's old touring car, which had been shipped on, still remained in our garage, Myers had certain seedy cronies whom he took riding in it or who simply sat in it in our driveway, as if anchored in a houseboat; but when the car went, they went or were banished. [9] Uncle Myers and Aunt Margaret had no friends, no couples with whom they exchanged visits—only a middle-aged, black-haired, small, emaciated woman with a German name and a yellowed skin whom we were taken to see one afternoon because she was dying of cancer. [10] This protracted death had the aspect of a public execution, which was doubtless why Myers took us to it; that is, it was a spectacle and it was free, and it inspired restlessness and depression. [11] Myers was the perfect type of rootless or municipalized man who finds his pleasures in the handouts or overflow of an industrial civilization. [12] He enjoyed standing on a curbstone, watching parades, the more nondescript the better, the

UNCLE MYERS: In "Tin Butterfly," copyright, 1951, by Mary McCarthy. Reprinted from her volume *Memories of a Catholic Girlhood* by permission of Harcourt Brace Jovanovich, Inc. Selection title by editor.

Labor Day parade being his favorite, and next to that a military parade, followed by the commercial parades with floats and girls dressed in costumes; he would even go to Lake Calhoun or Lake Harriet for doll-carriage parades and competitions of children dressed as Indians. [13] He liked bandstands, band concerts, public parks devoid of grass; sky writing attracted him; he was quick to hear of a department-store demonstration where colored bubbles were blown, advertising a soap, to the tune of "I'm Forever Blowing Bubbles," sung by a mellifluous soprano. [14] He collected coupons and tinfoil, bundles of newspaper for the old rag-and-bone man (thus interfering seriously with our school paper drives), free samples of cheese at Donaldson's, free tickets given out by a neighborhood movie house to the first installment of a serial—in all the years we lived with him, we never saw a full-length movie but only those truncated beginnings. [15] He was also fond of streetcar rides (could the system have been municipally owned?), soldiers' monuments, cemeteries, big, coarse flowers like cannas and cockscombs set in beds by city gardeners. [16] Museums did not appeal to him, though we did go one night with a large crowd to see Marshal Foch on the steps of the Art Institute. [17] He was always weighing himself on penny weighing machines. [18] He seldom left the house except on one of these purposeless errands, or else to go to a ball game, by himself. [19] In the winter, he spent the days at home in the den, or in the kitchen, making candy. [20] He often had enormous tin trays of decorated fondants cooling in the cellar, which leads my brother Kevin to think today that at one time in Myers' life he must have been a pastry cook or a confectioner. [21] He also liked to fashion those little figures made of pipe cleaners that were just then coming in as favors in the better candy shops, but Myers used *old* pipe cleaners, stained yellow and brown. [22] The bonbons, with their pecan or almond topping, that he laid out in such perfect rows were for his own use; we were permitted to watch him set them out, but never—and my brother Kevin confirms this—did we taste a single one.

QUESTIONS

1. At the beginning of the paragraph Mary McCarthy discusses Uncle Myers' history and proceeds to his friendships and interests. What are these interests?
2. Why is the information about the pipe cleaners and the candy

saved for the end of the paragraph? How would the impression of Uncle Myers have been changed if the paragraph ended with the details of his cronies and his collections?

3. The paragraph is unified because McCarthy discusses one thing at a time, without returning haphazardly to earlier considerations. What is the principle of order in the whole paragraph? What is gained by not dividing the paragraph into several shorter ones?

4. Does McCarthy directly state her attitude toward Uncle Myers, or does she let it emerge through what she shows about him? What is that attitude?

5. How else might the paragraph have been organized to develop a different idea or impression?

WRITING ASSIGNMENTS

Build a paragraph around a central impression of an unusual person, selecting details from different areas of experience to develop this impression. Do not state your attitude toward the person; let your details reveal it.

Rewrite the paragraph on Uncle Myers, presenting the details in a different order, and providing a new topic sentence. In a short second paragraph explain your reasons for organizing the new paragraph as you did.

TRANSITIONS

GEORGE ORWELL
The Army Parade-Step

[1]One rapid but fairly sure guide to the social atmosphere of a country is the parade-step of its army. [2]A military parade is really a kind of ritual dance, something like a ballet, expressing a certain philosophy of life. [3]The goose-step, for instance, is one of the most

THE ARMY PARADE-STEP: In "England Your England" in *Such, Such Were the Joys* by George Orwell. Reprinted by permission of Harcourt Brace Jovanovich, Inc., and by permission of A. M. Heath & Company, Ltd. for Mrs. Sonia Brownell Orwell and Secker & Warburg. Selection title by editor.

horrible sights in the world, far more terrifying than a dive-bomber. [4]It is simply an affirmation of naked power; contained in it, quite consciously and intentionally, is the vision of a boot crashing down on a face. [5]Its ugliness is part of its essence, for what it is saying is "Yes, I *am* ugly, and you daren't laugh at me," like the bully who makes faces at his victim. [6]Why is the goose-step not used in England? [7]There are, heaven knows, plenty of army officers who would be only too glad to introduce some such thing. [8]It is not used because the people in the street would laugh. [9]Beyond a certain point, military display is only possible in countries where the common people dare not laugh at the army. [10]The Italians adopted the goose-step at about the time when Italy passed definitely under German control, and, as one would expect, they do it less well than the Germans. [11]The Vichy government, had it survived, was bound to introduce a stiffer parade-ground discipline into what was left of the French army. [12]In the British army the drill is rigid and complicated, full of memories of the eighteenth century, but without definite swagger; the march is merely a formalized walk. [13]It belongs to a society which is ruled by the sword, no doubt, but a sword which must never be taken out of the scabbard.

DISCUSSION: TRANSITIONS

In Mary McCarthy's paragraph on Uncle Myers, transitions within and between blocks of ideas are made chiefly through identical sentence openers:

Sentence 12: *He enjoyed* standing on a curbstone . . .
Sentence 13: *He liked* bandstands, band concerts . . .
Sentence 14: *He collected* coupons and tinfoil . . .
Sentence 15: *He was also fond of* streetcar rides . . .

She depends on a single transitional question ("How had these two worlds impinged?") and on transitional words like "also" that specify the relationship of ideas—here amplification.

Where the relationship of ideas is not immediately clear, it may be pointed out by transitional words and phrases:

qualification: however, nonetheless, nevertheless
comparison: similarly, in the same way, by comparison, likewise

contrast: by contrast, on the one hand, on the other hand
illustration and explanation: for example, thus, so, to explain
consequence: thus, as a result, consequently, therefore, surely
concession: admittedly, nevertheless, at least
amplification: moreover, furthermore, also, in addition, indeed, surely
summation: all in all, in summary, in conclusion, finally, therefore

Within sentences, punctuation shows some of these relationships: a colon indicates that an expansion, explanation, or illustration of the previous idea follows; a semicolon, that the connected ideas are equal in importance or closely related. Transitions are best kept brief and unobtrusive. In the paragraph as in the whole essay, the reader should be able to discover the logical relation of ideas at first reading.

QUESTIONS

1. Which words or phrases in Orwell's paragraph are transitional? Could any be omitted without loss of clarity?
2. What sentence is wholly transitional—indicating the connection between ideas rather than stating an idea?
3. How does the whole paragraph explain the concluding phrase, "a sword which must never be taken out of the scabbard"?

WRITING ASSIGNMENTS

Write a paragraph discussing what you consider to be a "fairly sure guide to the social atmosphere" of the high school you attended or the college you are attending. You may wish to compare your high school and college to explain the phrase "social atmosphere." Underline your transitional words, phrases, and sentences.

The prevailing attitude toward policemen and other people in positions of authority might reveal a community's "social atmosphere," as Orwell uses this phrase. Discuss the evidence for such an attitude in your town or city, high school, or college, and relate that attitude to a point that Orwell makes in the paragraph.

BRUNO BETTELHEIM
The Hitler Salute

1. What was true of the inner responses of Germans to the concentration camps was also true for their overall reaction to total
mass control. But in the Hitler state it was always more than fear
for one's life that made it impossible to remain inwardly opposed to
the system. Every nonconformist was subject to many contra-
dictions. To cite the obvious dilemma: He could expose himself as
a dissenter and thus invite persecution, or he could profess faith in
something he not only did not believe, but hated and despised.
2. So the unwilling subject of the mass state had to begin to trick
himself, to look for excuses and subterfuges. But in so doing he
lost exactly the self respect he was trying to maintain. An example
of the way this works may be seen in the Hitler salute. The salute
was deliberately introduced so that everywhere—in the beer garden, the railroad, the place of work, and on the street—it would be
easy to recognize anyone who hung on to the old "democratic"
forms of greeting his friends.
3. To Hitler's followers, giving the salute was an expression of
self assertion, of power. Each time a loyal subject performed it, his
sense of well-being shot up. For an opponent of the regime it
worked exactly opposite. Every time he had to greet somebody in
public he had an experience that shook and weakened his integration. More specifically, if the situation forced him to salute, he immediately felt a traitor to his deepest convictions. So he had to
pretend to himself that it did not count. Or to put it another way:
he could not change his action—he *had* to give the Hitler salute.
Since one's integration rests on acting in accord with one's beliefs,
the only easy way to retain his integration was to change his beliefs. Things were made simpler by the fact that in most of us
there is a great desire to conform. Everyone knows how hard it is
to be deviant with even a casual acquaintance we meet on the
street; it is infinitely more so when being different puts one's very
life in danger. Thus many times a day the anti-Nazi had either to
become a martyr or abandon self respect.

THE HITLER SALUTE: In *The Informed Heart* by Bruno Bettelheim. Reprinted with
permission of Macmillan Publishing Co., Inc. Copyright © The Free Press.

4.   I once spoke with a young German psychologist who was a child at the beginning of the Hitler regime. Her father was a strong opponent of the Nazi movement and she felt as he did. But life went on and she had to go to school. At school she had to swear allegiance to the Führer, to give the Hitler salute repeatedly. For a long time she mentally crossed her fingers. She told herself that the oath and salute didn't count because she didn't mean them. But each time it became more difficult to hang on to her self respect and still keep up the pretense, until finally she gave up her mental reservation and swore allegiance like anybody else.

5.   While this development was still going on, a parallel process was taking place in her inner relation to her father. At first his morality had given the girl strength to go on without wavering in her convictions. But as time went on, she felt herself more and more projected into a most difficult conflict. First she had sided with the father and simply resented the state that forced such a conflict on her. But eventually there came a time when she blamed her father for being the source of her difficulties. Once this happened, she also began to resent her father's values. But values we resent can no longer give us strength, nor can they motivate us strongly. So after this point in her inner development, the father's values which had fortified her resistance became weaker and weaker and what had once been an asset became a liability.

6.   If a parent asks too much of us, we often end up complying even less than we might have done otherwise. By this time it was no longer a conflict between her and the Hitler state, with her father firmly on her side; the conflict was now within her, and her father could no longer support her because he was now a separate party in the conflict. Until she began to waver she took pride in his moral support; after that because she felt shame at her own behavior, he appeared to her as a critical figure, critical of her for doubting, for wishing to give in. So at the moment of indecision when she most needed to feel that her father respected her, he seemed to be pulling her still further apart. Here, then, is another example of how the personality splits under the impact of the coercive state if the individual tries to resist.

7.   What was true for the Hitler salute was of course true for all other features of the regime. The inescapable power of the total state rests exactly on this: not only that it reaches the minutest and most private life activities of the individual, but more, that it splits the inner person if he resists.

8.   To use another experience out of this young woman's student days: While attending *Gymnasium,* the girls in her school were asked to take a census of the population one day. To refrain from taking part would again have meant risking the well-being of herself and her family. Moreover, the request seemed innocuous enough. But in taking the census she suddenly found herself having to ask for private details from a Jewish family. She realized that these Jews saw her as a symbol of the regime and hated her. She resented this, and then realized that she was feeling just as the regime wanted her to: resentful of Jews. She also hated herself for helping to exterminate Jews. Certainly she hated the regime that forced the predicament on her, but she hated herself even more.

9.   And the total state finds almost daily tasks that each subject must perform or risk destruction. Most persons, in fulfilling these requirements, start out hating the system that forces them, but then end up hating themselves more. Moreover, the regime can stand their hatred, but they cannot endure the self hate, which is so destructive to integration.

QUESTIONS

1. In this section from Bettelheim's book on the effects of totalitarianism, Bettelheim turns from the attitudes in Nazi Germany toward the concentration camp to attitudes toward regimentation enforced by the government. The first sentence of paragraph 1 makes this transition. The second and third sentences state the subject of the nine paragraphs. Where does Bettelheim draw a conclusion?

2. If you wanted to group the nine paragraphs into larger paragraphs containing blocks of ideas, which paragraphs would form such blocks? Would transitions be needed within these larger blocks— or would the connection of ideas be clear without them?

3. One kind of effective transition between paragraphs is direct reference to a preceding idea. What paragraphs depend on this kind of transition?

4. Note the use of *moreover* in paragraphs 8 and 9. Could this formal transition be deleted without disturbing the coherence of the discussion? To what extent does Bettelheim depend on formal transitions between paragraphs?

5. Which sentences in paragraph 3 open with a formal transition? Could any of these transitions be deleted without obscuring the relation of ideas in the paragraph?

6. What purpose do the semicolons in paragraph 6 and the colons in paragraph 8 serve?

7. What implications do you find in the discussion for some sources of conflict between parents and children? Do you believe the particular conflict Bettelheim describes is restricted to totalitarian regimes?

WRITING ASSIGNMENTS

Orwell and Bettelheim are concerned with the psychology and power of totalitarian regimes. Write a paragraph stating the differences or similarities in what they are saying and the examples they provide.

Discuss a personal conflict that arose from an experience similar to that Bettelheim describes. Draw a conclusion from your discussion about one source of conflict between parents and children.

CLIMAX

LYTTON STRACHEY
Queen Victoria
at the End of Her Life

[1] She gave orders that nothing should be thrown away—and nothing was. [2] There, in drawer after drawer, in wardrobe after wardrobe, reposed the dresses of seventy years. [3] But not only the dresses—the furs and the mantles and subsidiary frills and the muffs and the parasols and the bonnets—all were ranged in chronological order, dated and complete. [4] A great cupboard was devoted to the dolls; in the china room at Windsor a special table held the mugs of her childhood, and her children's mugs as well. [5] Mementoes of the past surrounded her in serried accumulations. [6] In every room the tables were powdered thick with the photographs of relatives; their portraits, revealing them at all ages, covered the walls; their figures, in solid marble, rose up from pedestals, or gleamed from brackets in the form of gold and silver

QUEEN VICTORIA AT THE END OF HER LIFE: In *Queen Victoria* by Lytton Strachey, copyright, 1921, by Harcourt Brace Jovanovich, Inc.; renewed, 1949, by James Strachey. Reprinted by permission of the publishers. Selection title by editor.

statuettes. [7] The dead, in every shape—in miniatures, in porcelain, in enormous life-size oil-paintings—were perpetually about her. [8] John Brown stood upon her writing-table in solid gold.* [9] Her favorite horses and dogs, endowed with a new durability, crowded round her footsteps. [10] Sharp, in silver gilt, dominated the dinner table; Boy and Boz lay together among unfading flowers, in bronze. [11] And it was not enough that each particle of the past should be given the stability of metal or of marble: the whole collection, in its arrangement, no less than its entity, should be immutably fixed. [12] There might be additions, but there might never be alterations. [13] No chintz might change, no carpet, no curtain, be replaced by another; or, if long use at last made it necessary, the stuffs and the patterns must be so identically reproduced that the keenest eye might not detect the difference. [14] No new picture could be hung upon the walls at Windsor, for those already there had been put in their places by Albert, whose decisions were eternal. [15] So, indeed, were Victoria's. [16] To ensure that they should be the aid of the camera was called in. [17] Every single article in the Queen's possession was photographed from several points of view. [18] These photographs were submitted to Her Majesty, and when, after careful inspection, she had approved of them, they were placed in a series of albums, richly bound. [19] Then, opposite each photograph, an entry was made, indicating the number of the article, the number of the room in which it was kept, its exact position in the room and all its principal characteristics. [20] The fate of every object which had undergone this process was henceforth irrevocably sealed. [21] The whole multitude, once and for all, took up its steadfast station. [22] And Victoria, with a gigantic volume or two of the endless catalogue always beside her, to look through, to ponder upon, to expatiate over, could feel, with a double contentment, that the transitoriness of this world had been arrested by the amplitude of her might.

DISCUSSION: CLIMAX

There is a natural order of climax in certain sentences and paragraphs, as in Julius Caesar's famous statement, "I came, I saw, I conquered." In the same way, the last two sentences of the following

---

* John Brown (1826–1883) was the Scottish attendant to Victoria's husband, Prince Albert, and after the death of the Prince in 1861, to the Queen herself. Ed.

paragraph convey a sense of rising importance, as indeed the whole paragraph does:

> It was something formidable and swift, like the sudden smashing of a vial of wrath. It seemed to explode all round the ship with an overpowering concussion and a rush of great waters, as if an immense dam had been blown up to windward. In an instant the men lost touch of each other. This is the disintegrating power of a great wind: it isolates one from one's kind. An earthquake, a landslip, an avalanche, overtake a man incidentally, as it were—without passion. A furious gale attacks him like a personal enemy, tries to grasp his limbs, fastens upon his mind, seeks to rout his very spirit out of him.—Joseph Conrad. *Typhoon*

As in this paragraph, climax can be achieved by making one idea seem to anticipate another, and by giving weight to the concluding idea. The terminal position—a position of natural emphasis in English sentences and paragraphs—is in part responsible for this effect. The writer is free to make one idea seem more important by virtue of the position given it.

QUESTIONS

1. Queen Victoria's husband, Prince Albert, died of a sudden illness in 1861, at the age of 42. Victoria, the same age as her husband, entered a long period of private mourning, and until her death in 1901, she attempted to preserve her physical surroundings as they had existed in Albert's lifetime. In this portrait of Victoria in her old age, Strachey develops and illustrates several major ideas that build to his thesis idea. What are these ideas?
2. Strachey states in sentence 2 that Victoria saved the dresses of seventy years; in sentence 3, that she saved her furs and bonnets, as well as other articles of clothing—and arranged and dated them chronologically. How does the formal transition between these sentences help to show that Strachey is moving from one surprising, even astonishing, fact to an even more surprising one?
3. Compare sentences 11 and 12 with those that follow. How does Strachey indicate that he is building the paragraph to even more surprising details?
4. What contributes to the climactic effect of the final sentence of the paragraph?

WRITING ASSIGNMENTS

Write a character sketch of an unusual relative or friend or teacher, centering on a dominant trait and presenting related traits as Strachey does. Present these related traits in the order of rising importance—as illustrations of the dominant trait.

Rewrite Strachey's paragraph, beginning with his concluding sentence, and achieving a sense of climax in your reordering of ideas and details.

KATHERINE ANNE PORTER
The Bullfight

1.   I took to the bullfights with my Mexican and Indian friends. I sat with them in the cafés where the bullfighters appeared; more than once went at two o'clock in the morning with a crowd to see the bulls brought into the city; I visited the corral back of the ring where they could be seen before the corrida. Always, of course, I was in the company of impassioned adorers of the sport, with their special vocabulary and mannerisms and contempt for all others who did not belong to their charmed and chosen cult. Quite literally there were those among them I never heard speak of anything else; and I heard then all that can be said—the topic is limited, after all, like any other—in love and praise of bullfighting. But it can be tiresome, too. And I did not really live in that world, so narrow and so trivial, so cruel and so unconscious; I was a mere visitor. There was something deeply, irreparably wrong with my being there at all, something against the grain of my life; except for this (and here was the falseness I had finally to uncover): I loved the spectacle of the bullfights, I was drunk on it, I was in a strange, wild dream from which I did not want to be awakened. I was now drawn irresistibly to the bullring as before I had been drawn to the race tracks and the polo fields at home. But this had death in it, and it was the death in it that I loved. . . . And I was bitterly

THE BULLFIGHT: In "St. Augustine and the Bullfight" from *The Collected Essays and Occasional Writings of Katherine Anne Porter* by Katherine Anne Porter. Copyright © 1970 by Katherine Anne Porter. Reprinted by permission of Delacorte Press/Seymour Lawrence. Selection title by editor.

ashamed of this evil in me, and believed it to be in me only—no one had fallen so far into cruelty as this! These bullfight buffs I truly believed did not know what they were doing—but I did, and I knew better because I had once known better; so that spiritual pride got in and did its deadly work, too. How could I face the cold fact that at heart I was just a killer, like any other, that some deep corner of my soul consented not just willingly but with rapture? I still clung obstinately to my flattering view of myself as a unique case, as a humane, blood-avoiding civilized being, somehow a fallen angel, perhaps? Just the same, what was I doing there? And why was I beginning secretly to abhor Shelley as if he had done me a great injury, when in fact he had done me the terrible and dangerous favor of helping me to find myself out?

2.   In the meantime I was reading St. Augustine; and if Shelley had helped me find myself out, St. Augustine helped me find myself again. I read for the first time then his story of a friend of his, a young man from the provinces who came to Rome and was taken up by the gang of clever, wellborn young hoodlums Augustine then ran with; and this young man, also wellborn but severely brought up, refused to go with the crowd to the gladiatorial combat; he was opposed to them on the simple grounds that they were cruel and criminal. His friends naturally ridiculed such dowdy sentiments; they nagged him slyly, bedeviled him openly, and, of course, finally some part of him consented—but only to a degree. He would go with them, he said, but he would not watch the games. And he did not, until the time for the first slaughter, when the howling of the crowd brought him to his feet, staring: and afterward he was more bloodthirsty than any.

3.   Why, of course: oh, it might be a commonplace of human nature, it might be it could happen to anyone! I longed to be free of my uniqueness, to be a fellow-sinner at least with someone: I could not bear my guilt alone—and here was this student, this boy at Rome in the fourth century, somebody I felt I knew well on sight, who had been weak enough to be led into adventure but strong enough to turn it into experience. For no matter how we both attempted to deceive ourselves, our acts had all the earmarks of adventure: violence of motive, events taking place at top speed, at sustained intensity, under powerful stimulus and a willful seeking for pure sensation; willful, I say, because I was not kidnapped and forced, after all, nor was that young friend of St. Augustine's. We both proceeded under the power of our own weakness. When

the time came to kill the splendid black and white bull, I who had pitied him when he first came into the ring stood straining on tip-toe to see everything, yet almost blinded with excitement, and crying out when the crowd roared, and kissing Shelley on the cheekbone when he shook my elbow and shouted in the voice of one justified: "Didn't I tell you? Didn't I?"

QUESTIONS

1. In this excerpt from a long essay, Porter describes her first experience with bullfighting, to which she was introduced by her friend Shelley, a young Englishman living in Mexico. She describes also the effect of her reading the *Confessions* of St. Augustine; the passage she refers to concerns his friend Alypius, a law student who was enticed to the gladiatorial combats. The passage concludes:

> For so soon as he saw that blood, he therewith drunk down savageness; nor turned away, but fixed his eye, drinking in frenzy, unawares, and was delighted with that guilty fight, and intoxicated with the bloody pastime. Nor was he now the man he came, but one of the throng he came unto, yea, a true associate of theirs that brought him thither. Why say more? He beheld, shouted, kindled, carried thence with him the madness which should goad him to return not only with them who first drew him thither, but also before them, yea and to draw in others. (Book VI)

Notice that Porter's paragraphs end with a focus on similar ideas. What are these ideas, and how does this focus contribute to a sense of climax in the whole passage? Is the sense of climax greater at the end of the final paragraph?

2. How many blocks of ideas does paragraph 1 contain, and how is this division of ideas marked? Would the paragraph be more effective divided into several paragraphs?

3. To what extent does Porter rely on formal transitions to convey rising excitement?

WRITING ASSIGNMENT

Write several paragraphs describing and analyzing an exciting experience about which you had mixed feelings. Explain how you resolved—or failed to resolve—these feelings. Arrange the sentences of one of your paragraphs in climactic order.

POINT OF VIEW

GEOFFREY MOORHOUSE
Calcutta

1.   When the international and jet-propelled traveler disembarks at Dum Dum he finds, if he has come by the right airline, that a highly polished limousine awaits his pleasure. It will be 6.30 or thereabouts in the morning, and the atmosphere will already be faintly sticky with heat and so unmistakably sweetened with a compound of mainly vegetable odors that the visitor can almost taste it. He need fear no discomfort at this stage, however, for he is to be transported into the city in air-conditioned splendor behind delicately tinted windows. From this smooth and relaxing position he can begin to observe how the other half of humanity lives. From the outset he notices some things which are reassuringly familiar. Along the first mile of this wide and tarmacadamed airport road are spaced the very same collection of gaudy hoardings that signal the way in and out of Heathrow or J. F. Kennedy or Fiumicino; "Try a Little VC-10derness", says one—and some untidy idiot seems to have thrown up a collection of chicken coops in the shade of BOAC. Beside these homely reference points, however, the peculiarities of India are to be seen. The road is bordered by ditches and ponds, all brimming with water, in which women even at this hour are flogging garments clean, in which men are taking the first bath of the day. Beyond the spindle-elegant sodium lights, with buzzards and vultures perched on top, stand thickets of bamboo-and-thatch huts among avenues of palm. Along a canal, a large black barge top-heavy with hay is being poled inches at a time through a mass of pretty but choking mauve water hyacinth. And in the distance, lurking on the horizon, a range of tall factory chimneys is beginning to smoke.

2.   Calcutta is announced with a pothole or two. Then a bus is overtaken, such a vehicle as the traveler has never seen before; its bodywork is battered with a thousand dents, as though an army of

commuters had once tried to kick it to bits, and it is not only crammed with people, it has a score or so hanging off the platform and around the back like a cluster of grapes. It is lumbering and steaming into a suburban wasteland, stippled with blocks of dilapidated flats; and maybe Bishop Heber's imagery was not so far-fetched after all, for these are not at all unlike some of the homes for the workers you can see in Moscow today, though there they are not colored pink and they certainly haven't been decorated with the hammer and sickle in crude whitewash on the walls.* Swiftly, the outer Calcutta of these revolutionary symbols now co-agulates into the inner Calcutta which is unlike anywhere else on earth. The limousine now lurches and rolls, for there are too many potholes to avoid. It rocks down cobblestoned roads lined with high factory walls which have an air of South Lancashire about them. It begins to thread its way through traffic along thoroughfares that have something of Bishopsgate or Holborn in their buildings.

3.   It is the traffic that makes it all unique. A traffic in trams grinding round corners, a traffic in approximately London buses whose radiators seem ready to burst, in gypsy-green lorries with 'Ta-ta and By-by' and other slogans painted on the back, in taxis swerving all over the road with much blowing of horns, in rick-shaws springing unexpectedly out of sidestreets, in bullock carts swaying ponderously along to the impediment of everyone, in sacred Brahmani cows and bulls nonchalantly strolling down the middle of the tram-tracks munching breakfast as they go. A traffic, too, in people who are hanging on to all forms of public transport, who are squatting cross-legged upon the counters of their shops, who are darting in and out of the roadways between the vehicles, who are staggering under enormous loads, who are walking briskly with briefcases, who are lying like dead things on the pavements, who are drenching themselves with muddy water in the gutters, who are arguing, laughing, gesticulating, defecating, and who are sometimes just standing still as though wondering what to do. There never were so many people in a city at seven o'clock in the morning. Patiently the driver of the limousine steers his passage between and around them, while they pause in mid-stride to let him through, or leap to get out of his way, or stare at him blankly, or curse him roundly, or occasionally spit in the path of his highly

---

* Reginald Heber (1783–1826), who became bishop of Calcutta in 1823, compared the city to Moscow. He commented also on the large Greek-style houses and the city's hospitality. Ed.

polished Cadillac. Presently, and quite remarkably, he comes to the end of the journey without collision and deposits the traveler and his luggage upon the pavement in front of an hotel. And here, the traveler has his first encounter with a beggar. He had better make the best of it, for beggary is to be with him until the end of his days in Calcutta.

DISCUSSION: POINT OF VIEW

The *physical* point of view of a paragraph or an essay is the place from which something is observed. This kind of point of view, or angle of vision, is never exactly the same: no photographer is able to duplicate a landscape, even if he or she returns to it in the same season at the same time of day, and stands in exactly the same place. Some feature of the physical point of view will have changed. More than this, mood and feeling—so important to what we perceive, as photographers know—change from moment to moment. Mood, feeling, attitude—these constitute the *psychological* point of view. Every piece of writing reveals both, and both may change in the course of the paragraph or essay. However it is established, point of view must remain consistent, and when shifts are made, they must be made carefully. Abrupt shifts in point of view can make a piece of writing seem confusing or incoherent.

QUESTIONS

1. The traveler to India might see Calcutta for the first time from a taxi or bus rather than from "a highly polished limousine." What is gained by showing the city from Moorhouse's angle of vision?
2. The reference to the "very same collection of gaudy hoardings" leading in and out of Heathrow, J. F. Kennedy, and Fiumicino (the international airports of London, New York, and Rome, respectively) suggests that the traveler will at first think he is in a familiar world. He soon discovers that he is moving into an unfamiliar one. What other contrasts of this sort does Moorhouse imply?
3. How does Moorhouse establish not only the mental state of the typical traveler at the end of his journey to the hotel but also his own attitude toward Calcutta?
4. The reference to Bishopsgate and Holborn shows that Moorhouse is writing with a British audience in mind, people familiar with the architecture of these areas of London. What other statements call for knowledge of this kind?

WRITING ASSIGNMENT

Use Moorhouse's description of Calcutta as a model for a description of a section of a college town or your hometown. You may wish to portray the town as seen from a limousine, a Volkswagen, or a bicycle, but be careful to make the angle of vision contribute to the overall impression and the revelation of an attitude. Do not specify this attitude; let your selection of details reveal it.

WINSTON S. CHURCHILL
My First Introduction to the Classics

The school my parents had selected for my education was one of the most fashionable and expensive in the country. It modeled itself upon Eton and aimed at being preparatory for that Public School above all others. It was supposed to be the very last thing in schools. Only ten boys in a class; electric light (then a wonder); a swimming pond; spacious football and cricket grounds; two or three school treats, or "expeditions" as they were called, every term; the masters all M.A.'s in gowns and mortar-boards; a chapel of its own; no hampers allowed; everything provided by the authorities. It was a dark November afternoon when we arrived at this establishment. We had tea with the Headmaster, with whom my mother conversed in the most easy manner. I was preoccupied with the fear of spilling my cup and so making "a bad start." I was also miserable at the idea of being left alone among all these strangers in this great, fierce, formidable place. After all I was only seven, and I had been so happy in my nursery with all my toys. I had such wonderful toys: a real steam engine, a magic lantern, and a collection of soldiers already nearly a thousand strong. Now it was to be all lessons. Seven or eight hours of lessons every day except half-holidays, and football or cricket in addition.

When the last sound of my mother's departing wheels had died away, the Headmaster invited me to hand over any money I

MY FIRST INTRODUCTION TO THE CLASSICS: In *My Early Life* by Winston S. Churchill. Reprinted by permission of The Hamlyn Publishing Group Limited and Charles Scribner's Sons. Copyright 1930 Charles Scribner's Sons. Selection title by editor.

had in my possession. I produced my three half-crowns which were duly entered in a book, and I was told that from time to time there would be a "shop" at the school with all sorts of things which one would like to have, and that I could choose what I liked up to the limit of the seven and sixpence. Then we quitted the Headmaster's parlor and the comfortable private side of the house, and entered the more bleak apartments reserved for the instruction and accommodation of the pupils. I was taken into a Form Room and told to sit at a desk. All the other boys were out of doors, and I was alone with the Form Master. He produced a thin greeny-brown-covered book filled with words in different types of print.

"You have never done any Latin before, have you?" he said.

"No, sir."

"This is a Latin grammar." He opened it at a well-thumbed page. "You must learn this," he said, pointing to a number of words in a frame of lines. "I will come back in half an hour and see what you know."

Behold me then on a gloomy evening, with an aching heart, seated in front of the First Declension.

Mensa	a table
Mensa	O table
Mensam	a table
Mensae	of a table
Mensae	to or for a table
Mensa	by, with or from a table

What on earth did it mean? Where was the sense of it? It seemed absolute rigmarole to me. However, there was one thing I could always do: I could learn by heart. And I thereupon proceeded, as far as my private sorrows would allow, to memorize the acrostic-looking task which had been set me.

In due course the Master returned.

"Have you learnt it?" he asked.

"I think I can *say* it, sir," I replied; and I gabbled it off.

He seemed so satisfied with this that I was emboldened to ask a question.

"What does it mean, sir?"

"It means what it says. Mensa, a table. Mensa is a noun of the

First Declension. There are five declensions. You have learnt the singular of the First Declension."

"But," I repeated, "what does it mean?"

"Mensa means a table," he answered.

"Then why does mensa also mean O table," I enquired, "and what does O table mean?"

"Mensa, O table, is the vocative case," he replied.

"But why O table?" I persisted in genuine curiosity.

"O table,—you would use that in addressing a table, in invoking a table." And then seeing he was not carrying me with him, "You would use it in speaking to a table."

"But I never do," I blurted out in honest amazement.

"If you are impertinent you will be punished, and punished, let me tell you, very severely," was his conclusive rejoinder.

QUESTIONS

1. Churchill states in his autobiography that this episode was "my first introduction to the classics." The selection of details—and in particular the concluding conversation with the Form Master—reveals his attitude not only toward the preparatory school but toward children and education. What is that attitude? What details indicate that Churchill is not concerned merely with the misery of a seven-year-old boy left by his parents with strangers?
2. The Form Master is directly characterized through his responses to the boy's questions. Is the Headmaster characterized at all?
3. Churchill establishes an angle of vision through his setting. How does he establish his mental state?
4. Does Churchill the adult find humor in the episode, or does he write with bitterness and anger?

WRITING ASSIGNMENT

Write a carefully organized paragraph on one of the following topics, establishing a point of view and creating a single dominant impression:
  a. the first day at high school or college
  b. the first day in a college classroom
  c. a visit to a hospital or a prison
  d. an appearance in a courtroom
  e. a first view of a military barracks or college dormitory

WILLIAM L. SHIRER

Chautauqua

1.   For an Iowa highschool boy of sixteen or seventeen, his ego swollen by the realization that his mates on the tent crew were all in college—and three or four years older—those two summers on chautauqua, while filled with hard work, were a joy, and a further education. I loved the traveling, the variety of the land as we jolted along in a day coach through the rolling cornfields of Iowa, the lake-studded countryside of Minnesota, the flat wheatlands of the Dakotas, the hills of Missouri with its faint flavor of the South. And there was something in the life on the trains and in the red-painted depots, where we changed trains or arrived at our destination and departed, that was appealing to a raw youth. I sort of envied the life of the trainmen, who lived in a world of their own and had a camaraderie, a distinct life-style, that seemed to give them more satisfaction in their work than I had seen in offices and factories. They were, among other things, gargantuan eaters, and I remember the boardinghouses across the square from the depot where we would find sustenance during the week we were in town, and where we were joined, especially on early mornings, by the railroad men starting or finishing a shift and gobbling down immense breakfasts of oatmeal, bacon and eggs, pancakes, hot biscuits and coffee.

2.   After the last evening performance of the week, we would take down the big tent and stuff the canvas into large bags, pile our props into trunks and by midnight or shortly after catch a train (passenger trains swarmed even the branch lines in those days) for our next location, arriving there often by early morning or before noon and, after a hearty breakfast or lunch, pitching the tent on the lawn or the football field of a local high school or college. Soon the tent was up, the stage built, the lighting strung out, the bench seats arranged, our own little tent behind the stage, where the crew slept, erected, and we were ready for business. Strolling down Main Street to get an ice-cream soda, we could see that the advance man had done his job. Streamers stretched across the ave-

CHAUTAUQUA: In *20th-Century Journey* by William L. Shirer. Copyright © 1976 by William L. Shirer. Reprinted by permission of Simon & Schuster, a Division of Gulf & Western Corporation. Selection title by editor.

nue proclaiming "Chautauqua Is Coming!" The message was repeated on banners fluttering from automobiles, trucks, drays and
carriages, and all the businessmen on the sidewalks or in their offices and shops were wearing large buttons that said "I'll Be
There!"

3.   By the time chautauqua opened for the first matinee we were
back on the grounds for the last chores: rolling an upright piano
onto one corner of the stage, planting Old Glory behind it so that
our speakers could point to it with customary patriotic pride, and
fetching a pitcher of ice water and a glass to tide them over their
long-distance runs in the suffocating heat. The tent would fill up,
our preacher-superintendent would come beaming on stage and,
when the applause was over, open the week's festivities: "Well,
here we are, my friends, bringing you and this great town [men-
tioning it by name, if he could remember it] another great week of
chautauqua. And if you thought it was good last year, wait till you
see what we have in store for you *this* year—the greatest program,
I can say in all modesty, that chautauqua has ever presented anywhere. It's all here for you, afternoons and evenings, for the next
seven days." And he would spin through it with great aplomb.
"That peerless American statesman William Jennings Bryan"
would be back, but he could hardly finish his sentence because of
the applause. For Bryan was the great spellbinder of the chautauqua circuit, the biggest drawing card it ever had. There would
be other speakers, of course, and a new "Broadway hit," and the
Ben Greet Players with a new presentation of *Hamlet,* and two
orchestras, and, of course, Sousa's great band, a famous musical
sextet "straight from New York," an opera company "from Chicago" presenting *Pinafore,* a great "diva" from the "Metropolitan
Opera of New York"—and on and on he would go, the audience
breathless with anticipation, though it had known for weeks from
advance flyers just what the program would be.

4.   Finally the superintendent would present a beautiful young
lady (invariably a pert college girl trying to earn next year's tuition,
and a welcome member of our crew) who would be in charge of
"junior chautauqua." She would not only keep the youngsters occupied while their parents were absorbing culture, but would labor
doggedly all week to whip them into giving a pageant or a play on
the last afternoon, which, however terrible, would delight the fond
mothers and fathers and help to deepen their impression of all the
wholesome good that chautauqua had brought to the community.

QUESTIONS

1. Chautauqua was a traveling educational show that originated in Chautauqua, New York, in 1874, where people came to hear lectures and concerts. What feelings about chautauqua does Shirer share with the audience he describes? Does he see any aspects of chautauqua differently from these people?
2. How does Shirer establish a psychological point of view for the reader, in his opening paragraph?
3. How does Shirer establish a physical point of view in each paragraph? What use does he make of climactic development in these paragraphs?

WRITING ASSIGNMENT

Describe a summer work experience, or a similar experience that took you away from home, as Shirer does. Establish your point of view early in the paragraph or essay. Let your reader see and feel the experience as you did; don't merely summarize what happened to you.

DEFINITION

JEREMY BERNSTEIN

Skiing as a Child

1. I first took up skiing as a child of ten or so, in the late nineteen-thirties. Rochester, New York, where I grew up, had, and still does have, heavy, severe winters, and winter sports, especially ice-skating, were exceedingly popular. I soon found out that I had weak ankles, so ice-skating was a disaster for me; hence the skis. With the aid of a Boy Scout pamphlet, a small group of us attempted to teach ourselves skiing on a broad slope in Ellison Park, near where we lived. Lifts were unknown to us, and our ski equipment was such that the user of the oldest ski yet to be discovered—the ski was found in Hoting, Sweden, and is about forty-five

SKIING AS A CHILD: In "Le Poids Sur Le Ski Aval." Reprinted by permission; © 1974 The New Yorker Magazine, Inc. Selection title by editor.

hundred years old—would have felt himself in familiar territory among us. ("Ski" is the Norwegian word for "snowshoe," and the Hoting ski essentially resembles a snowshoe; there are, however, Scandinavian skis over two thousand years old with turned-up, pointed tips which resemble the modern version.) We had wooden skis—mainly hickory—with a groove carved in the bottom along the axis of the ski; this groove, which produced a small raised line in the middle of each ski track, was supposed to make the skis more stable. A rule of the day was that skis, whatever the skier's proficiency, should be one's height plus the length of an outstretched arm. Some of the more mechanical-minded among us tacked metal strips along the sides of our ski bottoms. These helped to preserve the wood from abrasion—without them our skis would have been chipped away after a season or so—and they also helped in controlling descents when the terrain was icy, for they could be edged into the ice. Waxing these wooden skis was a ritual that all but approached high alchemy. Waxes came in every color and variety, and were to be applied in layers with cheesecloth whenever the snow conditions warranted—whenever the snow was wet or sticky. (As I recall, the first wax I used was my mother's floor wax—a limited success.) We spent hours in basements happily applying and scraping off wax.
2.   The attachment of skis to the feet evolved somewhat during those years. At first, there had been a system of leather straps that more or less tied the boot to the ski. One put the toe of the boot in an open iron wedge, buckled the straps over the boot, and hoped for the best. Sometime in the early thirties, the cable binding was introduced. The old toe wedge remained, but the back of the boot had a groove carved in it, and through this groove went a metal cable—spring-wound—that wedged one's foot into the toe iron. These cables had three or four possible tensions, depending on how they were adjusted. (There was a gadget in front of the binding into which the cable could be set, in various positions. One then tightened the cable by pulling forward on a lever.) In adjusting the cable tension, one was faced with an unpleasant choice: either to attach the ski so loosely that it would fall off at the slightest movement of the foot or to attach it so tightly that it could never come off and there would inevitably be a tangle of skis and feet when one fell. It is a miracle that none of us broke a leg or an ankle with this arrangement, which was extremely dangerous, but, then, children are rarely hurt in ski falls. Our ski boots were

leather hiking boots with the soles modified—cut square by the manufacturer—to fit into the toe iron and with the groove cut into the heel for the cable. The system worked about as well with ordinary hiking boots, or even with gym shoes. Ski poles were made of light bamboo, and each pole had a large wheel of leather near the bottom. Special ski clothes were unknown to us.

DISCUSSION: DEFINITION

We have been discussing effective ways of organizing paragraphs. In this and succeeding sections we will consider some important ways of developing and analyzing ideas.

Definition is the most fundamental of these ways: readers must know the meaning of words essential to the discussion. How complete the definition is and what kind the writer uses depends on how much specific information the reader needs. The author of the following passage has been describing Carrie Nation's sometimes violent encounters with Kansas bartenders:

> The symbol of their authority was the bung starter, a handy tool for cooling hot skulls, which was beginning to take its revered place in informal brawling alongside the shillelagh and brass knucks.—Robert Lewis Taylor, *Vessel of Wrath*

Taylor might have given the reader a detailed description of the bung starter; he does not because the reader need only know how the bung starter was used.

The simplest kind of definition is to point to an object; in a museum I might merely point and say, "That's a bung starter" to explain the term. But usually we want to know the characteristics of the object—or at least know as much as can be stated. To inform us of these characteristics, the author may begin with the original meaning of the word—that is, with its etymology. The word *gravity* comes from the Latin word *gravitas*, meaning "weight" or "heaviness." These words help explain the word *gravity;* however, they are not the whole of its current meaning. The purpose of etymological definition is usually not to argue that a word must be used in its original sense, though an author may wish to argue that an original meaning of the word be restored if its meanings have changed. The word *silly* originally meant "innocent" or "blessed"; its meanings today suggest simple-mindedness or thoughtlessness ("a silly question").

Most definitions are concerned with current meanings—the usual meanings that people attach to words. The most common of these definitions are called *denotative* and *connotative. Denotative* definition singles out an object: it identifies the class (or *genus*) of objects to which the word belongs, then distinguishes the word from all other members of the class (*specific difference*). The genus may be extremely broad or extremely narrow:

> **hero** A man [*genus*] distinguished for exceptional courage, fortitude, or bold enterprise, especially in time of war or danger [*specific difference*]
> **hero** *U.S.* A sandwich [*genus*] made with a loaf of bread cut lengthwise [*specific difference*]—*Standard College Dictionary*

Notice that the author of the second definition might have begun with a broader genus: "Food, consisting of a loaf of bread. . . ." The broader the genus, the more detailed the specific difference. For words as broad in meaning as *thing,* the dictionary usually lists synonyms: *inanimate object, matter, concern,* and so on.

Connotative definition presents ideas and impressions, the emotional aura most or all of us associate with an object, an activity, or even a descriptive word. The word *rose* has a precise denotation—a particular flower with describable properties—and a range of connotations some of them deriving from the flower, as in the expression "a rosy future." Though both *inexpensive* and *cheap* mean low in price, *cheap* usually carries the connotation of poor quality or of something contemptible. *Inexpensive* is an emotionally neutral word; *cheap* usually is not. Some words like *cute* lack precise definition, expressing merely a range of emotive meanings.

Stipulative definition proposes a name or symbol for a newly discovered phenomenon, so that it can be referred to and talked about; occasionally a new name is proposed for something existing. The person who stipulates the definition is not claiming that the new term is necessarily the right or best one—an accurate description of the phenomenon. In the early 1960s the term *quasar* came into use for newly discovered, very distant and bright sources of light that look like stars—that are "quasi-stellar"—but seem to have properties not associated with known stars. A new word may someday be proposed as a substitute for *quasar* if the current word gathers connotations that make discussion difficult, or if these sources of light are no longer considered to be quasi-stellar in their properties.

Unlike stipulative definition, *theoretical* definition proposes an explanation or theory of the phenomenon—an account of its true nature. Einstein's definition of mass as the equivalent of energy in his Special Theory of Relativity is a theoretical definition. So are most textbook definitions of such abstract concepts as justice, democracy, and totalitarianism.

Precising definitions fix meanings that are indefinite, overlapping, or confused in popular usage. Recent Supreme Court decisions on obscenity and pornography are examples of precising definitions.

QUESTIONS

1. The formal definition of *ski* in one dictionary is as follows:

    > One of a pair of wooden or metal runners about 5 to 7 feet long and 3½ inches wide, with turned-up points, attached to the feet and used in sliding over snow, especially on slopes.— *Standard College Dictionary*

    How formal the definition in expository or informal writing is depends on how necessary this information is and on the complexity of the object or substance. How much of the formal definition above is included in Bernstein's discussion of the skis he used in childhood?

2. What purpose does the etymological definition of *ski* serve? Is Bernstein indicating that the original meaning of the word has changed since it came into existence?

3. Bernstein defines a number of objects as a way of indicating the difficulty he experienced as a child. How do these definitions help to suggest these difficulties?

4. Give the genus and the specific differences of the dictionary definitions of the following words: cucumber, geography, sun, proof, laurel, exile, hasp, inch, barn, jackal. For which of the words is the genus extremely general? Could a more restricted one have been provided?

5. In formal definition a word must not be circular—that is, it must not be used to define itself (for example: Logic is the science of logical thinking) and the specific difference must not exclude essential characteristics (for example: An automobile is a four-wheeled vehicle). Use your desk dictionary to determine whether the following formal definitions are complete and uncircular:

    a. A republic is a political union in which citizens qualified to vote are supreme.
    b. Democracy is government by the people.
    c. A constitutional monarchy is a government in which monarchical rule is constitutionally limited.
    d. Oligarchy is government by a few.
    e. Fascism is a system of government in which political opposition is prohibited and often ruthlessly suppressed.

WRITING ASSIGNMENTS

Write an account of a childhood sport, defining two or three pieces of equipment necessary to it. Introduce your definition as a way of commenting on the difficulties or challenge or enjoyment presented by the sport.

Use the *Oxford English Dictionary* and other reference books to investigate the etymology and properties of one of the following and write an account of the word:

    a. gyroscope   c. cotton gin
    b. alcohol   d. telescope

Use the *Oxford English Dictionary* and other reference books to show how etymology sheds light on current meanings of a word. Indicate the extent to which original meanings of the word have been retained in current usage. Here are possible words for investigation:

    a. puritan   c. tragic
    b. humorous   d. foolish

PAUL FUSSELL

World War One Trenches

1.   The two main British sectors duplicated each other also in their almost symbolic road systems. Each had a staging town behind: for Ypres it was Poperinghe (to the men, "Pop"); for the Somme, Amiens. From these towns troops proceeded with augmenting but usually well-concealed terror up a sinister road to the town of operations, either Ypres itself or Albert. And running into the enemy lines out of Ypres and Albert were the most sinister roads of all, one leading to Menin, the other to Bapaume, both in enemy territory. These roads defined the direction of ultimate attack and the hoped-for breakout. They were the goals of the bizarre inverse quest on which the soldiers were ironically embarked.

    But most of the time they were not questing. They were sit-

WORLD WAR ONE TRENCHES: In *The Great War and Modern Memory* by Paul Fussell. Copyright © 1975 by Oxford University Press, Inc. Reprinted by permission. Selection title by editor.

ting or lying or squatting in place below the level of the ground. "When all is said and done," Sassoon notes, "the war was mainly a matter of holes and ditches."[1] And in these holes and ditches extending for ninety miles, continually, even in the quietest times, some 7000 British men and officers were killed and wounded daily, just as a matter of course. "Wastage," the Staff called it.

2.   There were normally three lines of trenches. The front-line trench was anywhere from fifty yards or so to a mile from its enemy counterpart. Several hundred yards behind it was the support trench line. And several hundred yards behind that was the reserve line. There were three kinds of trenches: firing trenches, like these; communication trenches, running roughly perpendicular to the line and connecting the three lines; and "saps," shallower ditches thrust out into No Man's Land, providing access to forward observation posts, listening posts, grenade-throwing posts, and machine gun positions. The end of a sap was usually not manned all the time: night was the favorite time for going out. Coming up from the rear, one reached the trenches by following a communication trench sometimes a mile or more long. It often began in a town and gradually deepened. By the time pedestrians reached the reserve line, they were well below ground level.

3.   A firing trench was supposed to be six to eight feet deep and four or five feet wide. On the enemy side a parapet of earth or sandbags rose about two or three feet above the ground. A corresponding "parados" a foot or so high was often found on top of the friendly side. Into the sides of trenches were dug one- or two-man holes ("funk-holes"), and there were deeper dugouts, reached by dirt stairs, for use as command posts and officers' quarters. On the enemy side of a trench was a fire-step two feet high on which the defenders were supposed to stand, firing and throwing grenades, when repelling attack. A well-built trench did not run straight for any distance: that would have been to invite enfilade fire. Every few yards a good trench zig-zagged. It had frequent traverses designed to contain damage within a limited space. Moving along a trench thus involved a great deal of weaving and turning. The floor of a proper trench was covered with wooden duckboards, beneath which were sumps a few feet deep designed to collect water. The walls, perpetually crumbling, were supported by sandbags, corru-

---

[1] Siegfried Sassoon, *Memoirs of an Infantry Officer* (1930; New York, 1937), p. 228.

gated iron, or bundles of sticks or rushes. Except at night and in half-light, there was of course no looking over the top except through periscopes, which could be purchased in the "Trench Requisites" section of the main London department stores. The few snipers on duty during the day observed No Man's Land through loopholes cut in sheets of armor plate.

4.   The entanglements of barbed wire had to be positioned far enough out in front of the trench to keep the enemy from sneaking up to grenade-throwing distance. Interestingly, the two novelties that contributed most to the personal menace of the war could be said to be American inventions. Barbed wire had first appeared on the American frontier in the late nineteenth century for use in restraining animals. And the machine gun was the brainchild of Hiram Stevens Maxim (1840–1916), an American who, disillusioned with native patent law, established his Maxim Gun Company in England and began manufacturing his guns in 1889. He was finally knighted for his efforts. At first the British regard for barbed wire was on a par with Sir Douglas Haig's understanding of the machine gun. In the autumn of 1914, the first wire Private Frank Richards saw emplaced before the British positions was a single strand of agricultural wire found in the vicinity.[2] Only later did the manufactured article begin to arrive from England in sufficient quantity to create the thickets of mock-organic rusty brown that helped give a look of eternal autumn to the front.

5.   The whole British line was numbered by sections, neatly, from right to left. A section, normally occupied by a company, was roughly 300 yards wide. One might be occupying front-line trench section 51; or support trench S 51, behind it; or reserve trench SS 51, behind both. But a less formal way of identifying sections of trench was by place or street names with a distinctly London flavor. *Piccadilly* was a favorite; popular also were *Regent Street* and *Strand;* junctions were *Hyde Park Corner* and *Marble Arch.* Greater wit—and deeper homesickness—sometimes surfaced in the naming of the German trenches opposite. Sassoon remembers "Durley" 's account of the attack at Delville Wood in September, 1916: "Our objective was Pint Trench, taking Bitter and Beer and clearing Ale and Vat, and also Pilsen Lane."[3] Directional and traffic control signs were everywhere in the trenches, giving the

[2] Frank Richards, *Old Soldiers Never Die* (1933), pp. 44–45.
[3] *Memoirs of an Infantry Officer,* p. 151.

whole system the air of a parody modern city, although one literally "underground."

1. How is the description of the trenches related to the points Fussell makes about them in paragraph 2?
2. What details convey the feeling of life in the trenches? How does Fussell remind the reader that a war is being fought?
3. Why does he mention the names of the trench sections? Is this information essential to the definition of the trenches?

WRITING ASSIGNMENT

Write a definition of one of the following. Relate the details of your definition to an explanation of the uses of the object being defined:
   a. the interchange of a city expressway
   b. the playing board of a game like *Monopoly*
   c. an important part of a musical instrument (trumpet keys, violin bow)
   d. bicycle pedals
   e. lawn mower
   f. electric food mixer

MARCIA SELIGSON

The American Wedding

1.   Every culture, in every time throughout history, has commemorated the transition of a human being from one state in life to another. Birth, the emergence into manhood, graduation from school at various levels, birthdays, marriage, death—each of these outstanding steps is acknowledged by a ceremony of some sort, always public, the guests in effect becoming witnesses to the statement of life's ongoingness, of the natural order of history. To insure the special significance of the rite of passage, its apartness

THE AMERICAN WEDDING: In *The Eternal Bliss Machine* by Marcia Seligson. Reprinted by permission of William Morrow & Company, Inc. Copyright © 1973 by Marcia Seligson. Selection title by editor.

from any other event of the day, these rituals usually require pageantry, costumed adornment, and are accompanied by gift-bearing and feasting. We wear black to funerals, bring presents to christenings and birthday parties, get loaded at wakes, eat ourselves sick at bar mitzvahs. Birth, marriage and death, to be sure, are the most elemental and major steps, and as there is only one of those ritual commemorations for which we are *actually*, fully present, the wedding becomes, for mankind, its most vital rite of passage. And for this reason it is anchored at the very core of civilization.

2. For the rites of passage the ceremony itself is organic to the society for which the individual is being groomed, in his journey from one state to the next. In African hunting societies, for example, a boy at puberty is thrown naked into the jungle and required to kill a lion. His value as a man will be judged by how successful he can be in meeting the demands of his culture. In America, newlyweds are being prepared for their roles in a consumer society, so it is surely appropriate that all of the dynamics of wedding hoo-hah testify to these commercial, mercantile terms. Gifts are purchased not only by the "witnesses" but by bride for groom, groom for bride, bride for attendants, attendants for bride. Prenuptial parties, bachelor dinners, showers. The ever-mushrooming splash and flash circusness of the wedding itself. The American wedding is a ritual event of ferocious, gluttonous consuming, a debauch of intensified buying, never again to be repeated in the life of an American couple.

QUESTIONS

1. The first paragraph defines *rite of passage* denotatively. What theory of social reality does Seligson present in the second paragraph?
2. What is the principle of order in the first paragraph? Is the second paragraph developed in the same way?

WRITING ASSIGNMENTS

Describe a ceremony of high-school or college life—June graduation, the class play, the senior dance—and discuss the extent to which it is "organic" to the society of the institution.

Examine advertisements in magazines and newspapers that depict brides and festivities associated with weddings (bridal showers, the wedding ceremony, receptions, and the like). In a short essay describe these advertisements and discuss whether or not they support Seligson's statement that the American wedding is "a ritual event of ferocious, gluttonous consuming, a debauch of intensified buying."

JOSEPH WOOD KRUTCH

The Meaning of "Normal"

1.   The words we choose to define or suggest what we believe to be important facts exert a very powerful influence upon civilization. A mere name can persuade us to approve or disapprove, as it does, for example, when we describe certain attitudes as "cynical" on the one hand or "realistic" on the other. No one wants to be "unrealistic" and no one wants to be "snarling." Therefore his attitude toward the thing described may very well depend upon which designation is current among his contemporaries; and the less critical his mind, the more influential the most commonly used vocabulary will be.

2.   It is for this reason that, even as a mere verbal confusion, the use of "normal" to designate what ought to be called "average" is of tremendous importance and serves not only to indicate but actually to reinforce the belief that average ability, refinement, intellectuality, or even virtue is an ideal to be aimed at. Since we cannot do anything to the purpose until we think straight and since we cannot think straight without properly defined words it may be that the very first step toward an emancipation from the tyranny of "conformity" should be the attempt to substitute for "normal," as commonly used, a genuine synonym for "average."

3.   Fortunately, such a genuine and familiar synonym does exist. That which is "average" is also properly described as "mediocre." And if we were accustomed to call the average man, not "the common man" or still less "the normal man," but "the mediocre man" we should not be so easily hypnotized into believing that mediocrity is an ideal to be aimed at.

THE MEANING OF "NORMAL": In *Human Nature and the Human Condition*, by Joseph Wood Krutch. Copyright © 1959 by Joseph Wood Krutch. Reprinted by permission of Random House, Inc. Selection title by editor.

4.   A second step in the same direction would be to return to the word "normal" its original meaning. According to the Shorter Oxford Dictionary it derives from the Latin "norma," which has been Anglicized as "norm" and is, in turn, thus defined: "A rule or authoritative standard." The adjective "normative" is not commonly misused—no doubt because it is not part of that "vocabulary of the average man" by which educators now set so much store. It still generally means "establishing a norm or standard." But "normal" seldom means, as it should, "corresponding to the standard by which a thing is to be judged." If it did, "a normal man" would again mean, not what the average man *is* but what, in its fullest significance, the word "man" should imply, even "what a man *ought* to be." And that is a very different thing from the "average" or "mediocre" man whom we have so perversely accustomed ourselves to regard as most worthy of admiration.

5.   Only by defining and then attempting to reach up toward the "normal" as properly defined can a democratic society save itself from those defects which the enemies of democracy have always maintained were the necessary consequences of such a society. Until "preparation for life" rather than "familiarity with the best that has been thought and said" became the aim of education every schoolboy knew that Emerson had bid us hitch our wagons to a star. We now hitch them to a mediocrity instead.

6.   Unless, then, normal is a useless and confusing synonym for average it should mean what the word normative suggests, namely, a *concept of what ought to be* rather than a *description of what is*. It should mean what at times it has meant—the fullest possible realization of what the human being is capable of—the complete, not the aborted human being. It is an *entelechy,* not a mean; something excellent, not something mediocre; something rare, not common; not what the majority are, but what few, if any, actually measure up to.

7.   Where, it will be asked, do we get this norm, upon what basis does it rest? Upon the answer to that question depends what a civilization will be like and especially in what direction it will move. At various times religion, philosophy, law, and custom have contributed to it in varying degrees. When none of these is available poetry and literature may do so. But unless we can say in one way or another, "I have some idea of what men ought to be as well as some knowledge of what they are," then civilization is lost.

QUESTIONS

1. Krutch's definition of *normal* is a precising definition. He is not stipulating a new meaning for the word; instead, he is seeking to make an uncommon meaning its common one. How does Krutch try to persuade us of the need for this other definition?
2. How does Krutch account for the present differences in the connotations of *normative* and *normal*—which derive from the same word? Does he state or imply why *normal* came to mean *average*?
3. Can the meaning of *entelechy* be determined from its context? What help does the etymology of the word provide?
4. Use the synonym listings in your dictionary to determine the exact difference in meaning between the following pairs of words. Write sentences using ten of the italicized words to reflect their precise dictionary meanings:
   a. *essential;* necessary
   b. *predict;* prophesy
   c. *mimic;* mock
   d. sinister; *portentous*
   e. fortitude; *forbearance*
   f. phase; *facet*
   g. agent; *factor*
   h. recumbent; *prone*
   i. adroit; *deft*
   j. *dextrous;* handy
   k. blended; *mingled*
   l. *perturbed;* agitated

WRITING ASSIGNMENTS

Define one of the following words by stating what it is not as well as what it is. Comment on the significance of its etymology:

   a. tolerance   d. impeachment
   b. stinginess   e. tact
   c. contraband

Discuss the different meanings—denotative and connotative—of one of the following words, illustrating these meanings by your use of them:

   a. funny   d. crazy
   b. average   e. tacky
   c. cool   f. weird

GEOFFREY GORER
The Sissy

This concept of being a sissy is a key concept for the under-standing of American character; it has no exact parallel in any other society. It has nowadays become a term of opprobrium which can be applied to anyone, regardless of age or sex; although it is analogous to some English terms of opprobrium (e.g. milksop, cry-baby, nancy, mother's darling) it is more than any of them. Sche-matically, it means showing more dependence or fear or lack of initiative or passivity than is suitable for the occasion. It can be applied to a gambler hesitant about risking his money, to a mother overanxious about the pain her child may suffer at the hands of a surgeon, to a boy shy about asking a popular girl for a "date," to stage fright, to overt apprehension about a visit to the dentist, to a little girl crying because her doll is broken, just as well as to oc-casions which directly elicit courage or initiative or independence and which may be responded to more or less adequately. It is the overriding fear of all American parents that their child will turn into a sissy; it is the overriding fear of all Americans from the moment that they can understand language that they may be taken for a sissy; and a very great deal of American speech and ac-tivity, so often misinterpreted by non-Americans, is designed solely to avert this damning judgment. Particularly self-confident Ameri-cans may say "I guess I'm just a sissy . . ." when they feel quite sure that they are not. When applied to adult males (but only in that case) the term also implies sexual passivity.

QUESTIONS

1. Is Gorer's definition denotative or connotative—or both? Would he expect to find agreement among Americans on the meaning of the word?
2. How has Gorer tried to convey the nuance of *sissy* for the non-American reader?

THE SISSY: In *The American People* by Geoffrey Gorer, revised edition. Reprinted by permission of W. W. Norton & Company, Inc. Copyright 1948 by Geoffrey Gorer. Revised edition copyright © 1964 by Geoffrey Gorer. Selection title by editor.

WRITING ASSIGNMENTS

Discuss a current word like *cute*, whose meanings are chiefly connotative. Base your analysis of these meanings on your experience with and use of the word.

Develop by definition a paragraph on one of the following:
- a. Monday-morning quarterback
- b. buck-passing
- c. nagging
- d. needling
- e. hassling

DIVISION AND CLASSIFICATION

ALLAN NEVINS

The Newspaper

1. Obviously, it is futile to talk of accuracy or inaccuracy, authority or lack of authority, with reference to the newspaper as a whole. The newspaper cannot be dismissed with either a blanket endorsement or a blanket condemnation. It cannot be used as if all its parts had equal value or authenticity. The first duty of the historical student of the newspaper is to discriminate. He must weigh every separate department, every article, every writer, for what the department or article or writer seems to be worth. Clearly, a great part of what is printed in every newspaper is from official sources, and hence may be relied upon to be perfectly accurate. The weather report is accurate; so are court notices, election notices, building permits, lists of marriage licenses, bankruptcy lists. Though unofficial, other classes of news are almost totally free from error. The most complete precautions are taken to keep the stock market quotations minutely accurate, both by stock exchange authorities and by the newspaper staffs. An error in stock

THE NEWSPAPER: In *Allan Nevins on History,* edited by Ray Allan Billington. Reprinted by permission of Charles Scribner's Sons. Copyright © 1975 Columbia University. Selection title by editor.

quotations may have the most disastrous consequences, and mistakes are hence excluded by every means within human power. So with shipping news, news of deaths, and a considerable body of similar matter—sports records, registers of Congressional or legislative votes, and so on.

2.   Thus one great division of material in newspapers can be treated as completely authentic. There is another large division which may in general be treated as trustworthy and authoritative. This is the news which is prepared by experts under conditions exempt from hurry and favorable to the gathering of all the significant facts. The weekly review of a real estate expert is a case in point. The sporting news of the best newspapers, prepared by experts under conditions which make for accuracy, is singularly uniform, and this uniformity is the best evidence that it is truthful and well proportioned. Society news, industrial news, and similar intelligence, especially when it appears in the form of weekly surveys written by known specialists, is worthy of the utmost reliance.

3.   But in dealing with news which contains a large subjective element, and which is prepared under conditions of hurry and strain, the critical faculty must be kept constantly alert. Every conscientious correspondent at an inauguration, or a battle, or a political rally, or in an interview, tries to report the facts. But not one of them can help reporting, in addition to the facts, the impression that he has personally received of them. The most honest and careful observer ordinarily sees a little of what he wishes to see. It is through failure to make critical allowance for this fact that the historical student of newspapers is most likely to be led astray. Beveridge in his life of Lincoln remarks upon the striking difference between the Democratic reports and the Republican reports of the Lincoln-Douglas debates. At Ottawa, Illinois, for example, these two great leaders held their first joint debate on August 21, 1858. Lincoln came on a special train of fourteen cars crowded with shouting Republicans. It arrived at Ottawa at noon and, according to the Republican papers, when Lincoln alighted a shout went up from a dense and enthusiastic crowd which made the bluffs of the Illinois River and the woods along it ring and ring again. Lincoln entered a carriage; according to the *Chicago Tribune* men with evergreens, mottoes, fair young ladies, bands of music, military companies, and a dense mass of cheering humanity followed him through the streets in a scene of tumultuous excitement. But according to the *Philadelphia Press* and other

Douglas papers, Lincoln had only a chilly and lackadaisical reception. "As his procession passed," stated the *Philadelphia Press*, "scarcely a cheer went up. They marched along silently and sorrowfully, as if it were a funeral cortege following him to the grave." On the other hand, the Democratic papers declared that the reception of Douglas was perfectly tremendous; the cheers were so thundering, said the *Philadelphia Press,* that they seemed to rend the very air. But the *Chicago Tribune* said that Douglas had no reception of consequence; that the only cheers he got came from the Irish Catholics. Yet both reporters were probably fairly honest. They saw what they wished to see.

DISCUSSION: DIVISION AND CLASSIFICATION

Division in general is concerned with the parts of an object or class. When we name the various makes of American automobiles, we are dividing a class of objects. This class may be broad (automobiles) or limited (American automobiles), and the division can be made in a number of ways, depending on the purpose of the analysis. American automobiles may be divided by one of the following principles, to cite only a few: manufacturer, engine size, kind of transmission, fuel economy. And any of the subdivisions can in turn be treated as a class and divided by another principle:

> *class:* American automobiles
> *principle of division:* manufacturer
> *purpose of division:* to illustrate the variety of American automobiles
> *division according to manufacturer:* Ford, Chrysler, General Motors, American Motors automobiles, etc.

> *class:* General Motors automobiles
> *principle of subdivision:* names
> *purpose of division:* to illustrate the abundance of model names
> *division according to names:* Chevrolets, Buicks, Oldsmobiles, etc.

Chevrolets, in turn, can be divided by the same principle, or by another—engine size, for example. Each division and subdivision must be consistently worked out according to a single principle, and each should be as exhaustive as knowledge permits—if the division claims to be complete. If several principles of divisions are employed in an analysis, each division must be kept separate to avoid overlapping distinctions. Division can extend to ideas like discipline and justice, to people, to activities. The following paragraph employs division in a scientific definition:

purpose of analysis

For the investigator of meteorites the basic challenge is deducing the history of the *meteorites* from a bewildering abundance of evidence. The richness of the problem is

principle of division:
  types according to
  constituent material
  first type: stony
    meteorites
  second type: iron
    meteorites
  third type: stony-iron
    meteorites
subdivision of stony
  meteorites
principle of subdivision:
  presence or absence
  of chondrules
principles of further
  subdivisions

indicated by the sheer variety of *types* of meteorite. The two main classes are the *stony meteorites* and the *iron meteorites.* The stony meteorites consist mainly of silicates, with an admixture of nickel and iron. The iron meteorites consist mainly of nickel and iron in various proportions. A smaller class is the stony-iron meteorites, which are intermediate in composition between the other two. Stony meteorites are in turn divided into two groups: the chondrites and the achondrites, according to whether or not they contain chondrules, spherical aggregates of iron-magnesium silicate. Within each group there are further subdivisions based on mineralogical and chemical composition.

—I. R. Cameron,
"Meteorites and Cosmic Radiation"
(italics added)

Classification is the opposite kind of analysis. To classify is to place a subject in one (or more) of the possible classes to which it belongs. Oranges can be classified with citrus fruit, edible fruit, sources of Vitamin C, to name only a few classes. Two or more subjects may be placed in a single class: saws and hammers are tools; Pintos and Vegas are economy cars; Washington, Adams, and Jefferson were founding fathers, and also early Presidents of the United States.

QUESTIONS

1. Nevins divides materials in newspapers according to their degree of reliability: this is his principle of division. What are the three divisions he distinguishes?
2. What point is he making through these divisions?

3. In referring to the "large subjective element" of certain newspaper accounts, is Nevins referring to bias or prejudice? What does his example of the Lincoln-Douglas debates show?
4. What is the order of ideas in the three paragraphs? Why does Nevins save "news which contains a large subjective element" for last?
5. How many classes can you think of for newspapers?

WRITING ASSIGNMENTS

Divide materials in newspapers by another principle of division and use your division to make a point, as Nevins does.

Analyze the front-page stories of an issue of a newspaper according to the degree of their reliability. Discuss the "subjective element" of one of the stories, as Nevins discusses the account of the Lincoln-Douglas debates.

JOHN HOLT
Kinds of Discipline

1. A child, in growing up, may meet and learn from three different kinds of disciplines. The first and most important is what we might call the Discipline of Nature or of Reality. When he is trying to do something real, if he does the wrong thing or doesn't do the right one, he doesn't get the result he wants. If he doesn't pile one block right on top of another, or tries to build on a slanting surface, his tower falls down. If he hits the wrong key, he hears the wrong note. If he doesn't hit the nail squarely on the head, it bends, and he has to pull it out and start with another. If he doesn't measure properly what he is trying to build, it won't open, close, fit, stand up, fly, float, whistle, or do whatever he wants it to do. If he closes his eyes when he swings, he doesn't hit the ball. A child meets this kind of discipline every time he tries to *do* something, which is why it is so important in school to give children more chances to

KINDS OF DISCIPLINE: In *Freedom and Beyond* by John Holt, copyright © 1972 by John Holt. Reprinted by permission of the publisher, E. P. Dutton & Co., Inc. Selection title by editor.

do things, instead of just reading or listening to someone talk (or pretending to). This discipline is a great teacher. The learner never has to wait long for his answer; it usually comes quickly, often instantly. Also it is clear, and very often points toward the needed correction; from what happened he can not only see that what he did was wrong, but also why, and what he needs to do instead. Finally, and most important, the giver of the answer, call it Nature, is impersonal, impartial, and indifferent. She does not give opinions, or make judgments; she cannot be wheedled, bullied, or fooled; she does not get angry or disappointed; she does not praise or blame; she does not remember past failures or hold grudges; with her one always gets a fresh start, this time is the one that counts.

2.   The next discipline we might call the Discipline of Culture, of Society, of What People Really Do. Man is a social, a cultural animal. Children sense around them this culture, this network of agreements, customs, habits, and rules binding the adults together. They want to understand it and be a part of it. They watch very carefully what people around them are doing and want to do the same. They want to do right, unless they become convinced they can't do right. Thus children rarely misbehave seriously in church, but sit as quietly as they can. The example of all those grownups is contagious. Some mysterious ritual is going on, and children, who like rituals, want to be part of it. In the same way, the little children that I see at concerts or operas, though they may fidget a little, or perhaps take a nap now and then, rarely make any disturbance. With all those grownups sitting there, neither moving nor talking, it is the most natural thing in the world to imitate them. Children who live among adults who are habitually courteous to each other, and to them, will soon learn to be courteous. Children who live surrounded by people who speak a certain way will speak that way, however much we may try to tell them that speaking that way is bad or wrong.

3.   The third discipline is the one most people mean when they speak of discipline—the Discipline of Superior Force, of sergeant to private, of "you do what I tell you or I'll make you wish you had." There is bound to be some of this in a child's life. Living as we do surrounded by things that can hurt children, or that children can hurt, we cannot avoid it. We can't afford to let a small child find out from experience the danger of playing in a busy street, or of fooling with the pots on the top of a stove, or of eating

up the pills in the medicine cabinet. So, along with other precautions, we say to him, "Don't play in the street, or touch things on the stove, or go into the medicine cabinet, or I'll punish you." Between him and the danger too great for him to imagine we put a lesser danger, but one he can imagine and maybe therefore want to avoid. He can have no idea of what it would be like to be hit by a car, but he can imagine being shouted at, or spanked, or sent to his room. He avoids these substitutes for the greater danger until he can understand it and avoid it for its own sake. But we ought to use this discipline only when it is necessary to protect the life, health, safety, or well-being of people or other living creatures, or to prevent destruction of things that people care about. We ought not to assume too long, as we usually do, that a child cannot understand the real nature of the danger from which we want to protect him. The sooner he avoids the danger, not to escape our punishment, but as a matter of good sense, the better. He can learn that faster than we think. In Mexico, for example, where prople drive their cars with a good deal of spirit, I saw many children no older than five or four walking unattended on the streets. They understood about cars, they knew what to do. A child whose life is full of the threat and fear of punishment is locked into babyhood. There is no way for him to grow up, to learn to take responsibility for his life and acts. Most important of all, we should not assume that having to yield to the threat of our superior force is good for the child's character. It is never good for *anyone's* character. To bow to superior force makes us feel impotent and cowardly for not having had the strength or courage to resist. Worse, it makes us resentful and vengeful. We can hardly wait to make someone pay for our humiliation, yield to us as we were once made to yield. No, if we cannot always avoid using the Discipline of Superior Force, we should at least use it as seldom as we can.

4.   There are places where all three disciplines overlap. Any very demanding human activity combines in it the disciplines of Superior Force, of Culture, and of Nature. The novice will be told, "Do it this way, never mind asking why, just do it that way, that is the way we always do it." But it probably *is* just the way they always do it, and usually for the very good reason that it is a way that has been found to work. Think, for example, of ballet training. The student in a class is told to do this exercise, or that; to stand so; to do this or that with his head, arms, shoulders, abdomen, hips, legs, feet. He is constantly corrected. There is no argument. But behind

these seemingly autocratic demands by the teacher lie many decades of custom and tradition, and behind that, the necessities of dancing itself. You cannot make the moves of classical ballet unless over many years you have acquired, and renewed every day, the needed strength and suppleness in scores of muscles and joints. Nor can you do the difficult motions, making them look easy, unless you have learned hundreds of easier ones first. Dance teachers may not always agree on all the details of teaching these strengths and skills. But no novice could learn them all by himself. You could not go for a night or two to watch the ballet and then, without any other knowledge at all, teach yourself how to do it. In the same way, you would be unlikely to learn any complicated and difficult human activity without drawing heavily on the experience of those who know it better. But the point is that the authority of these experts or teachers stems from, grows out of their greater competence and experience, the fact that what they do *works*, not the fact that they happen to be the teacher and as such have the power to kick a student out of the class. And the further point is that children are always and everywhere attracted to that competence, and ready and eager to submit themselves to a discipline that grows out of it. We hear constantly that children will never do anything unless compelled to by bribes or threats. But in their private lives, or in extracurricular activities in school, in sports, music, drama, art, running a newspaper, and so on, they often submit themselves willingly and wholeheartedly to very intense disciplines, simply because they want to learn to do a given thing well. Our Little-Napoleon football coaches, of whom we have too many and hear far too much, blind us to the fact that millions of children work hard every year getting better at sports and games without coaches barking and yelling at them.

QUESTIONS

1. Does Holt divide discipline according to source or to the uses of discipline in education—or according to some other principle?
2. Is Holt's division exhaustive?
3. Holt states in paragraph 4 that the kinds of discipline distinguished overlap. How do they? Does he show that they nevertheless remain distinct?
4. The principle of division might have been the effects of discipline on the personality of the young person. Is Holt concerned with effects in the course of his discussion?

5. What other principles of division might be employed in a discussion of discipline and to what purpose?

WRITING ASSIGNMENTS

Divide discipline according to a different principle from Holt's. Make your divisions exclusive of one another and indicate how exhaustive you think they are.

Write an essay on jobs or fads, developing the topic by division. If you divide by more than one principle, keep each breakdown and discussion separate and consistent.

CAROLINE BIRD

Queue

1.   Queuing gets more things through a space-time bottleneck by lining them up in space or time. Schedules and appointment calendars line things and people up in time: queues, lists, or priority systems line them up in space. Like things can be lined up or queued to get more of them into a limited space. Canners do it when they line the anchovies up head by tail to get more into the can at a time (the anchovies *share* the time-space of the can when they are curled around something else, like a caper). You queue in space when you put all the tall books on one tall shelf so that you can get more shelves and hence more books on the wall at the same time.

2.   Staggering is a form of queuing which lines things up in time to get them through a limited space. Billing is staggered through the month to get more bills through the time-space of the billing department. New York City welfare checks can no longer all be sent out on the same day. French resorts are overloaded and Parisian services understaffed because Frenchmen who get a vacation insist on taking the whole month of August off at once. Staggering

QUEUE: In *The Crowding Syndrome*, published by David McKay Company, Inc. Copyright © 1972 by Caroline Bird. Reprinted by permission of the publisher.

will be eventually necessary to avert breakdown of the French economy.

3.   People and things can be lined up by the speed at which they move so that fast movers are not slowed to the pace of slow movers ahead of them. High-speed lanes for cars, toll lines reserved for those with exact change, and express check-out counters in supermarkets line up or queue the fast movers.

4.   People react strongly, and variously to being queued. Russians line themselves up without being told. Moscow theater audiences file out, last row first, like school children marching out of assemblies. In America, on the contrary, theatrical performances break up like the Arctic ice in springtime. Commuters and the constitutionally impatient gather themselves for a dash up the aisle, while the rest of the audience is still applauding. Fidgeters and people who can't bear having anyone ahead of them sidle across rows to emergency exits, while placid souls who seem to enjoy the presence of others drift happily up the aisle with the crowd. In Moscow, the theater is emptied faster. In New York, you can get out fast if you're willing to work at it.

5.   Even on a first-come, first-served basis, Americans don't like queues. Rather than put some people in front of other people, we prefer to row them up horizontally on the starting line and let the best man win, the way they did when they shot off a gun to open the Oklahoma land rush. West Indians like queuing even less. There were so many bus-boarding accidents in Bridgetown that the British-bred Barbados Assembly passed a law requiring passengers to form a line of not more than two abreast whenever six or more persons were waiting for a bus.

6.   Whether they like it or not, Americans are spending more time in queues. We now expect to queue for library books, cabs, movies, ski lifts, tees, subway tokens, and even campsites in the wilds of our national parks. Doctors, dentists, barbers, and employment interviewers line us up. So do headwaiters, sales clerks, cashiers, bank tellers, income tax adjusters, and the few remaining meat cutters. Lawn services line our lawns up for mowing. Plumbers line our emergencies up for fixing.

7.   The queue is standing operating procedure for any transaction which may not be free at the time it is demanded. Freight cars queue for unloading, telephone calls for circuits, and stacked airplanes for permission to land. In order to get through a big organi-

zation, decisions may have to wait in one line after another, as they
are bucked from desk to desk. Traffic control problems frequently
involve similar queues of queues.

8.   "Queuing theory" describes how queues grow and shrink. It
has become a hot branch of mathematics practiced by operations
researchers studying complicated traffic and transportation systems.

QUESTIONS

1. The queue is the general class—the general practice of lining people up—to which many kinds of queuing are fitted. "Staggering" is
   a kind of queuing, the author tells us. What other kinds does she
   discuss? How do the examples of queuing fit these kinds?
2. What does her analysis show about Americans? Is she singling out
   one quality of Americans, or does she illustrate several through attitudes toward queuing?
3. What do the contrasting examples of the problem of queuing in
   Moscow and Barbados show about Americans?
4. How do paragraphs 7 and 8 differ from earlier paragraphs in subject and focus? Why are these paragraphs saved for the end of the
   discussion?

WRITING ASSIGNMENT

Identify your attitude toward standing in line by discussing three or
four different queuing situations and your behavior in them. Arrange
these examples in the order of their importance to understanding or
defining your general attitude.

COMPARISON AND CONTRAST

ISAIAH BERLIN
Churchill and Roosevelt

1. Roosevelt, as a public personality, was a spontaneous, optimistic, pleasure-loving ruler who dismayed his assistants by the gay and apparently heedless abandon with which he seemed to delight in pursuing two or more totally incompatible policies, and astonished them even more by the swiftness and ease with which he managed to throw off the cares of office during the darkest and most dangerous moments. Churchill too loves pleasure, and he too lacks neither gaiety nor a capacity for exuberant self-expression, together with the habit of blithely cutting Gordian knots in a manner which often upset his experts; but he is not a frivolous man. His nature possesses a dimension of depth—and a corresponding sense of tragic possibilities, which Roosevelt's lighthearted genius instinctively passed by.

2. Roosevelt played the game of politics with virtuosity, and both his successes and his failures were carried off in splendid style; his performance seemed to flow with effortless skill. Churchill is acquainted with darkness as well as light. Like all inhabitants and even transient visitors of inner worlds, he gives evidence of seasons of agonized brooding and slow recovery. Roosevelt might have spoken of sweat and blood, but when Churchill offered his people tears, he spoke a word which might have been uttered by Lincoln or Mazzini or Cromwell but not Roosevelt, greathearted, generous, and perceptive as he was.

CHURCHILL AND ROOSEVELT: In "Mr. Churchill" by Isaiah Berlin; reprinted from *Jubilee*, edited by Edward Weeks and Emily Flint (Little, Brown and Company). Reprinted by permission of the author and John Murray Ltd. Selection title by editor.

DISCUSSION: COMPARISON AND CONTRAST

Two or more people, objects, actions, or ideas may be compared and contrasted for the purpose of arriving at a relative estimate or evaluation:

> If Socrates was as innocent as this at the age of seventy, it may be imagined how innocent Joan was at the age of seventeen. Now Socrates was a man of argument, operating slowly and peacefully on men's minds, whereas Joan was a woman of action, operating with impetuous violence on their bodies. That, no doubt, is why the contemporaries of Socrates endured him so long, and why Joan was destroyed before she was fully grown. But both of them combined terrifying ability with a frankness, personal modesty, and benevolence which made the furious dislike to which they fell victims absolutely unreasonable, and therefore inapprehensible by themselves.—George Bernard Shaw, Preface to *St. Joan*

The opening comparison tells us something important through the differences in Socrates' and Joan's ages and ways of operating on minds and bodies; the concluding sentence moves to similarities between them. The evaluation of both Socrates and Joan is made *through* the comparison and contrast; light is shed on both of them, not on one only. The comparison and contrast could have been organized differently: Shaw could have presented all of Socrates' qualities first, then all of Joan's, instead of interweaving them.

In general, comparison is concerned with resemblance, contrast with difference (however, comparison is sometimes used to mean a concern with resemblance and difference). When comparison and contrast occur in the same passage, they must be carefully distinguished to avoid confusing the reader. They can, of course, be combined with other methods of analysis: important terms may be defined before being compared; or comparison and contrast may serve to define these terms.

QUESTIONS

1. This excerpt from a portrait of Winston Churchill was written in 1949, when the wartime Prime Minister of England was still living. Franklin Roosevelt, the wartime President of the United States, had died in 1945. Both paragraphs are developed by comparison and contrast but are constructed differently. In paragraph 1 there is a contrast of wholes—first Roosevelt, then Churchill. How is para-

graph 2 different? What is gained by each kind of paragraph construction?

2. Why does paragraph 1 precede paragraph 2? Could the order be reversed without changing the meaning of either?

3. What are the essential similarities and differences between Roosevelt and Churchill? What relative evaluation do these establish?

4. Do you think the following statements are *implied* by the comparison and contrast?
   a. A "sense of tragic possibilities" is necessary in a wartime leader.
   b. A "sense of tragic possibilities" is synonymous with depth of character.
   c. Roosevelt knew little of human suffering.
   d. Roosevelt relied on instinct in policy decisions.
   e. Churchill was not a virtuoso in the game of politics.

WRITING ASSIGNMENT

In two well-developed paragraphs compare and contrast two of your relatives. Use paragraph 1 of the Berlin as a model for your first paragraph and paragraph 2 for your second. Where necessary use transitions to show that you are comparing and contrasting and to avoid awkward or abrupt shifts.

S. S. WILSON
Cycling and Walking

1.   The reason for the high energy efficiency of cycling compared with walking appears to lie mainly in the mode of action of the muscles. Whereas a machine only performs mechanical work when a force moves through a distance, muscles consume energy when they are in tension but not moving (doing what is sometimes called "isometric" work). A man standing still maintains his upright posture by means of a complicated system of bones in compression and muscles in tension. Hence merely standing consumes energy. Similarly, in performing movements with no external forces, as in shadowboxing, muscular energy is consumed

CYCLING AND WALKING: In "Bicycle Technology" by S. S. Wilson. Copyright ©
1973 by Scientific American, Inc. All rights reserved. Selection title by editor.

because of the alternate acceleration and deceleration of the hands and arms, although no mechanical work is done against any outside agency.

2.   In walking the leg muscles must not only support the rest of the body in an erect posture but also raise and lower the entire body as well as accelerate and decelerate the lower limbs. All these actions consume energy without doing any useful external work. Walking uphill requires that additional work be done against gravity. Apart from these ways of consuming energy, every time the foot strikes the ground some energy is lost, as evidenced by the wear of footpaths, shoes and socks. The swinging of the arms and legs also causes wear and loss of energy by chafing.

3.   Contrast this with the cyclist, who first of all saves energy by sitting, thus relieving his leg muscles of their supporting function and accompanying energy consumption. The only reciprocating parts of his body are his knees and thighs; his feet rotate smoothly at a constant speed and the rest of his body is still. Even the acceleration and deceleration of his legs are achieved efficiently, since the strongest muscles are used almost exclusively; the rising leg does not have to be lifted but is raised by the downward thrust of the other leg. The back muscles must be used to support the trunk, but the arms can also help to do this, resulting (in the normal cycling attitude) in a little residual strain on the hands and arms.

QUESTIONS

1. The author first compares standing still to shadowboxing to explain "the mode of action of the muscles." What are the points of similarity, and what does the comparison show? (The phrase compared to usually means that similarities will be indicated; compared with, that differences will be indicated.)
2. How is walking similar to and different from standing still, and what does the comparison show? Could the discussion of standing still and shadowboxing have been omitted without loss to the main contrast between cycling and walking?
3. What are the points of dissimilarity between walking and cycling?
4. The comparison of standing still with shadowboxing provides a relative estimate of these activities for the purpose of illustration. What is the purpose of the relative estimate provided by the contrast between cycling and walking?

WRITING ASSIGNMENT

Compare and contrast one of the following pairs of activities to arrive at a relative estimate of them and to make a point:

   a. softball and hardball   d. tennis and badminton
   b. football and touch football   e. checkers and chess
   c. jogging and running

HANNAH ARENDT

The Concentration-Camp Inmate

Forced labor as a punishment is limited as to time and intensity. The convict retains his rights over his body; he is not absolutely tortured and he is not absolutely dominated. Banishment banishes only from one part of the world to another part of the world, also inhabited by human beings; it does not exclude from the human world altogether. Throughout history slavery has been an institution within a social order; slaves were not, like concentration-camp inmates, withdrawn from the sight and hence the protection of their fellow-men; as instruments of labor they had a definite price and as property a definite value. The concentration-camp inmate has no price, because he can always be replaced; nobody knows to whom he belongs, because he is never seen. From the point of view of normal society he is absolutely superfluous, although in times of acute labor shortage, as in Russia and in Germany during the war, he is used for work.

QUESTIONS

1. Hannah Arendt might simply have described the typical existence of the concentration-camp inmate. Instead she defines that existence through contrast with other forms of imprisonment and servitude: through a relative estimate. What is the advantage of this procedure—defining by means of contrast—over other methods?

THE CONCENTRATION-CAMP INMATE: In *Origins of Totalitarianism*, new edition by Hannah Arendt. Copyright 1951. © 1958, 1966 by Hannah Arendt. Reprinted by permission of Harcourt Brace Jovanovich, Inc. Selection title by editor.

2. What accounts for the order of ideas? Are they presented in the order of their importance?

WRITING ASSIGNMENT

Make a list of significant similarities and differences between one of the following pairs and use it to write a paragraph. Use your comparison and contrast to arrive at a relative estimate—which is better or worse?—and to make a definite point.

    a. streetcar or bus nuisance and back-seat driver
    b. silent bore and talkative bore
    c. classroom comic and dormitory comic
    d. expectations of high-school English teachers and expectations of college English teachers

ANALOGY

MICHAEL COLLINS
Circling the Moon

1.   My command module chores now include an extra task: finding the LM on the surface. If I can see it through my sextant, center my cross hairs on it, and mark the instant of superposition, then my computer will know something it doesn't know now: where the LM actually is, instead of where it is supposed to be. This is a valuable—not vital, but valuable—piece of information for "Hal" to have, especially as a starting reference point for the sequence of rendezvous maneuvers which will come tomorrow (or sooner?). Of course, the ground can take its measurements as well, but it really has no way of judging where the LM came down, except by comparing Neil and Buzz's description of their surrounding terrain (lurain?) with the rather crude maps which Houston has. But I am far past the landing site now, about to swing around behind the left edge of the moon, so it will be awhile

CIRCLING THE MOON: In *Carrying the Fire* by Michael Collins. Excerpted and reprinted with the permission of Farrar, Straus & Giroux, Inc. Copyright © 1974 by Michael Collins. Selection title by editor.

before I get my first crack at looking for the LM. It takes me two hours to circle the moon once.

2. Meanwhile, the command module is purring along in grand shape. I have turned the lights up bright, and the cockpit reflects a cheeriness which I want very much to share. My concerns are exterior ones, having to do with the vicissitudes of my two friends on the moon and their uncertain return path to me, but inside, all is well as this familar machine and I circle and watch and wait. I have removed the center couch and stored it underneath the left one, and this gives the place an entirely different aspect. It opens up a central aisle between the main instrument panel and the lower equipment bay, a pathway which allows me to zip from upper hatch window to lower sextant and return. The main reason for removing the couch is to provide adequate access for Neil and Buzz to enter the command module through the side hatch, in the event that the probe and drogue mechanism cannot be cleared from the tunnel. If such is the case, we would have to open the hatch to the vacuum of space, and Neil and Buzz would have to make an extravehicular transfer from the LM, dragging their rock boxes behind them. All three of us would be in bulky pressurized suits, requiring a tremendous amount of space and a wide path into the lower equipment bay. In addition to providing more room, these preparations give me the feeling of being proprietor of a small resort hotel, about to receive the onrush of skiers coming in out of the cold. Everything is prepared for them; it is a happy place, and I couldn't make them more welcome unless I had a fireplace. I know from pre-flight press questions that I will be described as a lonely man ("Not since Adam has any man experienced such loneliness"), and I guess that the TV commentators must be reveling in my solitude and deriving all sorts of phony philosophy from it, but I hope not. Far from feeling lonely or abandoned, I feel very much a part of what is taking place on the lunar surface. I know that I would be a liar or a fool if I said that I have the best of the three Apollo 11 seats, but I can say with truth and equanimity that I am perfectly satisfied with the one I have. This venture has been structured for three men, and I consider my third to be as necessary as either of the other two.

3. I don't mean to deny a feeling of solitude. It is there, reinforced by the fact that radio contact with the earth abruptly cuts off at the instant I disappear behind the moon. I am alone now, truly alone, and absolutely isolated from any known life. I am it. If

a count were taken, the score would be three billion plus two over on the other side of the moon, and one plus God only knows what on this side. I feel this powerfully—not as fear or loneliness—but as awareness, anticipation, satisfaction, confidence, almost exultation. I like the feeling. Outside my window I can see stars—and that is all. Where I know the moon to be, there is simply a black void; the moon's presence is defined solely by the absence of stars. To compare the sensation with something terrestrial, perhaps being alone in a skiff in the middle of the Pacific Ocean on a pitchblack night would most nearly approximate my situation. In a skiff, one would see bright stars above and black sea below; I see the same stars, minus the twinkling, of course, and absolutely nothing below. In each case, time and distance are extremely important factors. In terms of distance, I am much more remote, but in terms of time, lunar orbit is much closer to civilized conversation than is the mid-Pacific. Although I may be nearly a quarter of a million miles away, I am cut off from human voices for only forty-eight minutes out of each two hours, while the man in the skiff—grazing the very surface of the planet—is not so privileged, or burdened. Of the two quantities, time and distance, time tends to be a much more personal one, so that I feel simultaneously closer to, and farther away from, Houston than I would if I were on some remote spot on earth which would deny me conversation with other humans for months on end.

DISCUSSION: ANALOGY

Illustrative analogy is a special kind of example, a comparison between two different things or activities for the purpose of explanation: a child growing like a tender plant and needing sun, water, and a receptive soil as well as proper care from a skilled gardener. The comparison may be point by point. But there are differences also, and if there is danger of the analogy being carried too far (the child is not so tender that he needs as much protection as the plant from the hazards of living), the writer may state these differences to limit the inferences that may be drawn. He or she has chosen the analogy for the sake of vivid illustration and nothing more. We shall see later that analogy is often used in argument: children *should* be fully protected from various hazards because they are tender plants. The argument will stand or fall depending on how convinced we are of the similarities and of the unimportance of the differences.

Analogy is often used in explanations of scientific ideas. One of the most famous is the analogy between the moving apart of the galaxies in the universe and the expanding raisin cake:

> Suppose the cake swells uniformly as it cooks, but the raisins themselves remain of the same size. Let each raisin represent a cluster of galaxies, and imagine yourself inside one of them. As the cake swells, you will observe that all the other raisins move away from you. Moreover, the farther away the raisin, the faster it will seem to move. When the cake has swollen to twice its initial dimensions, the distance between all the raisins will have doubled itself—two raisins that were initially an inch apart will now be two inches apart; two raisins that were a foot apart will have moved two feet apart. Since the entire action takes place within the same time interval, obviously the more distant raisins must move apart faster than those close at hand. So it happens with the clusters of galaxies.—Fred Hoyle, "When Time Began"

In another essay Hoyle employs another analogy: between the expanding galaxies and sewn dots on an expanding balloon. Each analogy has its advantages and disadvantages, depending on the points of similarity and dissimilarity. One advantage of the analogy quoted above is the disparity of size between a raisin and a galaxy—a system of sometimes billions of stars occupying an enormous amount of space. The disparity in size provides a relative estimate of size in the universe.

QUESTIONS

1. Collins is describing the 1969 moon landing of Neil Armstrong and Buzz Aldrin. What are the points of similarity between the returning astronauts and the returning skiers? Are these points of similarity stated or implied? (The "LM" is the landing module.)
2. What other analogy might Collins have employed to describe the returning astronauts? What would have been gained or lost in descriptive power or explanation had he employed it?
3. What is the similarity, and what are the differences, in the analogy between the skiff and the command module? What point is Collins making through the differences?

WRITING ASSIGNMENT

Explain the sensation of being alone in a car in heavy traffic or a storm, or traveling away from home for the first time, through analogy to another kind of experience similar enough to help make your experience vivid. Comment on the differences and their significance at some point in your explanation.

BENJAMIN LEE WHORF
The Background of Experience

1.   The familiar saying that the exception proves the rule contains a good deal of wisdom, though from the standpoint of formal logic it became an absurdity as soon as "prove" no longer meant "put on trial." The old saw began to be profound psychology from the time it ceased to have standing in logic. What it might well suggest to us today is that, if a rule has absolutely no exceptions, it is not recognized as a rule or as anything else; it is then part of the background of experience of which we tend to remain unconscious. Never having experienced anything in contrast to it, we cannot isolate it and formulate it as a rule until we so enlarge our experience and expand our base of reference that we encounter an interruption of its regularity. The situation is somewhat analogous to that of not missing the water till the well runs dry, or not realizing that we need air till we are choking.

2.   For instance, if a race of people had the physiological defect of being able to see only the color blue, they would hardly be able to formulate the rule that they saw only blue. The term blue would convey no meaning to them, their language would lack color terms, and their words denoting their various sensations of blue would answer to, and translate, our words "light, dark, white, black," and so on, not our word "blue." In order to formulate the rule or norm of seeing only blue, they would need exceptional moments in which they saw other colors. The phenomenon of gravitation forms a rule without exceptions; needless to say, the untutored person is utterly unaware of any law of gravitation, for it would never enter his head to conceive of a universe in which bodies behaved otherwise than they do at the earth's surface. Like the

THE BACKGROUND OF EXPERIENCE: In *Language, Thought, and Reality* by Benjamin Lee Whorf. © 1956 by M.I.T.; reprinted by permission of The M.I.T. Press, Cambridge, Massachusetts. Selection title by editor.

color blue with our hypothetical race, the law of gravitation is a part of the untutored individual's background, not something he isolates from that background. The law could not be formulated until bodies that always fell were seen in terms of a wider astronomical world in which bodies moved in orbits or went this way and that.

3.   Similarly, whenever we turn our heads, the image of the scene passes across our retinas exactly as it would if the scene turned around us. But this effect is background, and we do not recognize it; we do not see a room turn around us but are conscious only of having turned our heads in a stationary room. If we observe critically while turning the head or eyes quickly, we shall see, no motion it is true, yet a blurring of the scene between two clear views. Normally we are quite unconscious of this continual blurring but seem to be looking about in an unblurred world. Whenever we walk past a tree or house, its image on the retina changes just as if the tree or house were turning on an axis; yet we do not see trees or houses turn as we travel about at ordinary speeds. Sometimes ill-fitting glasses will reveal queer movements in the scene as we look about, but normally we do not see the relative motion of the environment when we move; our psychic makeup is somehow adjusted to disregard whole realms of phenomena that are so all-pervasive as to be irrelevant to our daily lives and needs.

QUESTIONS

1. How does the familiar saying "The exception proves the rule" help us to understand Whorf's point about the "background of experience"?
2. How is the situation analogous to those Whorf mentions briefly at the end of paragraph 1?
3. How is the law of gravitation analogous to that of the race of people discussed in paragraph 2?
4. What is gained in explanation by the example in paragraph 3? How is it similar to those in paragraph 2?

WRITING ASSIGNMENT

Illustrate Whorf's point through an example of your own. Then discuss its points of similarity and dissimilarity with one of Whorf's examples in paragraphs 2 and 3.

EXAMPLE

E. B. WHITE
New York

It is a miracle that New York works at all. The whole thing is implausible. Every time the residents brush their teeth, millions of gallons of water must be drawn from the Catskills and the hills of Westchester. When a young man in Manhattan writes a letter to his girl in Brooklyn, the love message gets blown to her through a pneumatic tube—*pfft*—just like that. The subterranean system of telephone cables, power lines, steam pipes, gas mains and sewer pipes is reason enough to abandon the island to the gods and the weevils. Every time an incision is made in the pavement, the noisy surgeons expose ganglia that are tangled beyond belief. By rights New York should have destroyed itself long ago, from panic or fire or rioting or failure of some vital supply line in its circulatory system or from some deep labyrinthine short circuit. Long ago the city should have experienced an insoluble traffic snarl at some impossible bottleneck. It should have perished of hunger when food lines failed for a few days. It should have been wiped out by a plague starting in its slums or carried in by ships' rats. It should have been overwhelmed by the sea that licks at it on every side. The workers in its myriad cells should have succumbed to nerves, from the fearful pall of smoke-fog that drifts over every few days from Jersey, blotting out all light at noon and leaving the high offices suspended, men groping and depressed, and the sense of world's end. It should have been touched in the head by the August heat and gone off its rocker.

DISCUSSION: EXAMPLE

An idea may be illustrated by a series of short examples or by a long example, if one is needed to make it clear. The word *example* originally referred to a sample or typical instance; the word still has this

NEW YORK: In *Here Is New York* by E. B. White, pp. 24–25. Copyright 1949 by E. B. White. Reprinted by permission of Harper & Row, Publishers, Inc. Selection title by editor.

EXAMPLE

77

meaning, and for many writers it is an outstanding instance, even one essential to understanding the idea under discussion:

> The world is full of things whose right-hand version is different from the left-hand version: a right-handed corkscrew as against a left-handed, a right snail as against a left one. Above all, the two hands; they can be mirrored one in the other, but they cannot be turned in such a way that the right hand and the left hand become interchangeable. That was known in Pasteur's time to be true also of some crystals, whose facets are so arranged that there are right-hand versions and left-hand versions.—J. Bronowski, *The Ascent of Man*

To write of right-hand and left-hand things in nature would be unclear to most readers without examples. In the same way, to write that New York is different today from the New York of fifty years ago would mean little without examples.

QUESTIONS

1. What examples does White give to show that "the whole thing is implausible"?
2. White explicitly compares New York City to a human being. What are the similarities, and how does the comparison help to emphasize the "miracle" he is describing?

WRITING ASSIGNMENTS

In a well-developed paragraph state an idea about your hometown or city and develop it by a series of short examples. Make your examples vivid and lively.

Develop one of the following statements by example:
   a. The insupportable labor of doing nothing.—Sir Richard Steele
   b. The first blow is half the battle.—Oliver Goldsmith
   c. Ask yourself whether you are happy, and you cease to be so.— John Stuart Mill
   d. Parentage is a very important profession; but no test of fitness for it is ever imposed in the interest of the children.—Bernard Shaw

TOM WOLFE

Thursday Morning
in a New York Subway Station

1.   Love! Attar of libido in the air! It is 8:45 A.M. Thursday morning in the IRT subway station at 50th Street and Broadway and already two kids are hung up in a kind of herringbone weave of arms
and legs, which proves, one has to admit, that love is not *confined*
to Sunday in New York. Still, the odds! All the faces come popping
in clots out of the Seventh Avenue local, past the King Size Ice
Cream machine, and the turnstiles start whacking away as if the
world were breaking up on the reefs. Four steps past the turnstiles
everybody is already backed up haunch to paunch for the climb up
the ramp and the stairs to the surface, a great funnel of flesh,
wool, felt, leather, rubber and steaming alumicron, with the blood
squeezing through everybody's old sclerotic arteries in hopped-up
spurts from too much coffee and the effort of surfacing from the
subway at the rush hour. Yet there on the landing are a boy and a
girl, both about eighteen, in one of those utter, My Sin, backbreak-
ing embraces.
2.   He envelops her not only with his arms but with his chest,
which has the American teen-ager concave shape to it. She has
her head cocked at a 90-degree angle and they both have their
eyes pressed shut for all they are worth and some incredibly fever-
ish action going with each other's mouths. All round them, ten,
scores, it seems like hundreds, of faces and bodies are perspiring,
trooping and bellying up the stairs with arteriosclerotic grimaces
past a showcase full of such novel items as Joy Buzzers, Squirting
Nickels, Finger Rats, Scary Tarantulas and spoons with realistic
dead flies on them, past Fred's barbershop, which is just off the
landing and has glossy photographs of young men with the kind of
baroque haircuts one can get in there, and up onto 50th Street into
a madhouse of traffic and shops with weird lingerie and gray hair-
dyeing displays in the windows, signs for free teacup readings and
a pool-playing match between the Playboy Bunnies and Downey's

EXAMPLE   **79**

Showgirls, and then everybody pounds on toward the Time-Life Building, the Brill Building or NBC.

3.   The boy and the girl just keep on writhing in their embroilment. Her hand is sliding up the back of his neck, which he turns when her fingers wander into the intricate formal gardens of his Chicago Boxcar hairdo at the base of the skull. The turn causes his face to start to mash in the ciliated hull of her beehive hairdo, and so she rolls her head 180 degrees to the other side, using their mouths for the pivot. But aside from good hair grooming, they are oblivious to everything but each other. Everybody gives them a once-over. Disgusting! Amusing! How touching! A few kids pass by and say things like "Swing it, baby." But the great majority in that heaving funnel up the stairs seem to be as much astounded as anything else. The vision of love at rush hour cannot strike anyone exactly as romance. It is a feat, like a fat man crossing the English Channel in a barrel. It is an earnest accomplishment against the tide. It is a piece of slightly gross heroics, after the manner of those knobby, varicose old men who come out from some place in baggy shorts every year and run through the streets of Boston in the Marathon race. And somehow that is the gaffe against love all week long in New York, for everybody, not just two kids writhing under their coiffures in the 50th Street subway station; too hurried, too crowded, too hard, and no time for dalliance.

QUESTIONS

1. Wolfe illustrates "the gaffe against love all week long in New York." What precisely is the "gaffe"? What do the details suggest about the Thursday morning mood of New Yorkers?
2. What does the description of the showcase and of 50th Street imply about the world of the lovers? Would they seem comical in any setting?

WRITING ASSIGNMENTS

Every piece of writing suggests something about the personality, interests, and ideas of the author, even when he speaks to us through a narrator. Discuss the impression you receive of the author of this selection.

Describe one or two people in a situation made comical by the setting. Allow your reader to visualize the setting as well as the situation.

PROCESS

FLORENCE H. PETTIT
How to Sharpen Your Knife

If you have never done any whittling or wood carving before, the first skill to learn is how to sharpen your knife. You may be surprised to learn that even a brand-new knife needs sharpening. Knives are never sold honed (finely sharpened), although some gouges and chisels are. It is essential to learn the firm stroke on the stone that will keep your blades sharp. The sharpening stone must be fixed in place on the table, so that it will not move around. You can do this by placing a piece of rubber inner tube or a thin piece of foam rubber under it. Or you can tack four strips of wood, if you have a rough worktable, to frame the stone and hold it in place. Put a generous puddle of oil on the stone—this will soon disappear into the surface of a new stone, and you will need to keep adding more oil. Press the knife blade flat against the stone in the puddle of oil, using your index finger. Whichever way the cutting edge of the knife faces is the side of the blade that should get a little more pressure. Move the blade around three or four times in a narrow oval about the size of your fingernail, going *counterclockwise* when the sharp edge is facing right. Now turn the blade over in the same spot on the stone, press hard, and move it around the small oval *clockwise,* with more pressure on the cutting edge that faces left. Repeat the ovals, flipping the knife blade over six or seven times, and applying lighter pressure to the blade the last two times. Wipe the blade clean with a piece of rag or tissue and rub it flat on the piece of leather strop at least twice on each side. Stroke *away* from the cutting edge to remove the little burr of metal that may be left on the blade.

HOW TO SHARPEN YOUR KNIFE: In *How to Make Whirligigs and Whimmy Diddles* by Florence H. Pettit. Copyright © 1972 by Florence H. Pettit. Reprinted with the permission of Thomas Y. Crowell Company, Inc., publisher. Selection title by editor.

DISCUSSION: PROCESS

An important method of paragraph development is that of tracing or analyzing a mechanical, natural, or historical process. In general, a process is a series of connected actions, each developing from the preceding one, that result in something: a decision, a product, an effect of some kind. Though the stages of a process are presented chronologically—that is, in the order in which they occur—the writer may interrupt the account to discuss the implications or details of a particular stage. In complex processes, various stages may individually contain a number of steps, each of which may be distinguished for the reader. Process analysis is often closely related to causal analysis, to be discussed in the next section, and may be combined with it.

QUESTIONS

1. What details help the reader to visualize the mechanical process described in the paragraph?
2. Are the stages of the process presented chronologically? If not, why not?
3. Are any terms defined in context—that is, in the description of how to sharpen a knife?

WRITING ASSIGNMENTS

Describe a mechanical process comparable to sharpening a knife—for example, sharpening the blades of a hand mower or pruning a tree or painting the exterior of a house.

Rewrite the paragraph on how to sharpen a knife, explaining the process to a child who is just beginning to learn how to carve wood.

IONA and PETER OPIE

Leapfrog

They say leapfrog can be played with any number, large or small (even by only one if there are posts or milk churns about),

LEAPFROG: In *Children's Games in Street and Playground* by Iona and Peter Opie, published by Oxford University Press. © Iona and Peter Opie 1969. Reprinted by permission of the publisher.

and it is a good game with just two: one bending down and the other vaulting over, running forward a few steps and making a back for the first boy to vault over. In this way leapfrog is "quite useful," or so an 11-year-old asserts, "because if anyone has to go a long distance walk it helps one to get along." But it is more fun if there are more players. They begin by lining up; one person bends down, and the first in the line jumps over him and runs forward a few steps, and makes a back himself; the second in the line jumps over each of these two players and runs forward a few more steps and makes a third back. Each player who follows has one more back to leap over, and makes another back himself, until everyone is stooping. Then the player who first bent down stands up, and himself jumps along the line of backs, and makes a further back at the other end of the line, and the second person who bent down gets up as soon as he has been jumped over, and starts jumping, and so on. In this way the game is continuous. Whoever is last in the line gets up and jumps over those in front of him, and whoever has cleared all the backs makes a new back at the far end of the line. The sport becomes more exciting if the last in the line stands up as soon as he has been jumped over, and straightway follows after the boy who has jumped over him: then there may be almost as many boys jumping as there are boys bending down, and when a boy comes to the end of the line of backs he has to be quick about bending down himself, for the person he first jumped over may be close on his heels ready, in his turn, to complete the line of jumps. Those who can are gasping "Keep the kettle boiling" to encourage the flow of jumpers which—in theory—may ripple onwards around the playground without stopping until the school bell rings. But the sport is not as simple as it looks. If a player does not vault properly, placing his hands evenly on the back of the bent figure and leaping lightly at the same time, the result, says an 11-year-old, will be "an unartistic heap of humans" on the ground. And as another boy remarks, "There is only one special rule and that is 'Do not push people over when you are jumping over them.' " In fact, holding oneself steady while being jumped over requires almost as much effort as does the jumping. When a person bends down he presents either his backside to the jumper, placing one leg forward with knee bent, resting his hands firmly on his knee, and tucking his head well in; or, perhaps more often, he bends down sideways to the oncomers, and grips an ankle. The higher the back he makes the more difficult it will be to jump over him, and the more likely he is to be knocked over. Likewise the nearer he is to the previous person who bent down the more difficult it will be to jump over him; and sometimes they insist that a player runs five or six yards before he bends down, while sometimes, to make the sport more difficult, the rule is that he must take only three or four steps after he has jumped. Sometimes they play "Higher and Higher," when those bending down make their backs a little higher after each turn, and a person who can no longer get over has to drop out. Sometimes they play in a circle and one person goes on jumping until he falls. Occasionally the rule is that a jumper may use only one hand when he vaults, a feat which needs practice. And sometimes those making the backs are allowed to sink down as the leaper places his hands on their back which, far from making it easier for the leaper "may mean that he goes flat on his face."

QUESTIONS

1. How do the authors define the basic game of leapfrog and distinguish the various ways of playing it? How does the purpose of the game emerge in the details? How do they convey the fun of the game?
2. At what points in the description of the game do the authors interrupt to comment on the details of the process?
3. What special skills are needed to play the game? Do the authors comment on these skills directly, or are they implied in the details?

WRITING ASSIGNMENT

Describe another game you played in childhood. Distinguish the stages of the game and the skills needed in them. Relate these to the purpose of the game—not only the rules of winning but the effect of the game on the players.

CAUSE AND EFFECT

KENNETH KENISTON
Big Man on Campus

1. With the extension of democratic rights in the first half of the nineteenth century and the ensuing decline of the Federalist establishment, a new conception of education began to emerge. Education was no longer a confirmation of a pre-existing status, but an instrument in the acquisition of higher status. For a new generation of upwardly mobile students, the goal of education was not to prepare them to live comfortably in the world into which they had been born, but to teach them new virtues and skills that would propel them into a different and better world. Education became training; and the student was no longer the gentleman-in-waiting, but the journeyman *apprentice* for upward mobility.

2. In the nineteenth century a college education began to be seen as a way to get ahead in the world. The founding of the land-grant colleges opened the doors of higher education to poor but aspiring boys from non-Anglo-Saxon, working-class, and lower-middle-class backgrounds. The myth of the poor boy who worked his way through college to success drew millions of poor boys to the new campuses. And with this shift, education became more vocational: its object was the acquisition of practical skills and useful information.

3. For the gentleman-in-waiting, virtue consisted above all in grace and style, in doing well what was appropriate to his position; education was merely a way of acquiring polish. And vice was manifested in gracelessness, awkwardness, in behaving inappropriately, discourteously, or ostentatiously. For the apprentice, however, virtue was evidenced in success through hard work. The requisite qualities of character were not grace or style, but drive, determination, and a sharp eye for opportunity. While casual liberality and even prodigality characterized the gentleman, frugality,

BIG MAN ON CAMPUS: In "Faces in the Lecture Room." Reprinted by permission of *Daedalus*, Journal of the American Academy of Arts and Sciences, Boston, Massachusetts. *The Contemporary University: U.S.A.*, edited by Robert S. Morison, 1966. Selection title by editor.

thrift, and self-control came to distinguish the new apprentice. And while the gentleman did not aspire to a higher station because his station was already high, the apprentice was continually becoming, striving, struggling upward. Failure for the apprentice meant standing still, not rising.

4.   In the early twentieth century still another type of student began to appear. As American society became more developed economically and more bureaucratized, upward mobility was no longer guaranteed by ambition, drive, and practical knowledge. In addition, those who aspired to success had to possess the ability to make friends and influence people. Mastering the human environment became more important than mastering the physical and economic environment. The function of education thus became not vocational training, but teaching the ability to be likable and persuasive and to get along with all kinds of people. College life was increasingly seen as an informal training ground for social skills; virtue was defined as popularity; and a new type, exemplified by the *Big Men on Campus*, began to emerge.

5.   Students who sought popularity and skill in dealing with people were naturally likely to emphasize the social rather than the academic or vocational aspects of higher education. Fraternities, student governments, even casual walks across the college campus, calling friends by name and saying "Hi" to strangers, were the new classrooms. Vocational skills became secondary—or, more precisely, the most important skills in *any* vocation were the capacity to make oneself respected, well liked, and a leader. The new sin was not gaucheness or standing still, but unpopularity. To the Big Man on Campus, academic and intellectual interests were irrelevant: whatever intelligence he possessed went into a rather calculated effort to please and impress others, win their respect, and dominate them without their knowing they were being dominated.

6.   The emergence of the Big Man on Campus as an ideal type among American students coincided with the appearance of a distinctively nonacademic youth culture. The gentleman and the apprentice were both oriented primarily to the adult world: their most relevant models were adults—either the parental generation of gentlemen or the older generation of upwardly mobile and successful entrepreneurs. For the Big Man on Campus, however, the adult world was less immediately important. He looked mainly to his peers, for only by establishing his popularity in their eyes could

he demonstrate his merit. Thus student cultures became more and more insulated both from academic culture and from adult society, developing their own rites, rituals, and traditions. The world of students became a separate world, not merely a reflection of or a preparation for adulthood. And as many observers have noted, the outlooks of this world were clearly distinguishable from the outlooks of adulthood—the student youth culture emphasized immediacy, enjoyment of the moment, popularity, attractiveness, sports, daring, and intellectual indifference. Walls, barricades, and fences of apathy, deafness, and blindness were built between students and the more academic, intellectual values of their teachers. The power of these fortifications is suggested by the monotonous finding of research done before World War II that so many students were so little affected by the values their colleges sought to promote.

7. Since that time, yet another type of student has begun to emerge. Today "superior academic performance" is a prerequisite for admission to any desirable college, let alone graduate school. Grace, ambition, and popularity have fallen into secondary position, for, without good grades and the ability to do well on IQ tests, the gentlemanly, ambitious, or popular student is not even considered by the admissions office. From an early age students are therefore exposed and overexposed to academic demands: they are taught from kindergarten onward that prestige and rewards are impossible without intellectual competence, cognitive efficiency, intellectual skill, and a high degree of specialization.

DISCUSSION: CAUSE AND EFFECT

Paragraphs and essays sometimes trace causes of an event or trace the effects. The word *cause* has been used in a number of ways. One of the oldest definitions—that of the Greek philosopher Aristotle—distinguishes four related causes: the material, the formal, the efficient, the final. The material cause of a dictionary, for example, is the paper, ink, and other materials used in its manufacture. The formal cause is the shape of the dictionary, the arrangement of words alphabetically, and the arrangement of definitions according to a plan—perhaps from the most common to the least common meanings. The efficient cause is the dictionary maker, who actually creates the dictionary; and the final cause is the use intended.

Another meaning of *cause* applies mainly to events. A writer may distinguish the remote cause from the immediate cause—those circumstances distant in time from the event and those just preceding it, respectively. Where there is a causal chain of events (a student fails to study for an exam, thus flunks the exam, thus flunks the course, thus falls below the minimum grade requirement of the college, and thus drops out of college), not studying for the exam is the immediate cause of flunking the exam, and it is the remote cause of dropping out of college.

Historical processes, which trace a chain of causes, can be extremely complex. The Japanese attack on Pearl Harbor was an immediate cause of the war between the United States and Japan. One remote cause was possibly the Immigration Act of 1924 which restricted Japanese immigration. The Immigration Act was in turn influenced by prevailing attitudes toward Asian and other foreign people.

Another complex kind of causal analysis distinguishes between necessary and sufficient conditions. This kind of analysis is most common in the sciences. A necessary condition must be present for an event to occur; the condition is sufficient if the event always occurs when it is present. A necessary condition of sunburn would be the sun, whose absence would prevent the sunburn; a sufficient condition would be prolonged exposure. The sun in itself is not a sufficient condition because sunburn does not always occur in its presence. Usually cause is analyzed as a complex interaction of conditions (sun, prolonged exposure, and so on). Such causal analysis is considered probable only—never certain—because unknown conditions may be present. If it were discovered that only a certain type of skin was susceptible to sunburn, that skin type would become one of the necessary conditions. Because of the constant possibility of unknown conditions, scientists can never be certain that they know all the conditions of an event or a phenomenon.

QUESTIONS

1. By what principle does Keniston divide students in the course of his analysis? Does he intend the division to be exhaustive?
2. How does he use this division of students to analyze attitudes toward education?
3. What causes does he cite for these attitudes? Does he single out a single cause for the emergence of the Big Man on Campus?
4. What conditions were necessary to the emergence of the "youth culture" discussed in paragraph 6?

WRITING ASSIGNMENTS

Discuss the extent to which students in your high school conform to one or more of the types Keniston distinguishes.

Discuss the extent to which students in your college are different from students you knew in high school. State what you consider to be the probable causes of these differences.

Analyze your educational goals and attitudes in light of Keniston's distinctions. Discuss the immediate and remote causes of your attitudes. Use your analysis to state which of the students in the essay you most resemble.

JOHN BROOKS

The Telephone

1.   What has the telephone done to us, or for us, in the hundred years of its existence? A few effects suggest themselves at once. It has saved lives by getting rapid word of illness, injury, or famine from remote places. By joining with the elevator to make possible the multistory residence or office building, it has made possible—for better or worse—the modern city. By bringing about a quantum leap in the speed and ease with which information moves from place to place, it has greatly accelerated the rate of scientific and technological change and growth in industry. Beyond doubt it has crippled if not killed the ancient art of letter writing. It has made living alone possible for persons with normal social impulses; by so doing, it has played a role in one of the greatest social changes of this century, the breakup of the multigenerational household. It has made the waging of war chillingly more efficient than formerly. Perhaps (though not provably) it has prevented wars that might have arisen out of international misunderstanding caused by written communication. Or perhaps—again not provably—by magnifying and extending irrational personal conflicts based on voice contact, it has caused wars. Certainly it has extended the

THE TELEPHONE: In *Telephone: The First Hundred Years* by John Brooks, pp. 8–9. Copyright © 1975, 1976 by John Brooks. Reprinted by permission of Harper & Row, Publishers, Inc. Selection title by editor.

scope of human conflicts, since it impartially disseminates the useful knowedge of scientists and the babble of bores, the affection of the affectionate and the malice of the malicious.

2.   But the question remains unanswered. The obvious effects just cited seem inadequate, mechanistic; they only scratch the surface. Perhaps the crucial effects are evanescent and unmeasurable. Use of the telephone involves personal risk because it involves exposure; for some, to be "hung up on" is among the worst of fears; others dream of a ringing telephone and wake up with a pounding heart. The telephone's actual ring—more, perhaps, than any other sound in our daily lives—evokes hope, relief, fear, anxiety, joy, according to our expectations. The telephone is our nerve-end to society.

3.   In some ways it is in itself a thing of paradox. In one sense a metaphor for the times it helped create, in another sense the telephone is their polar opposite. It is small and gentle—relying on low voltages and miniature parts—in times of hugeness and violence. It is basically simple in times of complexity. It is so nearly human, recreating voices so faithfully that friends or lovers need not identify themselves by name even when talking across oceans, that to ask its effects on human life may seem hardly more fruitful than to ask the effect of the hand or the foot. The Canadian philosopher Marshall McLuhan—one of the few who have addressed themselves to these questions—was perhaps not far from the mark when he spoke of the telephone as creating "a kind of extra-sensory perception."

QUESTIONS

1. Why does Brooks consider the effects he discusses in paragraph 1 less significant than those in paragraph 2? What does he mean by the statement, "Perhaps the crucial effects are evanescent and unmeasurable"?

2. In what ways is the telephone a paradox? Does the author show it to be a paradox in paragraphs 1 and 2?

3. Has Brooks stated all the effects of the telephone, or has he identified only a few? What central point is he making about the telephone?

WRITING ASSIGNMENTS

Develop one of the ideas in the essay from your personal experience. You might discuss your own positive and negative attitudes toward the telephone, and the reasons for them, or you might develop the statement, "In some ways it is in itself a thing of paradox."

Write an essay describing what it would be like to live without a telephone, or what a single day might be like without one.

Discuss the impact of the telephone on life in your home. Distinguish the various uses and effects of the telephone for various members of your family.

RUSSEL NYE
Television

1.   Television was radio with eyes, a newspaper without print, movies individualized. It involved its audience totally and instantaneously with a compelling combination of sight, sound, and motion that no other medium provided. Television fostered the illusion of intimacy—seen at home, individually or in a small group, positing a one-to-one relationship between the figure on the screen and the viewer at the set. Television also fostered the illusion of realism (like radio but more completely) because it showed what happened *when* it happened, visibly and audibly, with neither time-lag nor intervening agency. Films, newspapers, and the phonograph always involved intermediaries—a cameraman, a cutter or editor, a reporter, a selection of events, a choice of information—which television barely inferred. What appeared on the television screen (despite the fact that it was edited) appeared to be "the real thing." As philosopher-critic Marshall McLuhan pointed out, television is a "cool" medium in that as part of a new communications system (as opposed to "hot" or "linear" media like print) it makes the viewer a participant rather than a spectator. It is television's "all inclusive *nowness*," McLuhan wrote in *Under-*

TELEVISION: In *The Unembarrassed Muse: The Popular Arts in America* by Russel Nye. Copyright © 1970 by Russel Nye. Reprinted by permission of The Dial Press. Selection title by editor.

standing Media, which makes it very nearly the ultimate "instantaneous electronic environment . . . , a total field of instantaneous data in which . . . involvement is mandatory."

2. Television's most overwhelming characteristic is the size of its audience, always measured in millions, which makes it the greatest shared popular experience in history. Its life blood from the first was advertising, designed to sell products to a mass audience which in turn (as in other mass media) forced it toward conformity and standardization. Television is primarily a selling machine of great efficiency if properly handled. NBC's two-year study of its impact on the buying habits of a Midwestern town showed that advertising could increase sales from 48 per cent to 200 per cent (depending on the type of product) within a few weeks. (One recipe, presented on the Kraft Music Hall, almost immediately brought a half-million requests.) Television's grasp of its audience is all-encompassing. In 1967 95 per cent of all households owned at least one set while 25 per cent had two or more. During the peak viewing season (January and February) the average set is on forty-four hours a week; the potential audience for any single program is calculated at eighty-three–eighty-five million. (The "TV Dinner," that most McLuhanesque of culinary innovations, appeared in 1954.) The average American male at age sixty-five has spent three thousand days, or nearly nine years, watching television; a five-year-old American child has spent more hours before the set than a student spends in class during four years of college.

3. Television must therefore always see its audience not only as an audience but as a market; what it presents is not only entertainment but advertising. Nothing can be done on television without consideration of both sets of conditions. Studies have shown that a program that requires too much thought, elicits too much excitement, or stirs up too much controversy is likely to make the viewer neglect the sponsor's message; the element of mediocrity thus has a certain importance in programming.

4. Costs are far greater than those of film, radio, or print and therefore tend also to control programs. Television must produce each year over four hundred times as many hours of entertainment as Hollywood did during its prosperous era; television in ten days presents more hours of drama than Broadway in a year. Each network must fill about twenty-five to thirty hours of evening "prime time" each week with approximately fifty to seventy-five shows which cost from $130,000 to $500,000. Arthur Miller's play,

"Death of a Salesman," produced by CBS in 1966, cost the network $880,000, of which the sponsor, Xerox, paid only $250,000. Television's question in producing any program, therefore, is always how much does it cost to reach how many millions of viewers most effectively, and what will be the result to the sponsor in increased sales? As Robert Kintner of NBC said in 1960, "The ultimate responsibility [for television programs] is ours, but the ultimate power has to be the sponsor's, because without him you couldn't run a network."

QUESTIONS

1. What characteristics make television a powerful advertising medium?
2. What effects does advertising have on television programming? Why must television always "see its audience not only as an audience but as a market"?
3. What does Nye mean by "mediocrity" in paragraph 3? Is he using the word in the sense that Joseph Wood Krutch uses it (page 50)?
4. Exactly how do costs tend to control programming?

WRITING ASSIGNMENT

Evaluate the following statement—written in 1970—in light of current television programming on a single network, on a single evening of the week. Or compare the programming of two networks on the same evening:

Studies have shown that a program that requires too much thought, elicits too much excitement, or stirs up too much controversy is likely to make the viewer neglect the sponsor's message; the element of mediocrity thus has a certain importance in programming.

VARIETY OF PARAGRAPH DEVELOPMENT

DWIGHT MACDONALD
Functional Curiosity

Henry Luce has built a journalistic empire on this national weakness for being "well informed."* *Time* attributes its present two-million circulation to a steady increase, since it first appeared in 1925, in what it calls "functional curiosity." Unlike the old-fashioned idle variety, this is "a kind of searching, hungry interest in what is happening everywhere—born not of an idle desire to be entertained or amused, but of a solid conviction that the news intimately and vitally affects the lives of everyone now. Functional curiosity grows as the number of educated people grows." The curiosity exists, but it is not functional since it doesn't help the individual function. A very small part of the mass of miscellaneous Facts offered in each week's issue of *Time* (or, for that matter, in the depressing quantity of newspapers and magazines visible on any large newsstand) is useful to the reader; they don't help him make more money, take some political or other action to advance his interests, or become a better person. About the only functional gain (though the *New York Times,* in a recent advertising campaign, proclaimed that reading it would help one to "be more interesting") the reader gets out of them is practice in reading. And even this is a doubtful advantage. *Time's* educated people read too many irrelevant words—irrelevant, that is, to any thoughtful idea of their personal interests, either narrow (practical) or broad (cultural). Imagine a similar person of, say, the sixteenth century confronted with a copy of *Time* or the *New York Times*. He would take a whole day to master it, perhaps two, because he would be accustomed to take the time to think and even to feel about what he

---

* Henry Luce (1897–1963) was the editor and publisher of *Time*. He also published *Life, Fortune,* and *Sports Illustrated.* Ed.

FUNCTIONAL CURIOSITY: In *Against the American Grain* by Dwight Macdonald. Copyright © 1962 by Dwight Macdonald. Reprinted by permission of the author. Selection title by editor.

read; and he could take the time because there *was* time, there being comparatively little to read in that golden age. (The very name of Luce's magazine is significant: *Time,* just because we don't have it.) Feeling a duty—or perhaps simply a compulsion—at least to glance over the printed matter that inundates us daily, we have developed of necessity a rapid, purely rational, classifying habit of mind, something like the operations of a Mark IV calculating machine, making a great many small decisions every minute: read or not read? If read, then take in this, skim over that, and let the rest go by. This we do with the surface of our minds, since we "just don't have time" to bring the slow, cumbersome depths into play, to ruminate, speculate, reflect, wonder, *experience* what the eye flits over. This gives a greatly extended coverage to our minds, but also makes them, compared to the kind of minds similar people had in past centuries, coarse, shallow, passive, and unoriginal. Such reading habits have produced a similar kind of reading matter, since, except for a few stubborn old-fashioned types—the handcraftsmen who produce whatever is written today of quality, whether in poetry, fiction, scholarship or journalism—our writers produce work that is to be read quickly and then buried under the next day's spate of "news" or the next month's best seller; hastily slapped-together stuff which it would be foolish to waste much time or effort on either writing or reading. For those who, as readers or as writers, would get a little under the surface, the real problem of our day is how to *escape* being "well informed," how to resist the temptation to acquire too much information (never more seductive than when it appears in the chaste garb of duty), and how in general to elude the voracious demands on one's attention enough to think a little. The problem is as acute in the groves of Academe as in the profane world of journalism—one has only to consider the appalling mass of words available in any large college library on any topic of scholarly interest (that is, now that the "social sciences" have so proliferated, on any topic). The amount of verbal pomposity, elaboration of the obvious, repetition, trivia, low-grade statistics, tedious factification, drudging recapitulations of the half comprehended, and generally inane and laborious junk that one encounters suggest that the thinkers of earlier ages had one decisive advantage over those of today: they could draw on very little research.

DISCUSSION: VARIETY OF PARAGRAPH DEVELOPMENT

Paragraphs are often developed by more than one method: comparison and definition may be used to analyze the causes of an event, definition and analogy to explain a difficult idea. Earlier we considered the problem of unifying diverse ideas in a single paragraph so that the reader is able to give attention to one idea at a time. Obviously the greater number of ways we develop a paragraph, the more difficult it is to maintain unity; the greatest care must be given to the arrangement of ideas and transitions between them. Parallel phrasing and formal transitions help to clarify the relationship of ideas; another way is to subordinate some of the methods of analysis to the most important method.

QUESTIONS

1. What is the topic sentence of Macdonald's paragraph? How are division, causal analysis, example, and contrast used to develop it? Which of these methods is the most important, and how does Macdonald give it prominence in the paragraph?
2. How is the essay organized to deal with one idea at a time?
3. How does Macdonald account for the difference in the sixteenth-century attitude and the modern attitude? What causes does he cite for the latter?
4. What are the effects of our modern reading habits?

WRITING ASSIGNMENTS

Analyze a news story in *Time* or *Newsweek* to determine what interests it appeals to in its audience. Discuss what the magazine seeks to inform its readers about, and how it does so.

Analyze your daily consumption of news—from written material, television, or radio—to determine how exactly Macdonald describes your reading, viewing, and listening habits.

WILLIAM E. BURROWS
The American Vigilante

1.   The American vigilante phenomenon has gone through three distinct phases, though with considerable overlapping. The first was classic vigilantism, which erupted initially in South Carolina's back country on the eve of the Revolution and concerned itself with punishing ordinary badmen—horse and cattle thieves, counterfeiters, and assorted gangs of desperadoes. Classic vigilantism had as its main target the killers and spoilers who infested the early frontier. The second, or neovigilante, phase started with the great San Francisco committee of 1856 and had as its target ethnic and religious minorities and political opponents, usually clustered in urban areas. Neovigilantism was essentially urban and had little or nothing to do with cactus, horses, and gunslingers. The current phase, pseudo vigilantism, a less deadly but potentially volatile mixture of the first two, can be said to have started in response to the soaring crime and the racial upheavals of the 1960s. Both criminals and blacks have been the objects of pseudovigilante activities, and in a number of instances blacks themselves have organized vigilantelike groups to fight drug addiction among their own people.

2.   The American vigilante may have turned mean while growing up, but he started out as a helpful child, and one born of necessity. He was conceived as the only feasible defense against the perils of a constantly expanding frontier that usually left effective law enforcement far behind. Settlers who abandoned the relative security of the urban footholds back east, with their stabilizing schools, churches, municipal governments, courts, constables, and familiar neighborhoods, and pushed across the Appalachians into the great wilderness beyond were taking serious chances. They were laying their lives on the line, against Indians, desperadoes, and the elements, in order to grab timber, land, gold, and other resources. It was perfectly natural, given such a situation, that they would want to bring with them as much of the old stability as possible. In effect, those people wanted the best of two worlds: to carve up virgin

THE AMERICAN VIGILANTE: In *Vigilante!*, copyright © 1976 by William E. Burrows. Reprinted by permission of Harcourt Brace Jovanovich, Inc. Selection title by editor.

Kentucky or Ohio woodlands and mine unclaimed California and Montana gold, but to do so under the benevolent eyes of the Philadelphia or Boston police force and with the blessing of the New York or Baltimore political establishment. But that was obviously impossible. The price they had to pay in return for a chance to get the frontier's resources often was acute social instability, which translated into almost constant danger. They all knew that the alternative to establishing some kind of stability was to be plundered by the predators—to have their communities ravaged and their hard-earned wealth taken away from them. That was intolerable. Do-it-yourself law enforcement seemed to be the only answer.

3.   If the early pioneers took the law into their own hands begrudgingly—as was usually the case, since it was more profitable to plant crops or make chairs than it was to chase bandits—at least they were ideologically suited to it. The ideology of vigilantism, which began to take shape during the first few decades of the nineteenth century, had three basic components: popular sovereignty, the right of revolution, and the law of self-preservation. And those rested, like a tricorn, on a head of violence. As every nineteenth-century American schoolchild knew, violence worked. It had been spectacularly successful in yanking the colonies out from under the Crown in the first place. As a crucial tool for survival, in fact, it could be traced all the way back to Plymouth and Jamestown, when all those bloodthirsty savages, wild animals, and even an occasional renegade white had had to be subdued or liquidated for the apparent good of the majority.

4.   The concept of popular sovereignty—democracy—was the single most important political element contributing to the vigilante reaction. Obviously, no monarch would have allowed a bunch of armed subjects to ride around the countryside hanging the people they hated. If that kind of thing had caught on, the rabble might eventually have raised their sights, and then where would he have been? So one of the key reasons for vigilantism's taking hold in America was the belief that the rule of the people superseded all other rule. And from that followed the premise that they had the power to act in their own best interest in the absence of effective constituted authority. That's what Judge Henry Dow was getting at when he told Molly Wood that if people make the law they can and should be able to unmake it.

5.   The right of revolution justified the overturn by force of any authority considered by the people to be ineffective or harmful to

the maintenance of real law and order. It provided the philosophical basis for insurrection, as in the hackneyed but true-to-life scene in which the angry mob storms the jail, subdues the sheriff and deputies, and lynches the prisoner. In doing that, vigilantes and lynch mobs were perfectly aware of the fact that they were kicking the props out from under whatever lawful authority existed. But the vigilante credo had it that when lawful authorities contributed to injustice, either willingly or out of helplessness, they almost deserved what the redcoats had gotten in 1776.

6.　Finally, vigilante ideology rested on the ultimate argument of survival as the first law of nature—kill or be killed. If no one else was going to protect a man's life and property, natural law dictated that he had to do it himself or suffer the consequences. It was as simple as that, or so vigilantes assured one another time and again.

QUESTIONS

1. How does Burrows divide vigilantism in the whole discussion? How does he divide the ideology of vigilantism in paragraph 3?
2. What examples does Burrows give for each of the three components or causes of vigilantism in paragraphs 3–6? In what order are these causes arranged?
3. What were the immediate and remote causes of vigilantism on the American frontier? What does Burrows show to be a necessary cause, in paragraph 4?

WRITING ASSIGNMENT

Develop a short essay on one of the following topics, using division, causal analysis, and examples to develop a thesis. State your thesis in your opening paragraph, and restate it at the end of your essay, as a summing up of the discussion.

    a. cheating in high school
    b. driving habits of teenagers
    c. family arguments
    d. television and family life
    e. watching movies on television and in the theater
    f. watching and playing a sport

THE SENTENCE

ADDITION AND MODIFICATION

JANE JACOBS
Hudson Street

1. Under the seeming disorder of the old city, wherever the old city is working successfully, is a marvelous order for maintaining the safety of the streets and the freedom of the city. It is a complex order. Its essence is intricacy of sidewalk use, bringing with it a constant succession of eyes. This order is all composed of movement and change, and although it is life, not art, we may fancifully call it the art form of the city and liken it to the dance—not to a simple-minded precision dance with everyone kicking up at the same time, twirling in unison and bowing off en masse, but to an intricate ballet in which the individual dancers and ensembles all have distinctive parts which miraculously reinforce each other and compose an orderly whole. The ballet of the good city sidewalk never repeats itself from place to place, and in any one place is always replete with new improvisations.

2. The stretch of Hudson Street where I live is each day the scene of an intricate sidewalk ballet. I make my own first entrance into it a little after eight when I put out the garbage can, surely a prosaic occupation, but I enjoy my part, my little clang, as the droves of junior high school students walk by the center of the stage dropping candy wrappers. (How do they eat so much candy so early in the morning?)

3.   While I sweep up the wrappers I watch the other rituals of morning: Mr. Halpert unlocking the laundry's handcart from its mooring to a cellar door, Joe Cornacchia's son-in-law stacking out the empty crates from the delicatessen, the barber bringing out his sidewalk folding chair, Mr. Goldstein arranging the coils of wire which proclaim the hardware store is open, the wife of the tenement's superintendent depositing her chunky three-year-old with a toy mandolin on the stoop, the vantage point from which he is learning the English his mother cannot speak. Now the primary children, heading for St. Luke's, dribble through to the south; the children for St. Veronica's cross, heading to the west, and the children for P.S. 41, heading toward the east. Two new entrances are being made from the wings: well-dressed and even elegant women and men with brief cases emerge from doorways and side streets. Most of these are heading for the bus and subways, but some hover on the curbs, stopping taxis which have miraculously appeared at the right moment, for the taxis are part of a wider morning ritual: having dropped passengers from midtown in the downtown financial district, they are now bringing downtowners up to midtown. Simultaneously, numbers of women in house-dresses have emerged and as they crisscross with one another they pause for quick conversations that sound with either laughter or joint indignation, never, it seems, anything between. It is time for me to hurry to work too, and I exchange my ritual farewell with Mr. Lofaro, the short, thick-bodied, white-aproned fruit man who stands outside his doorway a little up the street, his arms folded, his feet planted, looking solid as earth itself. We nod; we each glance quickly up and down the street, then look back to each other and smile. We have done this many a morning for more than ten years, and we both know what it means: All is well.

4.   The heart-of-the-day ballet I seldom see, because part of the nature of it is that working people who live there, like me, are mostly gone, filling the roles of strangers on other sidewalks. But from days off, I know enough of it to know that it becomes more and more intricate. Longshoremen who are not working that day gather at the White Horse or the Ideal or the International for beer and conversation. The executives and business lunchers from the industries just to the west throng the Dorgene restaurant and the Lion's Head coffee house; meat-market workers and com-munications scientists fill the bakery lunchroom. Character dancers come on, a strange old man with strings of old shoes over

his shoulders, motor-scooter riders with big beards and girl friends who bounce on the back of the scooters and wear their hair long in front of their faces as well as behind, drunks who follow the advice of the Hat Council and are always turned out in hats, but not hats the Council would approve. Mr. Lacey, the locksmith, shuts up his shop for a while and goes to exchange the time of day with Mr. Slube at the cigar store. Mr. Koochagian, the tailor, waters the luxuriant jungle of plants in his window, gives them a critical look from the outside, accepts a compliment on them from two passersby, fingers the leaves on the plane tree in front of our house with a thoughtful gardener's appraisal, and crosses the street for a bite at the Ideal where he can keep an eye on customers and wigwag across the message that he is coming. The baby carriages come out, and clusters of everyone from toddlers with dolls to teen-agers with homework gather at the stoops.

5.   When I get home after work, the ballet is reaching its crescendo. This is the time of roller skates and stilts and tricycles, and games in the lee of the stoop with bottletops and plastic cowboys; this is the time of bundles and packages, zigzagging from the drug store to the fruit stand and back over to the butcher's; this is the time when teen-agers, all dressed up, are pausing to ask if their slips show or their collars look right; this is the time when beautiful girls get out of MG's; this is the time when the fire engines go through; this is the time when anybody you know around Hudson Street will go by.

6.   As darkness thickens and Mr. Halpert moors the laundry cart to the cellar door again, the ballet goes on under lights, eddying back and forth but intensifying at the bright spotlight pools of Joe's sidewalk pizza dispensary, the bars, the delicatessen, the restaurant and the drug store. The night workers stop now at the delicatessen, to pick up salami and a container of milk. Things have settled down for the evening but the street and its ballet have not come to a stop.

7.   I know the deep night ballet and its seasons best from waking long after midnight to tend a baby and, sitting in the dark, seeing the shadows and hearing the sounds of the sidewalk. Mostly it is a sound like infinitely pattering snatches of party conversation and, about three in the morning, singing, very good singing. Sometimes there is sharpness and anger or sad, sad weeping, or a flurry of search for a string of beads broken. One night a young man came roaring along, bellowing terrible language at two girls whom he

had apparently picked up and who were disappointing him. Doors opened, a wary semicircle formed around him, not too close, until the police came. Out came the heads, too, along Hudson Street, offering opinion, "Drunk . . . Crazy . . . A wild kid from the suburbs." *

8.   Deep in the night, I am almost unaware how many people are on the street unless something calls them together, like the bagpipe. Who the piper was and why he favored our street I have no idea. The bagpipe just skirled out in the February night, and as if it were a signal the random, dwindled movements of the sidewalk took on direction. Swiftly, quietly, almost magically a little crowd was there, a crowd that evolved into a circle with a Highland fling inside it. The crowd could be seen on the shadowy sidewalk, the dancers could be seen, but the bagpiper himself was almost invisible because his bravura was all in his music. He was a very little man in a plain brown overcoat. When he finished and vanished, the dancers and watchers applauded, and applause came from the galleries too, half a dozen of the hundred windows on Hudson Street. Then the windows closed, and the little crowd dissolved into the random movements of the night street.

9.   The strangers on Hudson Street, the allies whose eyes help us natives keep the peace of the street, are so many that they always seem to be different people from one day to the next. That does not matter. Whether they are so many always-different people as they seem to be, I do not know. Likely they are. When Jimmy Rogan fell through a plate-glass window (he was separating some scuffling friends) and almost lost his arm, a stranger in an old T shirt emerged from the Ideal bar, swiftly applied an expert tourniquet and, according to the hospital's emergency staff, saved Jimmy's life. Nobody remembered seeing the man before and no one has seen him since. The hospital was called in this way: a woman sitting on the steps next to the accident ran over to the bus stop, wordlessly snatched the dime from the hand of a stranger who was waiting with his fifteen-cent fare ready, and raced into the Ideal's phone booth. The stranger raced after her to offer the nickel too. Nobody remembered seeing him before, and no one has seen him since. When you see the same stranger three or four times on

---

* He turned out to be a wild kid from the suburbs. Sometimes, on Hudson Street, we are tempted to believe the suburbs must be a difficult place to bring up children.

Hudson Street, you begin to nod. This is almost getting to be an acquaintance, a public acquaintance, of course.

10. I have made the daily ballet of Hudson Street sound more frenetic than it is, because writing it telescopes it. In real life, it is not that way. In real life, to be sure, something is always going on, the ballet is never at a halt, but the general effect is peaceful and the general tenor even leisurely. People who know well such animated city streets will know how it is. I am afraid people who do not will always have it a little wrong in their heads—like the old prints of rhinoceroses made from travelers' descriptions of rhinoceroses.

11. On Hudson Street, the same as in the North End of Boston or in any other animated neighborhoods of great cities, we are not innately more competent at keeping the sidewalks safe than are the people who try to live off the hostile truce of Turf in a blind-eyed city. We are the lucky possessors of a city order that makes it relatively simple to keep the peace because there are plenty of eyes on the street. But there is nothing simple about that order itself, or the bewildering number of components that go into it. Most of those components are specialized in one way or another. They unite in their joint effect upon the sidewalk, which is not specialized in the least. That is its strength.

DISCUSSION: ADDITION AND MODIFICATION

As a paragraph usually begins with a topic sentence that states the subject or central idea, so may the sentence begin with a main clause that performs a similar job:

> *Character dancers come on,*
>> *a strange old man* with strings of old shoes over his shoulders,
>> *motor-scooter riders* with big beards and girl friends who bounce on the back of the scooters and wear their hair long in front of their faces as well as behind,
>> *drunks* who follow the advice of the Hat Council and are always turned out in hats,
> but not hats the Council would approve.

The three additions—*strange old man, motor-scooter riders, drunks*— make the main clause specific: they name the character dancers. Notice that these appositives are considerably longer than the main clause. Notice, too, that the third appositive is itself modified. English sentences can be modified endlessly. They are not, however, because the reader would soon lose sight of the central idea. The length of a sentence often depends on how many ideas and details a reader can grasp.

QUESTIONS

1. In the Jacobs, the main clause in the first sentence of paragraph 3 is followed by a series of appositives explaining the *rituals of morning.* How many appositives do you find? Which of them is modified?
2. The colon in the following sentence introduces an addition that explains the main clause:

   Two new entrances are being made from the wings: well-dressed and even elegant women and men with brief cases emerge from doorways and side streets.

   Does the colon in the succeeding sentences, in paragraph 2, serve the same purpose? What about the colon in the concluding sentence of the paragraph?
3. The second sentence of paragraph 5 might have been divided into four separate sentences. What is gained by joining the main clauses through semicolons? Are the semicolons in paragraph 3 used in the same way?
4. Notice that the main clause of the first sentence of paragraph 6 is modified by the opening subordinate clause and by the phrases that follow, beginning with *eddying.* Try rewriting the sentence, beginning with the main clause. Can the opening subordinate clause be put elsewhere in the sentence without obscuring the meaning?
5. What point is Jacobs making about "the daily ballet of Hudson Street"? How do the various details illustrate her point?

WRITING ASSIGNMENTS

Explain in your own words why the specialization in each of the "bewildering number of components" that make up the street is the source of its strength. Show how several of the examples in the essay illustrate this strength.

Develop the following main clauses through addition. Use colons and
semicolons if you wish:
   a. "Deep in the night, I am almost unaware how many people are
      on the street . . ."
   b. "The crowd could be seen on the shadowy sidewalk . . ."
   c. "People who know well such animated city streets will know
      how it is . . ."

Develop the following main clauses through modifications of the italicized word:
   a. "This is the time of roller skates and stilts and *tricycles* . . ."
   b. "The night workers stop now at the delicatessen to pick up
      salami and a container of *milk* . . ."
   c. "He was a very little man in a plain brown *overcoat* . . ."

EMPHASIS

MARK TWAIN
The Mesmerizer

[1] Every night for three nights I sat in the row of candidates on
the platform and held the magic disk in the palm of my hand and
gazed at it and tried to get sleepy, but it was a failure; I remained
wide awake and had to retire defeated, like the majority. [2] Also, I
had to sit there and be gnawed with envy of Hicks, our journeyman; I had to sit there and see him scamper and jump when
Simmons the enchanter exclaimed, "See the snake! See the
snake!" and hear him say, "My, how beautiful!" in response to the
suggestion that he was observing a splendid sunset; and so
on—the whole insane business. [3] I couldn't laugh, I couldn't applaud; it filled me with bitterness to have others do it and to have
people make a hero of Hicks and crowd around him when the
show was over and ask him for more and more particulars of the
wonders he had seen in his visions and manifest in many ways

THE MESMERIZER: In *The Autobiography of Mark Twain*, edited by Charles Neider,
pp. 51–52. Copyright © 1959 by The Mark Twain Company. Copyright © by
Charles Neider. Reprinted by permission of Harper & Row, Publishers, Inc. Selection title by editor.

that they were proud to be acquainted with him. [4] Hicks—the idea! [5] I couldn't stand it; I was getting boiled to death in my own bile.

[6] On the fourth night temptation came and I was not strong enough to resist. [7] When I had gazed at the disk a while I pretended to be sleepy and began to nod. [8] Straightway came the professor and made passes over my head and down my body and legs and arms, finishing each pass with a snap of his fingers in the air to discharge the surplus electricity; then he began to "draw" me with the disk, holding it in his fingers and telling me I could not take my eyes off it, try as I might; so I rose slowly, bent and gazing, and followed that disk all over the place, just as I had seen the others do. [9] Then I was put through the other paces. [10] Upon suggestion I fled from snakes, passed buckets at a fire, became excited over hot steamboat-races, made love to imaginary girls and kissed them, fished from the platform and landed mud cats that out-weighed me—and so on, all the customary marvels. [11] But not in the customary way. [12] I was cautious at first and watchful, being afraid the professor would discover that I was an imposter and drive me from the platform in disgrace; but as soon as I realized that I was not in danger, I set myself the task of terminating Hicks's usefulness as a subject and of usurping his place.

[13] It was a sufficiently easy task. [14] Hicks was born honest, I without that incumbrance—so some people said. [15] Hicks saw what he saw and reported accordingly, I saw more than was visible and added to it such details as could help. [16] Hicks had no imagination; I had a double supply. [17] He was born calm, I was born excited. [18] No vision could start a rapture in him and he was constipated as to language, anyway; but if I saw a vision I emptied the dictionary onto it and lost the remnant of my mind into the bargain.

DISCUSSION: EMPHASIS

When we speak we vary our sentences without much if any thought—interrupting the flow of ideas to emphasize a word or phrase, or to repeat an idea, for example. The speaker of the following sentence, a witness before a congressional committee, repeats certain phrases and qualifies his ideas in a typical way:

> My experience is that we hold people sometimes in jail, young people in jail, for days at a time with a complete lack of concern of the parents, if they do live in homes where parents live

together, a complete lack of concern in many instances on the part of the community or other agencies as to where these young people are or what they are doing.

Spoken sentences as complex and disjointed as this one seems when transcribed and printed can be understood easily because the speaker is able to vary the vocal inflection to stress key words and phrases. Written punctuation can sometimes clarify the points of emphasis but in a limited way:

My experience is that we hold people sometimes in jail— *young* people in jail—for days at a time, with a complete lack of concern of the parents—if they do live in homes where parents live together—a complete lack of concern in many in- stances on the part of the community or other agencies as to where these young people are or what they are doing.

Writers cannot depend directly on vocal inflection for clarity and em- phasis, so rather than using this many dashes they may break the sen- tence into several. However they can suggest these inflections by shaping the sentence in accord with ordinary speech patterns. Clear written sentences stay close to these patterns.

The core of most English sentences consists of a subject-verb- complement:

He read the book.

She was driving her new Porsche.

As we said earlier, this core can be expanded, and at length, if each modifier is clearly connected to what precedes it:

His emotions made him feel strange in the presence of men who talked excitedly of a prospective battle as of a drama they were about to witness, with nothing but eagerness and curiosity in their faces.—Stephen Crane, *The Red Badge of Courage*

Any variation from the familiar subject-verb-complement pattern will emphasize particular words. In the following sentences of Crane the subject and predicate are given emphasis through their separation:

When another night came *the columns,* changed to purple streaks, *filed across* two pontoon *bridges.* A glaring fire wine- tinted the waters of the river. *Its rays,* shining upon the moving masses of troops, *brought forth* here and there sudden *gleams* of silver or gold. Upon the other shore a dark and mysterious *range* of hills *was curved* against the sky.

These variations are natural to the way we speak; they need not have been planned. To achieve even greater emphasis the writer may vary the sentence even more, perhaps by making special use of the end of the sentence—the position that in English tends to be the most emphatic:

> The cold passed reluctantly from the earth, and the retiring fogs revealed an army stretched out on the hills, *resting.—The Red Badge of Courage.*

In one passage Crane breaks up the sentence so that individual ideas and experiences receive separate emphasis:

> The youth stopped. He was transfixed by this terrific medley of all noises. It was as if worlds were being rended. There was the ripping sound of musketry and the breaking crash of the artillery.

These sentences might have been coordinated with words like *and, but, for, yet, nor,* and *or* (or with a semicolon)—with a corresponding distribution of emphasis.

The relation of subordinate clauses to other elements in a sentence is controlled largely by the requirements of English word order. The position of subordinate clauses that serve as nouns or adjectives (sometimes called noun clauses and adjective clauses) is rather fixed; the position of subordinate clauses that serve as adverbs (sometimes called adverb clauses) is not. The position of the adverb clause depends on its importance as an idea and on its length:

> I majored in zoology *because I like working with animals.*

> *Because I like working with animals* I majored in zoology.

The position of the subordinate clause determines what information is stressed: in the first sentence the subordinate clause seems to express the more important idea because it follows the main clause. In the second sentence, the main clause receives the emphasis because it comes at the end of the sentence, the normally emphatic position. But the end of the sentence will not take the thrust of meaning if ideas appearing toward the beginning are given special emphasis, possibly through repetition.

Our informal spoken sentences show the least variation and depend heavily on coordination. The so-called *run-on sentence* in writing—a series of ideas strung together with *and* and other conjunctions—is a heavily coordinated sentence, without the usual vocal markers. The sentence *fragment* usually derives from the clipped sentences and phrases common in speech.

Any variation from normal speech pattern—for example, extremely short, disconnected sentences, or a large number of coordinated clauses, with relatively few modifiers—will create greater than usual emphasis. The kind of sentence variation is determined by the occasion and audience, the impression we want to give of ourselves, the mood we want to create, the formality or informality we consider appropriate. We will consider some of these matters in later discussions.

QUESTIONS

1. Compare the following sentences:
   a. Every night for three nights I sat in the row of candidates on the platform and held the magic disk in the palm of my hand and gazed at it and tried to get sleepy, but it was a failure.
   b. Every night for three nights, as I sat in the row of candidates on the platform, I held the magic disk in the palm of my hand, gazed at it, and tried to get sleepy, but it was a failure.
   How does Twain connect his verbs in *a* (the original sentence) to achieve special emphasis? In *b,* how does the omission of *and* before *held* and before *gazed* affect the degree of emphasis given these verbs in *a?*
2. Repetition of words and phrases provides additional emphasis. What words or phrases are repeated in sentences 2 and 3? What is the effect of this repetition on the mood of the first paragraph?
3. Rewrite sentence 5, subordinating one of the clauses. How does the revision affect the emphasis of ideas in the orginal sentence?
4. Does sentence 8 describe one connected experience, or could the sentence be divided into two without affecting the meaning? Would the meaning of sentences 12 and 18 be altered if they were similarly divided?
5. What personal emotions does Twain want to convey—rage, exultation, sober pride—and how does the sentence construction help to convey them and create a mood?

WRITING ASSIGNMENTS

Twain shows that deception requires abundant imagination. Write a short essay developing this idea from personal experience. Be as specific as Twain is in describing the deception.

Twain says earlier in his autobiography: "The truth is, a person's memory has no more sense than his conscience and no appreciation whatever of values and proportions." Develop this idea from your experience.

CARL SANDBURG

The Funeral of General Grant

[1] The Galesburg Marine Band marched past, men walking and their mouths blowing into their horns as they walked. [2] One man had a big horn that seemed to be wrapped around him and I was puzzled how he got into it. [3] They had on blue coats and pants and the stripe down the sides of the pants was either red or yellow and looked pretty. [4] Their music was slow and sad. [5] General Grant was dead and this was part of his funeral and the music should be sad. [6] It was only twenty years since the war ended and General Grant was the greatest general in the war and they wanted to show they were sad because he was dead. [7] That was the feeling I had and I could see there were many others had this same feeling. [8] Marching past came men wearing dark-blue coats and big black hats tied round with a little cord of what looked like gold with a knot and a little tassel. [9] They were the G.A.R., the Grand Army of the Republic, and I heard that some of these men had seen General Grant and had been in the war with him and could tell how he looked on a horse and what made him a great general. [10] Eight or ten of these G.A.R. men walked along the sides of a long black box on some kind of a black car pulled by eight black horses. [11] The body of General Grant wasn't in the box, but somewhere far away General Grant was being buried in a box like this one. [12] I could see everybody around was more quiet when this part of the parade passed.

QUESTIONS

1. What words are repeated in sentences 4–6? How does this repetition help establish a dominant mood?

THE FUNERAL OF GENERAL GRANT: In *Always the Young Strangers* by Carl Sandburg. Reprinted by permission of Harcourt Brace Jovanovich, Inc. Selection title by editor.

2. Sentences 2–7 are mainly simple and compound—mostly main clauses, with almost no variation. How does this evenness also help establish a dominant mood?
3. What other repetitions do you notice in the paragraph, and what do they contribute to the dominant mood?

WRITING ASSIGNMENTS

Rewrite Sandburg's paragraph, subordinating clauses wherever possible. Then discuss the effect of the changes you made on the original paragraph.

Describe a parade or celebration, and construct your sentences so that they convey the mood of the event.

NORMAN MAILER
The Death of Benny Paret

¹Paret was a Cuban, a proud club fighter who had become welterweight champion because of his unusual ability to take a punch. ²His style of fighting was to take three punches to the head in order to give back two. ³At the end of ten rounds, he would still be bouncing, his opponent would have a headache. ⁴But in the last two years, over the fifteen-round fights, he had started to take some bad maulings.

⁵This fight had its turns. ⁶Griffith won most of the early rounds, but Paret knocked Griffith down in the sixth. ⁷Griffith had trouble getting up, but made it, came alive and was dominating Paret again before the round was over. ⁸Then Paret began to wilt. ⁹In the middle of the eighth round, after a clubbing punch had turned his back to Griffith, Paret walked three disgusted steps away, showing his hindquarters. ¹⁰For a champion, he took much too long to turn back around. ¹¹It was the first hint of weakness Paret had ever shown, and it must have inspired a particular shame, because he fought the rest of the fight as if he were seek-

THE DEATH OF BENNY PARET: In *The Presidential Papers* by Norman Mailer. Reprinted by permission of G. P. Putnam's Sons. Copyright © 1960, 1961, 1962, 1963 by Norman Mailer. Selection title by editor.

ing to demonstrate that he could take more punishment than any man alive. [12] In the twelfth, Griffith caught him. [13] Paret got trapped in a corner. [14] Trying to duck away, his left arm and his head became tangled on the wrong side of the top rope. [15] Griffith was in like a cat ready to rip the life out of a huge boxed rat. [16] He hit him eighteen right hands in a row, an act which took perhaps three or four seconds, Griffith making a pent-up whimpering sound all the while he attacked, the right hand whipping like a piston rod which has broken through the crankcase, or like a baseball bat demolishing a pumpkin. [17] I was sitting in the second row of that corner—they were not ten feet away from me, and like everybody else, I was hypnotized. [18] I had never seen one man hit another so hard and so many times. [19] Over the referee's face came a look of woe as if some spasm had passed its way through him, and then he leaped on Griffith to pull him away. [20] It was the act of a brave man. [21] Griffith was uncontrollable. [22] His trainer leaped into the ring, his manager, his cut man, there were four people holding Griffith, but he was off on an orgy, he had left the Garden, he was back on a hoodlum's street. [23] If he had been able to break loose from his handlers and the referee, he would have jumped Paret to the floor and whaled on him there.

[24] And Paret? [25] Paret died on his feet. [26] As he took those eighteen punches something happened to everyone who was in psychic range of the event. [27] Some part of his death reached out to us. [28] One felt it hover in the air. [29] He was still standing in the ropes, trapped as he had been before, he gave some little half-smile of regret, as if he were saying, "I didn't know I was going to die just yet," and then, his head leaning back but still erect, his death came to breathe about him. [30] He began to pass away. [31] As he passed, so his limbs descended beneath him, and he sank slowly to the floor. [32] He went down more slowly than any fighter had ever gone down, he went down like a large ship which turns on end and slides second by second into its grave. [33] As he went down, the sound of Griffith's punches echoed in the mind like a heavy ax in the distance chopping into a wet log.

QUESTIONS

1. Each of the sentences in the second paragraph focuses on a distinct moment of the action. Could any of these sentences be combined without blurring the action?

2. Sentence 22 joins a number of actions occurring simultaneously. How does the sentence convey the jarring confusion of the moment?
3. Does sentence 29 describe a continuous action? Would the mood of the paragraph be changed if the sentence were broken up or punctuated differently?
4. How does repetition in sentence 32 reinforce the feeling Mailer is trying to communicate in the final paragraph?
5. Mailer's writing is closer to spoken patterns than the writing of others we have been studying. In how many of his sentences does Mailer depart from the subject-verb-complement pattern—and to what effect?

WRITING ASSIGNMENT

Summarize what you think are the implications of the passage, including what the passage suggests about Mailer's attitude toward Benny Paret.

LOOSE AND PERIODIC SENTENCES

JOHN STEINBECK
The Turtle

[1] The sun lay on the grass and warmed it, and in the shade under the grass the insects moved, ants and ant lions to set traps for them, grasshoppers to jump into the air and flick their yellow wings for a second, sow bugs like little armadillos, plodding restlessly on many tender feet. [2] And over the grass at the roadside a land turtle crawled, turning aside for nothing, dragging his high-domed shell over the grass. [3] His hard legs and yellow-nailed feet threshed slowly through the grass, not really walking, but boosting

THE TURTLE: In *The Grapes of Wrath* by John Steinbeck. Copyright 1939, Copyright © renewed 1967 by John Steinbeck. Reprinted by permission of The Viking Press, Inc. Selection title by editor.

and dragging his shell along. [4] The barley beards slid off his shell, and the clover burrs fell on him and rolled to the ground. [5] His horny beak was partly open, and his fierce, humorous eyes, under brows like fingernails, stared straight ahead. [6] He came over the grass leaving a beaten trail behind him, and the hill, which was the highway embankment, reared up ahead of him. [7] For a moment he stopped, his head held high. [8] He blinked and looked up and down. [9] At last he started to climb the embankment. [10] Front clawed feet reached forward but did not touch. [11] The hind feet kicked his shell along, and it scraped on the grass, and on the gravel. [12] As the embankment grew steeper and steeper, the more frantic were the efforts of the land turtle. [13] Pushing hind legs strained and slipped, boosting the shell along, and the horny head protruded as far as the neck could stretch. [14] Little by little the shell slid up the embankment until at last a parapet cut straight across its line of march, the shoulder of the road, a concrete wall four inches high. [15] As though they worked independently the hind legs pushed the shell against the wall. [16] The head upraised and peered over the wall to the broad smooth plain of cement. [17] Now the hands, braced on top of the wall, strained and lifted, and the shell came slowly up and rested its front end on the wall. [18] For a moment the turtle rested. [19] A red ant ran into the shell, into the soft skin inside the shell, and suddenly head and legs snapped in, and the armored tail clamped in sideways. [20] The red ant was crushed between body and legs. [21] And one head of wild oats was clamped into the shell by a front leg. [22] For a long moment the turtle lay still, and then the neck crept out and the old humorous frowning eyes looked about and the legs and tail came out. [23] The back legs went to work, straining like elephant legs, and the shell tipped to an angle so that the front legs could not reach the level cement plain. [24] But higher and higher the hind legs boosted it, until at last the center of balance was reached, the front tipped down, the front legs scratched at the pavement, and it was up. [25] But the head of wild oats was held by its stem around the front legs.

DISCUSSION: LOOSE AND PERIODIC SENTENCES

Sentences are sometimes classified as loose or periodic, as a way of describing their possible effects in a paragraph or essay—ranging from plodding monotony to extreme excitement. Loose sentences

begin with the core sentence, qualifying phrases and clauses following the core:

> *The squares were quite big,* and absolutely desert, save for
> the posts for clothes lines, and people passing, children play-
> ing on the hard earth.—D. H. Lawrence, "Nottingham and the
> Mining Countryside"

In a periodic sentence the core sentence comes toward the end, the
sentence opening with modifiers or a series of appositives:

> To believe your own thought, to believe that what is true for
> you in your private heart is true for all men—that is *genius.*—
> Ralph Waldo Emerson, "Self-Reliance"

> But not all the power and simplicity of Swift's prose, nor the
> imaginative effort that has been able to make not one but a
> whole series of impossible worlds more credible than the ma-
> jority of history books—none of this would enable us to enjoy
> Swift if his world-view were truly wounding or shocking.—
> George Orwell, "Politics vs. Literature"

The strongly periodic sentence is usually reserved for unusually
strong emphasis, as in Emerson's sentence.
   Most modern English sentences fall between the extremely loose
and the extremely periodic. Compound sentences seem loose when
succeeding clauses serve as afterthoughts or qualifications rather
than as ideas equal in importance to the opening idea:

> I was very conscious of the crowds at first, almost despairing
> to have to perform in front of them, and I never got used to
> it.—George Plimpton, *Paper Lion*

By contrast a sequence of clauses may increase gradually in emphasis, ending on a climactic note:

> Sometimes on the blocking sleds the players would gag
> around, and at the hike number I would be the only one to
> drive forward at the sled, the others holding up on some se-
> cret signal, and without the others to help, and with Binga-
> man's weight, it was like jarring a shoulder into a wall.—*Paper
> Lion*

Modern English uses periodic sentences sparingly, with a distribution
of emphasis more often through the whole sentence, as in Orwell's

sentence quoted above. Sometimes two moderately periodic sentences will be coordinated, with a corresponding distribution of emphasis:

> Though reliable narration is by no means the only way of conveying to the audience the facts on which dramatic irony is based, it is a useful way, and in some works, works in which no one but the author can conceivably know what needs to be known, it may be indispensable.—Wayne C. Booth, *The Rhetoric of Fiction*

QUESTIONS

1. In the Steinbeck paragraph, the essential element of sentence 2 is *a land turtle crawled.* If the concluding modifiers were moved toward the beginning of the sentence, would the shift in emphasis alter the meaning?
2. How does the moderately periodic construction of sentence 12 create a sense of action?
3. Convert sentence 3 into a periodic sentence. What is gained or lost by moving the phrase *dragging his shell along* to another part of the sentence?
4. Rewrite sentence 15 as a loose sentence. What is gained or lost in effect by your revision?
5. Combine sentences 7, 8, and 9 into one sentence. Which is more effective—your sentence or the original arrangement of sentences—and why?
6. Do the sentences in the passage, considered as a whole, seem predominantly loose or periodic? How does the dominant pattern affect the mood of the passage and contribute to its meaning? In general, what kind of sentence construction conveys a greater sense of anticipation and suspense, and why?
7. The following loose and periodic sentences are characteristic of some eighteenth- and nineteenth-century British and American prose. Rewrite them as loose or periodic sentences, changing the wording where necessary. Be ready to argue which is the more effective sentence and why.
   a. Considering that natural disposition in many men to lie, and in multitudes to believe, I have been perplexed what to do with that maxim so frequent in everybody's mouth, that truth will at last prevail.—Jonathan Swift
   b. To this knowledge which all men carry about with them, and to these sympathies in which without any other discipline than that of our daily life, we are fitted to take delight, the poet principally directs his attention.—William Wordsworth

c. Who first reduced lying into an art, and adapted it to politics, is not so clear from history, although I have made some diligent inquiries.—Swift
d. Plants and animals, biding their time, closely followed the retiring ice, bestowing quick and joyous animation on the new-born landscape.—John Muir

WRITING ASSIGNMENT

Write an interpretation of the passage, with particular attention to how Steinbeck may be using the turtle to make a general statement about life. Analyze the detail with care.

MAY SARTON
The Act of Writing

1. Choosing, defining, creating harmony, bringing that clarity and shape that is rest and light out of disorder and confusion—the work that I do at my desk is not unlike arranging flowers. Only it is much harder to get started on writing something! Teaching is also hard work, and probably (though in a different way) as creative as writing is, but there is always the class there to draw the best out of a teacher, so he does not have to make the same huge effort to "connect with" the work at hand. The writer, at his desk alone, must create his own momentum, draw the enthusiasm up out of his own substance, not just once, when he may feel inspired, but day after day when he often does not. The teacher is supported also by what he teaches, whereas the writer faces a daily battle with self-questioning, self-doubt, and conflict about his own work. Half the time what he finds on his desk in the morning looks hardly worth tinkering with; in the cool morning light every weakness is exposed.
2. Every writer has his own ways of getting started, from sharpening pencils, to reading the Bible, to pacing the floor. I often rinse out my mind by reading something, and I sometimes manage to

THE ACT OF WRITING: In *Plant Dreaming Deep* by May Sarton. Reprinted by permission of W. W. Norton & Company, Inc. Copyright © 1968 by May Sarton. Selection title by editor.

put off getting down to the hard struggle for an unconscionable time. Mostly I am helped through the barrier by music. I play records while I am writing and especially at the start of each day one particular record that accompanies the poem or chapter I am working at. During these last weeks it has been a record by Albinoni for strings and organ. I do not always play that key record, but it is there to draw on—the key to a certain piece of work, the key to that mood. The romantic composers, much as I enjoy listening to them at other times, are no help. Bach, Mozart, Vivaldi—they are what I need—clarity and structure.

QUESTIONS

1. Which sentence of paragraph 1 builds to the core sentence or main clause? Which sentences complete the essential thought of the sentence only in the final words? What do these sentences contribute to the general informality or formality of the writing?
2. Which sentences in paragraph 2 are periodic? How strong is the emphasis in these sentences?

WRITING ASSIGNMENTS

Compare the uses Sarton makes of loose and periodic sentences, in an expository piece of writing, with the use Steinbeck makes of them in a descriptive piece.

Discuss the ways you prepare for writing an essay or a letter, and the circumstances under which you do your best or worst writing.

PARALLELISM

JOSEPH CONRAD
The West Wind

[1] He is the war-lord who sends his battalions of Atlantic rollers to the assault of our seaboard. [2] The compelling voice of the West

THE WEST WIND: In *The Mirror of the Sea* by Joseph Conrad. Reprinted by permission of J. M. Dent and Sons, Ltd. Selection title by editor.

Wind musters up to his service all the might of the ocean. ³At the bidding of the West Wind there arises a great commotion in the sky above these Islands, and a great rush of waters falls upon our shores. ⁴The sky of the Westerly Weather is full of flying clouds, of great big white clouds coming thicker and thicker till they seem to stand welded into a solid canopy, upon whose grey face the lower wrack of the gale, thin, black, and angry-looking, flies past with vertiginous speed. ⁵Denser and denser grows this dome of vapors, descending lower and lower upon the sea, narrowing the horizon around the ship. ⁶And the characteristic aspect of Westerly Weather, the thick, grey, smoky, and sinister tone sets in, circumscribing the view of the men, drenching their bodies, oppressing their souls, taking their breath away with booming gusts, deafening, blinding, driving, rushing them onwards in a swaying ship towards our coasts lost in mists and rain.

DISCUSSION: PARALLELISM

The italicized words in the following sentences are parallel in structure, that is, they serve the same grammatical function in the sentence and are the same in form:

> He *replaced* the morsel of food on his plate
> and *read* the paragraph attentively. Then
> he *drank* a glass of water,
>   *pushed* his plate to one side,
>   *doubled* the paper down before him between his elbows and
>   *read* the paragraph over and over again.—James Joyce, "A Painful Case"

In speaking and writing we naturally make these verbs parallel. Only a person who has lost sight of the beginning of the sentence would say or write:

> Then he drank a glass of water, his plate was pushed to one side, doubled the paper down before him between his elbows and read the paragraph over and over again.

In short, we tend to continue and finish a sentence the way we begin it.

An old rule of style insists on strict parallelism following correlatives:

He wants not only *to see Rome* but also *to see Paris.*

Either *we visit Rome* or *we visit Paris:* we cannot visit both.

Today writers depart from strict parallelism, to avoid too formal an effect:

His evenings were spent either before his landlady's piano or roaming about the outskirts of the city.—"A Painful Case"

In modern English parallelism is not and need not be exact unless sentence clarity demands it.

QUESTIONS

1. Which words and phrases in sentences 4 and 6 by Conrad are parallel? Which phrases in sentence 5?
2. The two main clauses of sentence 3 are not parallel in structure. What change in the second clause would make it parallel to the first?
3. Conrad avoids too formal an effect by varying his sentences slightly. In which sentences is a close parallel structure of words and phrases impossible to avoid?
4. How does the sentence structure help to convey the effect of the West Wind?

WRITING ASSIGNMENT

Describe a lightning storm or a heavy snowfall or another natural phenomenon. Vary the construction of your sentences to avoid too formal an impression.

JOHN A. WILLIAMS

Driving Through Snowstorms

[1] Driving through snowstorms on icy roads for long distances is a most nerve-racking experience. [2] It is a paradox that the snow,

DRIVING THROUGH SNOWSTORMS: In *This Is My Country Too* by John A. Williams (New American Library, 1965). Reprinted by permission of the author. Selection title by editor.

coming down gently, blowing gleefully in a high wind, all the while lays down a treacherous carpet, freezes the windows, blocks the view. ³The might of automated man is muted. ⁴The horses, the powerful electrical systems, the deep-tread tires, all go for nothing. ⁵One minute the road feels firm, and the next the driver is sliding over it, light as a feather, in a panic, wondering what the heavy trailer trucks coming up from the rear are going to do. ⁶The trucks are like giants when you have to pass them, not at sixty or seventy as you do when the road is dry, but at twenty-five and thirty. ⁷Then their engines sound unnaturally loud. ⁸Snow, slush and chips of ice spray from beneath the wheels, obscure the windshield, and rattle off your car. ⁹Beneath the wheels there is plenty of room for you to skid and get mashed to a pulp. ¹⁰Inch by inch you move up, past the rear wheels, the center wheels, the cab, the front wheels, all sliding too slowly by. ¹¹Straight ahead you continue, for to cut over sharply would send you into a skid, right in front of the vehicle. ¹²At last, there is distance enough, and you creep back over, in front of the truck now, but with the sound of its engine still thundering in your ears.

QUESTIONS

1. How does Williams make phrases parallel in sentence 2 to emphasize similar ideas?
2. In what other sentences do you find a similar use of parallelism?
3. How does Williams construct sentence 10 to imitate the action it describes?

WRITING ASSIGNMENT

Describe the experience of driving or walking on icy or wet streets or sidewalks, and contrast this experience with the experience that Williams describes.

ERNESTO GALARZA

Boyhood in a Sacramento *Barrio*

1.   Our family conversations always occurred on our own kitchen porch, away from the gringos. One or the other of the adults would begin: *Se han fijado?* Had we noticed—that the Americans do not ask permission to leave the room; that they had no respectful way of addressing an elderly person; that they spit brown over the railing of the porch into the yard; that when they laughed they roared; that they never brought *saludos* to everyone in your family from everyone in their family when they visited; that *General Delibree* was only a clerk; that *zopilotes* were not allowed on the streets to collect garbage; that the policemen did not carry lanterns at night; that Americans didn't keep their feet on the floor when they were sitting; that there was a special automobile for going to jail; that a rancho was not a rancho at all but a very small hacienda; that the saloons served their customers free eggs, pickles, and sandwiches; that instead of bullfighting, the gringos for sport tried to kill each other with gloves?

2.   I did not have nearly the strong feelings on these matters that Doña Henriqueta expressed. I felt a vague admiration for the way Mr. Brien could spit brown. Wayne, my classmate, laughed much better than the Mexicans, because he opened his big mouth wide and brayed like a donkey so he could be heard a block away. But it was the kind of laughter that made my mother tremble, and it was not permitted in our house.

3.   Rules were laid down to keep me, as far as possible, *un muchacho bien educado.* If I had to spit I was to do it privately, or if in public, by the curb, with my head down and my back to people. I was never to wear my cap in the house and I was to take it off even on the porch if ladies or elderly gentlemen were sitting. If I wanted to scratch, under no circumstances was I to do it right then and there, in company, like the Americans, but I was to excuse myself. If Catfish or Russell yelled to me from across the street I was not to shout back. I was never to ask for tips for my errands or other

BOYHOOD IN A SACRAMENTO BARRIO: In *Barrio Boy* by Ernesto Galarza (University of Notre Dame Press, 1971). Reprinted by permission of the publisher. Selection title by editor.

services to the tenants of 418 L, for these were *atenciones* expected of me.

4.   Above all I was never to fail in *respeto* to grownups, no matter who they were. It was an inflexible rule; I addressed myself to *Señor* Big Singh, *Señor* Big Ernie, *Señora* Dodson, *Señor* Cho-ree Lopez.

5.   My standing in the family, but especially with my mother depended on my keeping these rules. I was not punished for breaking them. She simply reminded me that it gave her acute *vergüenza* to see me act thus, and that I would never grow up to be a correct *jefe de familia* if I did not know how to be a correct boy. I knew what *vergüenza* was from feeling it time and again; and the notion of growing up to keep a tight rein over a family of my own was somehow satisfying.

6.   In our musty apartment in the basement of 418 L, ours remained a Mexican family. I never lost the sense that we were the same, from Jalco to Sacramento. There was the polished cedar box, taken out now and then from the closet to display our heirlooms. I had lost the rifle shells of the revolution, and Tio Tonche, too, was gone. But there was the butterfly sarape, the one I had worn through the Battle of Peubla; a black lace mantilla Doña Henriqueta modeled for us; bits of embroidery and lace she had made; the tin pictures of my grandparents; my report card signed by Señorita Bustamante and Don Salvador; letters from Aunt Esther; and the card with the address of the lady who had kept the Ajax for us. When our mementos were laid out on the bed I plunged my head into the empty box and took deep breaths of the aroma of *puro cedro,* pure Jalcocotán mixed with camphor.

7.   We could have hung on the door of our apartment a sign like those we read in some store windows—*Aquí se habla español.* We not only spoke Spanish, we read it. From the *Librería Española,* two blocks up the street, Gustavo and I bought novels for my mother, like *Genoveva de Brabante,* a paperback with the poems of Amado Nervo and a handbook of the history of Mexico. The novels were never read aloud, the poems and the handbook were. Nervo was the famous poet from Tepic, close enough to Jalcocotán to make him our own. And in the history book I learned to read for myself, after many repetitions by my mother, about the deeds of the great Mexicans Don Salvador had recited so vividly to the class in Mazatlán. She refused to decide for me whether Abraham Lincoln was as great as Benito Juarez, or George Washington braver

than the priest Don Miguel Hidalgo. At school there was no opportunity to settle these questions because nobody seemed to know about Juarez or Hidalgo; at least they were never mentioned and there were no pictures of them on the walls.

8.   The family talk I listened to with the greatest interest was about Jalco. Wherever the conversation began it always turned to the pueblo, our neighbors, anecdotes that were funny or sad, the folk tales and the witchcraft, and our kinfolk, who were still there. I usually lay on the floor those winter evenings, with my feet toward the kerosene heater, watching on the ceiling the flickering patterns of the light filtered through the scrollwork of the chimney. As I listened once again I chased the *zopilote* away from Coronel, or watched José take Nerón into the forest in a sack. Certain things became clear about the *rurales* and why the young men were taken away to kill Yaqui Indians, and about the Germans, the Englishmen, the Frenchmen, the Spaniards, and the Americans who owned the haciendas, the railroads, the ships, the big stores, the breweries. They owned Mexico because President Porfirio Díaz had let them steal it, José explained as I listened. Now Don Francisco Madero had been assassinated for trying to get it back. On such threads of family talk I followed my own recollection of the years from Jalco—the attack on Mazatlán, the captain of Acaponeta, the camp at El Nanchi and the arrival at Nogales on the flatcar.

9.   Only when we ventured uptown did we feel like aliens in a foreign land. Within the *barrio* we heard Spanish on the streets and in the alleys. On the railroad tracks, in the canneries, and along the riverfront there were more Mexicans than any other nationality. And except for the foremen, the work talk was in our language. In the secondhand shops, where the *barrio* people sold and bought furniture and clothing, there were Mexican clerks who knew the Mexican ways of making a sale. Families doubled up in decaying houses, cramping themselves so they could rent an extra room to *chicano* boarders, who accented the brown quality of our Mexican *colonia*.

QUESTIONS

1. How is parallelism used in the second sentence of paragraph 1 to give equal emphasis to the various ideas?
2. How is the same use made of parallelism in paragraph 6?

3. Whole sentences can be parallel to one another. How much parallelism of this kind do you find in paragraph 3?
4. In general, how loose or how strict do you find the parallelism of Galarza's sentences? How formal an effect do his sentences create?

WRITING ASSIGNMENTS

Galarza uses his account to say something about Mexican and American folkways and the changes brought about in moving from one world to another. Discuss what Galarza is saying, and comment on his attitude toward the changes he experiences.

Discuss the increased importance manners have when you find yourself in a new environment, perhaps in a new school or neighborhood. You might want to discuss changes in speech habits as well as changes in behavior.

BALANCE

ROBERT ARDREY
The Herring Gull

[1] The herring gull is a creature of sufficient ingenuity that if he picks up a mussel with a shell too hard for his beak to break, he will carry it to a height and drop it on a hard road. [2] He is a creature of sufficient loyalty and perception to guarantee that he will never attack his own mate, and will recognize her among dozens flying into the colony at a distance to defy human binoculars. [3] He is a creature of sufficient social sophistication that, while many arrive in the spring already paired, definite areas in the colony which Tinbergen calls "clubs" will be set aside as meeting places for the unpaired. [4] He is a creature also, as we have seen, of such sensitive social adjustment that the arriving flock will make "decisions" of mood and readiness as if it were one being. [5] So dependent is the

THE HERRING GULL: In *The Territorial Imperative* by Robert Ardrey. Copyright ©
1966 by Robert Ardrey. Reprinted by permission of Atheneum Publishers. Selection
title by editor.

herring gull on the community of his citizenship that he would probably be unable to breed were he to return in the spring to the wrong gull town. [6] So powerful and incomprehensible is his attachment for home that, like the albatross, a pair may return year after year to nest in precisely the same spot, although the North Sea's winter storms will have effaced all landmarks to guide his eye.

DISCUSSION: BALANCE

A sentence is said to be balanced when parallel phrases or clauses are used to stress similarity in ideas or their difference:

> The savage bows down to idols of wood and stone: the civilized man to idols of flesh and blood.—George Bernard Shaw, *Man and Superman*

Exact balance extending to whole sentences, as well as to phrases and clauses, is found occasionally in writers of earlier centuries. The following passages describing the seventeenth-century English Puritans are extreme examples:

> If they were unacquainted with the works of philosophers and poets, they were deeply read in the oracles of God. If their names were not found in the registers of heralds, they were recorded in the Book of Life.

> Thus the Puritan was made up of two different men, the one all self-abasement, penitence, gratitude, passion; the other proud, calm, inflexible, sagacious. He prostrated himself in the dust before his Maker: but he set his foot on the neck of his king.—Thomas Babington Macaulay, *Milton* (1825)

Abraham Lincoln is less extreme in his use of balance in his description of the North and the South at war, in his Second Inaugural Address of 1865:

> Neither party expected for the war the magnitude or the duration which it has already attained. Neither anticipated that the cause of the conflict might cease with, or even before, the conflict itself should cease. Each looked for an easier triumph, and a result less fundamental and astounding. Both read the same Bible, and pray to the same God; and each invokes his aid against the other.

The marked rhythm of these sentences creates a highly formal effect by slowing the tempo. Exact balance interrupts the natural flow of the sentence, giving emphasis to most or all of its parts. For this reason writers today usually reserve exact sentence balance for speeches made on formal occasions. A moderate balance continues to be a useful way of achieving emphasis. A writer on modern English prose states:

> Many writers today, if they make two sentences elaborately parallel, are likely to qualify the effect by some means, perhaps by a contrast between the elaboration of the grammar and the colloquial tone of the vocabulary or between the high-flown expression and the humble content.*

QUESTIONS

1. In the Ardrey, what phrases and clauses in sentences 1–4 are balanced? How does this balance give emphasis to similar ideas?
2. What parts of sentences 5 and 6 are balanced for emphasis? Is the balance more or less exact than that of sentences 1–4?

WRITING ASSIGNMENT

Write a paragraph describing the effects of one of the following. Balance the opening of those sentences that describe the effects:
   a. a morning headache
   b. a runny nose
   c. a delicious lunch
   d. a gruff word from a friend

MAX LERNER

Sports in America

1.   The psychic basis of American mass sports is tribal and feudal. Baseball is a good example of the modern totem symbols

---

* James Sledd, *A Short Introduction to English Grammar* (Chicago, 1959), p. 293.

SPORTS IN AMERICA: In *America as a Civilization* by Max Lerner. Copyright 1957 by Max Lerner. Reprinted by permission of Simon and Schuster, Inc. Selection title by editor.

(Cubs, Tigers, Indians, Pirates, Dodgers, and Braves) and of sustained tribal animosities. The spectator is not *on* the team, but he can be *for* the team; he identifies himself with one team, sometimes with one player who becomes a jousting champion wearing his colors in a medieval tournament. Hence the hero symbolism in American sports and the impassioned hero worship which makes gods of mortals mediocre in every other respect, and gives them the place among the "Immortals" that the French reserve for their Academy intellectuals.

2. There is a stylized relation of artist to mass audience in the sports, especially in baseball. Each player develops a style of his own—the swagger as he steps to the plate, the unique windup a pitcher has, the clean-swinging and hard-driving hits, the precision quickness and grace of infield and outfield, the sense of surplus power behind whatever is done. There is the style of the spectator also: he becomes expert in the ritual of insult, provocation, and braggadocio; he boasts of the exaggerated prowess of his team and cries down the skill and courage of the other; he develops sustained feuds, carrying on a guerilla war with the umpires and an organized badinage with the players, while he consumes mountains of ritual hot dogs and drinks oceans of ritual soda pop.

3. Each sport develops its own legendry, woven around the "stars" who become folk heroes. The figures in baseball's Hall of Fame have their sagas told and retold in newspapers and biographies, and the Plutarchs who recount exploits become themselves notable figures in the culture. Some of these sports writers later become political columnists, perhaps on the assumption that politics itself is only a sport riddled with greater hypocrisy and that it takes a salty and hard-hitting sports writer to expose the politicians. The sports heroes become national possessions, like the Grand Canyon and the gold in Fort Knox. It is hard for a people who in their childhood have treasured the sports legendry as a cherished illusion to surrender it when they grow up.

QUESTIONS

1. The longer the phrases that are parallel in structure and meaning, the greater the sense of balance in sentences and paragraphs. How does Lerner vary the length of phrases and clauses balanced in the

second and third sentences of paragraph 2? How does this variation in length prevent the sentences from sounding too formal?
2. Is the balance of phrases in paragraph 1 tighter than in paragraph
   2? How does this balance of phrases give emphasis to key ideas
   and promote concision?
3. How exactly are sentences balanced in paragraph 3?

WRITING ASSIGNMENT

Discuss another American sport in light of one of the following statements:
a. "The psychic basis of American mass sports is tribal and feudal."
b. "There is a stylized relation of artist to mass audience in the
   sports."
c. "Each sport develops its own legendry, woven around the 'stars'
   who become folk heroes."

JOHN F. KENNEDY

The Space Program, 1962

1. If this capsule history of our progress teaches us anything, it
is that man, in his quest for knowledge and progress, is determined and cannot be deterred. The exploration of space will go
ahead, whether we join in it or not. And it is one of the great adventures of all time, and no nation which expects to be the leader
of other nations can expect to stay behind in this race for space.
2. Those who came before us made certain that this country rode
the first waves of the industrial revolution, the first waves of modern invention and the first wave of nuclear power, and this generation does not intend to founder in the backwash of the coming age
of space. We mean to be a part of it. We mean to lead it, for the
eyes of the world now look into space, to the moon and to the
planets beyond; and we have vowed that we shall not see it governed by a hostile flag of conquest, but by a banner of freedom and
peace. We have vowed that we shall not see space filled with

THE SPACE PROGRAM, 1962: In *The Burden and the Glory* by John F. Kennedy
(Harper & Row, Publishers, Inc., 1964). Selection title by editor.

weapons of mass destruction, but with instruments of knowledge and understanding.

3.   Yet the vows of this nation can only be fulfilled if we in this nation are first, and therefore we intend to be first. In short, our leadership in science and in industry, our hopes for peace and security, our obligations to ourselves as well as others, all require us to make this effort, to solve these mysteries, to solve them for the good of all men, and to become the world's leading space-faring nation.

4.   We set sail on this new sea because there is new knowledge to be gained, and new rights to be won, and they must be won and used for the progress of all people. For space science, like nuclear science and all technology, has no conscience of its own. Whether it will become a force for good or ill depends on man, and only if the United States occupies a position of pre-eminence can we help decide whether this new ocean will be a sea of peace or a new, terrifying theater of war. I do not say that we should or will go unprotected against the hostile misuse of space any more than we go unprotected against the hostile use of land or sea, but I do say that space can be explored and mastered without feeding the fires of war, without repeating the mistakes that man has made in extending his writ around this globe of ours.

5.   There is no strife, no prejudice, no national conflict in outer space as yet. Its hazards are hostile to us all. Its conquest deserves the best of all mankind, and its opportunity for peaceful cooperation may never come again. But why, some say, the moon? Why choose this as our goal? And they may well ask, why climb the highest mountain? Why, thirty-five years ago, fly the Atlantic? Why does Rice play Texas?

6.   We choose to go to the moon. We choose to go to the moon in this decade, and do the other things, not because they are easy but because they are hard; because that goal will serve to organize and measure the best of our energies and skills; because that challenge is one that we are willing to accept, one we are unwilling to postpone, and one which we intend to win—and the others, too.

QUESTIONS

1. This 1962 statement on space exploration is typical of President Kennedy's style of public address: phrases, clauses, and sentences are balanced in the course of the statement. Find examples of each

kind of balancing. To what extent is the formal balance of the examples you located varied by the length of sentences in individual paragraphs?

2. How is the formal balance qualified by "the colloquial tone of the vocabulary" or the "humble content," to quote James Sledd?

3. To what extent is the repetition of key words an element of formal balance in certain sentences?

WRITING ASSIGNMENT

Discuss the degree to which you are persuaded by the argument of paragraphs 4 and 5. Do you believe that the reason Rice plays Texas is a sufficient explanation for the space program?

ANTITHESIS

BERNARD SHAW
Don Juan Speaking to the Devil

DON JUAN. Pooh! why should I be civil to them or to you? In this Palace of Lies a truth or two will not hurt you. Your friends are all the dullest dogs I know. They are not beautiful: they are only decorated. They are not clean: they are only shaved and starched. They are not dignified: they are only fashionably dressed. They are not educated: they are only college passmen. They are not religious: they are only pew-renters. They are not moral: they are only conventional. They are not virtuous: they are only cowardly. They are not even vicious: they are only "frail." They are not artistic: they are only lascivious. They are not prosperous: they are only rich. They are not loyal, they are only servile; not dutiful, only sheepish; not public spirited, only patriotic; not courageous, only quarrelsome; not determined, only obstinate; not masterful, only domineering; not self-controlled, only obtuse; not self-respecting, only vain; not kind, only sentimental; not social, only gregarious;

DON JUAN SPEAKING TO THE DEVIL: In *Man And Superman* by Bernard Shaw. Reprinted by permission of The Society of Authors, as Agent for the Bernard Shaw Estate. Selection title by editor.

not considerate, only polite; not intelligent, only opinionated; not progressive, only factious; not imaginative, only superstitious; not just, only vindictive; not generous, only propitiatory; not disciplined, only cowed; and not truthful at all—liars every one of them, to the very backbone of their souls.

DISCUSSION: ANTITHESIS

When contrasting ideas are balanced in sentences and paragraphs, they are said to be in antithesis:

> But the arduous and dangerous deeds of individuals are taken *as romantic or eccentric* rather than *as epic and important.*
> But at present, instead of *being champions and persons,* the agents of great deeds *are becoming personnel of the collective.*—Paul Goodman

As in the first of these statements, the antithesis may be exact and epigrammatic. The second type of sentence appears more frequently, contrasting only roughly equivalent phrases. Whole sentences in antithesis are even more frequent:

> Rome did not invent education, but she developed it on a scale unknown before, gave it state support, and formed the curriculum that persisted till our harassed youth. She did not invent the arch, the vault, or the dome, but she used them with such audacity and magnificence that in some fields her architecture has remained unequaled. . . . She did not invent philosophy, but it was in Lucretius and Seneca that Epicureanism and Stoicism found their most finished form.—Will Durant, *Caesar and Christ*

The balancing of phrases within each sentence heightens the contrast of ideas in the whole passage.

QUESTIONS

1. In Act 3 of Shaw's *Man and Superman,* a dream sequence in the play, Don Juan tells the Devil, with whom he has been debating, that he finds Hell boring and its inhabitants "uncomfortable, false, restless, artificial, petulant, wretched creatures," existing as they did on earth in idleness and illusion. When the Devil asks Don Juan not to be "uncivil to my friends," Don Juan responds with this

famous speech. In it Shaw uses antithesis strictly. How strong is the emphasis achieved through this strict antithesis?
2. What use does Shaw make of semicolons and colons? Could the passage be punctuated without them?
3. What is the purpose of the dash in the final sentence of the speech?

WRITING ASSIGNMENTS

Use your dictionary to write sentences explaining any eight of the contrasted ideas in the passage.

Write an essay on one of these contrasted ideas, basing your discussion on observation and personal experience. Make use of antithesis in a few of your sentences.

MARTIN LUTHER KING, JR.
Nonviolent Resistance

1.   Oppressed people deal with their oppression in three characteristic ways. One way is acquiescence: the oppressed resign themselves to their doom. They tacitly adjust themselves to oppression, and thereby become conditioned to it. In every movement toward freedom some of the oppressed prefer to remain oppressed. Almost 2800 years ago Moses set out to lead the children of Israel from the slavery of Egypt to the freedom of the promised land. He soon discovered that slaves do not always welcome their deliverers. They become accustomed to being slaves. They would rather bear those ills they have, as Shakespeare pointed out, than flee to others that they know not of. They prefer the "fleshpots of Egypt" to the ordeals of emancipation.
2.   There is such a thing as the freedom of exhaustion. Some people are so worn down by the yoke of oppression that they give up. A few years ago in the slum areas of Atlanta, a Negro guitarist used to sing almost daily: "Ben down so long that down don't

NONVIOLENT RESISTANCE: In *Stride toward Freedom* by Martin Luther King, Jr., pp. 211–214. Copyright © 1958 by Martin Luther King, Jr. Reprinted by permission of Harper & Row, Publishers, Inc. Selection title by editor.

bother me." This is the type of negative freedom and resignation that often engulfs the life of the oppressed.

3.   But this is not the way out. To accept passively an unjust system is to coöperate with that system; thereby the oppressed become as evil as the oppressor. Noncoöperation with evil is as much a moral obligation as is coöperation with good. The oppressed must never allow the conscience of the oppressor to slumber. Religion reminds every man that he is his brother's keeper. To accept injustice or segregation passively is to say to the oppressor that his actions are morally right. It is a way of allowing his conscience to fall asleep. At this moment the oppressed fails to be his brother's keeper. So acquiescence—while often the easier way—is not the moral way. It is the way of the coward. The Negro cannot win the respect of his oppressor by acquiescing; he merely increases the oppressor's arrogance and contempt. Acquiescence is interpreted as proof of the Negro's inferiority. The Negro cannot win the respect of the white people of the South or the peoples of the world if he is willing to sell the future of his children for his personal and immediate comfort and safety.

4.   A second way that oppressed people sometimes deal with oppression is to resort to physical violence and corroding hatred. Violence often brings about momentary results. Nations have frequently won their independence in battle. But in spite of temporary victories, violence never brings permanent peace. It solves no social problem; it merely creates new and more complicated ones.

5.   Violence as a way of achieving racial justice is both impractical and immoral. It is impractical because it is a descending spiral ending in destruction for all. The old law of an eye for an eye leaves everybody blind. It is immoral because it seeks to humiliate the opponent rather than win his understanding; it seeks to annihilate rather than to convert. Violence is immoral because it thrives on hatred rather than love. It destroys community and makes brotherhood impossible. It leaves society in monologue rather than dialogue. Violence ends by defeating itself. It creates bitterness in the survivors and brutality in the destroyers. A voice echoes through time saying to every potential Peter, "Put up your sword." History is cluttered with the wreckage of nations that failed to follow this command.

6.   If the American Negro and other victims of oppression succumb to the temptation of using violence in the struggle for freedom, future generations will be the recipients of a desolate night of

bitterness, and our chief legacy to them will be an endless reign of meaningless chaos. Violence is not the way.

7. The third way open to oppressed people in their quest for freedom is the way of nonviolent resistance. Like the synthesis in Hegelian philosophy, the principle of nonviolent resistance seeks to reconcile the truths of two opposites—acquiescence and violence—while avoiding the extremes and immoralities of both. The nonviolent resister agrees with the person who acquiesces that one should not be physically aggressive toward his opponent; but he balances the equation by agreeing with the person of violence that evil must be resisted. He avoids the nonresistance of the former and the violent resistance of the latter. With nonviolent resistance, no individual or group need submit to any wrong, nor need anyone resort to violence in order to right a wrong.

8. It seems to me that this is the method that must guide the actions of the Negro in the present crisis in race relations. Through nonviolent resistance the Negro will be able to rise to the noble height of opposing the unjust system while loving the perpetrators of the system. The Negro must work passionately and unrelentingly for full stature as a citizen, but he must not use inferior methods to gain it. He must never come to terms with falsehood, malice, hate, or destruction.

9. Nonviolent resistance makes it possible for the Negro to remain in the South and struggle for his rights. The Negro's problem will not be solved by running away. He cannot listen to the glib suggestion of those who would urge him to migrate en masse to other sections of the country. By grasping his great opportunity in the South he can make a lasting contribution to the moral strength of the nation and set a sublime example of courage for generations yet unborn.

10. By nonviolent resistance, the Negro can also enlist all men of good will in his struggle for equality. The problem is not a purely racial one, with Negroes set against whites. In the end, it is not a struggle between people at all, but a tension between justice and injustice. Nonviolent resistance is not aimed against oppressors but against oppression. Under its banner consciences, not racial groups, are enlisted.

11. If the Negro is to achieve the goal of integration, he must organize himself into a militant and nonviolent mass movement. All three elements are indispensable. The movement for equality and justice can only be a success if it has both a mass and militant

character; the barriers to be overcome require both. Nonviolence is an imperative in order to bring about ultimate community.

12. A mass movement of militant quality that is not at the same time committed to nonviolence tends to generate conflict, which in turn breeds anarchy. The support of the participants and the sympathy of the uncommitted are both inhibited by the threat that bloodshed will engulf the community. This reaction in turn encourages the opposition to threaten and resort to force. When, however, the mass movement repudiates violence while moving resolutely toward its goal, its opponents are revealed as the instigators and practitioners of violence if it occurs. Then public support is magnetically attracted to the advocates of nonviolence, while those who employ violence are literally disarmed by overwhelming sentiment against their stand.

QUESTIONS

1. A moderate balancing and antithetical arrangement of phrases with a minimum balancing and antithetical arrangement of clauses creates a formal effect and, at the same time, moderates the tension of the passage. Note the sentences that conclude paragraph 1:

> They would rather *bear those ills they have,* as Shakespeare pointed out,
> > than *flee to others that they know not of.*
>
> They prefer *the "fleshpots of Egypt"*
> > to *the ordeals of emancipation.*

What sentences in paragraph 5 contain antithetical elements? How exact is the antithesis? How many of these sentences are balanced to emphasize similar ideas?
2. How exact is the antithesis of ideas in paragraphs 8 and 10?
3. One way to moderate the tension of a passage containing considerable balance and antithesis is to vary the length of sentences. To what extent are the sentences of paragraphs 5, 8, and 10 varied in their length?

WRITING ASSIGNMENTS

Compare King's sentence style with that of another of his writings, for example, "Letter from Birmingham Jail." Discuss how the relative exactness of sentence balance and antithesis is used to moderate or increase the tension of the writing.

Compare a letter by Saint Paul in the King James version of the Bible with the rendering of the same letter in the Goodspeed or the Revised Standard version. Comment on the differences you notice in the use of balance or antithesis.

THOMAS GRIFFITH

The American Image

1.   Why is it that we as a people tolerate what we at the same time lament? I think that in the double aspect of our objectives lies the explanation of some of our most respected lunacies. Take our appearance, for example: what we have made of our cities and done to our countryside. We may deplore our jerry-built look, the wastage of building up and tearing down, the lack of standards—but the other aspect of our appearance is that we prize variety and newness, insist on liberty, and resist regulation.

2.   Economic advantage, not aesthetics, determines the thrust of our cities. We have no dictator, no king, no Baron Haussmann to decree wide boulevards and parks, but only traffic pressures that create vast highway cut-throughs. We do not build for the ages, or to gratify a royal vanity; our buildings, which must conform to a profitable expectancy, have impermanence built into them. They are planned to be torn down. We assume changing needs and changing tastes, and know that the city may move on and leave a building isolated in a less desirable neighborhood; we anticipate the perfection of new materials: it would be economically unsound to project any structure's existence too far. Conscious that even in a building's brief life it may become functionally out of date, we now equip it with movable internal walls, for nothing is here to stay. What else can we do but plan for impermanence, when an urban hell like Los Angeles grows at the rate of 600 new residents a day, and for every three who come to stay two leave?

3.   Part of the American urban ugliness, and its provisional and unfinished look, then, stems from the rootless knowledge (unlike

THE AMERICAN IMAGE: In *The Waist-High Culture* by Thomas Griffith, pp. 169–171. Copyright © 1959 by Thomas Griffith. Reprinted by permission of Harper & Row, Publishers, Inc. Selection title by editor.

Europe's) that we do not intend to remain long in this particular place. We intend to move on, and to improve our lot (there may be another group moving because it is coming down in the world, but we do not talk about that). As a nation we are a volcano that is still heaving and puffing; it is asking too much to expect us at the same time to be conserving and prudent: perhaps when we reach the state where we are decently solicitous of what is being destroyed, decadence will have begun to set in—for creativity and custodianship are often warring qualities.

4. We pay a sentimental homage to the old, but do not really prize it. As a nation, we conceive of ourselves as having started from scratch; we did not build over Roman glories but slashed down trees and made squatter's cabins, and the feeling that we are "improving" sites, even when we are not, makes us slight the old: we may mourn the passing of something old and comfortable, but concede that its right to a particular patch of ground is economically untenable. Aesthetic regret, in the United States, is never a match for economic ambition. Depredation is always organized; preservation almost never. It might be formulated as a law of public pressure that the strength of interest is as twice the strength of numbers: those with a vague and intermittent goodwill are helpless against a sleepless and consuming want. The finest house, the handsomest street, is therefore at the mercy of any casual promoter who wants to tear it down. We are like an animal that casts off its skins too quickly: no wonder we look scraggly.

5. Progress is a hard word to fight in our land, and there are no exacting definitions of it. But though we may damn the despoilers and plead our helplessness, we are unwilling to limit impetus or to restrict variety to what a design commission will allow us. Americans cannot convince themselves that a frozen mold of the past—whether Beaux Arts Roman, baroque, or timbered English brought up to date—can outdo for our uses something that we can think up for ourselves, and the price of our license (which accounts for the happy audacity in the best of our architecture) is our random look, and the proliferation of bogus-modern or bogus-ancient by those who take a prevailing style and adulterate it. We do not believe in dictatorships of taste, and therefore must put up with Taj Mahal orange-juice stands, and roadside joints named the Leaning Tower of Pizza. The modern Voltaire would tell Helvetius: "I do not approve of your taste, but will defend in principle your right to make a buck as you see fit." It's a free country, isn't it?

QUESTIONS

1. What ideas are contrasted in the fourth sentence of paragraph 1? How is the sentence constructed to set these ideas in contrast?
2. How is this same contrast developed in paragraph 2? How exact is the antithesis within and between sentences?
3. The first three sentences of paragraph 4 contain contrasting ideas. How many do you find? What later sentence in paragraph 4 is constructed antithetically?
4. What sentences in paragraph 5 contain antithetical ideas? Is Griffith developing the same contrast of ideas as in earlier paragraphs?

WRITING ASSIGNMENT

Develop one of Griffith's ideas, illustrating from observations of your own, and arranging your examples antithetically, as Griffith arranges his in paragraph 2:

> We have no dictator, no king, no Baron Haussmann to decree wide boulevards and parks, but only traffic pressures that create vast highway cut-throughs.

LENGTH

ERNEST HEMINGWAY

The Shooting of the Buffalo

[1]The car was going a wild forty-five miles an hour across the open and as Macomber watched, the buffalo got bigger and bigger until he could see the gray, hairless, scabby look of one huge bull and how his neck was a part of his shoulders and the shiny black of his horns as he galloped a little behind the others that were strung out in that steady plunging gait; and then, the car swaying

THE SHOOTING OF THE BUFFALO: In "The Short Happy Life of Francis Macomber" by Ernest Hemingway. Copyright 1936 Ernest Hemingway; renewal copyright © 1964 Ernest Hemingway. Reprinted by permission of Charles Scribner's Sons from *The Short Stories of Ernest Hemingway.* Selection title by editor.

as though it had just jumped a road, they drew up close and he could see the plunging hugeness of the bull, and the dust in his sparsely haired hide, the wide boss of horn and his outstretched, wide-nostrilled muzzle, and he was raising his rifle when Wilson shouted, "Not from the car, you fool!" and he had no fear, only hatred of Wilson, while the brakes clamped on and the car skidded, plowing sideways to an almost stop and Wilson was out on one side and he on the other, stumbling as his feet hit the still speeding-by of the earth, and then he was shooting at the bull as he moved away, hearing the bullets whunk into him, emptying his rifle at him as he moved steadily away, finally remembering to get his shots forward into the shoulder, and as he fumbled to re-load, he saw the bull was down. ²Down on his knees, his big head tossing, and seeing the other two still galloping he shot at the leader and hit him. ³He shot again and missed and he heard the *carawonging* roar as Wilson shot and saw the leading bull slide forward onto his nose.

DISCUSSION: LENGTH

There is nothing intrinsically effective or ineffective, superior or inferior, about long or short sentences, just as there is nothing intrinsically effective in a single note of the scale. Effectiveness depends on the use or function of sentence length in a given context.

Ordinary exposition usually begins with the main idea and accumulates detail:

> She was a spirited-looking young woman, with dark curly hair cropped and parted on the side, a short oval face with straight eyebrows, and a large curved mouth.—Katherine Anne Porter, "Old Mortality"

How much detail a writer can provide depends on how effectively he can keep the main idea before the reader: detail becomes excessive when the main idea seems to disappear into it. In prose that describes physical action, the sentence may depict one connected action:

> Morrall would duck his head in the huddle and if it was feasible he would call a play which took the ball laterally across the field—a pitchout, perhaps, and the play would eat up ground toward the girls, the ball carrier sprinting for the sidelines, with his running guards in front of him, running low, and behind them the linemen coming too, so that twenty-two

men were converging on them at a fair clip.—George Plimp-
ton, *Paper Lion*

Sentences longer than this are rarely used, partly because of the difficulty of maintaining clarity.

By contrast, a paragraph may be constructed of very short, disconnected sentences, resulting in an effect that resembles "primer
style." Hemingway uses such sentences in a short story to express the
monotony felt by a veteran of the First World War on his return home:

> He sat there on the porch reading a book on the war. It was a
> history and he was reading about all the engagements he had
> been in. It was the most interesting reading he had ever done.
> He wished there were more maps. He looked forward with a
> good feeling to reading all the really good histories when they
> would come out with good detail maps. Now he was really
> learning about the war. He had been a good soldier. That
> made a difference.—Ernest Hemingway, "Soldier's Home"

QUESTIONS

1. Read aloud the first sentence of Hemingway's "The Shooting of the
   Buffalo," noting the main clauses. In light of the considerable
   length of the sentence, how are these clauses given emphasis?
   Read the sentence aloud again, this time breaking it into shorter
   sentences. What change in effect do you notice? Is there an *equiva-
   lence* between the original sentence, particularly in its length, and
   the experience described?
2. Why does Hemingway end the sentence with *he saw the bull was
   down* rather than continue into the next sentence?
3. Change the subordinate elements in sentence 2 into main clauses
   and the first two main clauses of sentence 3 into subordinate
   clauses. How do these changes affect the passage?
4. Use your dictionary to determine whether there are synonyms for
   the following words: *scabby, plunging, hugeness, speeding-by,
   whunk, carawonging*. Would any synonyms you found be more suitable than Hemingway's words? How do you explain the absence of
   some of these words in the dictionary?

WRITING ASSIGNMENT

Rewrite the entire passage by breaking it into shorter sentences. In a
second paragraph discuss the ways in which the revision alters the
mood.

RICHARD E. BYRD

Alone in the Antarctic

[1] May was a round boulder sinking before a tide. [2] Time sloughed off the last implication of urgency, and the days moved imperceptibly one into the other. [3] The few world news items which Dyer read to me from time to time seemed almost as meaningless and blurred as they might to a Martian. [4] My world was insulated against the shocks running through distant economies. [5] Advance Base was geared to different laws. [6] On getting up in the morning, it was enough for me to say to myself: Today is the day to change the barograph sheet, or, Today is the day to fill the stove tank. [7] The night was settling down in earnest. [8] By May 17th, one month after the sun had sunk below the horizon, the noon twilight was dwindling to a mere chink in the darkness, lit by a cold reddish glow. [9] Days when the wind brooded in the north or east, the Barrier became a vast stagnant shadow surmounted by swollen masses of clouds, one layer of darkness piled on top of the other. [10] This was the polar night, the morbid countenance of the Ice Age. [11] Nothing moved; nothing was visible. [12] This was the soul of inertness. [13] One could almost hear a distant creaking as if a great weight were settling.

QUESTIONS

1. In the winter of 1934, during his second Antarctic expedition, Admiral Byrd maintained by himself a meterological observation station some distance from the expedition base. What is the central impression or mood that he wishes to convey—that of time moving quickly or that of inertness?
2. How does the first sentence introduce a dominant image and motif? How is this image carried into later sentences? Pay particular attention to the adjectives and verbs in sentences 7–9 and 12–13.
3. Byrd's sentences are obviously much shorter than Hemingway's in "The Shooting of the Buffalo." Do Byrd's sentences or the clauses in his compound sentences seem clipped and abrupt? In the longer

ALONE IN THE ANTARCTIC: In *Alone* by Richard E. Byrd. Copyright, 1938, by Richard E. Byrd. Reprinted by permission of G. P. Putman's Sons. Selection title by editor.

sentences, are there many dependent elements, as in the first sentence by Hemingway?
4. Convert sentences 10–13 into one long, carefully constructed sentence. What is gained or lost in effect? In general, what does the sentence construction contribute to the overall mood?

WRITING ASSIGNMENT

Describe an experience that was exciting, but at the same time frightening or painful. Vary the length of your sentences to control the degree of excitement or emotion you want to convey.

CLIMAX

JOHN UPDIKE
My Grandmother

¹When we were all still alive, the five of us in that kerosene-lit house, on Friday and Saturday nights, at an hour when in the spring and summer there was still abundant light in the air, I would set out in my father's car for town, where my friends lived. ²I had, by moving ten miles away, at last acquired friends: an illustration of that strange law whereby, like Orpheus leading Eurydice, we achieve our desire by turning our back on it. ³I had even gained a girl, so that the vibrations were as sexual as social that made me jangle with anticipation as I clowned in front of the mirror in our kitchen, shaving from a basin of stove-heated water, combing my hair with a dripping comb, adjusting my reflection in the mirror until I had achieved just that electric angle from which my face seemed beautiful and everlastingly, by the very volumes of air and sky and grass that lay mutely banked about our home, beloved. ⁴My grandmother would hover near me, watching fearfully, as she had when I was a child, afraid that I would fall from a

tree. [5]Delirious, humming, I would swoop and lift her, lift her like a child, crooking one arm under her knees and cupping the other behind her back. [6]Exultant in my height, my strength, I would lift that frail brittle body weighing perhaps a hundred pounds and twirl with it in my arms while the rest of the family watched with startled smiles of alarm. [7]Had I stumbled, or dropped her, I might have broken her back, but my joy always proved a secure cradle. [8]And whatever irony was in the impulse, whatever implicit contrast between this ancient husk, scarcely female, and the pliant, warm girl I would embrace before the evening was done, direct delight flooded away: I was carrying her who had carried me, I was giving my past a dance, I had lifted the anxious caretaker of my childhood from the floor, I was bringing her with my boldness to the edge of danger, from which she had always sought to guard me.

DISCUSSION: CLIMAX

Our discussion of periodic sentences indicated one important way that climax can be achieved—by delaying the main idea or the completion of the main idea until the end of the sentence. We saw also that, even in loose sentences, modifying or qualifying phrases and clauses that follow the main idea can be arranged in the order of rising importance—as in *I came, I saw, I conquered.* A necessary condition of climax is a sense of anticipation, promoted chiefly through the ideas themselves. Obviously anticlimax will result if we make the culminating idea less significant than what has gone before. The letdown that results may be deliberately comic, as in this sentence by Thomas De Quincey:

> If once a man indulges himself in murder, very soon he comes to think little of robbery; and from robbing he next comes to drinking and Sabbath-breaking, and from that to incivility and procrastination.

QUESTIONS

1. In the Updike, how does the ending of sentence 3 vary the normal sentence pattern to take advantage of the strong terminal position? Is the double emphasis given to *beloved* justified by the context?
2. Sentence 3 develops through an accumulation of detail. Does the sentence develop a single idea? Could it be broken up without interrupting the meaning or disturbing the effect?

3. How is climax achieved in sentences 5 and 8? Is it achieved through the same kind of sentence construction?

WRITING ASSIGNMENTS

Describe an episode or a series of incidents involving a close relative or friend. Let your details reveal your attitude toward him or her; do not state the attitude directly.

Discuss how the sense of anticipation built into Updike's paragraph is conveyed through sentence climax.

ANNIE DILLARD

The Mystery of Beauty

1.   Cruelty is a mystery, and the waste of pain. But if we describe a world to compass these things, a world that is a long, brute game, then we bump against another mystery: the inrush of power and light, the canary that sings on the skull. Unless all ages and races of men have been deluded by the same mass hypnotist (who?), there seems to be such a thing as beauty, a grace wholly gratuitous. About five years ago I saw a mockingbird make a straight vertical descent from the roof gutter of a four-story building. It was an act as careless and spontaneous as the curl of a stem or the kindling of a star.

2.   The mockingbird took a single step into the air and dropped. His wings were still folded against his sides as though he were singing from a limb and not falling, accelerating thirty-two feet per second per second, through empty air. Just a breath before he would have been dashed to the ground, he unfurled his wings with exact, deliberate care, revealing the broad bars of white, spread his elegant, white-banded tail, and so floated onto the grass. I had just rounded a corner when his insouciant step caught my eye; there was no one else in sight. The fact of his free fall was like the old philosophical conundrum about the tree that falls in the forest.

THE MYSTERY OF BEAUTY: In *Pilgrim at Tinker Creek* by Annie Dillard, pp. 7–8. Copyright © 1974 by Annie Dillard. Reprinted by permission of Harper & Row, Publishers, Inc. Selection title by editor.

The answer must be, I think, that beauty and grace are performed whether or not we will or sense them. The least we can do is try to be there.

3.   Another time I saw another wonder: sharks off the Atlantic coast of Florida. There is a way a wave rises above the ocean horizon, a triangular wedge against the sky. If you stand where the ocean breaks on a shallow beach, you see the raised water in a wave is translucent, shot with lights. One late afternoon at low tide a hundred big sharks passed the beach near the mouth of a tidal river in a feeding frenzy. As each green wave rose from the churning water, it illuminated within itself the six- or eight-foot-long bodies of twisting sharks. The sharks disappeared as each wave rolled toward me; then a new wave would swell above the horizon, containing in it, like scorpions in amber, sharks that roiled and heaved. The sight held awesome wonders: power and beauty, grace tangled in a rapture with violence.

QUESTIONS

1. How does the colon help to create a sense of climax in the second sentence of paragraph 1? What use does the author make of the colon at the end of paragraph 3?
2. Notice that phrases such as *a grace wholly gratuitous* and *the kindling of a star* seem more important than phrases preceding them in their sentences by virtue of their position at the end. What similar uses does the author make of the end of sentences in paragraphs 2 and 3?
3. How does the author explain the phrase *a grace wholly gratuitous* later in the passage?

WRITING ASSIGNMENT

Develop one of the author's ideas from your own observations. Let the reader see and feel the experience as you saw and felt it. Build one or two of your sentences to convey a sense of climax, and if possible one of your paragraphs.

Diction

USAGE

ROBERT COLES

The South Goes North

1.   These newcomers to our cities, these émigrés who have never left our own borders, these long-standing American citizens who have fled in desperation from the South to the North, from the quiet and isolated mountains to the crowded flatlands, be they white men or black men, young women or old women, they talk about flights of stairs or door locks or street numbers or mailboxes or light switches. For a while one thinks the problem is that of language; "they" have their words, their dialect, their way of putting things, and it is a matter of time before an outsider will be able to get the point, to understand why those simple everyday words get mentioned so often—as if they are the keys to some mystery: "I've been here since the war, the Korean War. I came here from South Carolina. My husband was stationed up here, and he sent me a bus ticket. I never went back. I had my first baby inside me. The first surprise I had was the apartment building—I mean all the steps in it, the stairs and more stairs, until you think after climbing so many you'll be seeing the Lord himself." She goes on to remind her listener that in South Carolina there was exactly one step from the ground to the cabin in which she and her parents and her grandparents ("and the others before them") were born. That step was actually a stump of a tree half buried in the ground. The

THE SOUTH GOES NORTH: In Volume III of *Children of Crisis* by Robert Coles. Reprinted by permission of Little, Brown and Co. Copyright © 1967, 1968, 1969, 1970, 1971 by Robert Coles. Selection title by editor.

church she went to had "proper steps," two of them. And then suddenly she came to Boston, and encountered steps and steps and steps until she wondered in the beginning whether she could ever survive it all—lifting herself up and taking herself down again, and with no sunlight to help either. As for the hall lights in her "building," as she calls it, "they never have worked, not once."

2.   More than the steps get to her, though. The locks do, the endless numbers of door locks. She was poor in South Carolina and she is poor now. But back South one doesn't have to fasten down one's poverty, defend it fearfully, worry about its vulnerability. Up North it seems nothing can go unguarded, and indeed, "the nothing we have is all locked up." She does, however, lose her keys sometimes—yes, the three keys, to the front door of her apartment and the back door and the street door downstairs. Then she becomes irritated and half amused. She also becomes nostalgic for a minute: "I think to myself that before I came to the city I'd never seen a lock in my life. That was the first thing I told my mother when I went back to see her. I told her they're lock crazy up North. And it isn't as if they're millionaires, our people up there."

3.   She speaks about other matters to her mother. There are, again, those flights of stairs that go round and round and lead from one story to another. In one building she lived on the second story; in another on the fifth, the *fifth*—which means she was so high up she could imagine herself looking down on that small rural church she recalls being so tall. She wonders to this day whether the water tower she used to believe to be the tallest thing in the whole wide world is as tall as her apartment house, which she now certainly knows is far indeed from being the tallest building on her street, let alone other streets. And since she tries to keep in touch with her mother, even though neither of them is very good at writing, there are those numbers to keep in mind. Whoever got *that* idea anyway—of putting numbers on houses? Where do the numbers on her street start? Where does the street start, for that matter? In Dorchester County, South Carolina, so far as she knows, "there's not a number there on any home." She never had a post office box number, nor does her mother even today: "I write her name; I write the town; I write South Carolina—and it gets there faster than letters from her get to me."

4.   Of course she gets her mail put into a mailbox, another one of those newfangled devices that go with city living. Since letter boxes in her building are private but commonly trespassed, she

has to have a "mail key," too. For a long while the boxes in her apartment house were hopelessly inadequate—bent and punctured and covered with grime and scrawled words. Finally the postman complained, or higher officials in the post office did, or maybe it was the welfare department, which mails out checks. Someone did, she knows that, because the landlord was compelled to put in new boxes, and a policeman stood there watching while the job was done. It was a mixed blessing, needless to say: "I love the box, but the keys, all the keys you need—just to stay alive up here in the city." She told her mother about her new mailbox. Her mother told the news to the lady who runs the grocery store and gasoline station and post office down in Dorchester County, South Carolina. She is a white woman, and her name is Mrs. Chalmers, and she had a laugh over that. She told her informant to write back to "the poor girl" in Boston and ask how the mailman ever makes sense of them all, the hundreds of boxes he must have to fill up every morning.

5.   People manage to make their adjustments. There are spurts and lags, naturally. Some habits and customs are mastered more quickly than others. Some undreamed-of luxuries try the mind and soul more than others do. In Cleveland a man from "near Beckley," West Virginia, laughs about a few of his recent tribulations and compares them to what his ancestors had to go through—for they were also Americans who moved on (from the East Coast westward) when they had to: "I can't keep up with the light switches in this city. I think it's harder for me to figure out these lights than it was for my kin way back to cut a path through the hills and settle there. Everywhere you go here there's a switch. On and off, that's what you have to think about when you go into a room. Now who's supposed to know every minute of his life where the switch is? I've been up in this place over a year and I forget, and I have my wife on my back, saying, 'The switch is here, don't get dressed in darkness.' Well, what's so damned wrong about darkness when it's early in the morning!"

6.   In the cities late in the afternoon the lights appear, whether he or any other particular person likes it or not, and does or does not join in the act by turning a switch to ON. In the cities people seem to insist that darkness somehow be pushed into corners. There are plenty of those corners, especially in his neighborhood, but never in Ohio has he lived with the kind of darkness he everyday took for granted in West Virginia. He is the first one to point out that al-

most every street corner has lights, lights of all colors. There are streetlights—and the stores with their lights, and the gas stations with theirs, and the police cars with lights on their roofs, whirling around and around. And there are those signs, signs full of bulbs, signs that wait on the sun to leave so they can take over and say: look over here, look and remember and buy, and if you do, we'll stay around and get called a success, catchy and clever and able to do our job, which is to light up your mind with desire.

7.   He wants people to know he didn't live so far up a hollow that "this whole electric-light world up here in the city" is in and of itself strange to him. He had sockets with bulbs in them "back home" in his house, and he had television, also—so he really didn't expect to be as surprised as he was when he first came into Cleveland. He used to tighten the bulb in the evening, when he'd sit and smoke his pipe and get drowsy and half watch television. It was his children who often would pay full attention to it, "that picture box." And as a matter of fact, they were the ones who wanted him to loosen that bulb, so they could have the picture and nothing else all to themselves. But he liked to whittle, sometimes. And even if he didn't, the evening is the right time to have a little light around. Mind, he says a *little* light, no so much light that one feels in China during the night—which is where he sometimes thinks he might be as he sits in his Cleveland apartment. China, he learned from a teacher a long time ago, is where the day goes when we have night.

8.   In any event, now his children can't understand why he doesn't switch on all the lights, come dusk. Nor would they think of sitting and watching television in complete darkness. Why do his boys and girls require what they once would have abhorred, glowing lamps? He is quick to note the change and explain it: "It must be they used to want to have our cabin so pitch-black because that way they could lose themselves watching the programs and forget where they were. Now they're gone from there and up here. Now they're in the city, and the television programs are about the city. They don't have to imagine they're someplace else. They don't need it dark, so their minds can wander. *We've* wandered."

DISCUSSION: USAGE

None of us speaks or writes in the same way on all occasions: the differences depend on how formal the occasion is. A letter of application for a job will be more formal than a letter to a friend; a graduation speech will sound different from a locker-room conversation.

Each of us has a formal and informal language and, whether we know it or not, standards for judging their effectiveness. These standards we derive from the different groups we belong to—each group with its special idioms and vocabulary. Teenagers share a common language, which sometimes they have to translate for their parents; teenagers of a particular racial or ethnic background share a special dialect or language. So do teenagers of a particular city or region of the country. Though black teenagers in New York City share expressions and idioms with all other teenagers in the city, they may share a special dialect with their families and with their black friends. At school they may share a language with their teachers different from the dialect they speak at home. Even a family may have its own private language—special words and expressions to describe acts and feelings.

Cutting across these differences is a standardized English we hear on television and read in newspapers—a language sometimes less colorful and personal than these other languages, but serving as a medium for communication among diverse groups of people, not only in the United States but in other English-speaking countries. This standard is of long growth and it changes less than the informal language and slang of particular groups. This standard, represented in the readings in this book, falls between two extremes—one formal and abstract in its content and sentences, the other informal and concrete:

[*Formal*] Musical experiences of suspense are very similar to those experienced in real life. Both in life and in music the emotions thus arising have essentially the same stimulus situation: the situation of ignorance, the awareness of the individual's impotence and inability to act where the future course of events is unknown. Because these musical experiences are so very similar to those existing in the drama and in life itself, they are often felt to be particularly powerful and effective.— Leonard B. Meyer, *Emotion and Meaning in Music*

[*Informal*] It felt as I would have expected: wonderful. The lights went out; flickering matches transformed the Garden into a giant planetarium. Dylan and The Band came back for a reprise of "Most Likely You'll Go Your Way," left, came back again, and ended with a rousing electric version of "Blowin' in the Wind." I went home as high on Dylan as I'd ever been.—Ellen Willis, *The New Yorker,* February 18, 1974 (on Bob Dylan's Madison Square Garden concert)

The abstract ideas of the first passage could be stated in the most informal language. But usage is a matter of convention as well as personal choice, and if we would not be surprised to find Meyer's ideas stated in various ways, we probably would be surprised to find the Bob Dylan concert described in highly formal language. As a rule, informal writing is closer to the patterns of ordinary speech; formal writing often seems impersonal because it departs widely from these patterns (few people routinely speak Meyer's sentences). Much standard writing today has both formal and informal characteristics: we may combine colloquialisms with an abstract vocabulary in rather formal sentences containing striking parallelism and balance. We may even introduce slang (racy, hybrid, usually short-lived expressions) into an abstract discussion. The following sentence states a complex idea informally; the pauses and qualifications suggest the stop-and-start way we speak:

> There is a whole folklore, a whole tangle of something only a cultural anthropologist could begin to disentangle, that has grown up around the American frontier; there is—the already old-fashioned and somewhat disapproved word has to be used—a fascinating *myth* of the American frontier, the West.—Crane Brinton, *A History of Western Morals*

QUESTIONS

1. How do the words Coles quotes illustrate his statement that "it is a matter of time before an outsider will be able to get the point, to understand why those simple, everyday words get mentioned so often"?
2. How many varieties of usage do you find in this selection?
3. What points about Southern people living in the North is the author making through his details? What general truths about people and society do his statements suggest to you?

WRITING ASSIGNMENT

Discuss the changes that you experienced in moving from the city to the country, or from one environment to another completely different from it. At the end of your discussion draw conclusions from your details.

DERECK WILLIAMSON
Tell It Like It Was

1.   A browse through the Little League Baseball Official Rules indicates that times have changed since my sandlot baseball days. I'll tell it like it is now, and then try to tell it like it was then.

> PLAYING EQUIPMENT—Each team must have at least twelve conventional baseball uniforms. The Official Little League Shoulder Patch must be affixed to the upper left sleeve of the uniform blouse. Games may not be played except in uniforms. These uniforms are the property of the League, and are to be loaned to the players for such period as the League may determine.

2.   Playing equipment—Each guy came out to the ballfield looking like a bum. Shirts were optional. Patches went on pants because they were torn up sliding. Anybody wearing a clean or neat garment was jumped on, and rubbed around in the dirt.

> Each League must provide in each dugout at least six (6) protective helmets approved by Little League Headquarters. The wearing of such approved helmets by the batter, all base runners, and coaches is mandatory. Shoes with metal spikes or cleats are prohibited. Catchers must wear masks during practice, pitcher warm-up, and regular games.

3.   There were no dugouts—only the ditch that ran across the field just behind second base. In the ditch were at least sixty (60) frogs. Headgear was optional. The most popular were brimless caps and capless brims. There was only one helmet in the league—a leather aviator's helmet, with goggles, owned by Spike Snyder. Shoes with metal spikes or cleats could not be worn, because they all belonged to big brothers in high school and didn't fit. Catchers didn't wear masks. To avoid being hit in the head they stood eight feet behind the plate and let the ball bounce once.

TELL IT LIKE IT WAS: In Martin Levin's "Phoenix Nest," *Saturday Review*, June 21, 1969. Reprinted by permission of Martin Levin.

PITCHERS—Any player on the team roster may pitch. A player shall not pitch in more than six (6) innings in a calendar week. Delivery of a single pitch shall constitute having pitched in an inning.

4. Pitchers—Any player who owned the ball pitched. A player could not pitch on more than seven (7) days in a calendar week, or more than one hundred (100) innings a day, because it got too dark. Delivery of a pitch straight down and the pitcher falling senseless beside the ball constituted exhaustion.

EQUIPMENT—The ball shall weigh not less than five ounces or more than five and one-quarter (5¼) ounces avoirdupois. It shall measure not less than nine (9) inches nor more than nine and one-quarter (9¼) inches in circumference. The bat shall be round and made of wood. It shall not be more than thirty-three (33) inches in length. Bats may be taped for a distance not exceeding sixteen (16) inches from the small end. The first baseman is the only fielder who may wear a mitt. All other fielders must use fielder's gloves.

5. Equipment—The ball could be of any weight, and anybody stupid enough to say "avoirdupois" out loud deserved what he got. Circumferences of the ball depended on the amount of tape wrapped around it. Sometimes the tape came loose when you hit the ball, and the circumference changed rapidly. Sometimes it was just tape by the time it reached the fielder, and the circumference was zero (0).
6. Bats were made of wood and were round unless they had been used for hitting rocks. After bats were broken they were taped for their entire length and it was hard to tell which was the small end. The first baseman was lucky if he got either a mitt or a glove. The only mitt belonged to the fat right fielder, who wore it even when he was at bat.

PROTESTS—Protests shall be considered only when based on the violation or interpretation of a playing rule or the use of an ineligible player. No protest shall be considered on a decision involving an umpire's judgment.

7. Protests—A protest was considered only when you were aw-fully sure you could lick the other guy. There was no umpire, unless some kid was on crutches and couldn't play. Nobody paid any attention to his calls, because he was just another kid.

FIELD DECORUM—The actions of players, managers, coaches, umpires, and League officials must be above re-proach.

8. Field decorum—There were no managers, or coaches, or any of those big people. Only players who swore and spat. Anyone caught being above reproach got clobbered.

QUESTIONS

1. Williamson contrasts two kinds of baseball through two attitudes toward it—attitudes expressed not only in the details of the games but in ways of talking or writing about it. What is the chief dif-ference between the language of Little League Baseball Official Rules and that of his account of sandlot baseball?
2. Is Williamson approving of Little League baseball, critical of it, or merely amused? Or is his feeling neutral?

WRITING ASSIGNMENTS

Rewrite the Little League Baseball Official Rules for the information of children playing the game. Then analyze the changes that you made in vocabulary and sentence construction and the reasons for these changes.

Write a one-paragraph letter to a former high-school teacher asking for advice about a present course or a possible future career. Write a second one-paragraph letter to a friend who has taken the course or embarked on such a career, asking the same advice. In a third para-graph discuss the adjustments in usage you made and the reasons for them.

GEORGE A. PETTITT
Adolescents and Work

1. One problem is the shortage of meaningful work in which American adolescents may participate. The inherent needs of children for at least a limited role in the world of work has been lost sight of in enthusiasm for other cultural goals: production efficiency, protection of children from inappropriate labor for overly long hours, protection of the rights of the adult worker through unionization, and equalization of economic status by minimum wage laws without adequate consideration for the salability of the services offered by the immature and inexperienced.

2. The paradoxical attitude toward work, evidenced by indifference or opposition to work-experience for the young in a culture which expects everyone to paddle his own economic canoe, is further exemplified by the rejection of employment opportunity as one basic prophylactic against delinquency. Yet at the same time leading penologists urge the expansion of meaningful work opportunities in prisons as a means of rehabilitating criminals and combating recidivism. If work has even a minor value as an alternative to crime, it would seem to be common sense to make it available to delinquents before rather than after their trouble becomes chronic. When delinquency starts, those who turn to it are not demonstrably worse than non-delinquents. It is estimated that very few active young people reach the age of seventeen without taking a chance at some unlawful activity. Those whom the police apprehend each year are not much more than 2 percent of those who could legally have been apprehended if they had been identified. The overwhelming majority of youngsters manage to straighten themselves out, more by chance than inherent virtue, depending on whether reasonable alternatives are open, and provided that they are not given intensive training in delinquency while locked up in a reform school or its equivalent.

3. American society seems to be just as pigheaded about the kind of life children should lead as the automobile industry was a few years ago about the kind of automobiles their customers might

ADOLESCENTS AND WORK: In *Prisoners of Culture* by George A. Pettitt. Reprinted by permission of Charles Scribner's Sons. Copyright © 1970 George Pettitt. Selection title by editor.

buy. Not until a flood of foreign cars deluged the market did designers and producers realize that there might be more available garage space and more sales opportunity for cars slightly less massive than a battleship. Similarly, society seems unable to let young people experiment with small ambitions. There appears to be something reprehensible about admitting limited ability or being attracted to a job of no higher status than that held by a working parent. If this is not a reasonable interpretation of the contemporary American attitude, then insistence on schooling beyond the point where the return justifies the cost must be attributed to adult monopoly of the job market. This makes it impractical to hire inexperienced, immature minors even if jobs might be found for them. Many of the discontented may be kept in school solely in hope that they will get into less trouble there than they might if they walked the streets.

4. This hope might be reasonable if going to school were more widely recognized as an adult avocation, and if, somewhere along the line, a youngster were convinced that he had completed his term as a child and really begun a new regime as an apprentice adult. To the extent that school tags its clients as non-adults, it becomes progressively less attractive for those who are desperately in need of assurance as to how and where they fit into the adult world, when they well know they are headed for some level lower than that of the professions. Hope for the discontented in school would have more chance of realization if youngsters could find, within the approved educational structure, some of the assurances of progress toward adult goals that preliterate societies convey through membership in age-grades, with a few adult-related responsibilities and privileges.

5. In many instances, the only activity that makes sense to the juvenile may be membership in an organization like the junior traffic patrol. Here, at least, he has a meaningful job to do, a sense of responsibility to be discharged, a bit of privilege to enjoy, and some authority to wield. For the first time in his life, perhaps, he is distinguished from the "lonely crowd" by a uniform or some insignia to be worn, by a code of disciplined behavior, and by participation in a learning group which has an immediate, practical application for the instruction it receives. Junior traffic patrol groups are about as close to highly successful, primitive age-grades as anything that civilization has to offer. But for older adolescents, as their personal need for identity becomes more urgent,

there may be nothing but athletic teams or student activities, which are sometimes described as playing in the "economy size sandbox." These have their place, and are highly challenging to some adolescents. But to others, they are "kid stuff," and for want of something better to do, the discontented organize social clubs, exclusive cliques, and undercover "in groups," which do their best to create purposes sanctioned neither by school authorities nor parents. If supervision cannot be avoided in these organizations, the most adventuresome may turn to out-of-school gangs. It is not delinquency and crime, *per se,* which *attract* young people, as much as it is the orthodox pattern laid down for adolescents that *repels* them. Unruly or delinquent behavior in young people may represent legitimate revolt against the external environment.

QUESTIONS

1. Insurance policies and many government documents are written in a highly formal, abstract style. In them we are seldom aware of a real person speaking to us and revealing his or her interests and background; the voice is wholly impersonal. Technical writing in the social sciences is often highly formal also, but in this kind of writing, the greater number of concrete examples the author provides, the more we are likely to be aware of the author as an observer. What impression do you get of Pettitt through the concrete examples he provides?
2. The vocabulary of much technical writing, whether in the social sciences or in other fields, uses abstract rather than concrete words—words that point to ideas rather than experiences or things. Such words are more often written than spoken. What kind of words do you find in paragraph 1? Is this prose more easily written than spoken?
3. How does the junior traffic patrol help the reader understand the phrase "age-grades"? What other examples might illustrate this kind of activity?
4. How tight is the parallelism in sentences of paragraphs 2 and 4? Do you find a concern for sentence balance in the whole selection?

WRITING ASSIGNMENT

Discuss Pettitt's final statement in light of your own experience and observations. Provide an example of your own—comparable to the junior traffic patrol.

JOYCE MAYNARD
The Pressure of The Group

1. The pressure of The Group is strong in any period. There was a new kind of pressure affecting us during the sixties though—not just the push toward conformity and the fear and distrust that people have by nature (and that public schools seem to reinforce) of anything that's different. In the fifties, I think, groups pretty rigidly conformed, but they were indiscriminating too. A pair of bobby sox, a V-necked sweater, and you were *in*. The sixties were a more critical-minded, sophisticated time, full of more negative adjectives than lavish superlatives, a time when it was easier to do things wrong than to do them right. Products, ourselves, of hours spent listening to TV commercials, we had become comparative shoppers, suspicious and demanding, minutely analyzing one another's actions and appearances—new haircuts with unevenly trimmed sideburns, cowlicks, unmatched socks, Band-Aids that, we suspected, concealed pimples, new dresses, new shoes. We knew each other's faces and bodies and wardrobes so well that any change was noticed at once, the fuel for endless notes. That's why I dressed so carefully mornings—I was about to face the scrutiny of fifteen gossip-seeking girls, ten only slightly less observant boys ready to imitate my voice and walk, and one stern, prune-faced teacher who would check my spelling and my long division with the care my enemies gave to my hems. At every moment—even at home, with no one but family there—I'd be conscious of what the other kids, The Group, would think if they could see me now.
2. They ruled over us all—and over each other—like a supreme court. Their presence was frightening, their judgments quick and firm and often damning, and the tightness of the circle when I was in it only made the times when I was outside seem more miserable. The hierarchy was re-established a hundred times a day—in choosing partners for science experiments, in study halls, when the exchange of homework problems began, and at lunch. But most of all in note passing. We rarely needed to take notes, and so we passed them. We could have whispered easily enough, of

course, or remained silent. (It wasn't ever that we had important things to say.) But note passing was far more intriguing, spylike. (Those were "The Man from U.N.C.L.E." days, all of us playing Illya Kuryakin.) Most of all, note passing was exclusive. Whispers were impermanent and could be overheard. Notes could be tightly sealed and folded, their journeys followed down the rows to make sure none was intercepted along the way. Getting a note, even an angry one, was always a compliment. Whenever I received one, I was amazed and grateful that I had made some slight impression on the world, that I was worthy of someone's time and ink. There were kids, I knew, whose letters died, like anonymous fan mail, unanswered and unread.

3. I think it was in notes, more than in conversations or Girl Scout meetings or Saturday mornings together on our bikes, that friendships and hatreds were established. We committed ourselves on paper to things we never would have said out loud (this seems odd to me now) and we saved them all—round-lettered, backhand messages written on blue-lined loose-leaf paper, the corners of old workbook pages, candy wrappers, lunch bags; they circulated around the classroom from desk to desk and year to year (once, in the seventh grade, we even had a pulley between desks). These were, I think, the greatest writing practice we got in school. Sometimes the notes contained news, stretched out in soap opera–type installment doses, to last us through an uneventful day. Stories leaked slowly—"Guess what?" would travel down my row to Becky till, at last, the teacher's mind deep in another matter, my note would cross the hardest point along its course, the latitudinal gulch between our rows (not within them) and she would unwrap it, folded like an origami bird, and write her answer, "What?" and pass it back to me. We wrote about TV shows watched the night before, about how much we hated math and what our weekend and after-school plans were ("Are you going to walk home or take the bus?" "Short cut or long way around?").

4. Great wars, or so they seemed to us, were waged in notes, based on elaborate strategies we worked out, like homework, the night before. If things were getting dull, I'd plan to pick a fight, with accusations of two-facedness (talking about someone behind his back was the most common offense) or cruelty to an underdog. Realizing early that I wasn't going to be a leader among the *in,* and refusing to simply follow, I became the champion of the class failures. The boy with the harelip, the girl who lived in a trailer

and smelled bad, the one who tended to drool a little on her collar, I defended (enjoying the image of myself as kind and gentle benefactress, protecting the sensitive, the poet soul) from the group I loved and envied—for their coolness—and hated for the fact that they had never quite admitted me. I lectured Margie in suffering, histrionic moralistic tones ("You, who have always been popular, cannot know what it's like not to be. Think, for a moment, what Franny feels like when you laugh at her or lead her on to make a fool of herself, because she thinks that then you'll be her friend. I *know*—I know what it's like on this side of the fence . . .") Margie, a genuinely friendly girl, would be first puzzled and defensive. And then, as her troops moved in on me, sarcastic and coldly vicious. She'd write back to deny the charges, and there would be the ghastly period I always forgot about, setting out on my battles, when I seemed to be sinking and friendless, and wished I'd never started the whole thing.

QUESTIONS

1. How many words in paragraphs 1 and 2 would you classify as formal—that is, as words you would not use in ordinary conversation? How tightly constructed are the sentences in which these words occur?
2. Formal writing makes use of passive constructions more so than informal writing. Does Maynard favor passive constructions, or does she favor the use of personal pronouns?
3. In general, how much does Maynard depend on colloquialisms, contractions, and other features of informal speech? Are her sentences tighter than those we ordinarily speak?
4. How does the discussion of note-passing illustrate "the pressure of The Group"? Is Maynard saying that the pressure exerted by girls was different from that exerted by boys, or is she not concerned with this difference?

WRITING ASSIGNMENTS

Analyze the pressures exerted by "The Group" in your high school experience. In the course of this analysis compare your experience with Maynard's.

Discuss the similarities and differences you observe between boys in a group and girls in a group, at a particular age. Draw a conclusion about boys and girls in the seventies.

TONE

CHARLES DICKENS
A Sunday Evening in London

[1] It was a Sunday evening in London, gloomy, close and stale. [2] Maddening church bells of all degrees of dissonance, sharp and flat, cracked and clear, fast and slow, made the brick-and-mortar echoes hideous. [3] Melancholy streets, in a penitential garb of soot, steeped the souls of the people who were condemned to look at them out of windows in dire despondency. [4] In every thoroughfare, up almost every alley, and down almost every turning, some doleful bell was throbbing, jerking, tolling, as if the Plague were in the city and the dead-carts were going round. [5] Everything was bolted and barred that could by possibility furnish relief to an overworked people. [6] No pictures, no unfamiliar animals, no rare plants or flowers, no natural or artificial wonders of the ancient world—all *taboo* with that enlightened strictness, that the ugly South Sea gods in the British Museum might have supposed themselves at home again. [7] Nothing to see but streets, streets, streets. [8] Nothing to breathe but streets, streets, streets. [9] Nothing to change the brooding mind, or raise it up. [10] Nothing for the spent toiler to do, but to compare the monotony of his seventh day with the monotony of his six days, think what a weary life he led, and make the best of it—or the worst, according to the probabilities.

DISCUSSION: TONE

We have referred to the *tone* of a piece of writing, and we can define it now as the reflection of the writer's attitude toward his or her subject or reader. Writers may be mildly or strongly sarcastic, bitter, angry, mocking, whimsical, jocular, facetious, admiring, joyful, awe-struck—perhaps indifferent. They will reveal their attitude in one or more ways, depending on what they assume about their audience and depending on the effect they want to produce. If they do not state their attitude directly, they will indicate it indirectly: they may exaggerate to the point of absurdity for a humorous effect; or understate so that there is an obvious discrepancy between what is shown or what is said, producing an ironic effect; or they may merely present the facts without deliberate exaggeration or understatement, so that their attitude emerges gradually but unmistakably from their selection of detail. They will be aware that the tone of a statement can *qualify* meaning— in the way a sarcastic tone of voice indicates that we intend our words to be caustic.

In short, the tone of a paragraph or an essay is to be found in the voice we hear as we read. Whether or not they intend to do so, all writers express themselves in a voice that conveys an impression—if nothing else, an impression of unreflecting, dull people whose monotonous sentences indicate that they take little interest in what they say or how they say it. Writers interested in their subject and their audience are not likely to be dull; their positive attitude will be obvious. Occasionally, in the course of writing, writers will discover something about themselves or their subject—perhaps even that they have made a false start and need to begin again. False starts in writing are often failures to discover the voice—that is, the proper tone—to use in expressing an idea or developing an impression. And just as our ideas and attitudes will change from one piece of writing to another, the tone of an essay may change in response to shifts in attitude and emphasis. For an essay need not reveal one dominant tone: the voice of the writer may take on the nuances we hear in speech. In writing, these shifts in voice will be reflected in the modulations and rhythms of the sentences and paragraphs, which in turn reflect something of the rhythms and stresses of speech.

QUESTIONS

1. List the adjectives Dickens uses to describe the atmosphere of a Sunday evening in London. How do these adjectives help to specify the tone? How early in the paragraph is the tone evident?
2. What effect does the repetition in sentences 8–10 have on the tone?
3. How has Dickens exaggerated in order to convey the depression and monotony of a London Sunday?

WRITING ASSIGNMENT

Describe Sunday morning or Sunday evening in your home town or city. Let your details suggest your attitude toward the experience and perhaps toward the town or city. Don't state the attitude directly.

JAMES BALDWIN

Fifth Avenue, Uptown

1. There is a housing project standing now where the house in which we grew up once stood, and one of those stunted city trees is snarling where our doorway used to be. This is on the rehabilitated side of the avenue. The other side of the avenue—for progress takes time—has not been rehabilitated yet and it looks exactly as it looked in the days when we sat with our noses pressed against the windowpane, longing to be allowed to go "across the street." The grocery store which gave us credit is still there, and there can be no doubt that it is still giving credit. The people in the project certainly need it—far more, indeed, than they ever needed the project. The last time I passed by, the Jewish proprietor was still standing among his shelves, looking sadder and heavier but scarcely any older. Farther down the block stands the shoe-repair store in which our shoes were repaired until reparation became impossible and in which, then, we bought all our "new" ones. The Negro proprietor is still in the window, head down, working at the leather.

2. These two, I imagine, could tell a long tale if they would (perhaps they would be glad to if they could), having watched so many, for so long, struggling in the fishhooks, the barbed wire, of this avenue.

3. The avenue is elsewhere the renowned and elegant Fifth. The area I am describing, which, in today's gang parlance, would be called "the turf," is bounded by Lenox Avenue on the west, the Harlem River on the east, 135th Street on the north, and 130th Street on the south. We never lived beyond these boundaries; this is where we grew up. Walking along 145th Street—for example— familiar as it is, and similar, does not have the same impact because I do not know any of the people on the block. But when I turn east on 131st Street and Lenox Avenue, there is first a sodapop joint, then a shoeshine "parlor," then a grocery store, then a dry cleaners', then the houses. All along the street there are people

FIFTH AVENUE, UPTOWN: In "Fifth Avenue: Uptown: A Letter from Harlem" from the book *Nobody Knows My Name* by James Baldwin. Copyright © 1960 by James Baldwin. Originally published in *Esquire*. Reprinted by permission of The Dial Press.

who watched me grow up, people who grew up with me, people I watched grow up along with my brothers and sisters; and, sometimes in my arms, sometimes underfoot, sometimes at my shoulder—or on it—their children, a riot, a forest of children, who include my nieces and nephews.

4.   When we reach the end of this long block, we find ourselves on wide, filthy, hostile Fifth Avenue, facing that project which hangs over the avenue like a monument to the folly, and the cowardice, of good intentions. All along the block, for anyone who knows it, are immense human gaps, like craters. These gaps are not created merely by those who have moved away, inevitably into some other ghetto; or by those who have risen, almost always into a greater capacity for self-loathing and self-delusion; or yet by those who, by whatever means—War II, the Korean war, a policeman's gun or billy, a gang war, a brawl, madness, an overdose of heroin, or, simply, unnatural exhaustion—are dead. I am talking about those who are left, and I am talking principally about the young. What are they doing? Well, some, a minority, are fanatical churchgoers, members of the more extreme of the Holy Roller sects. Many, many more are "moslems," by affiliation or sympathy, that is to say that they are united by nothing more—and nothing less—than a hatred of the white world and all its works. They are present, for example, at every Buy Black street-corner meeting—meetings in which the speaker urges his hearers to cease trading with white men and establish a separate economy. Neither the speaker nor his hearers can possibly do this, of course, since Negroes do not own General Motors or RCA or the A & P, nor, indeed, do they own more than a wholly insufficient fraction of anything else in Harlem (those who *do* own anything are more interested in their profits than in their fellows). But these meetings nevertheless keep alive in the participators a certain pride of bitterness without which, however futile this bitterness may be, they could scarcely remain alive at all. Many have given up. They stay home and watch the TV screen, living on the earnings of their parents, cousins, brothers, or uncles, and only leave the house to go to the movies or to the nearest bar. "How're you making it?" one may ask, running into them along the block, or in the bar. "Oh, I'm TV-ing it"; with the saddest, sweetest, most shamefaced of smiles, and from a great distance. This distance one is compelled to respect; anyone who has traveled so far will not easily be dragged again into the world. There are further retreats, of course, than the

TV screen or the bar. There are those who are simply sitting on their stoops, "stoned," animated for a moment only, and hideously, by the approach of someone who may lend them the money for a "fix." Or by the approach of someone from whom they can purchase it, one of the shrewd ones, on the way to prison or just coming out.

5.   And the others, who have avoided all of these deaths, get up in the morning and go downtown to meet "the man." They work in the white man's world all day and come home in the evening to this fetid block. They struggle to instill in their children some private sense of honor or dignity which will help the child to survive. This means, of course, that they must struggle, stolidly, incessantly, to keep this sense alive in themselves, in spite of the insults, the indifference, and the cruelty they are certain to encounter in their working day. They patiently browbeat the landlord into fixing the heat, the plaster, the plumbing; this demands prodigious patience; nor is patience usually enough. In trying to make their hovels habitable, they are perpetually throwing good money after bad. Such frustration, so long endured, is driving many strong, admirable men and women whose only crime is color to the very gates of paranoia.

6.   One remembers them from another time—playing handball in the playground, going to church, wondering if they were going to be promoted at school. One remembers them going off to war—gladly, to escape this block. One remembers their return. Perhaps one remembers their wedding day. And one sees where the girl is now—vainly looking for salvation from some other embittered, trussed, and struggling boy—and sees the all-but-abandoned children in the streets.

QUESTIONS

1. What is Baldwin's general attitude toward upper Fifth Avenue and the Harlem of the late 1950s, when this description was written? Is his attitude toward the inhabitants of the street markedly different from his attitude toward the street itself? Does he state his attitude directly, or instead imply it in his details?
2. Does Baldwin maintain an overall tone in these paragraphs, or does his tone shift at some point?
3. Is he writing to persuade the reader to take action on the social evils suffered by the people on the street, or is he merely describing a street he knows well?

4. What impression do you get of Baldwin? What seem to be his most prominent qualities as an observer and writer?

WRITING ASSIGNMENTS

Analyze three paragraphs from different articles in an issue of a newspaper or newsmagazine to show how usage varies according to subject, attitude, and the approach of individual writers. You might compare the diction of two reports of the same event—in two newsmagazines or newspapers—to illustrate the possible variations.

Describe a street you remember well from your high-school days. Establish a dominant tone as you write. If you shift your tone, do so without being abrupt.

CONCRETENESS

CLAUDE BROWN
A Building in Upper Harlem

[1] There is a building in upper Harlem on a shabby side street with several other buildings that resemble it in both appearance and condition. [2] "This building" is in an advanced state of deterioration; only cold water runs through the water pipes, the rats here are as large as cats. [3] The saving grace of this building might very well be the erratic patterns of the varied and brilliant colors of the graffiti which adorn it internally and externally from basement to roof. [4] This building has no electricity in the apartments, but the electricity in the hallway lamp fixtures is still on. [5] Some of the apartments have garbage piled up in them five feet high and that makes opening the door a very difficult task for those whose nasal passages are sufficiently insensitive to permit entry. [6] In some of the apartments and on the rooftop, the garbage and assorted debris are piled only one or two feet high, and the trash has been there so long that plant life has generated. [7] The most rapid tour possible

A BUILDING IN UPPER HARLEM: © 1973 by The New York Times Company. Reprinted by permission. Selection title by editor.

through this building will necessitate boiling oneself in a hot tub of strong disinfectant for a couple of hours, and even then this astonishingly formidable breed of lice will continue to make its presence felt throughout a long itchy night. [8] This building is adjacent to a fully occupied tenement whose inhabitants are families, some of which include several children. [9] This building has a few steps missing from the staircase above the second floor and there are no lightbulbs in the hallway; it's a very unsafe place for trespassers, even during the day. [10] This building's last family of tenants was emancipated several weeks ago; they hit the numbers and moved to the Bronx, shouting, "Free at last, free at last; thank God for the number man." [11] Prior to their liberation, the "last family" had lived a most unusual existence. [12] Somebody had to be at home at all times to protect the family's second-hand-hot television from becoming a third-hand-hot television; there were too many junkies in and out who used the vacant apartments to stash their loot until they could "down" it and who also used some of the apartments for sleeping and as "shooting galleries." [13] For protection, the last family had a large, vicious German shepherd. [14] This dog was needed for the rats as well as the junkies. [15] A cat would be no help at all. [16] The sight of the rats in this building would give any cat smaller than a mountain lion instant heart failure. [17] The last family considered itself fortunate, despite the many unpleasant, unhealthy and unsafe aspects of its residence. [18] "We ain't paid no rent in two years. [19] I guess the city just forgot that we was here or they was just too embarrassed to ask for it," said the head of the last family. [20] This building has holes in the walls large enough for a man to walk through two adjacent apartments. [21] This building has holes in the ceilings on the fourth and fifth floors, and when it rains, the rain settles on the floor of a fourth-story apartment. [22] This building is not unique, there are many others like it in the ghettos of New York City; and like many others . . . this building is owned by the City of New York.

DISCUSSION: CONCRETENESS

Writing is concrete when it makes an abstract idea or impression perceptible to the senses and gives it immediacy. Graham Greene makes concrete a feeling shared by Londoners during the German bombing of the city in 1940:

One gets used to anything: that is what one hears on many lips these days, though everybody, I suppose, remembers the sense of shock he felt at the first bombed house he saw. I think of one in Woburn Square neatly sliced in half. With its sideways exposure it looked like a Swiss chalet: there were a pair of skiing sticks hanging in the attic, and in another room a grand piano cocked one leg over the abyss.—*The Lost Childhood*

Specific detail is one way to make an idea or impression concrete; another way is to use imagery and figurative language, as well as specific details, as in Virginia Woolf's impression of a London street (written in 1924):

London is enchanting. I step out upon a tawny colored magic carpet, it seems, and get carried into beauty without raising a finger. The nights are amazing, with all the white porticos and broad silent avenues. And people pop in and out, lightly, divertingly like rabbits; and I look down Southampton Row, wet as a seal's back or red and yellow in sunshine, and watch the omnibuses going and coming and hear the old crazy organs.—*A Writer's Diary*

Whatever the purpose of the writer may be, excessive detail will blur the focus and perhaps make the writing incoherent. Voltaire said, "The secret of being a bore is to tell everything." A boring film may show everything in a seemingly endless stream of detail; a boring paragraph or essay does the same thing. Effective detail is *selected* to develop an idea or impression; good writing reveals an economy of style.

QUESTIONS

1. Brown's description of a Harlem slum building depends little on simile, metaphor, and personification and much on an accretion of detail. From what physical angle of vision is the building described in sentences 1–9? Are we given an overall view from a single point of observation?
2. What is gained by reserving the information about the adjacent building for the middle of the paragraph—following the description of the deserted building? What is gained in the whole paragraph by saving the information about the owner of the building for the end? What is the principle of order in the whole paragraph?

3. The final sentence indicates that the author is making the building representative or symbolic of an *attitude,* reflected in a particular environment. What is that attitude and how does the selection of detail help us to understand it?

WRITING ASSIGNMENT

Discuss the implications of the details of the paragraph: what the building reveals about the city that owns it and what it suggests about the lives of its inhabitants.

JOHN UPDIKE
Central Park

On the afternoon of the first day of spring, when the gutters were still heaped high with Monday's snow but the sky itself was swept clean, we put on our galoshes and walked up the sunny side of Fifth Avenue to Central Park. There we saw:

Great black rocks emerging from the melting drifts, their craggy skins glistening like the backs of resurrected brontosaurs.

A pigeon on the half-frozen pond strutting to the edge of the ice and looking a duck in the face.

A policeman getting his shoe wet testing the ice.

Three elderly relatives trying to coax a little boy to accompany his father on a sled ride down a short but steep slope. After much balking, the boy did, and, sure enough, the sled tipped over and the father got his collar full of snow. Everybody laughed except the boy, who sniffled.

Four boys in black leather jackets throwing snowballs at each other. (The snow was ideally soggy, and packed hard with one squeeze.)

Seven men without hats.

Twelve snowmen, none of them intact.

CENTRAL PARK: In *Assorted Prose* by John Updike. Copyright © 1956 by John Updike. First appeared in *The New Yorker*. Reprinted by permission of Alfred A. Knopf, Inc.

Two men listening to the radio in a car parked outside the Zoo; Mel Allen was broadcasting the Yanks-Cardinals game from St. Petersburg.

A tahr (*Hemitragus jemlaicus*) pleasantly squinting in the sunlight.

An aoudad absently pawing the mud and chewing.

A yak with its back turned.

Empty cages labeled "Coati," "Orang-outang," "Ocelot."

A father saying to his little boy, who was annoyed almost to tears by the inactivity of the seals, "Father [Father Seal, we assumed] is very tired; he worked hard all day."

Most of the cafeteria's out-of-doors tables occupied.

A pretty girl in black pants falling on them at the Wollman Memorial Rink.

"BILL & DORIS" carved on a tree. "REX & RITA" written in the snow.

Two old men playing, and six supervising, a checkers game.

The Michael Friedsam Foundation Merry-Go-Round, nearly empty of children but overflowing with calliope music.

A man on a bench near the carrousel reading, through sunglasses, a book on economics.

Crews of shinglers repairing the roof of the Tavern-on-the-Green.

A woman dropping a camera she was trying to load, the film unrolling in the slush and exposing itself.

A little colored boy in aviator goggles rubbing his ears and saying, "He really hurt me." "No, he didn't," his nursemaid told him.

The green head of Giuseppe Mazzini staring across the white softball field, unblinking, though the sun was in its eyes.

Water murmuring down walks and rocks and steps. A grown man trying to block one rivulet with snow.

Things like brown sticks nosing through a plot of cleared soil.

A tire track in a piece of mud far removed from where any automobiles could be.

Footprints around a KEEP OFF sign.

Two pigeons feeding each other.

Two showgirls, whose faces had not yet thawed the frost of their makeup, treading indignantly through the slush.

A plump old man saying "Chick, chick" and feeding peanuts to squirrels.

Many solitary men throwing snowballs at tree trunks.

Many birds calling to each other about how little the Ramble has changed.

One red mitten lying lost under a poplar tree.

An airplane, very bright and distant, slowly moving through the branches of a sycamore.

QUESTIONS

1. Has Updike described what he saw at random, or do you see a principle of order in the essay—spatial perhaps, or climactic?
2. How do his details create a dominant impression, or is Updike trying to avoid creating a dominant impression?
3. What is gained by presenting these impressions in phrases—actually shortened sentences?
4. What impression do you get of Updike from the essay—particularly from what he notices and chooses to describe?

WRITING ASSIGNMENT

Describe an afternoon in a park or athletic field, as Updike does. Make your details as vivid as you can, without developing each impression.

RALPH RAPHAEL
The County Fair

1. "We are about to give away *free samples* of a *manufacturer's product,*" announces a salesman on the midway of the Humboldt County Fair in Ferndale. His overly groomed hair and blue sports suit set him apart from the down-home folks who walk by his booth. On the velvet table in front of him his delicate fingers are stacking up neat little piles of fancy gold pen-and-pencil sets. People gather around, lured by the prospect of receiving, for free, some of these pretty artifacts of the modern-day world. "This is a new version of an old product, the only really *new* invention in a writing implement or instrument since the quill," the salesman says immodestly. He proceeds to demonstrate the "gravity lock" on

THE COUNTY FAIR: In *Edges* by Ralph Raphael. Copyright © 1973, 1976 by Ralph Raphael. Reprinted by permission of Alfred A. Knopf, Inc. Selection title by editor.

the pen, which means that the pen point retracts automatically when it is held upside down. "This is a principle as old as the one that built the pyramids, but it is the first time it's been adopted to anything so small as a pen."

2.   The gold pen-and-pencil sets, however, are not the "free samples" to be given away. Instead, what the salesman distributes to each eager spectator is one free cartridge apiece. He then proceeds to demonstrate yet another new product: a pen which hooks into a telephone and also functions as a letter opener and magnifying glass. The telephone pen (regularly $3.95) and the pen-and-pencil set (regularly $7.95) are being sold together for "only *two dollars*" (said boldly, with two fingers waving in the air) "and ninety-eight cents" (said softly, as if it were an afterthought). Actually, the salesman tells the crowd, they will be purchasing only the telephone pen and receiving the rest absolutely free—and that includes a special gold ink cartridge "which is not only gold, but this one is *perfumed*. Now that's something *really* new." He scribbles some lines on a piece of paper and passes it around; sure enough, it smells just like a synthetic flower.

3.   When the salesman announces he can only "give away" gold gravity-lock pen-and-pencil sets to the first eight people purchasing telephone pens, people rush to the front waving their money. By now the $2.98 has been rounded off to an even three dollars, plus tax. Then, with the first round of sales completed, a *silver* pen-and-pencil set suddenly appears ("a $9.95 value," he claims) and the whole thing starts all over again.

4.   This is no isolated event. Throughout the county fair, salespeople are demonstrating and peddling their water distillers, electric blenders, no-stick cookware, liquid embroidery, sewing machines, vacuum cleaners, encyclopedias, electric organs. Everyone, it seems, has something to push. A large trailer entitled "Energy and the Environment" turns out to be a Pacific Gas & Electric propaganda venture justifying its nuclear power plants and demonstrating that it cares about the environment by showing a picture of a transmission tower painted green. The Marines, meanwhile, continue their search "for a few good men."

5.   The salesmen are all professionals who follow the country fair circuit. The pen vendor, aged forty-three, has been a drummer ever since he was eighteen years old. His sales pitch, repeated verbatim every hour or so, seems to have a will of its own which has little or nothing to do with the stone-faced man who delivers it. It's

just a job like any other job, although it demands that he have no home other than the camper in which he travels. Like the barkers and peddlers of years past, the people of the fair are creatures of the road who remain forever on the outskirts of the communities they serve.

6. But the salesmen are not alone. The "carnies," as the amusement-park folks call themselves, have transformed the county-fair circuit into a way of life. Traveling together in one continuous party, they wear "carny power" insignia on the back of their Levi's jackets and like to hang together when the local toughs start hankering for a fight. They are proud to belong to a select group of "gypsies, tramps, and thieves," self-appointed outcasts from the small-town societies in which they set up shop. Like the salesmen who travel beside them, they live off the suckers ("Everyone loves being a sucker," a barker tells me authoritatively) who come to the fair to blow a few bucks and catch a passing glimpse of bright lights and fancy things.

QUESTIONS

1. Raphael moves from example to idea—from an illustration of carnival selling, to the carnival itself. How is the illustration shown to be typical of what happens at carnivals?
2. How is the salesman shown to be typical of the carnival itself?
3. In general, what is the order of ideas in the six paragraphs? Why does Raphael end with the discussion of the "carnies"?

WRITING ASSIGNMENT

Describe an event like the county fair—for example, a bloodmobile or school carnival—through one activity that is typical of the event and through the people participating in it.

IMAGERY

RACHEL CARSON
Walking to the Seacoast

1.   One of my own favorite approaches to a rocky seacoast is by a rough path through an evergreen forest that has its own peculiar enchantment. It is usually an early morning tide that takes me along that forest path, so that the light is still pale and fog drifts in from the sea beyond. It is almost a ghost forest, for among the living spruce and balsam are many dead trees—some still erect, some sagging earthward, some lying on the floor of the forest. All the trees, the living and the dead, are clothed with green and silver crusts of lichens. Tufts of the bearded lichen or old man's beard hang from the branches like bits of sea mist tangled there. Green woodland mosses and a yielding carpet of reindeer moss cover the ground. In the quiet of that place even the voice of the surf is reduced to a whispered echo and the sounds of the forest are but the ghosts of sound—the faint sighing of evergreen needles in the moving air; the creaks and heavier groans of half-fallen trees resting against their neighbors and rubbing bark against bark; the light rattling fall of a dead branch broken under the feet of a squirrel and sent bouncing and ricocheting earthward.

2.   But finally the path emerges from the dimness of the deeper forest and comes to a place where the sound of surf rises above the forest sounds—the hollow boom of the sea, rhythmic and insistent, striking against the rocks, falling away, rising again.

3.   Up and down the coast the line of the forest is drawn sharp and clean on the edge of a seascape of surf and sky and rocks. The softness of the sea fog blurs the contours of the rocks; gray water and gray mists merge offshore in a dim and vaporous world that might be a world of creation, stirring with new life.

WALKING TO THE SEACOAST: In *The Edge of the Sea*. Copyright 1955 by Rachel L. Carson. Reprinted by permission of Houghton Mifflin Company. Selection title by editor.

DISCUSSION: IMAGERY

Images convey sensory impressions: impressions of sight, hearing, smell, taste, or touch. The following passage from a story by James Joyce illustrates most of these:

> The cold air stung us and we played till our bodies glowed. Our shouts echoed in the silent street. The career of our play brought us through the dark muddy lanes behind the houses where we ran the gauntlet of the rough tribes from the cottages, to the back doors of the dark dripping gardens where odors arose from the ashpits, to the dark odorous stables where a coachman smoothed and combed the horse or shook music from the buckled harness.—"Araby"

We think through images constantly. Joyce could not have expressed his sense of a particular street on a particular night in abstract language. The more evocative our imagery, when the situation calls for vivid impressions, the more directly will our words express experience. A passage will seem over-written if a vivid representation of experience is not needed; so-called fine writing tries to be too evocative of sense experience. In the passage quoted above, Joyce selects only those details that will give the reader an impression of the physical sensations experienced in the darkness. The imagery suggests the vitality of imagination with which the story is concerned; that vitality could not have been conveyed without it.

QUESTIONS

1. Rachel Carson appeals to our sense of sight and sound in describing her walk to the seacoast. At what point do sounds become important? How many sounds does she describe? What contrasts does she develop, and why are these important to her dominant impression?
2. How does sight reinforce sound in the passage? Does Carson appeal to other senses for reinforcement?

WRITING ASSIGNMENTS

Describe a walk you have taken, selecting details to create a dominant impression, and appealing to more than one of the senses as Carson does.

Rooms as well as places outdoors look different to us in different seasons or times of the day or night. Select a room or a place and show these differences, appealing to as many senses as you need to.

TRUMAN CAPOTE

A Christmas Memory

1. Morning. Frozen rime lusters the grass; the sun, round as an orange and orange as hot-weather moons, balances on the horizon, burnishes the silvered winter woods. A wild turkey calls. A renegade hog grunts in the undergrowth. Soon, by the edge of knee-deep, rapid-running water, we have to abandon the buggy. Queenie wades the stream first, paddles across barking complaints at the swiftness of the current, the pneumonia-making coldness of it. We follow, holding our shoes and equipment (a hatchet, a burlap sack) above our heads. A mile more: of chastising thorns, burs and briers that catch at our clothes; of rusty pine needles brilliant with gaudy fungus and molted feathers. Here, there, a flash, a flutter, an ecstasy of shrillings remind us that not all the birds have flown south. Always, the path unwinds through lemony sun pools and pitch vine tunnels. Another creek to cross: a disturbed armada of speckled trout froths the water round us, and frogs the size of plates practice belly flops; beaver workmen are building a dam. On the farther shore, Queenie shakes herself and trembles. My friend shivers, too: not with cold but enthusiasm. One of her hat's ragged roses sheds a petal as she lifts her head and inhales the pine-heavy air. "We're almost there; can you smell it, Buddy?" she says, as though we were approaching an ocean.
2. And, indeed, it is a kind of ocean. Scented acres of holiday trees, prickly leafed holly. Red berries shiny as Chinese bells: black crows swoop upon them screaming. Having stuffed our burlap sacks with enough greenery and crimson to garland a dozen windows, we set about choosing a tree. "It should be," muses my friend, "twice as tall as a boy. So a boy can't steal the

star." The one we pick is twice as tall as me. A brave handsome
brute that survives thirty hatchet strokes before it keels with a
creaking rending cry. Lugging it like a kill, we commence the long
trek out. Every few yards we abandon the struggle, sit down and
pant. But we have the strength of triumphant huntsmen; that and
the tree's virile, icy perfume revive us, goad us on. Many compli-
ments accompany our sunset return along the red clay road to
town; but my friend is sly and noncommittal when passers-by
praise the treasure perched on our buggy: what a fine tree and
where did it come from? "Yonderways," she murmurs vaguely.
Once a car stops and the rich mill owner's lazy wife leans out and
whines: "Giveya two-bits cash for that ol tree." Ordinarily my
friend is afraid of saying no; but on this occasion she promptly
shakes her head: "We wouldn't take a dollar." The mill owner's
wife persists. "A dollar, my foot! Fifty cents. That's my last offer.
Goodness, woman, you can get another one." In answer, my friend
gently reflects: "I doubt it. There's never two of anything."

QUESTIONS

1. "There's never two of anything," the woman of "sixty-something"
   and a distant cousin of the seven-year-old boy says, and the details
   of the passage show us why. What aspects of the scene does the
   speaker focus on? To what senses does he appeal in his description of the morning?
2. At various points the speaker refers to the distance he and his
   friend had to travel and to the vastness of the field where they cut
   the tree. How different would the experience seem if they had cut
   the tree in a nearby wood?
3. How has Capote transformed an ordinary event—the cutting of a
   Christmas tree—into an experience that seems epic to the boy?
4. How does Capote convey the importance of odor to the total experience? Notice that smells, like taste, are difficult to describe. But
   we can be reminded of objects we associate with vivid odors, and
   this reminder makes the odors alive to us.
5. What impressions do you get of the character of the friend? How
   does Capote convey that impression?

WRITING ASSIGNMENT

Describe a Christmas morning or another holiday that stands apart
from other such mornings in your memory. Try to render the sights

and smells of the morning through images that you think will convey the experience to others.

FIGURATIVE LANGUAGE

ROBERT PENN WARREN
Jeff York

¹You have seen him a thousand times. ²You have seen him standing on the street corner on Saturday afternoon, in the little county-seat towns. ³He wears blue jean pants, or overalls washed to a pale pastel blue like the color of sky after a shower in spring, but because it is Saturday he has on a wool coat, an old one, perhaps the coat left from the suit he got married in a long time back. ⁴His long wrist bones hang out from the sleeves of the coat, the tendons showing along the bone like the dry twist of grapevine still corded on the stove-length of a hickory sapling you would find in his wood box beside his cookstove among the split chunks of gum and red oak. ⁵The big hands, with the knotted, cracked joints and the square, horn-thick nails, hang loose off the wrist bone like clumsy, home-made tools hung on the wall of a shed after work. ⁶If it is summer, he wears a straw hat with a wide brim, the straw fraying loose around the edge. ⁷If it is winter, he wears a felt hat, black once, but now weathered with streaks of dark gray and dull purple in the sunlight. ⁸His face is long and bony, the jawbone long under the drawn-in cheeks. ⁹The flesh along the jawbone is nicked in a couple of places where the unaccustomed razor has been drawn over the leather-coarse skin. ¹⁰A tiny bit of blood crusts brown where the nick is. ¹¹The color of the face is red, a dull red like the red clay mud or clay dust which clings to the bottom of his pants and to the cast-iron-looking brogans on his feet, or a red like the color of a piece of hewed cedar which has been left in the weather. ¹²The face does not look alive. ¹³It seems to be

JEFF YORK: In "The Patented Gate and the Mean Hamburger," copyright, 1947, by Robert Penn Warren. Reprinted from his volume *The Circus in the Attic and Other Essays* by permission of Harcourt Brace Jovanovich, Inc. Selection title by editor.

molded from the clay or hewed from the cedar. [14] When the jaw moves, once, with its deliberate, massive motion on the quid of tobacco, you are still not convinced. [15] That motion is but the cunning triumph of a mechanism concealed within.

DISCUSSION: FIGURATIVE LANGUAGE

A simile is an explicit comparison (using *like* or *as*) that usually develops or implies more than one simple point of resemblance:

> Will Brangwen ducked his head and looked at his uncle with swift, mistrustful eyes, like a caged hawk.—D. H. Lawrence, *The Rainbow*

A metaphor is an implicit comparison in which an object is presented as if it were something else:

> Some people are molded by their admirations, others by their hostilities.—Elizabeth Bowen, *The Death of the Heart.*

Personification is the attribution of human qualities to abstract ideas or objects:

> So some random light directing them with its pale footfall upon stair and mat, from some uncovered star, or wandering ship, or the Lighthouse even, the little airs mounted the staircase and nosed round bedroom doors.—Virginia Woolf, *To the Lighthouse*

Simile, metaphor, and personification unite in the following passage:

> Then Sunday light raced over the farm as fast as the chickens were flying. Immediately the first straight shaft of heat, solid as a hickory stick, was laid on the ridge.—Eudora Welty, *Losing Battles*

One purpose of figures of speech is to evoke the qualities of experience and give shape or substance to an emotion or awareness that up to the moment of its expression may be indefinite. In exposition a writer will depend on metaphor because of its property of expressing an attitude as well as representing an idea:

> England is not the jewelled isle of Shakespeare's much-quoted passage, nor is it the inferno depicted by Dr. Goeb-

bels. More than either it resembles a family, a rather stuffy Victorian family, with not many black sheep in it but with all its cupboards bursting with skeletons. It has rich relations who have to be kow-towed to and poor relations who are horribly sat upon, and there is a deep conspiracy of silence about the source of the family income. It is a family in which the young are generally thwarted and most of the power is in the hands of irresponsible uncles and bedridden aunts.—George Orwell, "England, Your England"

QUESTIONS

1. Sentence 3 of "Jeff York" develops through an accretion of detail and simile that specifies the blue jeans. What is made specific in sentence 4 through a similar accretion of detail?
2. How do the hanging wristbones and hands, described in sentences 4 and 5, make concrete the dominant impression that concludes the passage? How does sentence 5 extend the impression developed in sentence 4?
3. How do similes in sentences 4 and 5 help to characterize Jeff York's world? Where else is simile employed for the same purpose?
4. How is the detail in sentences 9 and 10 related to the sentences that follow them? Why does Warren mention the razor nicks?
5. According to what principle is the detail of the description of Jeff York organized?

WRITING ASSIGNMENT

Describe a friend or relative through the clothing he or she wears and the world you associate with the person.

SEAN O'CASEY

Dublin Houses

¹There were the houses, too—a long, lurching row of discontented incurables, smirched with the age-long marks of ague, fe-

DUBLIN HOUSES: In *Inishfallen, Fare Thee Well* by Sean O'Casey. Reprinted with permission of Macmillan Publishing Co., Inc. and Macmillan, London and Basingstoke. Copyright © 1949 by Sean O'Casey. Selection title by editor.

vers, cancer, and consumption, the soured tears of little children, and the sighs of disappointed newly-married girls. ²The doors were scarred with time's spit and anger's hasty knocking; the pillars by their sides were shaky, their stuccoed bloom long since peeled away, and they looked like crutches keeping the trembling doors standing on their palsied feet. ³The gummy-eyed windows blinked dimly out, lacquered by a year's tired dust from the troubled street below. ⁴Dirt and disease were the big sacraments here—outward and visible signs of an inward and spiritual disgrace. ⁵The people bought the cheapest things in food they could find in order to live, to work, to worship: the cheapest spuds, the cheapest tea, the cheapest meat, the cheapest fat; and waited for unsold bread to grow stale that they might buy that cheaper, too. ⁶Here they gathered up the fragments so that nothing would be lost. ⁷The streets were long haggard corridors of rottenness and ruin. ⁸What wonderful mind of memory could link this shrinking wretchedness with the flaunting gorgeousness of silk and satin; with bloom of rose and scent of lavender? ⁹A thousand years must have passed since the last lavender lady was carried out feet first from the last surviving one of them. ¹⁰Even the sun shudders now when she touches a roof, for she feels some evil has chilled the glow of her garment. ¹¹The flower that here once bloomed is dead forever. ¹²No wallflower here has crept into a favoured cranny; sight and sign of the primrose were far away; no room here for a dance of daffodils; no swallow twittering under a shady eave; and it was sad to see an odd sparrow seeking a yellow grain from the mocking dust; not even a spiky-headed thistle, purple mitred, could find a corner here for a sturdy life. ¹³No Wordsworth here wandered about as lonely as a cloud.

QUESTIONS

1. The description of Dublin houses is governed by a basic figure of speech, the personification of the houses as *discontented incurables.* What emotional aura does the personification evoke? What is gained by making the houses seem alive, rather than merely describing them as rickety?
2. How does sentence 3 develop the initial personification?
3. People are usually described as *haggard,* not streets. How does the word differ connotatively from *worn* and *tired?* What is gained by the use of *haggard?*

4. What other words and phrases involve personification, and what do they contribute to the general impression of Dublin houses?

5. O'Casey might have written *discolored* rather than *smirched* in the first sentence. Which word is better suited to the passage and why?

WRITING ASSIGNMENTS

Paraphrase sentences 10, 11, and 12. Then discuss what is missing in tone and meaning when figurative words are replaced by literal equivalents.

Describe an unusual room or building. Use imagery and figurative language to create an overall impression. Try to control the emotional response of your reader through a chain of images and associations, as O'Casey does.

EDMUND WILSON

The Old Car Pound

¹On the dreary yellow Michigan waste with its gray stains of frozen water, the old cars wait like horses at the pound. ²Since the spring before last, Henry Ford has been buying them up at twenty dollars apiece, and people drive them in every day. ³Old, battered, muddy roadsters, sedans, limousines, touring cars and trucks—in strings of two or three they are dragged off to the disassembly building, following foolishly and gruesomely like corpses shaken up into life, hoods rickety and wheels turning backwards. ⁴Once inside, they are systematically and energetically dismantled: the flat road-ruined tires are stripped away; the rush-flare of an acetylene torch attacks the stems of the steering wheels; the motors are cleaned out like a bull's tripes and sent to make scrap iron for the blast furnace; the glass is taken out and kept to replace broken factory panes; the leather from the hoods and seats goes for aprons and handpads for the workers; the hair stuffing of the seats is sold

THE OLD CAR POUND: In *The American Earthquake* by Edmund Wilson. Copyright © 1958 by Edmund Wilson. Excerpted and reprinted with the permission of Farrar, Straus & Giroux, Inc. Selection title by editor.

again; even the bronze and babbitt metal are scraped out of the connecting rods and melted up to line new connecting rods. ⁵ Then the picked and gutted carcass of the old car is shoved into a final death chamber—crushed flat by a five-ton press, which makes it scrunch like a stepped-on beetle.

QUESTIONS

1. What is the dominant comparison of the paragraph? In how many ways is it developed in the course of the paragraph?
2. What point is Wilson making implicitly about the process he describes?
3. Why does Wilson combine the series of main clauses in sentence 4 with semicolons, instead of punctuating them as separate sentences?

WRITING ASSIGNMENT

Compare an automobile or a similar object to something that resembles it in several important ways. Draw a conclusion from this comparison, perhaps defining the quality of the object that seems most striking or unusual to you.

JAMES AGEE
Buster Keaton

¹ No other comedian could do as much with the dead pan. ² He used this great, sad, motionless face to suggest various related things: a one-track mind near the track's end of pure insanity; mulish imperturbability under the wildest of circumstances; how dead a human being can get and still be alive; an awe-inspiring sort of patience and power to endure, proper to granite but uncanny in flesh and blood. ³ Everything that he was and did bore out this rigid face and played laughs against it. ⁴ When he moved his

BUSTER KEATON: In *Agee on Film, I* by James Agee. Copyright 1958 by the James Agee Trust. Reprinted by permission of Ivan Obolensky, Inc. Selection title by editor.

eyes, it was like seeing them move in a statue. [5] His short-legged body was all sudden, machinelike angles, governed by a daft aplomb. [6] When he swept a semaphore-like arm to point, you could almost hear the electrical impulse in the signal block. [7] When he ran from a cop his transitions from accelerating walk to easy jog-trot to brisk canter to headlong gallop to flogged-piston sprint—always floating, above this frenzy, the untroubled, untouchable face—were as distinct and as soberly in order as an automatic gearshift.

QUESTIONS

1. What do the similes and metaphors in sentences 5 and 7 have in common? What are the explicit or implied points of resemblance? In sentence 7 what image does *flogged-piston sprint* bring to mind? What is described as *floating,* and is the word meant literally or metaphorically?
2. How are the similes and metaphors in sentences 5 and 7 connected to the statement in sentence 2 that Keaton's face suggested "a one-track mind near the track's end of pure insanity"?
3. Analyze the similes and metaphors of sentences 3, 4, and 6. How are they connected to those of 5 and 7?
4. What is the essence of Keaton's comic style for Agee? How do the similes and metaphors focus on the key aspect of this style?

WRITING ASSIGNMENTS

Rewrite Agee's paragraph, eliminating the similes and metaphors. Then discuss the ideas you found it difficult to express without them.

Describe a contemporary comedian, using similes and metaphors to reveal his style.

FAULTY DICTION

GEORGE ORWELL
Politics and the English Language

1.   Most people who bother with the matter at all would admit
that the English language is in a bad way, but it is generally assumed that we cannot by conscious action do anything about it.
Our civilization is decadent and our language—so the argument
runs—must inevitably share in the general collapse. It follows that
any struggle against the abuse of language is a sentimental archaism, like preferring candles to electric light or hansom cabs to
aeroplanes. Underneath this lies the half-conscious belief that language is a natural growth and not an instrument which we shape
for our own purposes.
2.   Now, it is clear that the decline of a language must ultimately
have political and economic causes: it is not due simply to the bad
influence of this or that individual writer. But an effect can become a cause, reinforcing the original cause and producing the
same effect in an intensified form, and so on indefinitely. A man
may take to drink because he feels himself to be a failure, and then
fail all the more completely because he drinks. It is rather the
same thing that is happening to the English language. It becomes
ugly and inaccurate because our thoughts are foolish, but the slovenliness of our language makes it easier for us to have foolish
thoughts. The point is that the process is reversible. Modern English, especially written English, is full of bad habits which spread
by imitation and which can be avoided if one is willing to take the
necessary trouble. If one gets rid of these habits one can think
more clearly, and to think clearly is a necessary first step toward
political regeneration: so that the fight against bad English is not
frivolous and is not the exclusive concern of professional writers. I
will come back to this presently, and I hope that by that time the

POLITICS AND THE ENGLISH LANGUAGE: In *Shooting an Elephant and Other Essays*
by George Orwell, copyright, 1945, 1946, 1949, 1950, by Sonia Brownell Orwell.
Reprinted by permission of Harcourt Brace Jovanovich, Inc. Also by permission of
A. M. Heath & Company, Ltd. for Mrs. Sonia Brownell Orwell and Secker & Warburg.

meaning of what I have said here will have become clearer. Meanwhile, here are five specimens of the English language as it is now habitually written. .

3.   These five passages have not been picked out because they are especially bad—I could have quoted far worse if I had chosen—but because they illustrate various of the mental vices from which we now suffer. They are a little below the average, but are fairly representative samples. I number them so that I can refer back to them when necessary:

(1) I am not, indeed, sure whether it is not true to say that the Milton who once seemed not unlike a seventeenth-century Shelley had not become, out of an experience ever more bitter in each year, more alien [*sic*] to the founder of that Jesuit sect which nothing could induce him to tolerate.

Professor Harold Laski (Essay in *Freedom of Expression*)

(2) Above all, we cannot play ducks and drakes with a native battery of idioms which prescribes such egregious collocations of vocables as the Basic *put up with* for *tolerate* or *put at a loss* for *bewilder*.

Professor Lancelot Hogben (*Interglossa*)

(3) On the one side we have the free personality: by definition it is not neurotic, for it has neither conflict nor dream. Its desires, such as they are, are transparent, for they are just what institutional approval keeps in the forefront of consciousness; another institutional pattern would alter their number and intensity; there is little in them that is natural, irreducible, or culturally dangerous. But *on the other side,* the social bond itself is nothing but the mutual reflection of these self-secure integrities. Recall the definition of love. Is not this the very picture of a small academic? Where is there a place in this hall of mirrors for either personality or fraternity?

Essay on psychology in *Politics* (New York)

(4) All the "best people" from the gentlemen's clubs, and all the frantic fascist captains, united in common hatred of Socialism and bestial horror of the rising tide of the mass revolutionary movement, have turned to acts of provocation, to foul incendiarism, to medieval legends of poisoned

wells, to legalize their own destruction of proletarian organizations, and rouse the agitated petty-bourgeoisie to
chauvinistic fervor on behalf of the fight against the revolutionary way out of the crisis.

Communist pamphlet

(5) If a new spirit *is* to be infused into this old country,
there is one thorny and contentious reform which must be
tackled, and that is the humanization and galvanization of
the B.B.C. Timidity here will bespeak canker and atrophy
of the soul. The heart of Britain may be sound and of
strong beat, for instance, but the British lion's roar at
present is like that of Bottom in Shakespeare's *Midsummer
Night's Dream*—as gentle as any sucking dove. A virile
new Britain cannot continue indefinitely to be traduced in
the eyes or rather ears, of the world by the effete languors
of Langham Place, brazenly masquerading as "standard
English." When the Voice of Britain is heard at nine
o'clock, better far and infinitely less ludicrous to hear
aitches honestly dropped than the present priggish, inflated, inhibited, school-ma'amish arch braying of blameless
bashful mewing maidens!

Letter in *Tribune*

4.   Each of these passages has faults of its own, but, quite apart
from avoidable ugliness, two qualities are common to all of them.
The first is staleness of imagery; the other is lack of precision. The
writer either has a meaning and cannot express it, or he inadver-
tently says something else, or he is almost indifferent as to
whether his words mean anything or not. This mixture of
vagueness and sheer incompetence is the most marked characteristic of modern English prose, and especially of any kind of political writing. As soon as certain topics are raised, the concrete melts
into the abstract and no one seems able to think of turns of speech
that are not hackneyed: prose consists less and less of *words* chosen for the sake of their meaning, and more and more of *phrases*
tacked together like the sections of a prefabricated henhouse. I list
below, with notes and examples, various of the tricks by means of
which the work of prose-construction is habitually dodged:
5.   *Dying metaphors.* A newly invented metaphor assists thought
by evoking a visual image, while on the other hand a metaphor

which is technically "dead" (e.g. *iron resolution*) has in effect reverted to being an ordinary word and can generally be used without loss of vividness. But in between these two classes there is a huge dump of worn-out metaphors which have lost all evocative power and are merely used because they save people the trouble of inventing phrases for themselves. Examples are: *Ring the changes on, take up the cudgels for, toe the line, ride roughshod over, stand shoulder to shoulder with, play into the hands of, no axe to grind, grist to the mill, fishing in troubled waters, on the order of the day, Achilles' heel, swan song, hotbed.* Many of these are used without knowledge of their meaning (what is a "rift," for instance?), and incompatible metaphors are frequently mixed, a sure sign that the writer is not interested in what he is saying. Some metaphors now current have been twisted out of their original meaning without those who use them even being aware of the fact. For example, *toe the line* is sometimes written *tow the line.* Another example is *the hammer and the anvil,* now always used with the implication that the anvil gets the worst of it. In real life it is always the anvil that breaks the hammer, never the other way about: a writer who stopped to think what he was saying would be aware of this, and would avoid perverting the original phrase.

6.   *Operators* or *verbal false limbs.* These save the trouble of picking out appropriate verbs and nouns, and at the same time pad each sentence with extra syllables which give it an appearance of symmetry. Characteristic phrases are *render inoperative, militate against, make contact with, be subjected to, give rise to, give grounds for, have the effect of, play a leading part (role) in, make itself felt, take effect, exhibit a tendency to, serve the purpose of,* etc., etc. The keynote is the elimination of simple verbs. Instead of being a single word, such as *break, stop, spoil, mend, kill,* a verb becomes a *phrase,* made up of a noun or adjective tacked on to some general-purpose verb such as *prove, serve, form, play, render.* In addition, the passive voice is wherever possible used in preference to the active, and noun constructions are used instead of gerunds (*by examination of* instead of *by examining*). The range of verbs is further cut down by means of the *-ize* and *de-* formations, and the banal statements are given an appearance of profundity by means of the *not un-* formation. Simple conjunctions and prepositions are replaced by such phrases as *with respect to, having regard to, the fact that, by dint of, in view of, in the interests of, on the hypothesis that;* and the ends of sentences are

saved from anticlimax by such resounding commonplaces as *greatly to be desired, cannot be left out of account, a development to be expected in the near future, deserving of serious consideration, brought to a satisfactory conclusion,* and so on and so forth.

7.   *Pretentious diction.* Words like *phenomenon, element, individual* (as noun), *objective, categorical, effective, virtual, basic, primary, promote, constitute, exhibit, exploit, utilize, eliminate, liquidate,* are used to dress up simple statement and give an air of scientific impartiality to biased judgments. Adjectives like *epoch-making, epic, historic, unforgettable, triumphant, age-old, inevitable, inexorable, veritable,* are used to dignify the sordid processes of international politics, while writing that aims at glorifying war usually takes on an archaic color, its characteristic words being: *realm, throne, chariot, mailed fist, trident, sword, shield, buckler, banner, jackboot, clarion.* Foreign words and expressions such as *cul de sac, ancien régime, deus ex machina, mutatis mutandis, status quo, gleichschaltung, weltanschauung,* are used to give an air of culture and elegance. Except for the useful abbreviations *i.e., e.g., and etc.,* there is no real need for any of the hundreds of foreign phrases now current in English. Bad writers, and especially scientific, political, and sociological writers, are nearly always haunted by the notion that Latin or Greek words are grander than Saxon ones, and unnecessary words like *expedite, ameliorate, predict, extraneous, deracinated, clandestine, subaqueous,* and hundreds of others constantly gain ground from their Anglo-Saxon opposite numbers.* The jargon peculiar to Marxist writing (*hyena, hangman, cannibal, petty bourgeois, these gentry, lackey, flunkey, mad dog, White Guard,* etc.) consists largely of words and phrases translated from Russian, German, or French; but the normal way of coining a new word is to use a Latin or Greek root with the appropriate affix and, where necessary, the size formation. It is often easier to make up words of this kind (*deregionalize, impermissible, extramarital, nonfragmentary* and so forth) than to think up the English words that will cover one's meaning. The result, in general, is an increase in slovenliness and vagueness.

---

*An interesting illustration of this is the way in which the English flower names which were in use till very recently are being ousted by Greek ones, *snapdragon* becoming *antirrhinum,* *forget-me-not* becoming *myosotis,* etc. It is hard to see any practical reason for this change of fashion: it is probably due to an instinctive turning away from the more homely word and a vague feeling that the Greek word is scientific.

8. *Meaningless words.* In certain kinds of writing, particularly in art criticism and literary criticism, it is normal to come across long passages which are almost completely lacking in meaning.* Words like *romantic, plastic, values, human, dead, sentimental, natural, vitality,* as used in art criticism, are strictly meaningless, in the sense that they not only do not point to any discoverable object, but are hardly ever expected to do so by the reader. When one critic writes, "The outstanding feature of Mr. X's work is its living quality," while another writes, "The immediately striking thing about Mr. X's work is its peculiar deadness," the reader accepts this as a simple difference of opinion. If words like *black* and *white* were involved, instead of the jargon words *dead* and *living,* he would see at once that language was being used in an improper way. Many political words are similarly abused. The word *Fascism* has now no meaning except in so far as it signifies "something not desirable." The words *democracy, socialism, freedom, patriotic, realistic, justice,* have each of them several different meanings which cannot be reconciled with one another. In the case of a word like *democracy,* not only is there no agreed definition, but the attempt to make one is resisted from all sides. It is almost universally felt that when we call a country democratic we are praising it: consequently the defenders of every kind of régime claim that it is a democracy, and fear that they might have to stop using the word if it were tied down to any one meaning. Words of this kind are often used in a consciously dishonest way. That is, the person who uses them has his own private definition, but allows his hearer to think he means something quite different. Statements like *Marshal Pétain was a true patriot, The Soviet press is the freest in the world, The Catholic Church is opposed to persecution,* are almost always made with intent to deceive. Other words used in variable meanings, in most cases more or less dishonestly, are: *class, totalitarian, science, progressive, reactionary, bourgeois, equality.*

9. Now that I have made this catalogue of swindles and perversions, let me give another example of the kind of writing that they lead to. This time it must of its nature be an imaginary one. I am

---

* Example: "Comfort's catholicity of perception and image, strangely Whitmanesque in range, almost the exact opposite in aesthetic compulsion, continues to evoke that trembling atmospheric accumulative hinting at a cruel, an inexorably serene timelessness. . . . Wrey Gardiner scores by aiming at simple bull's-eyes with precision. Only they are not so simple, and through this contented sadness runs more than the surface bittersweet of resignation." (*Poetry Quarterly.*)

going to translate a passage of good English into modern English of the worst sort. Here is a well-known verse from *Ecclesiastes:*

> I returned and saw under the sun, that the race is not to the swift, nor the battle to the strong, neither yet bread to the wise, nor yet riches to men of understanding, nor yet favour to men of skill; but time and chance happeneth to them all.

Here it is in modern English:

> Objective consideration of contemporary phenomena compels the conclusion that success or failure in competitive activities exhibits no tendency to be commensurate with innate capacity, but that a considerable element of the unpredicatable must invariably be taken into account.

10. This is a parody, but not a very gross one. Exhibit (3), above, for instance, contains several patches of the same kind of English. It will be seen that I have not made a full translation. The beginning and ending of the sentence follow the original meaning fairly closely, but in the middle the concrete illustrations—race, battle, bread—dissolve into the vague phrase "success or failure in competitive activities." This had to be so, because no modern writer of the kind I am discussing—no one capable of using phrases like "objective consideration of contemporary phenomena"—would ever tabulate his thoughts in that precise and detailed way. The whole tendency of modern prose is away from concreteness. Now analyze these two sentences a little more closely. The first contains forty-nine words but only sixty syllables, and all its words are those of everyday life. The second contains thirty-eight words of ninety syllables: eighteen of its words are from Latin roots, and one from Greek. The first sentence contains six vivid images, and only one phrase ("time and chance") that could be called vague. The second contains not a single fresh, arresting phrase, and in spite of its ninety syllables it gives only a shortened version of the meaning contained in the first. Yet without a doubt it is the second kind of sentence that is gaining ground in modern English. I do not want to exaggerate. This kind of writing is not yet universal, and outcrops of simplicity will occur here and there in the worst-written page. Still, if you or I were told to write a few lines on the uncer-

tainty of human fortunes, we should probably come much nearer to my imaginary sentence than to the one from *Ecclesiastes*.

11. As I have tried to show, modern writing at its worst does not consist in picking out words for the sake of their meaning and inventing images in order to make the meaning clearer. It consists in gumming together long strips of words which have already been set in order by someone else, and making the results presentable by sheer humbug. The attraction of this way of writing is that it is easy. It is easier—even quicker, once you have the habit—to say *In my opinion it is not an unjustifiable assumption that* than to say *I think*. If you use ready-made phrases, you not only don't have to hunt about for words; you also don't have to bother with the rhythms of your sentences, since these phrases are generally so arranged as to be more or less euphonious. When you are composing in a hurry—when you are dictating to a stenographer, for instance, or making a public speech—it is natural to fall into a pretentious, Latinized style. Tags like *a consideration which we should do well to bear in mind* or *a conclusion to which all of us would readily assent* will save many a sentence from coming down with a bump. By using stale metaphors, similes, and idioms, you save much mental effort, at the cost of leaving your meaning vague, not only for your reader but for yourself. This is the significance of mixed metaphors. The sole aim of a metaphor is to call up a visual image. When these images clash—as in *The Fascist octopus has sung its swan song, the jackboot is thrown into the melting pot*—it can be taken as certain that the writer is not seeing a mental image of the objects he is naming; in other words he is not really thinking. Look again at the examples I gave at the beginning of this essay. Professor Laski (1) uses five negatives in fifty-three words. One of these is superfluous, making nonsense of the whole passage, and in addition there is the slip—*alien* for akin—making further nonsense, and several avoidable pieces of clumsiness which increase the general vagueness. Professor Hogben (2) plays ducks and drakes with a battery which is able to write prescriptions, and, while disapproving of the everyday phrase *put up with,* is unwilling to look *egregious* up in the dictionary and see what it means; (3), if one takes an uncharitable attitude towards it, is simply meaningless: probably one could work out its intended meaning by reading the whole of the article in which it occurs. In (4), the writer knows more or less what he wants to say, but an accumulation of stale phrases chokes him like tea leaves blocking a sink. In

(5), words and meaning have almost parted company. People who write in this manner usually have a general emotional meaning—they dislike one thing and want to express solidarity with another—but they are not interested in the detail of what they are saying. A scrupulous writer, in every sentence that he writes, will ask himself at least four questions, thus: What am I trying to say? What words will express it? What image or idiom will make it clearer? Is this image fresh enough to have an effect? And he will probably ask himself two more: Could I put it more shortly? Have I said anything that is avoidably ugly? But you are not obliged to go to all this trouble. You can shirk it by simply throwing your mind open and letting the ready-made phrases come crowding in. They will construct your sentences for you—even think your thoughts for you, to a certain extent—and at need they will perform the important service of partially concealing your meaning even from yourself. It is at this point that the special connection between politics and the debasement of language becomes clear.

12. In our time it is broadly true that political writing is bad writing. Where it is not true, it will generally be found that the writer is some kind of rebel, expressing his private opinions and not a "party line." Orthodoxy, of whatever color, seems to demand a lifeless, imitative style. The political dialects to be found in pamphlets, leading articles, manifestoes, White Papers and the speeches of undersecretaries do, of course, vary from party to party, but they are all alike in that one almost never finds in them a fresh, vivid, homemade turn of speech. When one watches some tired hack on the platform mechanically repeating the familiar phrases—*bestial atrocities, iron heel, bloodstained tyranny, free peoples of the world, stand shoulder to shoulder*—one often has a curious feeling that one is not watching a live human being but some kind of dummy: a feeling which suddenly becomes stronger at moments when the light catches the speaker's spectacles and turns them into blank discs which seem to have no eyes behind them. And this is not altogether fanciful. A speaker who uses that kind of phraseology has gone some distance toward turning himself into a machine. The appropriate noises are coming out of his larynx, but his brain is not involved as it would be if he were choosing his words for himself. If the speech he is making is one that he is accustomed to make over and over again, he may be almost unconscious of what he is saying, as one is when one utters the

responses in church. And this reduced state of consciousness, if not indispensable, is at any rate favorable to political conformity.

13. In our time, political speech and writing are largely the defense of the indefensible. Things like the continuance of British rule in India, the Russian purges and deportations, the dropping of the atom bombs on Japan, can indeed be defended, but only by arguments which are too brutal for most people to face, and which do not square with the professed aims of political parties. This political language has to consist largely of euphemism, question-begging and sheer cloudy vagueness. Defenseless villages are bombarded from the air, the inhabitants driven out into the countryside, the cattle machine-gunned, the huts set on fire with incendiary bullets: this is called *pacification*. Millions of peasants are robbed of their farms and sent trudging along the roads with no more than they can carry: this is called *transfer of population* or *rectification of frontiers*. People are imprisoned for years without trial, or shot in the back of the neck or sent to die of scurvy in Arctic lumber camps: this is called *elimination of unreliable elements*. Such phraseology is needed if one wants to name things without calling up mental pictures of them. Consider for instance some comfortable English professor defending Russian totalitarianism. He cannot say outright, "I believe in killing off your opponents when you can get good results by doing so." Probably, therefore, he will say something like this:

"While freely conceding that the Soviet régime exhibits certain features which the humanitarian may be inclined to deplore, we must, I think, agree that a certain curtailment of the right to political opposition is an unavoidable concomitant of transitional periods, and that the rigors which the Russian people have been called upon to undergo have been amply justified in the sphere of concrete achievement."

14. The inflated style is itself a kind of euphemism. A mass of Latin words falls upon the facts like soft snow, blurring the outlines and covering up all the details. The great enemy of clear language is insincerity. When there is a gap between one's real and one's declared aims, one turns as it were instinctively to long words and exhausted idioms, like a cuttlefish squirting out ink. In our age there is no such thing as "keeping out of politics." All issues are political issues, and politics itself is a mass of lies, evasions, folly, hatred, and schizophrenia. When the general atmo-

sphere is bad, language must suffer. I should expect to find—this is a guess which I have not sufficient knowledge to verify—that the German, Russian and Italian languages have all deteriorated in the last ten or fifteen years, as a result of dictatorship.

15. But if thought corrupts language, language can also corrupt thought. A bad usage can spread by tradition and imitation, even among people who should and do know better. The debased language that I have been discussing is in some ways very convenient. Phrases like *a not unjustifiable assumption, leaves much to be desired, would serve no good purpose, a consideration which we should do well to bear in mind,* are a continuous temptation, a packet of aspirins always at one's elbow. Look back through this essay, and for certain you will find that I have again and again committed the very faults I am protesting against. By this morning's post I have received a pamphlet dealing with conditions in Germany. The author tells me that he "felt impelled" to write it. I open it at random, and here is almost the first sentence that I see:"[The Allies] have an opportunity not only of achieving a radical transformation of Germany's social and political structure in such a way as to avoid a nationalistic reaction in Germany itself, but at the same time of laying the foundations of a co-operative and unified Europe." You see, he "feels impelled" to write—feels, presumably, that he has something new to say—and yet his words, like cavalry horses answering the bugle, group themselves automatically into the familiar dreary pattern. This invasion of one's mind by ready-made phrases (*lay the foundations, achieve a radical transformation*) can only be prevented if one is constantly on guard against them, and every such phrase anaesthetizes a portion of one's brain.

16. I said earlier that the decadence of our language is probably curable. Those who deny this would argue, if they produced an argument at all, that language merely reflects existing social conditions, and that we cannot influence its development by any direct tinkering with words and constructions. So far as the general tone or spirit of a language goes, this may be true, but it is not true in detail. Silly words and expressions have often disappeared, not through any evolutionary process but owing to the conscious action of a minority. Two recent examples were *explore every avenue* and *leave no stone unturned,* which were killed by the jeers of a few journalists. There is a long list of flyblown metaphors which

could similarly be got rid of if enough people would interest themselves in the job; and it should also be possible to laugh the *not
un-* formation out of existence,* to reduce the amount of Latin and
Greek in the average sentence, to drive out foreign phrases and
strayed scientific words, and, in general, to make pretentiousness
unfashionable. But all these are minor points. The defense of the
English language implies more than this, and perhaps it is best to
start by saying what it does *not* imply.

17. To begin with it has nothing to do with archaism, with the sal-
vaging of obsolete words and turns of speech, or with the setting
up of a "standard English" which must never be departed from.
On the contrary, it is especially concerned with the scrapping of
every word or idiom which has outworn its usefulness. It has nothing to do with correct grammar and syntax, which are of no importance so long as one makes one's meaning clear, or with the
avoidance of Americanisms, or with having what is called a "good
prose style." On the other hand it is not concerned with fake simplicity and the attempt to make written English colloquial. Nor
does it even imply in every case preferring the Saxon word to the
Latin one, though it does imply using the fewest and shortest
words that will cover one's meaning. What is above all needed is to
let the meaning choose the word, and not the other way about. In
prose, the worst thing one can do with words is to surrender to
them. When you think of a concrete object, you think wordlessly,
and then, if you want to describe the thing you have been visualiz-
ing you probably hunt about till you find the exact words that
seem to fit it. When you think of something abstract you are more
inclined to use words from the start, and unless you make a conscious effort to prevent it, the existing dialect will come rushing in
and do the job for you, at the expense of blurring or even changing
your meaning. Probably it is better to put off using words as long
as possible and get one's meaning as clear as one can through pictures or sensations. Afterward one can choose—not simply *accept*—the phrases that will best cover the meaning, and then
switch round and decide what impression one's words are likely to
make on another person. This last effort of the mind cuts out all
stale or mixed images, all prefabricated phrases, needless repeti-

---

* One can cure oneself of the *not un-* formation by memorizing this sentence: *A not
unblack dog was chasing a not unsmall rabbit across a not ungreen field.*

tions, and humbug and vagueness generally. But one can often be in doubt about the effect of a word or a phrase, and one needs rules that one can rely on when instinct fails. I think the following rules will cover most cases:

(i) Never use a metaphor, simile, or other figure of speech which you are used to seeing in print.

(ii) Never use a long word where a short one will do.

(iii) If it is possible to cut a word out, always cut it out.

(iv) Never use the passive where you can use the active.

(v) Never use a foreign phrase, a scientific word, or a jargon word if you can think of an everyday English equivalent.

(vi) Break any of these rules sooner than say anything outright barbarous.

These rules sound elementary, and so they are, but they demand a deep change of attitude in anyone who has grown used to writing in the style now fashionable. One could keep all of them and still write bad English, but one could not write the kind of stuff that I quoted in those five specimens at the beginning of this article.

18. I have not here been considering the literary use of language, but merely language as an instrument for expressing and not for concealing or preventing thought. Stuart Chase and others have come near to claiming that all abstract words are meaningless, and have used this as a pretext for advocating a kind of political quietism. Since you don't know what Fascism is, how can you struggle against Fascism? One need not swallow such absurdities as this, but one ought to recognize that the present political chaos is connected with the decay of language, and that one can probably bring about some improvement by starting at the verbal end. If you simplify your English, you are freed from the worst follies of orthodoxy. You cannot speak any of the necessary dialects, and when you make a stupid remark its stupidity will be obvious, even to yourself. Political language—and with variations this is true of all political parties, from Conservatives to Anarchists—is designed to make lies sound truthful and murder respectable, and to give an appearance of solidity to pure wind. One cannot change this all in a moment, but one can at least change one's own habits, and from time to time one can even, if one jeers loudly enough, send some worn-out and useless phrase—some *jackboot, Achilles' heel, hot-*

bed, melting pot, acid test, veritable inferno, or other lump of verbal refuse—into the dustbin where it belongs.

DISCUSSION: FAULTY DICTION

Diction can be faulty for the same reasons sentences are: imprecision, inflation, inappropriateness. These faults sometimes arise, as Orwell points out, because writers wish to disguise their thoughts and intentions. Faults also arise when, in seeking to avoid the looseness that can be found in speech, we depart too far from the usual speech patterns. The following suggestions may help you avoid awkward, monotonous, or overloaded sentences:

1. Needless repetition of a word can be awkward and monotonous; it may also be confusing if the word is used to express a different meaning each time it occurs:

   We entertained a motion to provide entertainment and food for the guests.

2. Trying to avoid repeating a word in the same sentence can lead to confusion or misunderstanding:

   The person who entered the room was not the individual we were expecting.

   Individual is a common synonym for *person,* but there is no reason to avoid using *person* a second time. Since *individual* has other meanings, the reader may think we intend one of these. H. W. Fowler calls needless substitution of this kind "elegant variation."

3. The following sentence contains deadwood—needless repetition and words and phrases for which there are simple, precise equivalents:

   There are necessary skills a writer needs to make his ideas easy to grasp and comprehensible to each and every reader.

4. Euphemism is a mild substitute for a possibly shocking or offensive or blunt expression. Readers of Victorian novels routinely decipher such euphemisms as *ruined* and *betrayed* as descriptions of certain women; these readers, in turn, employ euphemisms that people fifty years from now will have to decipher. (We still use *limbs* to refer to a person's legs without realizing that the word was originally a euphemism; some know they are employing euphemism when asking for *white meat* when chicken is on the table). We may

employ euphemism to avoid giving offense. In a film about a young widow and her family living in New York City, offended children complain, "Momma! You went out with a *garbage man?*" This useful, but often despised, occupation may seem a little more desirable if any of the standard, and sometimes absurd, euphemisms are substituted for garbage man: *janitor, custodian, sanitary engineer.* The last of these can be confused with other occupations. And confusion and pain may result when unspecified qualities are made to seem sinister or contemptible by being left unnamed, as in the widely-used term *exceptional* to describe certain kinds of children. But are the words *slow* and *retarded* kinder to the less intelligent child or to the mentally deficient? What words should be used in speaking to them or about them? There is no easy advice to give: writers must be as honest, and at the same time as considerate of feelings, as they can.

5. Clichés and bromides rob prose of conviction and vigor. A cliché is a phrase or saying that once may have been original and startling but has become trite through overuse: *honey of a girl, sweet as sugar, conspicuous by his absence, more sinned against than sinning.* A bromide is a dull platitude thought to be comforting: *It's the effort that counts, not the winning.*

6. Mixed metaphors can make sentences unintentionally comic:

Blows to one's pride stick in the craw.

7. Overlapping words will obscure the meaning of a sentence. Fowler cites this example:

The *effect* of the tax is not likely to be *productive* of much real damage.

The italicized words mean the same thing.

8. Awkwardness may result when we needlessly avoid splitting infinitives, ending sentences with prepositions, or opening them with *but* and *and;* Fowler refers to these "rules" as superstitions and fetishes. Formal and informal English sentences have ended with prepositions and will continue to do so—and opened with *and* and *but.* The following sentence comes about because the writer wishes not to break a rule:

That's the ladder up which I climbed.

No one would speak such a sentence, but sentences like it are written in a mistaken effort to be correct. Similarly, we must sometimes split the infinitive. Note the ambiguous effect of avoiding the split in the following sentence:

Our object is further to cement trade relations. [Fowler]

The ear must be the guide in most instances; a sensible practice is not to split the infinitive with long modifiers.

QUESTIONS

1. How does the third example in Orwell's paragraph 3 help to explain the statement in paragraph 4 that "the concrete melts into the abstract"?
2. What visual image did *iron resolution* in paragraph 5 originally convey? What other dead metaphors can you cite, and what was the original significance?
3. Among the characteristic phrases cited in paragraph 6, Orwell might have included *in terms of*. Compare the following:

   He explained his failure in terms of his attitude toward school.

   Einstein was a creative thinker in physics because he thought in terms of mathematics instead of mystical concepts.

   In which sentence is the phrase used less awkwardly, and why?
4. Why is the passage cited in the footnote to paragraph 8 "almost completely lacking in meaning"? Given Orwell's criticisms in paragraph 8, what would be the proper use of language in art criticism?
5. Compare the passage from *Ecclesiastes* quoted in paragraph 9 (King James Version) with modern renderings of it. Do you think these modern renderings are superior to Orwell's parody or to the King James version? Why?
6. "If you or I were told to write a few lines on the uncertainty of human fortunes," why would the writing come nearer to Orwell's parody than to the sentence from *Ecclesiastes?*
7. Given the assumptions Orwell makes in the whole essay, why are all issues "political issues"?
8. Orwell says in paragraph 17 that his concern has not been to promote a "standard English" or "to make written English colloquial." Explain what he means here. Has he not recommended the use of plain English words? What exceptions would he allow?
9. Rewrite the following sentences to eliminate the faults in diction:
   a. Once you have heard him speak in his highly unorthodox manner, his grating rasping voice and his often repeated phrases that are hackneyed, you will never forget him.

b. Her version of the story was not the rendering we had heard a week before.
c. He has more regard for his honor than he has respect for money.
d. There is a not uncommon way of expressing that idea.
e. She had unfortunate luck in dealing with the man who owned the premises where she lived and to whom she paid rent.
f. There is no candy in the jar there.
g. He is the man with whom she came with.
h. A free economy is the linchpin on which a progressive tariff policy must be built.
i. The result of the conference is certain to effect a change in the present tariff policy.

WRITING ASSIGNMENTS

Analyze a paragraph from the catalog of your college or university to discover its tone and judge the writing according to the criteria Orwell proposes.

Analyze a letter to the editor of a newspaper or magazine and indicate the self-impression the writer wishes to create, the qualities of the prose, and the virtues or defects of the letter.

Analyze three paragraphs from a current textbook in one of your courses to determine how much needless jargon is employed and how well the writing meets the standard of good writing Orwell proposes.

Analyze a published speech of a major political figure (see *The New York Times* or *Vital Speeches* or *Congressional Record*). How honest is the use of language? Compare this speech with another by the same person. How consistent is he or she in use of language?

THOMAS H. MIDDLETON
Yay, Team?

1.　During the hearings concerning the confirmation of Representative Gerald Ford as Vice President in 1973, Ford commented,

YAY, TEAM?: In *Saturday Review/World,* January 26, 1974. Reprinted by permission of the author.

"You don't go out and tackle your quarterback once he has called the play," to which Senator Harrison A. Williams, Jr., countered, "If your quarterback was running toward the wrong goal line, wouldn't you tackle him?"

2. "Yes," said Ford, "but that would be the exception rather than the rule."

3. The football metaphor has become an accepted commonplace in recent years. In my opinion, it's a bad one. It's simply inept.

4. Literate people are sensitive to jumbled metaphors. "The arms of the American Minuteman will be the scourge that stems the rising tide of vermin swooping down on the sleeping giant of outraged citizenry" collapses of its own disharmony, but "You don't go out and tackle your quarterback" may sound okay but it doesn't do the job.

5. The trouble is that football, though it's big business, is still basically a game. It is not comparable to government. To use football as a metaphor for government—and particularly for war—is to oversimplify, perhaps with deadly results. It's easy to see why football terminology is seized upon by politicians. It has a simple, pragmatic, virile ring to it. And I suppose everyone who makes money from football, with the exception of some of the players, has in one way or another fostered the idea that football is contained warfare. "He hasn't used the bomb yet" means merely that the quarterback or the coach or whoever really calls the plays has not yet called for a long forward pass. And have you ever watched those films of the glorious moments from the preceding week's games?—slow-motion pictures of enormous bodies hurtling high in the air and landing on their heads to the accompaniment of tympani and Götterdämmerung-oriented music. The narrator, with a deeply resonant voice, sounds like the same one who used to say, "But France's military might crumbled rapidly before the invincible onslaught of Hitler's Wehrmacht" over shots of thundering panzer divisions. During the Vietnam war, there were constant references to "our team" and "our quarterback," and I once heard a man urging a hawkish policy say, "When you're on your opponent's five-yard line, you don't punt!" He didn't mention that, in football, neither do you saturate your opponent's city with high explosives from five miles in the air. Killing is equated with a game in this metaphor, and now there are a lot of people who deal with the fortunes of the American political system in the same terms.

6. The hackneyed, timeworn old Ship of State works much bet-

ter. There is a real matter of life and death in the fortunes of a ship. I'd feel more comfortable with a man who said, "You don't get rid of your captain once he's set his course" than with one who used quarterbacks calling plays. If it's discovered that the captain's chosen course leads to Suicide Shoals, or that he and some of his fellow officers have been hacking holes in the hull below the waterline, it will occasion a greater sense of urgency than if the quarterback chooses to try for a field goal instead of a first down.

7.   I think we have a tendency to think of the world in terms of winning, losing, happy endings, unhappy endings, and that sort of thing, as though the world were a game or a stage and all the men and women merely players. I'm a frequent listener to listener-response radio, as well as an ardent Letters-to-the-Editor fan. The other day I heard a woman who called in to one of the local talk stations say she'd like to live to be at least 100 "because I want to see how it all turns out."

8.   World without end is a tough conception, but it doesn't help to picture the world in terms of opening kickoffs and final guns. In fact, thinking in terms of final guns, we just might *get* final guns.

QUESTIONS

1. Is Middleton saying that the football metaphor is inappropriate to the situations it has been applied to, or that it is dangerous to think about these situations in metaphorical terms?
2. Are there situations to which the football metaphor is applicable, in your opinion? How about a selling situation—for example selling shoes or used cars? Isn't the relationship between customer and salesman often an adversary relationship?

WRITING ASSIGNMENT

Analyze the use of metaphor in letters to the editor or in columns of your daily newspaper. Comment on their appropriateness, giving attention to points of similarity and dissimilarity.

PART TWO

The
Whole
Essay

Exposition

THESIS

PEGGY AND PIERRE STREIT

A Well in India

1. The hot dry season in India. . . . A corrosive wind drives rivu-
lets of sand across the land; torpid animals stand at the edge of
dried-up water holes. The earth is cracked and in the rivers the
sluggish, falling waters have exposed the sludge of the mud flats.
Throughout the land the thoughts of men turn to water. And in
the village of Rampura these thoughts are focused on the village
well.

2. It is a simple concrete affair, built upon the hard earth worn
by the feet of five hundred villagers. It is surmounted by a wooden
structure over which ropes, tied to buckets, are lowered to the
black, placid depths twenty feet below. Fanning out from the well
are the huts of the villagers—their walls white from sun, their
thatched roofs thick with dust blown in from the fields.

3. At the edge of the well is a semi-circle of earthen pots and,
crouched at some distance behind them, a woman. She is an untouchable—a sweeper in Indian parlance—a scavenger of the village. She cleans latrines, disposes of dead animals and washes
drains. She also delivers village babies, for this—like all her
work—is considered unclean by most of village India.

4. Her work—indeed, her very presence—is considered polluting, and since there is no well for untouchables in Rampura, her
water jars must be filled by upper-caste villagers.

5. There are dark shadows under her eyes and the flesh has fallen away from her neck, for she, like her fellow outcastes, is at the end of a bitter struggle. And if, in her narrow world, shackled by tradition and hemmed in by poverty, she had been unaware of the power of the water of the well at whose edge she waits—she knows it now.

6. Shanti, 30 years old, has been deserted by her husband, and supports her three children. Like her ancestors almost as far back as history records, she has cleaned the refuse from village huts and lanes. Hers is a life of inherited duties as well as inherited rights. She serves, and her work calls for payment of one chapatty—a thin wafer of unleavened bread—a day from each of the thirty families she cares for.

7. But this is the hiatus between harvests; the oppressive lull before the burst of monsoon rains; the season of flies and dust, heat and disease, querulous voices and frayed tempers—and the season of want. There is little food in Rampura for anyone, and though Shanti's chores have continued as before, she has received only six chapatties a day for her family—starvation wages.

8. Ten days ago she revolted. Driven by desperation, she defied an elemental law of village India. She refused to make her sweeper's rounds—refused to do the work tradition and religion had assigned her. Shocked at her audacity, but united in desperation, the village's six other sweeper families joined in her protest.

9. Word of her action spread quickly across the invisible line that separates the untouchables' huts from the rest of the village. As the day wore on and the men returned from the fields, they gathered at the well—the heart of the village—and their voices rose, shrill with outrage: a *sweeper* defying them all! Shanti, a sweeper *and* a woman challenging a system that had prevailed unquestioned for centuries! Their indignation spilled over. It was true, perhaps, that the sweepers had not had their due. But that was no fault of the upper caste. No fault of theirs that sun and earth and water had failed to produce the food by which they could fulfill their obligations. So, to bring the insurgents to heel, they employed their ultimate weapon; the earthern water jars of the village untouchables would remain empty until they returned to work. For the sweepers of Rampura the well had run dry.

10. No water: thirst, in the heat, went unslaked. The embers of the hearth were dead, for there was no water for cooking. The crumbling walls of outcaste huts went untended, for there was no

water for repairs. There was no fuel, for the fires of the village were fed with dung mixed with water and dried. The dust and the sweat and the filth of their lives congealed on their skins and there it stayed, while life in the rest of the village—within sight of the sweepers—flowed on.

11. The day began and ended at the well. The men, their dhotis wrapped about their loins, congregated at the water's edge in the hushed post-dawn, their small brass water jugs in hand, their voices mingling in quiet conversation as they rinsed their bodies and brushed their teeth. The buffaloes were watered, their soft muzzles lingering in the buckets before they were driven off to the fields. Then came the women, their brass pots atop their heads, to begin the ritual of water drawing: the careful lowering of the bucket in the well, lest it come loose from the rope; the gratifying splash as it touched the water; the maneuvering to make it sink; the squeal of rope against wooden pulley as it ascended. The sun rose higher. Clothes were beaten clean on the rocks surrounding the well as the women gossiped. A traveler from a near-by road quenched his thirst from a villager's urn. Two little boys, hot and bored, dropped pebbles into the water and waited for their hollow splash, far below.

12. As the afternoon wore on and the sun turned orange through the dust, the men came back from the fields. They doused the parched, cracked hides of their water buffaloes and murmured contentedly, themselves, as the water coursed over their own shoulders and arms. And finally, as twilight closed in, came the evening procession of women, stately, graceful, their bare feet moving smoothly over the earth, their full skirts swinging about their ankles, the heavy brass pots once again balanced on their heads.

13. The day was ended and life was as it always was—almost. Only the fetid odor of accumulated refuse and the assertive buzz of flies attested to strife in the village. For, while tradition and religion decreed that sweepers must clean, it also ordained that the socially blessed must not. Refuse lay where it fell and rotted.

14. The strain of the water boycott was beginning to tell on the untouchables. For two days they had held their own. But on the third their thin reserve of flesh had fallen away. Movements were slower; voices softer; minds dull. More and more the desultory conversation turned to the ordinary; the delicious memory of sliding from the back of a wallowing buffalo into a pond; the feel of

bare feet in wet mud; the touch of fresh water on parched lips; the anticipation of monsoon rains.

15. One by one the few tools they owned were sold for food. A week passed, and on the ninth day two sweeper children were down with fever. On the tenth day Shanti crossed the path that separated outcaste from upper caste and walked through familiar, winding alleyways to one of the huts she served.

16. "Your time is near," she told the young, expectant mother. "Tell your man to leave his sickle home when he goes to the fields. I've had to sell mine." (It is the field sickle that cuts the cord of newborn babies in much of village India.) Shanti, the instigator of the insurrection, had resumed her ancestral duties; the strike was broken. Next morning, as ever, she waited at the well. Silently, the procession of upper-caste women approached. They filled their jars to the brim and without a word they filled hers.

17. She lifted the urns to her head, steadied them, and started back to her quarters—back to a life ruled by the powers that still rule most of the world: not the power of atoms or electricity, nor the power of alliances or power blocs, but the elemental powers of hunger, of disease, of tradition—and of water.

DISCUSSION: THESIS

The thesis of an essay is its central or controlling idea, the proposition or chief argument—the point of the essay. The topic sentence of a paragraph may be a full or partial statement of the controlling idea: the thesis is always a full statement of it. Where the thesis appears in an essay depends on what writers assume about their audience. If they know the audience well and believe no introduction to the thesis is necessary, they may state it in the very first sentence. The Federalist papers of Hamilton, Jay, and Madison often start in this way:

> A firm Union will be of the utmost moment to the peace and liberty of the States, as a barrier against domestic faction and insurrection.—Alexander Hamilton, *The Federalist* No. 9

So do many newspaper editorials. Most writers, however, prefer to build to the thesis, stating it partially or fully later in the introductory paragraphs. If the thesis needs background and extended discussion to be understood, or perhaps is so controversial that it is preferable to build to it slowly, the writer may position it at the end of the essay. The following opening sentences of an essay state the subject only—the topics to be explored:

> Saints should always be judged guilty until they are proved innocent, but the tests that have to be applied to them are not, of course, the same in all cases. In Gandhi's case the questions one feels inclined to ask are: to what extent was Gandhi moved by vanity—by the consciousness of himself as a humble, naked old man, sitting on a praying mat and shaking empires by sheer spiritual power—and to what extent did he compromise his own principles by entering politics, which of their nature are inseparable from coercion and fraud?— George Orwell, "Reflections on Gandhi"

Important terms need to be defined, attitudes clarified, and a climate of opinion and the world of Gandhi portrayed before Orwell can state his thesis fully.

In some essays the writer leads the reader to draw conclusions from the details provided and their presentation. In these instances the thesis is said to be *implicit*.

Considerations of audience have much to do with where the thesis appears in the essay. Such rhetorical considerations also influence the uses made of the beginning and the ending of the essay, its tone and transitions, its order of ideas, and its unity and style.

QUESTIONS

1. The Streits build to a statement of their thesis at the end of paragraph 5. Why is it necessary to portray the world of the untouchable before stating the thesis?
2. Where in the essay is the thesis restated? Is the restatement more informative or detailed than the original statement of it?
3. What is the attitude of the authors toward the world they portray and the fate of Shanti? Do they seem to be taking sides?
4. Is it important to the thesis that Shanti is a woman? Are the authors concerned with her as a woman, in addition to their concern for her as an untouchable?
5. Is the concern of the essay equally with the power of water and the power of tradition? Or are these considerations subordinate to the portrayal of the untouchable and the courage shown?
6. Are we given a motive directly for what Shanti does—or is the motive implied?
7. How are transitions made through the seventeen short paragraphs?

WRITING ASSIGNMENTS

Develop an idea relating to the power of tradition and illustrate it from personal experience and observation. Provide enough background so that your reader understands why the tradition is important to the people who observe it.

Describe a conflict between you and your parents or school officials or between a person and a group of some sort. Explain how the conflict arises from a basic difference in attitude, ideas or feelings—a difference that reveals something important about you and the other people involved.

GEORGE ORWELL

Shooting an Elephant

1.   In Moulmein, in lower Burma, I was hated by large numbers of people—the only time in my life that I have been important enough for this to happen to me. I was sub-divisional police officer of the town, and in an aimless, petty kind of way anti-European feeling was very bitter. No one had the guts to raise a riot, but if a European woman went through the bazaars alone somebody would probably spit betel juice over her dress. As a police officer I was an obvious target and was baited whenever it seemed safe to do so. When a nimble Burman tripped me up on the football field and the referee (another Burman) looked the other way, the crowd yelled with hideous laughter. This happened more than once. In the end the sneering yellow faces of young men that met me everywhere, the insults hooted after me when I was at a safe distance, got badly on my nerves. The young Buddhist priests were the worst of all. There were several thousands of them in the town and none of them seemed to have anything to do except stand on street corners and jeer at Europeans.
2.   All this was perplexing and upsetting. For at that time I had already made up my mind that imperialism was an evil thing and the sooner I chucked up my job and got out of it the better. Theo-

retically—and secretly, of course—I was all for the Burmese and all against their oppressors, the British. As for the job I was doing, I hated it more bitterly than I can perhaps make clear. In a job like that you see the dirty work of Empire at close quarters. The wretched prisoners huddling in the stinking cages of the lock-ups, the gray, cowed faces of the long-term convicts, the scarred buttocks of the men who had been flogged with bamboos—all these oppressed me with an intolerable sense of guilt. But I could get nothing into perspective. I was young and ill educated and I had had to think out my problems in the utter silence that is imposed on every Englishman in the East. I did not even know that the British Empire is dying, still less did I know that it is a great deal better than the younger empires that are going to supplant it. All I knew was that I was stuck between my hatred of the empire I served and my rage against the evil-spirited little beasts who tried to make my job impossible. With one part of my mind I thought of the British Raj as an unbreakable tyranny, as something clamped down, in *saecula saeculorum,* upon the will of prostrate peoples; with another part I thought that the greatest joy in the world would be to drive a bayonet into a Buddhist priest's guts. Feelings like these are the normal by-products of imperialism; ask any Anglo-Indian official, if you can catch him off duty.

3.   One day something happened which in a roundabout way was enlightening. It was a tiny incident in itself, but it gave me a better glimpse than I had had before of the real nature of imperialism—the real motives for which despotic governments act. Early one morning the sub-inspector at a police station the other end of the town rang me up on the 'phone and said that an elephant was ravaging the bazaar. Would I please come and do something about it? I did not know what I could do, but I wanted to see what was happening and I got on to a pony and started out. I took my rifle, an old .44 Winchester and much too small to kill an elephant, but I thought the noise might be useful *in terrorem.* Various Burmans stopped me on the way and told me about the elephant's doings. It was not, of course, a wild elephant, but a tame one which had gone "must." It had been chained up, as tame elephants always are when their attack of "must" is due, but on the previous night it had broken its chain and escaped. Its mahout, the only person who could manage it when it was in that state, had set out in pursuit, but had taken the wrong direction and was now twelve hours' journey away, and in the morning the elephant had suddenly reap-

peared in the town. The Burmese population had no weapons and were quite helpless against it. It had already destroyed somebody's bamboo hut, killed a cow and raided some fruit-stalls and devoured the stock; also it had met the muncipal rubbish van and, when the driver jumped out and took to his heels, had turned the van over and inflicted violences upon it.

4.   The Burmese sub-inspector and some Indian constables were waiting for me in the quarter where the elephant had been seen. It was a very poor quarter, a labyrinth of squalid bamboo huts, thatched with palm-leaf, winding all over a steep hillside. I remember that it was a cloudy, stuffy morning at the beginning of the rains. We began questioning the people as to where the elephant had gone and, as usual, failed to get any definite information. That is invariably the case in the East; a story always sounds clear enough at a distance, but the nearer you get to the scene of events the vaguer it becomes. Some of the people said that the elephant had gone in one direction, some said that he had gone in another, some professed not even to have heard of any elephant. I had almost made up my mind that the whole story was a pack of lies, when we heard yells a little distance away. There was a loud, scandalized cry of "Go away, child! Go away this instant!" and an old woman with a switch in her hand came round the corner of a hut, violently shooing away a crowd of naked children. Some more women followed, clicking their tongues and exclaiming; evidently there was something that the children ought not to have seen. I rounded the hut and saw a man's dead body sprawling in the mud. He was an Indian, a black Dravidian coolie, almost naked, and he could not have been dead many minutes. The people said that the elephant had come suddenly upon him round the corner of the hut, caught him with its trunk, put its foot on his back and ground him into the earth. This was the rainy season and the ground was soft, and his face had scored a trench a foot deep and a couple of yards long. He was lying on his belly with arms crucified and head sharply twisted to one side. His face was coated with mud, the eyes wide open, the teeth bared and grinning with an expression of unendurable agony. (Never tell me, by the way, that the dead look peaceful. Most of the corpses I have seen looked devilish.) The friction of the great beast's foot had stripped the skin from his back as neatly as one skins a rabbit. As soon as I saw the dead man I sent an orderly to a friend's house nearby to borrow an elephant rifle. I had already sent back the pony, not wanting it to go mad

with fright and throw me if it smelt the elephant.

5.   The orderly came back in a few minutes with a rifle and five cartridges, and meanwhile some Burmans had arrived and told us that the elephant was in the paddy fields below, only a few hundred yards away. As I started forward practically the whole population of the quarter flocked out of the houses and followed me. They had seen the rifle and were all shouting excitedly that I was going to shoot the elephant. They had not shown much interest in the elephant when he was merely ravaging their homes, but it was different now that he was going to be shot. It was a bit of fun to them, as it would be to an English crowd; besides they wanted the meat. It made me vaguely uneasy. I had no intention of shooting the elephant—I had merely sent for the rifle to defend myself if necessary—and it is always unnerving to have a crowd following you. I marched down the hill, looking and feeling a fool, with the rifle over my shoulder and an ever-growing army of people jostling at my heels. At the bottom, when you got away from the huts, there was a metalled road and beyond that a miry waste of paddy fields a thousand yards across, not yet ploughed but soggy from the first rains and dotted with coarse grass. The elephant was standing eight yards from the road, his left side toward us. He took not the slightest notice of the crowd's approach. He was tearing up bunches of grass, beating them against his knees to clean them, and stuffing them into his mouth.

6.   I had halted on the road. As soon as I saw the elephant I knew with perfect certainty that I ought not to shoot him. It is a serious matter to shoot a working elephant—it is comparable to destroying a huge and costly piece of machinery—and obviously one ought not to do it if it can possibly be avoided. And at that distance, peacefully eating, the elephant looked no more dangerous than a cow. I thought then and I think now that his attack of "must" was already passing off; in which case he would merely wander harmlessly about until the mahout came back and caught him. Moreover, I did not in the least want to shoot him. I decided that I would watch him for a little while to make sure that he did not turn savage again, and then go home.

7.   But at that moment I glanced round at the crowd that had followed me. It was an immense crowd, two thousand at the least and growing every minute. It blocked the road for a long distance on either side. I looked at the sea of yellow faces above the garish clothes—faces all happy and exited over this bit of fun, all certain

that the elephant was going to be shot. They were watching me as they would watch a conjurer about to perform a trick. They did not like me, but with the magical rifle in my hands I was momentarily worth watching. And suddenly I realized that I should have to shoot the elephant after all. The people expected it of me and I had got to do it; I could feel their two thousand wills pressing me forward, irresistibly. And it was at this moment, as I stood there with the rifle in my hands, that I first grasped the hollowness, the futility of the white man's dominion in the East. Here was I, the white man with his gun, standing in front of the unarmed native crowd—seemingly the leading actor of the piece; but in reality I was only an absurd puppet pushed to and fro by the will of those yellow faces behind. I perceived in this moment that when the white man turns tyrant it is his own freedom that he destroys. He becomes a sort of hollow, posing dummy, the conventionalized figure of a sahib. For it is the condition of his rule that he shall spend his life in trying to impress the "natives," and so in every crisis he has got to do what the "natives" expect of him. He wears a mask, and his face grows to fit it. I had got to shoot the elephant. I had committed myself to doing it when I sent for the rifle. A sahib has got to act like a sahib; he has got to appear resolute, to know his own mind and do definite things. To come all that way, rifle in hand, with two thousand people marching at my heels, and then to trail feebly away, having done nothing—no, that was impossible. The crowd would laugh at me. And my whole life, every white man's life in the East, was one long struggle not to be laughed at.

8.   But I did not want to shoot the elephant. I watched him beating his bunch of grass against his knees with that preoccupied grandmotherly air that elephants have. It seemed to me that it would be murder to shoot him. At that age I was not squeamish about killing animals, but I had never shot an elephant and never wanted to. (Somehow it always seems worse to kill a *large* animal.) Besides, there was the beast's owner to be considered. Alive, the elephant was worth at least a hundred pounds; dead, he would only be worth the value of his tusks, five pounds, possibly. But I had got to act quickly. I turned to some experienced-looking Burmans who had been there when we arrived, and asked them how the elephant had been behaving. They all said the same thing: he took no notice of you if you left him alone, but he might charge if you went too close to him.

9.   It was perfectly clear to me what I ought to do. I ought to walk

up to within, say, twenty-five yards of the elephant and test his behavior. If he charged, I could shoot; if he took no notice of me, it
would be safe to leave him until the mahout came back. But also I
knew that I was going to do no such thing. I was a poor shot with
a rifle and the ground was soft mud into which one would sink at
every step. If the elephant charged and I missed him, I should
have about as much chance as a toad under a steam-roller. But
even then I was not thinking particularly of my own skin, only of
the watchful yellow faces behind. For at that moment, with the
crowd watching me, I was not afraid in the ordinary sense, as I
would have been if I had been alone. A white man mustn't be
frightened in front of "natives"; and so, in general, he isn't frightened. The sole thought in my mind was that if anything went
wrong those two thousand Burmans would see me pursued,
caught, trampled on, and reduced to a grinning corpse like that
Indian up the hill. And if that happened it was quite probable that
some of them would laugh. That would never do. There was only
one alternative. I shoved the cartridges into the magazine and lay
down on the road to get a better aim.

10. The crowd grew very still, and a deep, low, happy sigh, as of
people who see the theater curtain go up at last, breathed from in-
numerable throats. They were going to have their bit of fun after
all. The rifle was a beautiful German thing with crosshair sights. I
did not then know that in shooting an elephant one would shoot to
cut an imaginary bar running from ear-hole to ear-hole. I ought,
therefore, as the elephant was sideways on, to have aimed straight
at his ear-hole; actually I aimed several inches in front of this,
thinking the brain would be further forward.

11. When I pulled the trigger I did not hear the bang or feel the
kick—one never does when a shot goes home—but I heard the
devilish roar of glee that went up from the crowd. In that instant,
in too short a time, one would have thought, even for the bullet to
get there, a mysterious, terrible change had come over the elephant. He neither stirred nor fell, but every line of his body had altered. He looked suddenly stricken, shrunken, immensely old, as
though the frightful impact of the bullet had paralyzed him without knocking him down. At last, after what seemed a long time—it
might have been five seconds, I dare say—he sagged flabbily to his
knees. His mouth slobbered. An enormous senility seemed to have
settled upon him. One could have imagined him thousands of
years old. I fired again into the same spot. At the second shot he

did not collapse but climbed with desperate slowness to his feet and stood weakly upright, with legs sagging and head drooping. I fired a third time. That was the shot that did for him. You could see the agony of it jolt his whole body and knock the last remnant of strength from his legs. But in falling he seemed for a moment to rise, for as his hind legs collapsed beneath him he seemed to tower upward like a huge rock toppling, his trunk reaching skyward like a tree. He trumpeted, for the first and only time. And then down he came, his belly toward me, with a crash that seemed to shake the ground even where I lay.

12. I got up. The Burmans were already racing past me across the mud. It was obvious that the elephant would never rise again, but he was not dead. He was breathing very rhythmically with long rattling gasps, his great mound of a side painfully rising and falling. His mouth was wide open—I could see far down into caverns of pale pink throat. I waited a long time for him to die, but his breathing did not weaken. Finally I fired my two remaining shots into the spot where I thought his heart must be. The thick blood welled out of him like red velvet, but still he did not die. His body did not even jerk when the shots hit him, the tortured breathing continued without a pause. He was dying, very slowly and in great agony, but in some world remote from me where not even a bullet could damage him further. I felt that I had got to put an end to that dreadful noise. It seemed dreadful to see the great beast lying there, powerless to move and yet powerless to die, and not even to be able to finish him. I sent back for my small rifle and poured shot after shot into his heart and down his throat. They seemed to make no impression. The tortured gasps continued as steadily as the ticking of a clock.

13. In the end I could not stand it any longer and went away. I heard later that it took him half an hour to die. Burmans were bringing dahs and baskets even before I left, and I was told they had stripped his body almost to the bones by the afternoon.

14. Afterward, of course, there were endless discussions about the shooting of the elephant. The owner was furious, but he was only an Indian and could do nothing. Besides, legally I had done the right thing, for a mad elephant has to be killed, like a mad dog, if its owner fails to control it. Among the Europeans opinion was divided. The older men said I was right, the younger men said it was a damn shame to shoot an elephant for killing a coolie, because an elephant was worth more than any damn Coringhee

coolie. And afterward I was very glad that the coolie had been killed; it put me legally in the right and it gave me a sufficient pretext for shooting the elephant. I often wondered whether any of the others grasped that I had done it solely to avoid looking a fool.

QUESTIONS

1. Orwell states in paragraph 3: "One day something happened which in a roundabout way was enlightening. It was a tiny incident in itself, but it gave me a better glimpse than I had had before of the real nature of imperialism—the real motives for which despotic governments act." The incident, in all its particularity, reveals the psychology of the imperialist ruler. What effect do the atmosphere (the stuffy, cloudy weather) and the behavior of the Burmans and their attitude toward the elephant have on this psychology? Why is the dead coolie described in detail in paragraph 4? Why is the shooting of the elephant described in detail in paragraph 11? In general, how does the incident reveal the motives Orwell mentions?

2. The incident reveals more than just the motives of the imperialist ruler: it reveals much about mob and crisis psychology and the man in the middle. What does it reveal specifically?

3. Where in the essay is the thesis stated, and how do you account for its placement?

4. The exactness of the diction contributes greatly to the development of the thesis, for Orwell does not merely *tell* us, he makes us see. In paragraph 11, for example, he states: ". . . I heard the devilish roar of *glee* that went up from the crowd." He might have chosen *laughter, hilarity,* or *mirth* to describe the behavior of the crowd, but *glee* is the exact word because it connotes something that the other three words do not—malice. And the elephant "*sagged* flabbily to his knees," not *dropped* or *sank,* because *sagged* connotes weight and, in the context of the passage, age. What does Orwell mean in the same paragraph by "His mouth slobbered" and "An enormous senility seemed to have settled upon him"? In paragraph 12 why "*caverns* of pale pink throat" rather than *depths*? In paragraph 4 why is the corpse *grinning* rather than *smiling*? (Consult the synonym listings in your dictionary, or compare definitions.)

WRITING ASSIGNMENTS

Illustrate the last sentence of the essay from your own experience. Build the essay to the moment when you acted to avoid looking like a fool. Make your reader see and feel what you saw and felt.

Orwell states: "And my whole life, every white man's life in the East, was one long struggle not to be laughed at." Drawing on your experience and observation, discuss what you see as the feelings and motives of people charged with enforcing rules of some sort—perhaps hall monitors in high school, or lifeguards at a swimming pool, or supervisors at a playground, or babysitters. Use your discussion to draw a conclusion, as Orwell does.

ROBERT BENCHLEY
Saturday's Smells

1.   Never, even in my best form, what you would call a "drone" or "worker" at heart, I have been having a particularly tough time of it lately just sitting at my desk.

2.   Specialists and psychoanalysts from all over the world have been working on my case, and it was only yesterday that I myself was able to give them the key to my inability to work. It is my new pipe tobacco. It smells like Saturday, and consequently puts me in a chronic holiday mood.

3.   This may take a little explaining. The main thesis on which I am going to build my case is that, when you were a child, certain days had their individual smells, and that these smells, when experienced today, take you back to your state of mind when you experienced them in childhood. Do I make myself clear, or must I say that all over again?

4.   Sunday smells were, of course, the most distinctive, and, when they assail me today, I become restless and depressed and want to go to sea. In my section of the country, the first Sunday smell was of the fish-balls for breakfast. This was not so depressing, as fish-balls were good, and anyway, Sunday didn't begin to get you down until later in the day.

5.   Then came, in slow succession, the musty draughts of the Sunday-school vestry, laden with the week's dust on the maps of Palestine and the hymnals, and freshened that morning only by the smell of black silk dresses sprinkled with lavender and the starch from little girls' petticoats and sashes. Then the return to

SATURDAY'S SMELLS: In *The Benchley Roundup*, edited by Nathaniel Benchley. Copyright 1934 by Robert C. Benchley. Reprinted by permission of Harper & Row, Publishers, Inc.

the home, where fish-cakes had given way to fricasseeing chicken and boiling onions, which, in turn, gave way to the aroma of the paternal cigar as you started out on that Sunday afternoon walk, during which you passed all the familiar spots where you had been playing only the day before with the gang, now desolate and small-looking in the pall of Sunday.

6. But, sure as the smells of Sunday were, those of Saturday were none the less distinctive and a great deal more cheery. In our house we began getting whiffs of Saturday as early as Friday evening, when the bread was "set" on the kitchen table and the beans put to soak nearby. The smell of the cold bread-dough when the napkins were lifted from the pans always meant "no school tomorrow," and was a preliminary to the "no school today" smells of Saturday, which are at the basis of my present trouble.

7. On Saturday morning early these "no school today" smells began to permeate the kitchen, and, as the kitchen was the sole port of entry and exit during the morning's play outside, they became inextricably mixed up with not only cooking, but "duck-on-the-rock," "Indian guide" and that informal scrimmaging which boys indulge in in back yards, which goes by the name of either "football" or "baseball" according to the season of the year.

8. In New England, of course, the *leit motif* among the Saturday smells was the one of beans baking, but the bread and pies ran it a close second. A good cake in the oven could hold its own, too. Then, along about eleven-thirty the Saturday noon dinner began to loom up, being more plebeian than the Sunday noon dinner, it usually took the combined form of cabbage, turnips, beets and corned beef, all working together in one pot, with the potatoes, to make what is known as the "New England boiled dinner." That put a stop to any other smells that thought they were something earlier in the morning.

9. On the outside, Saturday morning contributed the smell of burning leaves, and of shingles on the new house that was always being built in the neighborhood; and, although sounds do not come into our lecture today, there was the sound of carpenters hammering, and the re-echoing beat of rugs being dusted, which became almost smells in their affinity to them.

10. Now, here is the point about my pipe tobacco. A month or so ago I tried out a new blend, which, I discovered only yesterday, smells exactly like beans in an oven. So, when I settle down to a morning's work and light my pipe, I am gradually overcome with

the delicious feeling that there is "no school today," and that I really ought to be outdoors playing.

11. So, without knowing why, I have been leaving my work and getting out my skates and yielding to the Saturday spirit. The only trouble has been that, under this subtle influence, every day has been Saturday, because every day has smelled like Saturday.

12. I don't suppose that the tradesmen to whom I owe money will think much of this explanation, but it satisfies me and the psychoanalysts perfectly. And, as yet, I have made no move to buy a less insidious-smelling pipe tobacco.

QUESTIONS

1. How does Benchley lead the reader to his "main thesis"? How does he establish a point of view in this lead to it?
2. Why does he begin with Sunday smells, and indeed mention them at all?
3. Does Benchley discuss Saturday's smells in any particular order, or is the connection of ideas a random one?
4. How does he make the transition to his pipe tobacco, in paragraph 10? Is he making a new point at the end of the essay, or are paragraphs 10–12 mainly a restatement of his main thesis?

WRITING ASSIGNMENT

Write an essay contrasting the smells of Saturday with those of another day, as you experience them today, or experienced them in childhood. At the end of your essay return to the ideas or experiences that opened your discussion.

ERIC SEVAREID
Velva, North Dakota

1. My home town has changed in these thirty years of the American story. It is changing now, will go on changing as America changes. Its biography, I suspect, would read much the same as

VELVA, NORTH DAKOTA: In *This Is Eric Sevareid* by Eric Sevareid. Copyright 1964 by Eric Sevareid. Reprinted by permission of Harold Matson Company Inc. Selection title by editor.

that of all other home towns. Depression and war and prosperity have all left their marks; modern science, modern tastes, manners, philosophies, fears and ambitions have touched my town as indelibly as they have touched New York or Panama City.

2. Sights have changed: there is a new precision about street and home, a clearing away of chicken yards, cow barns, pigeon-crested cupolas, weed lots and coulees, the dim and secret adult-free rendezvous of boys. An intricate metal "jungle gym" is a common backyard sight, the sack swing uncommon. There are wide expanses of clear windows designed to let in the parlor light, fewer ornamental windows of colored glass designed to keep it out. Attic and screen porch are slowly vanishing and lovely shades of pastel are painted upon new houses, tints that once would have embarrassed farmer and merchant alike.

3. Sounds have changed; I heard not once the clopping of a horse's hoof, nor the mourn of a coyote. I heard instead the shriek of brakes, the heavy throbbing of the once-a-day Braniff airliner into Minot, the shattering sirens born of war, the honk of a diesel locomotive which surely cannot call to faraway places the heart of a wakeful boy like the old steam whistle in the night. You can walk down the streets of my town now and hear from open windows the intimate voices of the Washington commentators in casual converse on the great affairs of state; but you cannot hear on Sunday morning the singing in Norwegian of the Lutheran hymns; the old country seems now part of a world left long behind and the old-country accents grow fainter in the speech of my Velva neighbors.

4. The people have not changed, but the *kinds* of people have changed: there is no longer an official, certified town drunk, no longer a "Crazy John," spitting his worst epithet, "rotten chicken legs," as you hurriedly passed him by. People so sick are now sent to places of proper care. No longer is there an official town joker, like the druggist MacKnight, who would spot a customer in the front of the store, have him called to the phone, then slip to the phone behind the prescription case, and imitate the man's wife to perfection with orders to bring home more bread and sausage and Cream of Wheat. No longer anyone like the early attorney, J. L. Lee, who sent fabulous dispatches to that fabulous tabloid, the *Chicago Blade,* such as his story of the wild man captured on the prairie and chained to the wall in the drugstore basement. (This, surely, was Velva's first notoriety; inquiries came from anthropologists all over the world.)

5.   No, the "characters" are vanishing in Velva, just as they are vanishing in our cities, in business, in politics. The "well-rounded, socially integrated" personality that the progressive schoolteachers are so obsessed with is increasing rapidly, and I am not at all sure that this is good. Maybe we need more personalities with knobs and handles and rugged lumps of individuality. They may not make life more smooth; more interesting they surely make it.

6.   They eat differently in Velva now; there are frozen fruits and sea food and exotic delicacies we only read about in novels in those meat-and-potato days. They dress differently. The hard white collars of the businessmen are gone with the shiny alpaca coats. There are comfortable tweeds now, and casual blazers with a touch in their colors of California, which seems so close in time and distance.

7.   It is distance and time that have changed the most and worked the deepest changes in Velva's life. The telephone, the car, the smooth highway, radio and television are consolidating the entities of our country. The county seat of Towner now seems no closer than the state capital of Bismarck; the voices and concerns of Presidents, French premiers and Moroccan pashas are no farther away than the portable radio on Aunt Jessey's kitchen table. The national news magazines are stacked each week in Harold Anderson's drugstore beside the new soda fountain, and the excellent *Minot Daily News* smells hot from the press each afternoon.

8.   Consolidation. The nearby hamlets of Sawyer and Logan and Voltaire had their own separate banks and papers and schools in my days of dusty buggies and Model Ts marooned in the snowdrifts. Now these hamlets are dying. A bright yellow bus takes the Voltaire kids to Velva each day for high school. Velva has grown— from 800 to 1,300—because the miners from the Truax coal mine can commute to their labors each morning and the nearby farmers can live in town if they choose. Minot has tripled in size to 30,000. Once the "Magic City" was a distant and splendid Baghdad, visited on special occasions long prepared for. Now it is a twenty-five minute commuter's jump away. So P. W. Miller and Jay Louis Monicken run their businesses in Minot but live on in their old family homes in Velva. So Ray Michelson's two girls on his farm to the west drive up each morning to their jobs as maids in Minot homes. Aunt Jessey said, "Why, Saturday night I counted sixty-five cars just between here and Sawyer, all going up to the show in Minot."

9. The hills are prison battlements no longer; the prairies no heart-sinking barrier, but a passageway free as the swelling ocean, inviting you to sail home and away at your whim and your leisure. (John and Helen made an easy little jaunt of 700 miles that weekend to see their eldest daughter in Wyoming.)

10. Consolidation. Art Kumm's bank serves a big region now; its assets are $2,000,000 to $3,000,000 instead of the $200,000 or $300,000 in my father's day. Eighteen farms near Velva are under three ownerships now. They calculate in sections; "acres" is an almost forgotten term. Aunt Jessey owns a couple of farms, and she knows they are much better run. "It's no longer all take out and no put in," she said. "Folks strip farm now; they know all about fertilizers. They care for it and they'll hand on the land in good shape." The farmers gripe about their cash income, and not without reason at the moment, but they will admit that life is good compared with those days of drought and foreclosure, manure banked against the house for warmth, the hand pump frozen at 30 below and the fitful kerosene lamp on the kitchen table. Electrification has done much of this, eased back-breaking chores that made their wives old as parchment at forty, brought life and music and the sound of human voices into their parlors at night.

11. And light upon the prairie. "From the hilltop," said Aunt Jessey, "the farms look like stars at night."

12. Many politicians deplore the passing of the old family-size farm, but I am not so sure. I saw around Velva a release from what was like slavery to the tyrannical soil, release from the ignorance that darkens the soul and from the loneliness that corrodes it. In this generation my Velva friends have rejoined the general American society that their pioneering fathers left behind when they first made the barren trek in the days of the wheat rush. As I sit here in Washington writing this, I can feel their nearness. I never felt it before save in my dreams.

13. But now I must ask myself: Are they nearer to one another? And the answer is no; yet I am certain that this is good. The shrinking of time and distance has made contrast and relief available to their daily lives. They do not know one another quite so well because they are not so much obliged to. I know that democracy rests upon social discipline, which in turn rests upon personal discipline; passions checked, hard words withheld, civic tasks accepted, work well done, accountings honestly rendered. The old-fashioned small town was this discipline in its starkest, most primi-

tive form; without this discipline the small town would have blown itself apart.

14. For personal and social neuroses festered under this hard scab of conformity. There was no place to go, no place to let off steam; few dared to voice unorthodox ideas, read strange books, admire esoteric art or publicly write or speak of their dreams and their soul's longings. The world was not "too much with us," the world was too little with us and we were too much with one another.

15. The door to the world stands open now, inviting them to leave anytime they wish. It is the simple fact of the open door that makes all the difference; with its opening the stale air rushed out. So, of course, the people themselves do not have to leave, because, as the stale air went out, the fresh air came in.

16. Human nature is everywhere the same. He who is not forced to help his neighbor for his own existence will not only give him help, but his true good will as well. Minot and its hospital are now close at hand, but the people of Velva put their purses together, built their own clinic and homes for the two young doctors they persuaded to come and live among them. Velva has no organized charity, but when a farmer falls ill, his neighbors get in his crop; if a townsman has a financial catastrophe his personal friends raise a fund to help him out. When Bill's wife, Ethel, lay dying so long in the Minot hospital and nurses were not available, Helen and others took their turns driving up there just to sit with her so she would know in her gathering dark that friends were at hand.

17. It is personal freedom that makes us better persons, and they are freer in Velva now. There is no real freedom without privacy, and a resident of my home town can be a private person much more than he could before. People are able to draw at least a little apart from one another. In drawing apart, they gave their best human instincts room for expansion.

QUESTIONS

1. Where does Sevareid indicate his attitude toward his home town? What is his thesis?
2. How does the selection of detail in the whole essay support the dominating impression Sevareid creates of the town in his opening paragraph? Is any of this detail unrelated to this dominant impression?
3. What is the tone of the comment on the story of the wild man, and how is it related to the thesis?

4. How does Sevareid emphasize the causes of the change in life in Velva? Does he indicate a main cause?
5. What does Sevareid mean by the statement that concludes paragraph 13, "without this discipline the small town would have blown itself apart"?
6. Sevareid points up a series of paradoxes toward the end. What are these, and what do they contribute to the tone of the conclusion?

WRITING ASSIGNMENTS

Analyze the shifts in tone and relate these to Sevareid's thesis. Analyze also how Sevareid introduces his thesis and keeps it before the reader.

Describe the changes that have occurred in the neighborhood in which you grew up and discuss the reasons for these changes.

W. S. MERWIN
Unchopping a Tree

1.   Start with the leaves, the small twigs, and the nests that have been shaken, ripped, or broken off by the fall; these must be gathered and attached once again to their respective places. It is not arduous work, unless major limbs have been smashed or mutilated. If the fall was carefully and correctly planned, the chances of anything of the kind happening will have been reduced. Again, much depends upon the size, age, shape, and species of the tree. Still, you will be lucky if you can get through this stage without having to use machinery. Even in the best of circumstances it is a labor that will make you wish often that you had won the favor of the universe of ants, the empire of mice, or at least a local tribe of squirrels, and could enlist their labors and their talents. But no, they leave you to it. They have learned, with time. This is men's work. It goes without saying that if the tree was hollow in whole or in part, and contained old nests of bird or mammal or insect, or hoards of nuts or such structures as wasps or bees build for their

survival, the contents will have to be repaired where necessary, and reassembled, insofar as possible, in their original order, including the shells of nuts already opened. With spiders' webs you must simply do the best you can. We do not have the spider's weaving equipment, nor any substitute for the leaf's living bond with its point of attachment and nourishment. It is even harder to simulate the latter when the leaves have once become dry—as they are bound to do, for this is not the labor of a moment. Also it hardly needs saying that this is the time for repairing any neighboring trees or bushes or other growth that may have been damaged by the fall. The same rules apply. Where neighboring trees were of the same species it is difficult not to waste time conveying a detached leaf back to the wrong tree. Practice, practice. Put your hope in that.

2.   Now the tackle must be put into place or the scaffolding, depending on the surroundings and the dimensions of the tree. It is ticklish work. Almost always it involves, in itself, further damage to the area, which will have to be corrected later. But as you've heard, it can't be helped. And care now is likely to save you considerable trouble later. Be careful to grind nothing into the ground.

3.   At last the time comes for the erecting of the trunk. By now it will scarcely be necessary to remind you of the delicacy of this huge skeleton. Every motion of the tackle, every slight upward heave of the trunk, the branches, their elaborately reassembled panoply of leaves (now dead) will draw from you an involuntary gasp. You will watch for a leaf or a twig to be snapped off yet again. You will listen for the nuts to shift in the hollow limb and you will hear whether they are indeed falling into place or are spilling in disorder—in which case, or in the event of anything else of the kind—operations will have to cease, of course, while you correct the matter. The raising itself is no small enterprise, from the moment when the chains tighten around the old bandages until the bole hangs vertical above the stump, splinter above splinter. Now the final straightening of the splinters themselves can take place (the preliminary work is best done while the wood is still green and soft, but at times when the splinters are not badly twisted most of the straightening is left until now, when the torn ends are face to face with each other). When the splinters are perfectly complementary the appropriate fixative is applied. Again we have no duplicate of the original substance. Ours is extremely strong, but it is rigid. It is limited to surfaces, and there is no play

in it. However the core is not the part of the trunk that conducted life from the roots up into the branches and back again. It was relatively inert. The fixative for this part is not the same as the one for the outer layers and the bark, and if either of these is involved in the splintered section they must receive applications of the appropriate adhesives. Apart from being incorrect and probably ineffective, the core fixative would leave a scar on the bark.

4.   When all is ready the splintered trunk is lowered onto the splinters of the stump. This, one might say, is only the skeleton of the resurrection. Now the chips must be gathered, and the sawdust, and returned to their former positions. The fixative for the wood layers will be applied to chips and sawdust consisting only of wood. Chips and sawdust consisting of several substances will receive applications of the correct adhesives. It is as well, where possible, to shelter the materials from the elements while working. Weathering makes it harder to identify the smaller fragments. Bark sawdust in particular the earth lays claim to very quickly. You must find your own ways of coping with this problem. There is a certain beauty, you will notice at moments, in the pattern of the chips as they are fitted back into place. You will wonder to what extent it should be described as natural, to what extent man-made. It will lead you on to speculations about the parentage of beauty itself, to which you will return.

5.   The adhesive for the chips is translucent, and not so rigid as that for the splinters. That for the bark and its subcutaneous layers is transparent and runs into the fibers on either side, partially dissolving them into each other. It does not set the sap flowing again but it does pay a kind of tribute to the preoccupations of the ancient thoroughfares. You could not roll an egg over the joints but some of the mine-shafts would still be passable, no doubt. For the first exploring insect who raises its head in the tight echoless passages. The day comes when it is all restored, even to the moss (now dead) over the wound. You will sleep badly, thinking of the removal of the scaffolding that must begin the next morning. How you will hope for sun and a still day!

6.   The removal of the scaffolding or tackle is not so dangerous, perhaps, to the surroundings, as its installation, but it presents problems. It should be taken from the spot piece by piece as it is detached, and stored at a distance. You have come to accept it there, around the tree. The sky begins to look naked as the chains and struts one by one vacate their positions. Finally the moment

arrives when the last sustaining piece is removed and the tree stands again on its own. It is as though its weight for a moment stood on your heart. You listen for a thud of settlement, a warning creak deep in the intricate joinery. You cannot believe it will hold. How like something dreamed it is, standing there all by itself. How long will it stand there now? The first breeze that touches its dead leaves all seems to flow into your mouth. You are afraid the motion of the clouds will be enough to push it over. What more can you do? What more can you do?

7.   But there is nothing more you can do.

8.   Others are waiting.

9.   Everything is going to have to be put back.

QUESTIONS

1. What are the chief indications of the writer's purpose in this essay? Does he state that purpose directly?

2. Examine the following statement from paragraph 4 carefully: "You will wonder to what extent it should be described as natural, to what extent man-made. It will lead you on to speculations about the parentage of beauty itself, to which you will return." What is the tone of the statement—that is, what seems to be the writer's attitude toward his reader as well as toward the act of unchopping a tree? Is an attitude *implied* in the whole essay that no single statement expresses? Could you accept such an implication as embodying the thesis?

3. The writer has chosen a strategy to deal with his idea—that is, he approaches his reader in a particular way to achieve a particular effect. What does he want his reader to think and feel at the end of the essay, and what is his strategy in realizing these aims?

4. The essay ends with three single-sentence paragraphs. To what effect? What is Merwin saying?

WRITING ASSIGNMENT

Write an essay on a similar topic, for example, undoing an insult. Be consistent in conveying a tone and in building to your conclusion.

E. B. WHITE
About Myself

1. I am a man of medium height. I keep my records in a Weis Folder Re-order Number 8003. The unpaid balance of my estimated tax for the year 1945 is item 3 less the sum of items 4 and 5. My eyes are gray. My Selective Service order number is 10789. The serial number is T1654. I am in Class IV-A, and have been variously in Class 3-A, Class I-A(H), and Class 4-H. My social security number is 067-01-9841. I am married to U.S. Woman Number 067-01-9807. Her eyes are gray. This is not a joint declaration, nor is it made by an agent; therefore it need be signed only by me—and, as I said, I am a man of medium height.

2. I am the holder of a quit-claim deed recorded in Book 682, Page 501, in the county where I live. I hold Fire Insurance Policy Number 424747, continuing until the 23 day of October in the year nineteen hundred forty-five, at noon, and it is important that the written portions of all policies covering the same property read exactly alike. My cervical spine shows relatively good alignment with evidence of proliferative changes about the bodies consistent with early arthritis. (Essential clinical data: pain in neck radiating to mastoids and occipito-temporal region, not constant, moderately severe; patient in good general health and working.) My operator's licence is Number 16200. It expired December 31, 1943, more than a year ago, but I am still carrying it and it appears to be serving the purpose. I shall renew it when I get time. I have made, published, and declared my last will and testament, and it thereby revokes all other wills and codicils at any time heretofore made by me. I hold Basic A Mileage Ration 108950, O.P.A. Form R-525-C. The number of my car is 18-388. Tickets A-14 are valid through March 21st.

3. I was born in District Number 5903, New York State. My birth is registered in Volume 3/58 of the Department of Health. My father was a man of medium height. His telephone number was 484. My mother was a housewife. Her eyes were blue. Neither parent had a social security number and neither was secure socially. They drove to the depot behind an unnumbered horse.

4. I hold Individual Certificate Number 4320-209 with the Equitable Life Assurance Society, in which a corporation hereinafter called the employer has contracted to insure my life for the sum of two thousand dollars. My left front tire is Number 48KE8846, my right front tire is Number 63T6895. My rear tires are, from left to right, Number 6N4M5384 and Number A26E5806D. I brush my hair with Whiting-Adams Brush Number 010 and comb my hair with Pro-Phy-Lac-Tic Comb Number 1201. My shaving brush is sterilized. I take Pill Number 43934 after each meal and I can get more of them by calling ELdorado 5-6770. I spray my nose with De Vilbiss Atomizer Number 14. Sometimes I stop the pain with Squibb Pill, Control Number 3K49979 (aspirin). My wife (Number 067-01-9807) takes Pill Number 49345.

5. I hold War Ration Book 40289EW, from which have been torn Airplane Stamps Numbers 1, 2, and 3. I also hold Book 159378CD, from which have been torn Spare Number 2, Spare Number 37, and certain other coupons. My wife holds Book 40288EW and Book 159374CD. In accepting them, she recognized that they remained the property of the United States Government.

6. I have a black dog with cheeks of tan. Her number is 11032. It is an old number. I shall renew it when I get time. The analysis of her prepared food is guaranteed and is Case Number 1312. The ingredients are: Cereal Flaked feeds (from Corn, Rice, Bran, and Wheat), Meat Meal, Fish Liver and Glandular Meal, Soybean Oil Meal, Wheat Bran, Corn Germ Meal, 5% Kel-Centrate [containing Dried Skim Milk, Dehydrated Cheese, Vitamin B_1 (Thiamin), Flavin Concentrate, Carotene, Yeast, Vitamin A and D Feeding Oil (containing 3,000 U.S.P. units Vitamin A and 400 U.S.P. units Vitamin D per gram), Diastase (Enzyme), Wheat Germ Meal, Rice Polish Extract], 1½% Calcium Carbonate, .00037% Potassium Iodide, and ¼% Salt. She prefers offal.

7. When I finish what I am now writing it will be late in the day. It will be about half past five. I will then take up Purchase Order Number 245-9077-B-Final, which I received this morning from the Office of War Information and which covers the use of certain material they want to translate into a foreign language. Attached to the order are Standard Form Number 1034 (white) and three copies of Standard Form Number 1034a (yellow), also "Instructions for Preparation of Voucher by Vendor and Example of Prepared Voucher." The Appropriation Symbol of the Purchase Order is 1153700.001-501. The requisition number is B-827. The allotment

is X5-207.1-R2-11. Voucher shall be prepared in ink, indelible pencil, or typewriter. For a while I will be vendor preparing voucher.
Later on, when my head gets bad and the pain radiates, I will be
voucher preparing vendor. I see that there is a list of twenty-one
instructions which I will be following. Number One on the list is:
"Name of payor agency as shown in the block 'appropriation symbol and title' in the upper left-hand corner of the Purchase Order."
Number Five on the list is: "Vendor's personal account or invoice
number," but whether that means Order Number 245-9077-B-
Final, or Requisition B-827, or Allotment X5-207.1-R2-11, or Appropriation Symbol 1153700.001-501, I do not know, nor will I
know later on in the evening after several hours of meditation, nor
will I be able to find out by consulting Woman 067-01-9807, who
is no better at filling out forms than I am, nor after taking Pill
Number 43934, which tends merely to make me drowsy.
8.   I owe a letter to Corporal 32413654, Hq and Hq Sq., VII AAF
S.C., APO 953, c/o PM San Francisco, Calif., thanking him for the
necktie he sent me at Christmas. In 1918 I was a private in the
Army. My number was 4,345,016. I was a boy of medium height. I
had light hair. I had no absences from duty under G.O. 31, 1912,
or G.O. 45, 1914. The number of that war was Number One.

QUESTIONS

1. E. B. White develops his thesis *implicitly.* Before we try to state the
   thesis, we shall have to consider the details and the nature of the
   presentation. Let us begin with paragraph 2. Why does White state
   "My cervical spine shows relatively good alignment with evidence
   of proliferative changes about the bodies consistent with early arthritis" instead of "I have the symptoms of arthritis"? Why does he
   provide the number of his fire insurance policy and paraphrase its
   language? Why in paragraph 3 does he say that neither of his
   parents was "secure socially" instead of "had much money"? And
   why does he tell us the number of the district in which he was
   born? On what aspect of his life does this detail focus?
2. How does the detail of paragraphs 2 and 3 resemble that of paragraph 1? What do the numbers and classifications, even the
   reorder number of his Weis folder, tell us about him? What do they
   not tell us? In short, what impression of him do they create?
3. Up to paragraph 6 White has been talking about himself. In paragraph 6, however, he lists the ingredients of dogfood. Why does
   he? What is the implication of "She prefers offal"?

4. In the last paragraph why does White give the full address of the corporal and then indicate that he is writing to thank him for the necktie?
5. Why in the concluding paragraph does he repeat the fact that he "was a boy of medium height"? Why does he conclude the essay as he does? How serious is the tone of the last sentence? Is the tone of the essay as a whole serious? Is it humorous in any way?
6. State the thesis explicitly and be ready to discuss how the precise, exhaustive detail develops it.
7. White does not state his thesis directly. What is the value of being indirect, given his thesis?
8. How else might White have presented his thesis? To what kind of audience is he writing? To state the question in another way, what can you tell about the audience from how he approaches it?

WRITING ASSIGNMENT

Write a paragraph developing an impression of yourself through details about your life. Organize it to reveal a series of characteristics or one dominant characteristic. Do not comment on these details. In a second paragraph develop the same impression by stating the characteristic(s) and illustrating them. In the first paragraph, your thesis should be implicit in the details; in the second, it should be explicit.

ART BUCHWALD

Clean Your Room

You don't really feel the generation gap in this country until a son or daughter comes home from college for Christmas. Then it strikes you how out of it you really are.

This dialogue probably took place all over America last Christmas week:

"Nancy, you've been home from school for three days now. Why don't you clean up your room?"

"We don't have to clean up our rooms at college, Mother."

"That's very nice, Nancy, and I'm happy you're going to such

CLEAN YOUR ROOM: In *I Never Danced at the White House* by Art Buchwald. Reprinted by permission of G. P. Putnam's Sons. Copyright © 1971, 1972, 1973 by Art Buchwald.

a freewheeling institution. But while you're in the house, your father and I would like you to clean up your room."

"What difference does it make? It's *my* room."

"I know, dear, and it really doesn't mean that much to me. But your father has a great fear of the plague. He said this morning if it is going to start anywhere in this country, it's going to start in your room."

"Mother, you people aren't interested in anything that's relevant. Do you realize how the major corporations are polluting our environment?"

"Your father and I are very worried about it. But right now we're more concerned with the pollution in your bedroom. You haven't made your bed since you came home."

"I never make it up at the dorm."

"Of course you don't, and I'm sure the time you save goes toward your education. But we still have these old-fashioned ideas about making beds in the morning, and we can't shake them. Since you're home for such a short time, why don't you do it to humor us?"

"For heaven's sake, Mother, I'm grown up now. Why do you have to treat me like a child?"

"We're not treating you like a child. But it's very hard for us to realize you're an adult when you throw all your clothes on the floor."

"I haven't thrown all my clothes on the floor. Those are just the clothes I wore yesterday."

"Forgive me. I exaggerated. Well, how about the dirty dishes and empty soft-drink cans on your desk? Are you collecting them for a science project?"

"Mother, you don't understand us. You people were brought up to have clean rooms. But our generation doesn't care about things like that. It's what you have in your head that counts."

"No one respects education more than your father and I do, particularly at the prices they're charging. But we can't see how living in squalor can improve your mind."

"That's because of your priorities. You would rather have me make up my bed and pick up my clothes than become a free spirit who thinks for myself."

"We're not trying to stifle your free spirit. It's just that our Blue Cross has run out, and we have no protection in case anybody in the family catches typhoid."

"All right, I'll clean up my room if it means that much to you. But I want you to know you've ruined my vacation."

"It was a calculated risk I had to take. Oh, by the way, I know this is a terrible thing to ask of you, but would you mind helping me wash the dinner dishes?"

"Wash dishes? Nobody washes dishes at school."

"Your father and I were afraid of that."

QUESTIONS

1. Do you think Buchwald is making some real point, or is his purpose merely to amuse the reader?
2. Is he poking fun at both Nancy and her parents—or at one of them only?
3. What is gained by presenting the parents and daughter through dialogue rather than through a summary of what happened?

WRITING ASSIGNMENT

Write a dialogue or an essay on a humorous situation involving teenagers and parents that reveals something about both of them—perhaps an attitude typical of these groups. Let the reader discover this truth through your details; don't state the truth directly.

MAIN AND SUBORDINATE IDEAS

IRWIN EDMAN

Sincerity as a Fine Art

1. I remember often during my early adolescence listening to older people making conversation. I vowed I would never willingly be a conspirator at such transparent hypocrisies. When *I* went out

SINCERITY AS A FINE ART: In *Under Whatever Sky* by Irwin Edman. Copyright 1951 by Irwin Edman. Reprinted by permission of The Viking Press, Inc.

to dinner, I found myself saying, I should speak only when I felt like it, and I should say only what was on my mind. I used to listen while my elders pretended to have a fascinated interest in visitors with whom I knew they had only the most remote concern, and hear them discuss with affected animation matters that I knew bored them to pain. I remember having had it explained to me that this was the least that good manners demanded. It was at this moment that I came to the conclusion that good manners and dubious morals had much in common.

2.   In these matters, I have become subdued to the general color of civilized society. It has long ago been brought home to me that a guest has obligations in addition to that of eating the food provided by his host. It is fair enough that one should, if not sing, at least converse for one's supper. I have even come to believe that my elders of long ago were more interested in their visitors than I had supposed. I have lighted upon the fact that questions asked out of politeness may elicit answers that are fascinating on their own. An enchanting story may be the unearned increment of a conventional inquiry.

3.   And yet I have not ceased to be troubled at the momentum with which on a social occasion one is embarked on a brief career of insincerity. I have found myself expressing opinions on Russia or on psychiatry that I had not known I possessed. I have sometimes, out of sheer inability to get out of it, maintained a position on old-age security, or on old age itself, that, save for some impulsive remark I had let fall, I should not have considered it a point of honor to defend as my considered philosophy on the subject. On shamefully numerous occasions, I have repeated an anecdote by which I was myself bored to death. I have talked with dowagers about literature, art, and education, at moments when all three of these lofty themes seemed to me insufferably tedious and stuffy.

4.   I have come to admire those sturdy individualists who say—as I once planned to say—only whatever comes into their minds, and speak only when they are spoken to, and perhaps not even then. But I must admit I find them difficult socially, these high-minded boors who can be pricked into only the most minimal of replies, these dedicated roughnecks who find a savage pleasure in telling you without compromise what they think of everything, including your loyalties and your enthusiasms—and possibly yourself.

5.   There must be some way of acting both agreeably and sincerely. It is a fine art, practiced, one is told, by a few witty

eighteenth-century courtiers. But wits today are rather celebrated for their malignity. It is a difficult alternative, that between truth and charm, and I confess that I am tempted to seek the easier and more genial path. If one plumped for sincerity, one would get to be known simply as a bear, a bear who would soon be walking alone, a boorish bear who at any rate would seldom be invited out to dinner. As Santayana remarks somewhere, "For a man of sluggish mind and bad manners, there is decidedly no place like home."

DISCUSSION: MAIN AND SUBORDINATE IDEAS

One way to distinguish the main idea or thesis of the essay from subordinate ideas and details that develop it or introduce related considerations is to repeat or restate it at key points. As in the paragraph, transitions may be used to show the relative weight of ideas. Essays and paragraphs in which all ideas seem equal in importance are difficult to read.

Outlining is one way to think out the logical relationship of ideas in the essay. Here is a partial sentence outline of Edman:

I. In my youth I was disturbed by the hypocrisy of adults.
   A. I vowed that I would be different when I grew up.
      1. I would speak only when I wanted to.
      2. I would speak only the truth.
   B. I observed my parents with their guests.
      1. They pretended to be interested in boring conversations.
      2. They explained that good manners required that they seem interested.
   C. I concluded that good manners and dubious morals had much in common.
II. As an adult I see the matter somewhat differently.
   A. I misunderstood several things.
      1. A guest has an obligation to his host.
      2. My parents were interested in their guests.
      3. Polite questions may produce fascinating answers.

Notice that the first heading (I) is a generalization stated in the first two sentences of the first paragraph. A, B, and C under it are its logical breakdown—its detail.

A topic outline consists of short, parallel phrases—not complete sentences:

    I. My youthful dislike of adult hypocrisy
       A. My vow to be different when I grew up
          1. Speaking only when I wanted to
          2. Speaking only the truth
       B. Observing my parents with their guests
          1. Their pretense in interest at boring conversations
          2. Their explanation that good manners require a show of interest

If you use it properly, the outline is a preliminary plan only, and you should revise it as new ideas and details occur to you as you write.

QUESTIONS

1. Finish the sentence outline of Edman's essay. Notice that the first division corresponds to the first paragraph. The second division, however, may include more than only the second paragraph: it may cover the remainder of the essay. There is, in other words, no necessary correspondence between the number of paragraphs in the essay and the number of divisions in the outline.
2. Finish the topic outline, using your completion of the sentence outline as the basis.
3. To what extent does Edman depend on transitions to show which are the main and subordinate ideas? What is his thesis?
4. Does Edman offer a solution to the problem he presents in paragraphs 1–4? Is he suggesting, for example, that he found a middle course between two extremes?

WRITING ASSIGNMENT

Write a sentence or topic outline for one of the following. Then write an essay from your outline:
    a. The art of keeping friends
    b. On not giving advice
    c. The art of persuading children
    d. On getting along with neighbors
    e. On getting along with a roommate
    f. On living away from home

MARGARET MEAD AND RHODA METRAUX

The Gift of Autonomy

1. Every gift we give carries with it our idea of what a present is. Perhaps it expresses our personality; perhaps, on the contrary, it is what we believe the recipient really wants, a choice based on careful listening for the slightest hint of what he longs for or needs or should have, even though he may not realize it.

2. Gifts from parents to children always carry the most meaningful messages. The way parents think about presents goes one step beyond the objects themselves—the ties, dolls, sleds, record players, kerchiefs, bicycles and model airplanes that wait by the Christmas tree. The gifts are, in effect, one way of telling boys and girls, "We love you even though you have been a bad boy all month" or, "We love having a daughter" or, "We treat all our children alike" or, "It is all right for girls to have some toys made for boys" or, "This alarm clock will help you get started in the morning all by yourself." Throughout all the centuries since the invention of a Santa Claus figure who represented a special recognition of children's behavior, good and bad, presents have given parents a way of telling children about their love and hopes and expectations for them.

3. When I was a child, my parents used to give me a pair of books each Christmas. One was "light," easy reading; the other was "heavy," a book I had to think about if I was to enjoy it. This combination carried with it the message that there are different kinds of pleasure to be gained through reading and that I should discover each kind for myself.

4. If we think about all the presents we have given our children over the years, we will see how they fit into the hopes we have for each child. I do not mean this in the simple sense that we delight in a little girl's femininity, and so give her dolls, or that we implement a boy's masculinity by giving him model planes and boxing gloves. We do, of course, speak to our children in this simplest form of symbolism. And we do, of course, personalize what we say

when we give our outdoors son a fishing rod and his experiment-minded brother a microscope.

5.   However, our giving also carries more subtle and complex messages. For example, we can ask ourselves: "What am I saying to my children about growing up to be independent, autonomous people?" An abstract question of this kind can be posed in relation to a whole range of presents for children of both sexes and of different ages. Where the choice to be made is between a simple toy engine that the child himself can wind up and a more complicated one that I shall have to wind up for him, which one do I give him? Choosing a doll for a little girl, do I buy her a perishable costume doll with one beautiful dress, a washable doll with a wardrobe or a doll for which she will make dresses out of the materials I also give her? The costume doll can perhaps be dressed and undressed, but that is all. A bath would be ruinous. A sturdy doll with a ready-made wardrobe places choice in the child's own hands. She herself can dress and undress it, bathe it safely and decide whether her "little girl" will wear pink or blue, plaid or plain. Giving my child materials out of which to fashion doll dresses is a lovely idea, and may perhaps encourage her to learn how to sew. But choice and autonomy both are reduced because now I must help her at every step.

6.   We can ask questions of this kind also about the presents of money that are given our children by grandparents and godparents, aunts and uncles and family friends. What do we tell our children about the bright silver dollar tucked into the toe of a Christmas stocking or the grown-up-looking check that is made out in the child's own name? Is the money meant to be used now for some specific purpose—for the charm bracelet a little girl has admired or the radio a boy wants for his own room? Or is it an inducement, perhaps, to begin saving for the car a teen-ager must wait five years to own? Is the child told, directly or indirectly: "This is your money to do with as you like"? Or is the child asked: "Would you rather spend it or put in in the bank?"

7.   By defining the alternatives so sharply, we are, in effect, robbing the child of choice. In fact, when you tell him that the money is his and then give directions, hint at alternatives or reproach him for spending it in one way instead of another, the gift carries a very definite message: "I don't really trust your choices. I don't really want you to choose." If, on the other hand, the message is simple and direct ("This is your money, yours, to dispose of as you like"),

then the child may even solicit your advice. But there is no real turning back once you have said, "This is your money."

8.   Over the years, there are always new ways of reinforcing or detracting from our children's growing sense of independence. For example, if you give a boy a box of stationery imprinted with his name and a supply of postage stamps, you are showing him that you expect him to write, address and mail his own letters. This means, of course, that you may never see the letters he writes, or you may become a consultant on appropriate terms of address or the correct abbreviations of names of states. At this point you can give him an almanac in which he himself can look up the answers to his questions—or you can keep the almanac on your own desk and become the mediator between his questions and the information he needs.

9.   Giving a girl a diary with a key is a way in which a mother can tell her daughter (boys, on the whole, do not keep diaries) that she respects her child's growing sense of identity and independence. Giving a boy a desk is one way of fostering his sense of personal privacy; but if we continually tidy it up or complain about its untidiness, as we see it, the original message miscarries.

10.   In many families the climax, and in some the crisis, of their individual pattern of giving comes as the children approach college, when their parents prepare to give them the most expensive "gift" of all—a college education. Of course, parents are not, as a rule, literally "giving" their children an education. What they are giving them is the opportunity to become educated.

11.   Many parents today meet the responsibility of supporting their children through the college years, wholly or in part, by taking out insurance policies for this special purpose. Usually such policies, whatever their specific form, are payable to the parents. Then the choice of a college and the course of study remains firmly in the parents' hands. Americans believe very strongly that he who pays the piper calls the tune.

12.   This is the *customary* way of doing things. It carries with it the message that our children, although approaching adulthood, are still children in our eyes. But this need not be. The money instead can be set up as a fund available to the boy or girl. Its purpose can be specified: This is not money for just anything. It is money for higher education, intended to give you freedom and choice within this area of your life.

13.   For children who have grown up with an ever-enlarging sense

of their own autonomy and independence, intelligent handling of the opportunity for further education will come naturally and easily. They are free, if they like, to postpone going to college for a year. Or they can drop out for a semester or a year without fearing that the tuition money will have vanished when they want to go back. A girl can marry before she goes to college, or while she is still a student, knowing that the choice of when and where she will continue her education remains open to her. Next year or ten years from now the money will be there, waiting, ready for her when she wants and needs it.

14. Like the small presents of early childhood that carry the message "You need my help," the educational insurance policy in the parents' name places responsibility in the parents' hands. In many cases parents are not even required to spend the money on the education of the child in whose interest the policy was acquired. But when money is placed in the child's own name, a trust for a special purpose, the parents are saying: "This is what I hope to give you—the right of choice. I respect your right to choose. My gift is intended to underwrite your freedom to be a person. Long ago I gave you stamps so you could mail your own letters. I gave you an allowance so you could move more freely in your own world. Now, as then, I want you to be an autonomous, self-starting person, someone who enjoys interdependence with other people because instead of fighting for your independence, you have grown into it."

15. All our giving carries with it messages about ourselves, our feelings about those to whom we give, how we see them as people and how we phrase the ties of relationship. Christmas giving, in which love and hope and trust play such an intrinsic part, can be an annual way of telling our children that we think of each of them as a person, as we also hope they will come to think of us.

QUESTIONS

1. If the statement in paragraph 11—"Americans believe very strongly that he who pays the piper calls the tune"—were the thesis of the essay, how might the essay have been organized to develop it? What parts of the present essay would you omit?
2. Where does the thesis first appear, and how is it restated later in the essay?
3. In what order are the various problems of giving presents discussed in paragraphs 4–10?

4. Why do the authors devote a considerable part of the essay to the educational insurance policy?
5. Is the purpose of the essay to analyze the practice of gift giving, or to give advice to parents and others on this matter? Do the authors address their readers as colleagues, or clients seeking advice, or merely as general readers?

WRITING ASSIGNMENTS

Analyze the gifts you gave members of your family last Christmas or Chanukah, and discuss the reasons for your choices. Give particular attention to your expectations in choosing the gift for each person.

Discuss the ways high school teachers can encourage or discourage students from doing their best work. Distinguish the problems that arise in two different subjects like English and mathematics.

BEGINNING AND ENDING

WALT KELLY
Commerce

1.   Private enterprise roared unregulated during the twenties and among the rugged individualists of those times were entrepreneurs in knee pants who occupied themselves with painstaking projects which were either mildly successful, but operated at a loss, or failures and operated at a loss.
2.   Most of us were for the strenuous life and believed in starting from scratch, preferably out of doors, when it came to running a business. I put this feeling to good use one time when my mother offered to pay me a penny for every ten flies swatted around the house. She didn't specify where; they could be smacked in the kitchen, parlor, or bedroom. So I went off hunting through the hall, upstairs, downstairs, and managed to snag half a dozen

scrawny specimens. As a matter of fact I remember that there was one big one which came apart in two sections when he was smashed against a bookcase. Naturally, I counted him as two. My mother was not the sort of woman to examine the carcass of an insect with the eye of authority.

3.   However, that was the bag. I waited in vain for a welcome buzz—but the other four needed to fill out the quota for the penny were not showing in the preserve. With rare presence of mind, I went down into the cellar and opened the outside cellar doors and presently the basement was aswarm with horseflies as big as robins which droned and zoomed against the ceiling and banged into the light bulb. It wasn't long before I had seventeen dead and a couple of wounded which eluded the *coup de grâce* by hiding behind the furnace. I took the seventeen, plus the original six, throwing in for good measure a moth that had perished of natural causes and two spiders that had growled at me, and went upstairs.

4.   Mother may not have been an expert on insects, but she was an expert on justice and fair play, and besides she had good ears. She had heard the entire campaign from cellar door opening to close and she told me that I was cheating. Forthwith she threw out the seventeen horseflies over my protests—I claimed that a few might have been resident in the cellar before I lured in the others. This she would not allow; but she accepted as *bona fide* the moth, to my surprise, and the spiders. Truthfully, I don't think she looked at the spiders too closely, not being an arachnid fan, and she may have considered they were flies of a sort. At any rate, even with the admission of the three last, I was still one short of a penny's worth.

5.   "Where do most of the houseflies get in at anyway?" I asked. Mother replied that most of them came in through the back door. I wondered out loud why none of them came in the front and Mother said, "Oh, they do, but only on Sunday!" This was a pretty good joke for her and, pleased with herself, she beat the air around her head with a Japanese fan and said, "My land! The heat."

6.   It occurred to me then that an ounce of prevention was worth a pound of cure and the place to get the flies was at the point of entry. So I stationed myself outside the screen door on the porch, feeling that everything would work out well now that I was operating in the familiar out-of-doors. Whenever a fly landed on the screen door I'd smack him with the virtuous feeling of having defended the house from imminent invasion. With this method, I

soon amassed about fifty flies, one of which was indeed retrieved inside the house when I slammed it through a hole in the mesh.

7.   Naturally, my mother would not admit that the fifty were legitimate, but did relent enough to accept the single that had been driven through the screen. In vain I pleaded that the exterior defense of the home was just as important as an inside mop-up job. Mother gave me a penny for what she considered the morning's work and went back to pounding underwear against a washboard.

8.   Moodily I set about catching two grasshoppers in the back yard and hitching them to a matchbox with thread. The grasshoppers were pretty unruly, but every once in a while they would pull together and the team and cart would go flying through the air in a highly satisfactory fashion. Chance, a black dog who was living with us at the time, thought this was all pretty exciting and barked wildly enough to scare the chickens, which set up a clatter of their own. Mother came to the door to discover the cause of the uproar. I pointed out the charms of having trained grasshoppers and she was enchanted for about three minutes while we watched the matchbox go soaring over the grass. Then she decided that the enterprise was too cruel and ordered me to cut the insects loose. This I did with a heavy heart, having envisioned myself as ringmaster in a grasshopper circus, and world famous.

9.   Mother went into the house and came out with another penny. She gave it to me with instructions to spend it wisely, praised me for being clever, and told me never to hurt anybody smaller than myself. I wondered vaguely about my chances for hurting anybody bigger and went off to inspect Mr. Rowinsky's licorice. It had been a good business day.

DISCUSSION: BEGINNING AND ENDING

Unless writers have no interest in anyone except themselves, they will want to capture their readers' attention and hold it. Writers will lose their readers if they describe in too much detail how they intend to proceed. Usually they will indicate a point of view and perhaps also the ways their subject is to be developed. There may be excellent reasons for beginning an essay with a statement of the thesis, as Hamilton and Madison do in certain of the Federalist papers, but in most instances the thesis needs an introduction: writers will build to their thesis by showing why the subject is worth discussing and why the thesis is worth the reader's attention. The following opening paragraphs effectively accomplish this purpose:

The administration of criminal justice and the extent of individual moral responsibility are among the crucial problems of a civilized society. They are indissolubly linked, and together they involve our deepest personal emotions. We often find it hard to forgive ourselves for our own moral failures. All of us, at some time or other, have faced the painful dilemma of when to punish and when to forgive those we love—our children, our friends. How much harder it is, then, to deal with the stranger who transgresses.—David L. Bazelon, "The Awesome Decision"

The aim of this book is to delineate two types of clever schoolboy: the converger and the diverger. The earlier chapters offer a fairly detailed description of the intellectual abilities, attitudes and personalities of a few hundred such boys. In the later chapters, this description is then used as the basis for a more speculative discussion—of the nature of intelligence and originality and of the ways in which intellectual and personal qualities interact. Although the first half of the book rests heavily on the results of psychological tests, and the last two chapters involve psychoanalytic theory, I have done my best to be intelligible, and, wherever possible, interesting to everyone interested in clever schoolboys: parents, schoolteachers, dons, psychologists, administrators, clever schoolboys.—Liam Hudson, *Contrary Imaginations*

In the first of these opening paragraphs, readers are eased into the subject: their interest is aroused by the personal consideration—their attitude toward themselves, their children, their friends. The author assumes that this interest needs to be aroused. In the second opening paragraph, interest is challenged: no easing into the subject here, for the opening sentence announces both the subject of the book and a key distinction. The bonus is the wit of the author—and the promise of more.

An effective ending will not let the discussion drop; the reader should not have a sense of loose ends, of lines of thought left uncompleted. In the formal essay, the ending may be used for a restatement of the thesis or perhaps a full statement of it—if the writer has chosen to build to it. One of the most effective conclusions is the reference back to ideas that opened the essay.

QUESTIONS

1. How does Kelly state his subject in his opening paragraph and establish a tone?

2. Does he maintain the same tone throughout, or does the tone change?
3. What qualities of childhood is Kelly illustrating? Are these qualities stated directly? Does Kelly state a thesis?
4. How does he conclude the discussion? What is the tone of the final sentence?

WRITING ASSIGNMENT

Write an essay on the same topic—private enterprise as you practiced it in childhood. State your subject and establish a dominant tone in your opening paragraph. In your concluding paragraph draw a conclusion about yourself or about childhood. Remember that you are writing to people who know little or nothing about you or your childhood experiences.

VERONICA GENG

Quote Commitment Unquote

> An awful lot of worrying was done in the Fifties about whether people were able To Love or not. . . . all that talk about "commitment" and "permanent relationships" . . .
>
> —Philip Roth, "Marriage à la Mode" *American Review #18*

1.   Roth's way with the capital letter and the quotation mark suggests that he writes with an amused backward glance, as if the terms *able to love, commitment,* and *permanent relationships* were artifacts as remote as the series of Hogarth paintings from which he has drawn his story's title. This cool posture is a little démodé. The language Roth calls Fifties-feminese is back in style—for both sexes—and sneer at your own risk.
2.   The term *commitment* is the operative one, for it is widely supposed to be the key to the other two: *Love without commitment is just fooling around; love with commitment is (or inexorably*

leads to) a permanent relationship. A lot of people find it hard to think in any other way about love or permanent relationships. A mystique of committedness has taken hold and grabs everybody by the lapels to inform them of its imperatives.

3.   I am irritated by the number of times per day this word breathes on me. I have begun to shrink from it, to view it with suspicion, as though it were propaganda for some unnamed special interest. I am wondering if people know what they mean by it, or if they are dupes.

4.   "I believe in being able to commit myself to another person." What does that mean? A contract? Why not say so? My friend the speaker allows that *commitment* and *contract* have in common certain implications of the long haul and of voluntary giving over— "but, uh, it's more than that." It would have to be more than that to have the power it does, but an explanation of the more is hard to elicit. As far as I can tell, my friend's primary attachment to *commitment* is that it has become a value-loaded word and *contract* hasn't. A contract is something one either does or does not enter into, as suits one's purpose; as yet, no halo radiates from the brow of the person "able" to sign papers for auto insurance payments. But ah, *commitment:* it carries with it the virtue of committedness, the so-called ability to commit oneself. In fact, like other virtues on which people preen themselves, committedness, despite its literal meaning, is often found to exist without an object. ("I'm a very committed person.")

5.   "Sorry, but I don't want any heavy commitments right now"—a familiar male (and maybe increasingly female) kiss-off. The kissed-off is thrown into a hell of excruciating vagueness: what exactly is it that is not wanted? The burdens feared by Paul, the Prince Charming figure in Donald Barthelme's *Snow White* ("her responsibilities of various sorts . . . teeth . . . piano lessons. . . .")? Then why not break up with clarity? ("Sorry, but I don't want to have to: pay your bills/talk to you/make love to you every night/ever see you again/other.")

6.   But mystiques do not thrive on clarity. The entire point of a word like *commitment* is its maddening vagueness. One is simply supposed to have a "sense" of what it signifies. That vagueness serves to reinforce the mental and emotional laziness of those who succumb to the mystique ("Commitment—or togetherness or masculinity, etc.—is just a natural thing, it doesn't need to be taken apart and analyzed") and to discomfit those who reject it ("How

can I reject something so nebulous? What am I rejecting? Maybe they're right—maybe there's something to it").

7.   It was this sort of discomfort that sent me to my dictionaries. Commitment has been used in English since the 1400s, mostly with reference to such loveless matters as war and politics, prisons and madhouses, storage and burial ("to engage as opponents; to charge with a duty or office; to consign officially to confinement; to consign for safekeeping or disposal"). The definition nearest the sense of the commitment cant one hears around is this: "to give in trust; to put into charge or keeping." *Webster's Second New International Dictionary* points out that the word used this way "may express merely the general idea of delivering into another's charge . . . or may have the special sense of an absolute transfer to a superior power or final custody." But nowhere is it suggested that such delivery or transfer is a virtue.

8.   The Latin *committere* makes current usage seem downright deformed. None of the Latin definitions implies virtue, and some are negative ("to incur a punishment; to sin"). Most of the others do not even suggest permanence, stability, or duration, but something very nearly the opposite: "to begin; to set on foot; to venture; to risk oneself." These do not imply contracts, custodies, or eternities, but, in Noel Coward's phrase, "something a little less binding": beginnings, chances, first steps.

9.   Obviously our words acquire the meanings we need them for. Why did a word once used for venture and risk come to imply that there is virtue in handing oneself over to a future decided in advance? Perhaps because "commitment" makes life easy. It relieves you of the difficult businesses of venture and risk, autonomy and choice. It protects you from trusting or testing yourself by providing a handy external coercion to make you do right. It absolves you of responsibility for your actions—you were, after all, only following through on a "commitment." Without this prop, there would be troublesome evaluations to be made at every turn and you would be forced to reconcile conflicting feelings and beliefs (hard work ahead there), or even live with the fact of the irreconcilable. Easier to give yourself over to *another's charge,* to *a superior power,* to *custody,* for *confinement, storage,* or *disposal.*

10. A "commitment" also provides you with many convenient excuses. Your failures can be explained in comfortingly global terms. (Your love affair did not collapse because you were a liar or ate with your feet on the table but because you were "unable to com-

mit yourself.") You can use your "commitment" to justify your fears. ("Sorry, I can't take up this offer because I have another commitment.") You can use it to rationalize your promiscuities. ("I deserve some fun because of this dreary commitment I've gotten myself tied to.") You can even use it to get power over other people. ("We've committed ourselves to each other, so I have a weapon to hit you with when you don't do what I want.")

11. One of the more practical aspects of "commitment" is The Rule That Dare Not Speak Its Name. No one will admit this, but you do not actually have to abide by a "commitment" unless you feel like it. Although people who use "lack of commitment" as an excuse for passivity like to pretend that a "commitment" is as difficult to extricate oneself from as a military engagement or a mental ward, that is not true. A "commitment" applies until it no longer applies. Of course, bolting for this exit involves a massive exercise in bad faith, but many people find that a small price to pay for the advantage: taking the dread out of permanence.

12. "Commitment" is especially useful to institutionalized power, which cannot afford to trust anyone. A group of "committed" citizens is less threatening than a group of citizens who have not abdicated their ability to make judgments. The witnesses before the Senate Watergate Committee were the most "committed" individuals in recent history. "Commitments" keep your toe to the line; without them, a madman like you might do most anything—blow a whistle, change direction, take a chance.

13. Perhaps we are afraid to trust ourselves. And so we agree that "commitments" are natural and good and hand ourselves over to them like washing machines whose futures are set by the inflexible terms of a contract. Till death or the Department of Consumer Affairs do us part.

QUESTIONS

1. One job of the writer concerned with a current issue is, first, to acquaint the reader with its details—including its background—and, second, to explain why the issue is important enough to write about. How does Geng identify the issue, and show the reader why the issue is important to her?

2. How does she keep before the reader the importance she attaches to attitudes connected with *commitment*? What are these attitudes?

3. What is the purpose of the dictionary meanings of *commitment,*

given in paragraphs 7 and 8? In general, what attitude toward language do you find implied in these paragraphs? Does the author make her attitude explicit later in the essay?

4. What conclusions does she draw from the use of *commitment,* in paragraphs 9–13? What is the principle of order in these paragraphs?

5. How does she conclude the essay—by stating or restating her thesis, by reviewing her main evidence for it, by suggesting an application of it, or by drawing a final conclusion about the use of the word *commitment* today?

6. Do you agree with the author's conclusions about the word *commitment?* Do you have a different explanation for its widespread use? Do you use the word in a way other than the author specifies?

WRITING ASSIGNMENT

Discuss the meanings you attach, and hear attached, to one of the following words:

    a. sincere   c. cool
    b. viable   d. tough

SHIRLEY JACKSON

My Life with R. H. Macy

1.   And the first thing they did was segregate me. They segregated me from the only person in the place I had even a speaking acquaintance with; that was a girl I had met going down the hall who said to me: "Are you as scared as I am?" And when I said, "Yes," she said, "I'm in lingerie, what are you in?" and I thought for a while and then said, "Spun glass," which was as good an answer as I could think of, and she said, "Oh. Well, I'll meet you here in a sec." And she went away and was segregated and I never saw her again.

2.   Then they kept calling my name and I kept trotting over to

MY LIFE WITH R. H. MACY: In *The Lottery* by Shirley Jackson. Reprinted with the permission of Farrar, Straus & Giroux, Inc. Copyright 1948, 1949 by Shirley Jackson, copyright renewed © 1976 by Laurence Hyman, Barry Hyman, Mrs. Sarah Webster, and Mrs. Joanne Schnurer.

wherever they called it and they would say ("They" all this time being startlingly beautiful young women in tailored suits and with shortclipped hair), "Go with Miss Cooper, here. She'll tell you what to do." All the women I met my first day were named Miss Cooper. And Miss Cooper would say to me: "What are you in?" and I had learned by that time to say, "Books," and she would say, "Oh, well, then, you belong with Miss Cooper here," and then she would call "Miss Cooper?" and another young woman would come and the first one would say, "13-3138 here belongs with you," and Miss Cooper would say, "What is she in?" and Miss Cooper would answer, "Books," and I would go away and be segregated again.

3.   Then they taught me. They finally got me segregated into a classroom, and I sat there for a while all by myself (that's how far segregated I was) and then a few other girls came in, all wearing tailored suits (I was wearing a red velvet afternoon frock) and we sat down and they taught us. They gave us each a big book with R. H. Macy written on it, and inside this book were pads of little sheets saying (from left to right): "Comp. keep for ref. cust. d.a. no. or c.t. no. salesbook no. salescheck no. clerk no. dept. date M." After M there was a long line for Mr. or Mrs. and the name, and then it began again with "No. item. class. at price, total." And down at the bottom was written ORIGINAL and then again, "Comp. keep for ref.," and "Paste yellow gift stamp here." I read all this very carefully. Pretty soon a Miss Cooper came, who talked for a little while on the advantages we had in working at Macy's, and she talked about the salesbooks, which it seems came apart into a sort of road map and carbons and things. I listened for a while, and when Miss Cooper wanted us to write on the little pieces of paper, I copied from the girl next to me. That was training.

4.   Finally someone said we were going on the floor, and we descended from the sixteenth floor to the first. We were in groups of six by then, all following Miss Cooper doggedly and wearing little tags saying BOOK INFORMATION. I never did find out what that meant. Miss Cooper said I had to work on the special sale counter, and showed me a little book called *The Stage-Struck Seal,* which it seemed I would be selling. I had gotten about halfway through it before she came back to tell me I had to stay with my unit.

5.   I enjoyed meeting the time clock, and spent a pleasant half-hour punching various cards standing around, and then someone came in and said I couldn't punch the clock with my hat on. So I had to leave, bowing timidly at the time clock and its prophet, and

I went and found out my locker number, which was 1773, and my time-clock number, which was 712, and my cash-box number, which was 1336, and my cash-register number, which was 253, and my cash-register-drawer number, which was K, and my cash-register-drawer-key number, which was 872, and my department number, which was 13. I wrote all these numbers down. And that was my first day.

6.   My second day was better. I was officially on the floor. I stood in a corner of a counter, with one hand possessively on *The Stage-Struck Seal,* waiting for customers. The counter head was named 13-2246, and she was very kind to me. She sent me to lunch three times, because she got me confused with 13-6454 and 13-3141. It was after lunch that a customer came. She came over and took one of my stage-struck seals, and said "How much is this?" I opened my mouth and the customer said "I have a D. A. and I will have this sent to my aunt in Ohio. Part of that D. A. I will pay for with a book dividend of 32 cents, and the rest of course will be on my account. Is this book price-fixed?" That's as near as I can remember what she said. I smiled confidently, and said "Certainly; will you wait just one moment?" I found a little piece of paper in a drawer under the counter: it had "Duplicate Triplicate" printed across the front in big letters. I took down the customer's name and address, her aunt's name and address, and wrote carefully across the front of the duplicate triplicate "1 Stg. Strk. Sl." Then I smiled at the customer again and said carelessly: "That will be seventy-five cents." She said "But I have a D. A." I told her that all D. A.'s were suspended for the Christmas rush, and she gave me seventy-five cents, which I kept. Then I rang up a "No Sale" on the cash register and I tore up the duplicate triplicate because I didn't know what else to do with it.

7.   Later on another customer came and said "Where would I find a copy of Ann Rutherford Gwynn's *He Came Like Thunder?*" and I said "In medical books, right across the way," but 13-2246 came and said "That's philosophy, isn't it?" and the customer said it was, and 13-2246 said "Right down this aisle, in dictionaries." The customer went away, and I said to 13-2246 that her guess was as good as mine, anyway, and she stared at me and explained that philosophy, social sciences and Bertrand Russell were all kept in dictionaries.

8.   So far I haven't been back to Macy's for my third day, because that night when I started to leave the store, I fell down the stairs

and tore my stockings and the doorman said that if I went to my department head Macy's would give me a new pair of stockings and I went back and I found Miss Cooper and she said, "Go to the adjuster on the seventh floor and give him this," and she handed me a little slip of pink paper and on the bottom of it was printed "Comp. keep for ref. cust. d.a. no. or c.t. no. salesbook no. salescheck no. clerk no. dept. date M." And after M, instead of a name, she had written 13-3138. I took the little pink slip and threw it away and went up to the fourth floor and bought myself a pair of stockings for $.69 and then I came down and went out the customers' entrance.

9.   I wrote Macy's a long letter, and I signed it with all my numbers added together and divided by 11,700, which is the number of employees in Macy's. I wonder if they miss me.

QUESTIONS

1. What information does Jackson provide about herself and her job, in her opening paragraph? What information does she not provide? How does this selection of detail establish a focus of interest?
2. What is her thesis, and where does she first state it? How does she keep this thesis before the reader throughout the essay?
3. In what order does she present her experiences at Macy's?
4. How is the concluding paragraph related to the opening one? Do you find it an effective conclusion?
5. What is the overall tone of the essay, and how is it established?

WRITING ASSIGNMENTS

Describe your first day on a new job. Use your opening paragraph to suggest a thesis, and state it fully toward the end of your essay, or in your concluding paragraph. Keep in mind that your reader knows nothing about you or your place of work. Select your details carefully; don't tell the reader everything.

Rewrite one or two paragraphs of Jackson's essay from the point of view of a customer or another salesperson who is observing the speaker of the essay. Decide before you write what tone you wish to establish.

ANALYSIS

JOHN CIARDI

Is Everybody Happy?

1.   The right to pursue happiness is issued to Americans with their birth certificates, but no one seems quite sure which way it ran. It may be we are issued a hunting license but offered no game. Jonathan Swift seemed to think so when he attacked the idea of happiness as "the possession of being well-deceived," the felicity of being "a fool among knaves." For Swift saw society as Vanity Fair, the land of false goals.

2.   It is, of course, un-American to think in terms of fools and knaves. We do, however, seem to be dedicated to the idea of buying our way to happiness. We shall all have made it to Heaven when we possess enough.

3.   And at the same time the forces of American commercialism are hugely dedicated to making us deliberately unhappy. Advertising is one of our major industries, and advertising exists not to satisfy desires but to create them—and to create them faster than any man's budget can satisfy them. For that matter, our whole economy is based on a dedicated insatiability. We are taught that to possess is to be happy, and then we are made to want. We are even told it is our duty to want. It was only a few years ago, to cite a single example, that car dealers across the country were flying banners that read "You Auto Buy Now." They were calling upon Americans, as an act approaching patriotism, to buy at once, with money they did not have, automobiles they did not really need, and which they would be required to grow tired of by the time the next year's models were released.

4.   Or look at any of the women's magazines. There, as Bernard DeVoto once pointed out, advertising begins as poetry in the front pages and ends as pharmacopoeia and therapy in the back pages. The poetry of the front matter is the dream of perfect beauty. This is the baby skin that must be hers. These, the flawless teeth. This,

IS EVERYBODY HAPPY?: In *Manner of Speaking* (Rutgers University Press, 1972). Reprinted by permission of the author.

the perfumed breath she must exhale. This, the sixteen-year-old figure she must display at forty, at fifty, at sixty, and forever.

5.   Once past the vaguely uplifting fiction and feature articles, the reader finds the other face of the dream in the back matter. This is the harness into which Mother must strap herself in order to display that perfect figure. These, the chin straps she must sleep in. This is the salve that restores all, this is her laxative, these are the tablets that melt away fat, these are the hormones of perpetual youth, these are the stockings that hide varicose veins.

6.   Obviously no half-sane person can be completely persuaded either by such poetry or by such pharmacopoeia and orthopedics. Yet someone is obviously trying to buy the dream as offered and spending billions every year in the attempt. Clearly the happiness market is not running out of customers, but what are we trying to buy?

7.   The idea "happiness," to be sure, will not sit still for easy definition: the best one can do is to try to set some extremes to the idea and then work in toward the middle. To think of happiness as acquisitive and competitive will do to set the materialistic extreme. To think of it as the idea one senses in, say, a holy man of India will do to set the spiritual extreme. That holy man's ideal of happiness is in needing nothing from outside himself. In wanting nothing, he lacks nothing. He sits immobile, rapt in contemplation, free even of his own body. Or nearly free of it. If devout admirers bring him food he eats it; if not, he starves indifferently. Why be concerned? What is physical is an illusion to him. Contemplation is his joy and he achieves it through a fantastically demanding discipline, the accomplishment of which is itself a joy within him.

8.   Is he a happy man? Perhaps his happiness is only another sort of illusion. But who can take it from him? And who will dare say it is more illusory than happiness on the installment plan?

9.   But, perhaps because I am Western, I doubt such catatonic happiness, as I doubt the dreams of the happiness market. What is certain is that his way of happiness would be torture to almost any Western man. Yet these extremes will still serve to frame the area within which all of us must find some sort of balance. Thoreau—a creature of both Eastern and Western thought—had his own firm sense of that balance. His aim was to save on the low levels in order to spend on the high.

10. Possession for its own sake or in competition with the rest of the neighborhood would have been Thoreau's idea of the low

levels. The active discipline of heightening one's perception of what is enduring in nature would have been his idea of the high. What he saved from the low was time and effort he could spend on the high. Thoreau certainly disapproved of starvation, but he would put into feeding himself only as much effort as would keep him functioning for more important efforts.

11. Effort is the gist of it. There is no happiness except as we take on life-engaging difficulties. Short of the impossible, as Yeats put it, the satisfactions we get from a lifetime depend on how high we choose our difficulties. Robert Frost was thinking in something like the same terms when he spoke of "the pleasure of taking pains." The mortal flaw in the advertised version of happiness is in the fact that it purports to be effortless.

12. We demand difficulty even in our games. We demand it because without difficulty there can be no game. A game is a way of making something hard for the fun of it. The rules of the game are an arbitrary imposition of difficulty. When the spoilsport ruins the fun, he always does so by refusing to play by the rules. It is easier to win at chess if you are free, at your pleasure, to change the wholly arbitrary rules, but the fun is in winning within the rules. No difficulty, no fun.

13. The buyers and sellers at the happiness market seem too often to have lost their sense of the pleasure of difficulty. Heaven knows what they are playing, but it seems a dull game. The Indian holy man seems dull to us, I suppose, because he seems to be refusing to play anything at all. The Western weakness may be in the illusion that happiness can be bought. Perhaps the Eastern weakness is in the idea that there is such a thing as perfect (and therefore static) happiness.

14. Happiness is never more than partial. There are no pure states of mankind. Whatever else happiness may be, it is neither in having nor in being, but in becoming. What the Founding Fathers declared for us as an inherent right, we should do well to remember, was not happiness but the *pursuit* of happiness. What they might have underlined, could they have foreseen the happiness market, is the cardinal fact that happiness is in the pursuit itself, in the meaningful pursuit of what is life-engaging and life-revealing, which is to say, in the idea of *becoming*. A nation is not measured by what it possesses or wants to possess, but by what it wants to become.

15. By all means let the happiness market sell us minor satisfactions and even minor follies so long as we keep them in scale and buy them out of spiritual change. I am no customer for either puritanism or asceticism. But drop any real spiritual capital at those bazaars, and what you come home to will be your own poorhouse.

DISCUSSION: ANALYSIS

The methods of paragraph development—definition, division, comparison and contrast, and the like—are the methods we find in complete essays, and, as in most paragraphs, they do not occur alone. As we saw in Veronica Geng's essay on commitment, definition and example can reinforce each other: each of the uses of the word *commitment* is carefully illustrated and related to one of its meanings.

The reader of an essay should understand at every point why a particular method of analysis is being used, and how each method helps to develop the thesis, regardless of whether the thesis is stated or implied. Often transitional sentences are needed to make these relations clear. Writers must keep in mind that they know more about their subject than their readers do: they are illustrating ideas for their readers, and the kind and number of examples they provide depend on how much help is needed in understanding the thesis. No matter how logically developed the writer's ideas may be, if they are not explained clearly or illustrated, the essay will communicate nothing; it will convince no one except the writer.

QUESTIONS

1. Ciardi organizes his discussion of happiness as an extended definition. What kind of definition of happiness does he employ—denotative, connotative, stipulative, or theoretical?
2. Ciardi builds to his full definition of happiness through a consideration of advertising and the Eastern holy man. Given his opening comments on Swift and the American way of thinking, why does he delay his definition until late in the essay? How do his comments on advertising and the Eastern holy man help to establish his definition?
3. Where, finally, does he state his definition?
4. The "pursuit of happiness" is so familiar a phrase that we are likely not to examine its full implications. Is Ciardi defining this phrase according to what he believes the founding fathers meant by it, or is he proposing his own definition?

WRITING ASSIGNMENTS

Ciardi deals with an abstract idea through everyday experiences. Select another phrase in common use and define it as Ciardi does. Examine its implications fully.

Discuss the statement "We demand difficulty even in our games" through two different games that you enjoy playing. Indicate the extent of your agreement with Ciardi.

Develop the following statement through your personal observations: "Whatever else happiness may be, it is neither in having nor in being, but in becoming."

Ciardi analyzes women's magazines in light of the idea of happiness they purvey. Analyze a man's magazine in the same way, giving attention to the articles and the advertisements.

EDWARD T. HALL

The English and the Americans

1.   It has been said that the English and the Americans are two great people separated by one language. The differences for which language gets blamed may not be due so much to words as to communications on other levels beginning with English intonation (which sounds affected to many Americans) and continuing to ego-linked ways of handling time, space, and materials. If there ever were two cultures in which differences of the proxemic details are marked it is in the educated (public school) English and the middle-class Americans. One of the basic reasons for this wide disparity is that in the United States we use space as a way of classifying people and activities, whereas in England it is the social system that determines who you are. In the United States, your address is an important cue to status (this applies not only to one's home but to the business address as well). The Joneses from Brooklyn and Miami are not as "in" as the Joneses from Newport and Palm Beach. Greenwich and Cape Cod are worlds apart from

Newark and Miami. Businesses located on Madison and Park avenues have more tone than those on Seventh and Eighth avenues. A corner office is more prestigious than one next to the elevator or at the end of a long hall. The Englishman, however, is born and brought up in a social system. He is still Lord—— no matter where you find him, even if it is behind the counter in a fishmonger's stall. In addition to class distinctions, there are differences between the English and ourselves in how space is allotted.

2. The middle-class American growing up in the United States feels he has a right to have his own room, or at least part of a room. My American subjects, when asked to draw an ideal room or office, invariably drew it for themselves and no one else. When asked to draw their present room or office, they drew only their own part of a shared room and then drew a line down the middle. Both male and female subjects identified the kitchen and the master bedroom as belonging to the mother or the wife, whereas Father's territory was a study or a den, if one was available; otherwise, it was "the shop," "the basement," or sometimes only a workbench or the garage. American women who want to be alone can go to the bedroom and close the door. The closed door is the sign meaning "Do not disturb" or "I'm angry." An American is available if his door is open at home or at his office. He is expected not to shut himself off but to maintain himself in a state of constant readiness to answer the demands of others. Closed doors are for conferences, private conversations, and business, work that requires concentration, study, resting, sleeping, dressing, and sex.

3. The middle- and upper-class Englishman, on the other hand, is brought up in a nursery shared with brothers and sisters. The oldest occupies a room by himself which he vacates when he leaves for boarding school, possibly even at the age of nine or ten. The difference between a room of one's own and early conditioning to shared space, while seeming inconsequential, has an important effect on the Englishman's attitude toward his own space. He may never have a permanent "room of his own" and seldom expects one or feels he is entitled to one. Even Members of Parliament have no offices and often conduct their business on the terrace overlooking the Thames. As a consequence, the English are puzzled by the American need for a secure place in which to work, an office. Americans working in England may become annoyed if they are not provided with what they consider appropriate enclosed work space. In regard to the need for walls as a screen for

the ego, this places the Americans somewhere between the Germans and the English.

4.   The contrasting English and American patterns have some remarkable implications, particularly if we assume that man, like other animals, has a built-in need to shut himself off from others from time to time. An English student in one of my seminars typified what happens when hidden patterns clash. He was quite obviously experiencing strain in his relationships with Americans. Nothing seemed to go right and it was quite clear from his remarks that we did not know how to behave. An analysis of his complaints showed that a major source of irritation was that no American seemed to be able to pick up the subtle clues that there were times when he didn't want his thoughts intruded on. As he stated it, "I'm walking around the apartment and it seems that whenever I want to be alone my roommate starts talking to me. Pretty soon he's asking 'What's the matter?' and wants to know if I'm angry. By then I am angry and say something."

5.   It took some time but finally we were able to identify most of the contrasting features of the American and British problems that were in conflict in this case. When the American wants to be alone he goes into a room and shuts the door—he depends on architectural features for screening. For an American to refuse to talk to someone else present in the same room, to give them the "silent treatment," is the ultimate form of rejection and a sure sign of great displeasure. The English, on the other hand, lacking rooms of their own since childhood, never developed the practice of using space as a refuge from others. They have in effect internalized a set of barriers, which they erect and which others are supposed to recognize. Therefore, the more the Englishman shuts himself off when he is with an American the more likely the American is to break in to assure himself that all is well. Tension lasts until the two get to know each other. The important point is that the spatial and architectural needs of each are not the same at all.

QUESTIONS

1. What is Hall's thesis, and where is it first stated? Where does he restate it later in the essay?
2. How is the contrast between the English and the Americans organized? Does Hall contrast the English and American patterns point

by point, or instead deal with one set of patterns first, another set afterwards? Or does he mix these methods of organization?

3. How does he illustrate these patterns? Does he illustrate all of them?

4. Hall traces cause-and-effect relations through contrast of living patterns. What are the chief relations he traces?

5. How do the examples explain the phrase *internalized a set of barriers,* in the concluding paragraph? What does Hall mean by *screening?*

6. What use does Hall make of classification in the whole essay? On what basis does he divide the English and the Americans?

WRITING ASSIGNMENTS

Discuss the extent to which your study habits fit the English or the American pattern. Use your analysis to comment on the accuracy of Hall's thesis.

Contrast two of your friends or relatives on the basis of their attitude toward space and architecture. State the similarities before commenting on the differences. Notice that the differences may be slight ones, and even slight differences may be revealing of people.

LEWIS THOMAS
Social Talk

1. Not all social animals are social with the same degree of commitment. In some species, the members are so tied to each other and interdependent as to seem the loosely conjoined cells of a tissue. The social insects are like this; they move, and live all their lives, in a mass; a beehive is a spherical animal. In other species, less compulsively social, the members make their homes together, pool resources, travel in packs or schools, and share the food, but any single one can survive solitary, detached from the rest. Others are social only in the sense of being more or less congenial, meeting from time to time in committees, using social gatherings as *ad hoc* occasions for feeding and breeding. Some animals simply nod

at each other in passing, never reaching even a first-name relationship.

2.   It is not a simple thing to decide where we fit, for at one time or another in our lives we manage to organize in every imaginable social arrangement. We are as interdependent, especially in our cities, as bees or ants, yet we can detach if we wish and go live alone in the woods, in theory anyway. We feed and look after each other, constructing elaborate systems for this, even including vending machines to dispense ice cream in gas stations, but we also have numerous books to tell us how to live off the land. We cluster in family groups, but we tend, unpredictably, to turn on each other and fight as if we were different species. Collectively, we hanker to accumulate all the information in the universe and distribute it around among ourselves as though it were a kind of essential foodstuff, ant-fashion (the faintest trace of real news in science has the action of a pheromone, lifting the hairs of workers in laboratories at the ends of the earth), but each of us also builds a private store of his own secret knowledge and hides it away like untouchable treasure. We have names to label each as self, and we believe without reservation that this system of taxonomy will guarantee the entity, the absolute separateness of each of us, but the mechanism has no discernible function in the center of a crowded city; we are essentially nameless, most of our time.

3.   Nobody wants to think that the rapidly expanding mass of mankind, spreading out over the surface of the earth, blackening the ground, bears any meaningful resemblance to the life of an anthill or a hive. Who would consider for a moment that the more than three billion of us are a sort of stupendous animal when we become linked together? We are not mindless, nor is our day-to-day behavior coded out to the last detail by our genomes, nor do we seem to be engaged together, compulsively, in any single, universal, stereotyped task analogous to the construction of a nest. If we were ever to put all our brains together in fact, to make a common mind the way the ants do, it would be an unthinkable thought, way over our heads.

4.   Social animals tend to keep at a particular thing, generally something huge for their size; they work at it ceaselessly under genetic instructions and genetic compulsion, using it to house the species and protect it, assuring permanence.

5.   There are, to be sure, superficial resemblances in some of the things we do together, like building glass and plastic cities on all

the land and farming under the sea, or assembling in armies, or landing samples of ourselves on the moon, or sending memoranda into the next galaxy. We do these together without being quite sure why, but we can stop doing one thing and move to another whenever we like. We are not committed or bound by our genes to stick to one activity forever, like the wasps. Today's behavior is no more fixed than when we tumbled out over Europe to build cathedrals in the twelfth century. At that time we were convinced that it would go on forever, that this was the way to live, but it was not; indeed, most of us have already forgotten what it was all about. Anything we do in this transient, secondary social way, compulsively and with all our energies but only for a brief period of our history, cannot be counted as social behavior in the biological sense. If we can turn it on and off, on whims, it isn't likely that our genes are providing the detailed instructions. Constructing Chartres was good for our minds, but we found that our lives went on, and it is no more likely that we will find survival in Rome plows or laser bombs, or rapid mass transport or a Mars lander, or solar power, or even synthetic protein. We do tend to improvise things like this as we go along, but it is clear that we can pick and choose.

6.   For practical purposes, it would probably be best for us not to be biologically social, in the long run. Not that we have a choice, of course, or even a vote. It would not be good news to learn that we are all roped together intellectually, droning away at some featureless, genetically driven collective work, building something so immense that we can never see the outlines. It seems especially hard, even perilous, for this to be the burden of a species with the unique attribute of speech, and argument. Leave this kind of life to the insects and birds, and lesser mammals, and fish.

7.   But there is just that one thing. About human speech.

8.   It begins to look, more and more disturbingly, as if the gift of language is the single human trait that marks us all genetically, setting us apart from all the rest of life. Language is, like nest-building or hive-making, the universal and biologically specific activity of human beings. We engage in it communally, compulsively, and automatically. We cannot be human without it; if we were to be separated from it our minds would die, as surely as bees lost from the hive.

9.   We are born knowing how to use language. The capacity to recognize syntax, to organize and deploy words into intelligible

sentences, is innate in the human mind. We are programmed to identify patterns and generate grammar. There are invariant and variable structures in speech that are common to all of us. As chicks are endowed with an innate capacity to read information in the shapes of overhanging shadows, telling hawk from other birds, we can identify the meaning of grammar in a string of words, and we are born this way. According to Chomsky, who has examined it as a biologist looks at live tissue, language "must simply be a biological property of the human mind." The universal attributes of language are genetically set; we do not learn them, or make them up as we go along.

10. We work at this all our lives, and collectively we give it life, but we do not exert the least control over language, not as individuals or committees or academies or governments. Language, once it comes alive, behaves like an active, motile organism. Parts of it are always being changed, by a ceaseless activity to which all of us are committed; new words are invented and inserted, old ones have their meaning altered or abandoned. New ways of stringing words and sentences together come into fashion and vanish again, but the underlying structure simply grows, enriches itself, expands. Individual languages age away and seem to die, but they leave progeny all over the place. Separate languages can exist side by side for centuries without touching each other, maintaining their integrity with the vigor of incompatible tissues. At other times, two languages may come together, fuse, replicate, and give rise to nests of new tongues.

11. If language is at the core of our social existence, holding us together, housing us in meaning, it may also be safe to say that art and music are functions of the same universal, genetically determined mechanism. These are not bad things to do together. If we are social creatures because of this, and therefore like ants, I for one (or should I say we for one?) do not mind.

QUESTIONS

1. How does the contrast with the social insects define what human beings are not?
2. Does Thomas fully define what human beings are?
3. How exactly is the "social talk" of human beings different from that of the social insects?

4. In general, how is the essay organized? What is the thesis, and where is it first stated?
5. What "names" is Thomas referring to in the final sentence of paragraph 2?

WRITING ASSIGNMENT

Develop one of the following statements from your personal experience. Or use your experience to disagree with Thomas, or to qualify the statement:

a. "We are as interdependent, especially in our cities, as bees or ants. . . ."
b. "We cluster in family groups, but we tend, unpredictably, to turn on each other and fight as if we were different species."
c. "We have names to label each as self . . . but the mechanism has no discernible function in the center of a crowded city; we are essentially nameless, most of our time."
d. "We do tend to improvise things . . . as we go along, but it is clear that we can pick and choose."

JAMES THURBER

What a Lovely Generalization!

1.   I have collected, in my time, derringers, snowstorm paper-weights, and china and porcelain dogs, and perhaps I should explain what happened to these old collections before I go on to my newest hobby, which is the true subject of this monograph. My derringer collection may be regarded as having been discontinued, since I collected only two, the second and last item as long ago as 1935. There were originally seventeen snowstorm paperweights, but only four or five are left. This kind of collection is known to the expert as a "diminished collection," and it is not considered cricket to list it in your *Who's Who* biography. The snowstorm paper-weight suffers from its easy appeal to the eye and the hand. House guests like to play with paperweights and to slip them into their luggage while packing up to leave. As for my china and porcelain

WHAT A LOVELY GENERALIZATION!: In *Thurber Country,* published by Simon & Schuster. Copr. © 1953 James Thurber. Originally published in *The Bermudian.*

dogs, I disposed of that collection some two years ago. I had decided that the collection of actual objects, of any kind, was too much of a strain, and I determined to devote myself, instead, to the impalpable and the intangible.

2.   Nothing in my new collection can be broken or stolen or juggled or thrown at cats. What I collect now is a certain kind of Broad Generalization, or Sweeping Statement. You will see what I mean when I bring out some of my rare and cherished pieces. All you need to start a collection of generalizations like mine is an attentive ear. Listen in particular to women, whose average generalization is from three to five times as broad as a man's. Generalizations, male or female, may be true ("Women don't sleep very well"), untrue ("There are no pianos in Japan"), half true ("People would rather drink than go to the theater"), debatable ("Architects have the wrong idea"), libelous ("Doctors don't know what they're doing"), ridiculous ("You never see foreigners fishing"), fascinating but undemonstrable ("People who break into houses don't drink wine"), or idiosyncratic ("Peach ice cream is never as good as you think it's going to be").

3.   "There are no pianos in Japan" was the first item in my collection. I picked it up at a reception while discussing an old movie called "The Battle," or "Thunder in the East," which starred Charles Boyer, Merle Oberon, and John Loder, some twenty years ago. In one scene, Boyer, as a Japanese naval captain, comes upon Miss Oberon, as his wife, Matsuko, playing an old Japanese air on the piano for the entertainment of Loder, a British naval officer with a dimple, who has forgotten more about fire control, range finding, marksmanship, and lovemaking than the Japanese commander is ever going to know. "Matsuko," says the latter, "why do you play that silly little song? It may be tedious for our fran." Their fran, John Loder, says, "No, it is, as a matter of—" But I don't know why I have to go into the whole plot. The lady with whom I was discussing the movie, at the reception, said that the detail about Matsuko and the piano was absurd, since "there are no pianos in Japan." It seems that this lady was an authority on the musical setup in Japan because her great-uncle had married a singsong girl in Tokyo in 1912.

4.   Now, I might have accepted the declarations that there are no saxophones in Bessarabia, no banjo-mandolins in Mozambique, no double basses in Zanzibar, no jew's-harps in Rhodesia, no zithers in Madagascar, and no dulcimers in Milwaukee, but I could not

believe that Japan, made out in the movie as a great imitator of Western culture, would not have any pianos. Some months after the reception, I picked up an old copy of the *Saturday Evening Post* and, in an article on Japan, read that there were, before the war, some fifteen thousand pianos in Japan. It just happened to say that, right there in the article.

5.   You may wonder where I heard some of the other Sweeping Statements I have mentioned above. Well, the one about peach ice cream was contributed to my collection by a fifteen-year-old girl. I am a chocolate man myself, but the few times I have eaten peach ice cream it tasted exactly the way I figured it was going to taste, which is why I classify this statement as idiosyncratic; that is, peculiar to one individual. The item about foreigners never fishing, or, at any rate, never fishing where you can see them, was given to me last summer by a lady who had just returned from a motor trip through New England. The charming generalization about people who break into houses popped out of a conversation I overheard between two women, one of whom said it was not safe to leave rye, Scotch, or bourbon in your summer house when you closed it for the winter, but it was perfectly all right to leave your wine, since intruders are notoriously men of insensitive palate, who cannot tell the difference between Nuits-St.-Georges and saddle polish. I would not repose too much confidence in this theory if I were you, however. It is one of those Comfortable Conclusions that can cost you a whole case of Château Lafite.

6.   I haven't got space here to go through my entire collection, but there is room to examine a few more items. I'm not sure where I got hold of "Gamblers hate women"—possibly at Bleeck's—but, like "Sopranos drive men crazy," it has an authentic ring. This is not true, I'm afraid, of "You can't trust an electrician" or "Cops off duty always shoot somebody." There may be something in "Dogs know when you're despondent" and "Sick people hear everything," but I sharply question the validity of "Nobody taps his fingers if he's all right" and "People who like birds are queer."

7.   Some twenty years ago, a Pittsburgh city editor came out with the generalization that "Rewrite men go crazy when the moon is full," but this is perhaps a little too special for the layman, who probably doesn't know what a rewrite man is. Besides, it is the abusive type of Sweeping Statement and should not be dignified by analysis or classification.

8.   In conclusion, let us briefly explore "Generals are afraid of

their daughters," vouchsafed by a lady after I had told her my General Wavell anecdote. It happens, for the sake of our present record, that the late General Wavell, of His Britannic Majesty's forces, discussed his three daughters during an interview a few years ago. He said that whereas he had millions of men under his command who leaped at his every order, he couldn't get his daughters down to breakfast on time when he was home on leave, in spite of stern directives issued the night before. As I have imagined it, his ordeal went something like this. It would get to be 7 A.M., and then 7:05, and General Wavell would shout up the stairs demanding to know where everybody was, and why the girls were not at table. Presently, one of them would call back sharply, as a girl has to when her father gets out of hand, "For heaven's sake, Daddy, will you be quiet! Do you want to wake the neighbors?" The General, his flanks rashly exposed, so to speak, would fall back in orderly retreat and eat his kippers by himself. Now, I submit that there is nothing in this to prove that the General was afraid of his daughters. The story merely establishes the fact that his daughters were not afraid of him.

9.   If you are going to start collecting Sweeping Statements on your own, I must warn you that certain drawbacks are involved. You will be inclined to miss the meaning of conversations while lying in wait for generalizations. Your mouth will hang open slightly, your posture will grow rigid, and your eyes will take on the rapt expression of a person listening for the faint sound of distant sleigh bells. People will avoid your company and whisper that you are probably an old rewrite man yourself or, at best, a finger tapper who is a long way from being all right. But your collection will be a source of comfort in your declining years, when you can sit in the chimney corner cackling the evening away over some such gems, let us say, as my own two latest acquisitions: "Jewelers never go anywhere" and "Intellectual women dress funny."

10. Good hunting.

QUESTIONS

1. Is Thurber's statement that a woman's "average generalization is from three to five times as broad as a man's" any better founded than other generalizations he cites? How do you think he wants the reader to take this statement?

2. How does each of the examples in paragraph 2 illustrate the labels

Thurber gives them? Why is the statement that "People would rather drink than go to the theater" half true?
3. What is the overall tone of the essay, and how is it established? How is this tone related to Thurber's purpose in writing the essay?

WRITING ASSIGNMENTS

Collect examples of generalizations like those in paragraph 2, classifying them, and build your examples to a conclusion about the purpose such generalizations serve.

Write a characterization of Thurber from the way he talks about himself and talks to the reader of the essay. Consider his qualities as a humorist.

C. NORTHCOTE PARKINSON
Imperative Tense

1.   Our ideas of authority derive from fatherhood and our terms of respect, in nearly every language, are the proof of it. Among human beings the young are dependent on their parents for a long time. The father is protector and teacher for so many years that the obedience he has to exact becomes habitual, creating in successive generations an attitude of respect towards seniority as such. Such an attitude of deference is also traditionally displayed by the mother. With her, however, the father's relationship is more complex, for the survival of the kinship group or tribe depends more upon its women than its men. In general, however, the father's rule extends over the whole group and the childen's sense of subordination is firmly based upon common sense and tradition. Their attitude towards authority comprises three distinct elements: wonder, at the father's greater knowledge and skill; affection for one who is at least interested in ensuring the child's survival; and fear of punishment for disobedience. These three elements go to make up a sense of security. More particularly essential is the element of fear, for if the child does not fear his father he can hardly suppose

IMPERATIVE TENSE: In *The Law of Delay*. Copyright © 1970 by C. Northcote Parkinson. Reprinted by permission of Houghton Mifflin Company.

that his father will be feared by anyone else. And what is the protection worth of a man whom no one fears?

2.   As the community grows larger the idea of fatherhood turns into kingship. From early times there have been two types of monarchy, the mobile and the static. Over a pastoral tribe, eternally on the move, the king is the leader, deciding the route, choosing the day and marking the camp site. Over an agricultural people the king is more of a priest, interceding with the gods so as to ensure the sunshine when it is wanted and the rain at the proper time. There is still room in the world for both types of authority. During World War II Lord Montgomery typified the leader in the field but Lord Alanbrooke was seldom ever seen, his authority looming behind the successive doors of the War Office. One was needed to give immediate direction, the other to intercede with higher authority for the army's proper share of the available manpower. Both types of authority have the same remote origin and both imply a mixture of reputation and power. Where the reputation has been lost, the power soon vanishes. Where the power has gone the reputation cannot survive. The world is full of high-sounding titles from which all meaning has been drained. This has always been so, however. What is new is our present doubt as to whether authority itself can survive.

3.   The first weakening of current authority resulted from the female revolution which took place in Britain and USA after about 1900. Skirts became trousers, women were to graduate and vote and the sexes were to be equal in nearly every way. But the revolution ended in compromise and confusion. Allowed to be equal in the areas where they had once been submissive, women remained superior in the areas where their superiority had always been acknowledged. The gentleman might cease to be a gentleman but the lady remained a lady, with the result that (in USA more especially) the husband ended as the inferior. What has been lost is the wife's deference to the husband, that wisdom which led to her publicly accepting a male decision which could well have resulted from her previous and private advice. Wives have forgotten how to offer an open submission in return for a frequently decisive influence.

4.   The sequel to this change in attitude is that the wife has lost control over the children. The Victorian wife used her husband's authority to quell the children; an authority which she had strengthened by her own example of calculated deference. The

modern wife tries to reason with the children who therefore lack, from the outset, the security they need. She ends by hoping that the school will provide the discipline that the home has come to lack. This proves impossible because the sense of authority needs to be established before the age of five and quite possibly before the age of three. Schools can do all too little in this respect and universities can, of course, do nothing. The result is that we are faced in public and business administration by the need to establish some sort of authority over young people who may never have known any discipline at all. This is no easy task and we must feel sometimes that our failure is inevitable.

5.   This feeling of hopelessness underlies the current talk about group decision. Do we *need* discipline after all? Perhaps the better way is to take a majority vote? Are we so sure, after all, that older people are wiser than the young? The fashion of today is to call youth into counsel and ask the advice of those whose careers have scarcely begun. Heaven forbid that we should be thought surly and despotic! We must also remind each other that the technological trend goes against the claims of seniority. Significant changes of method used to occur about once in thirty years. Each generation could learn from the last, make its own contribution and look forward to another ten years of superior knowledge and valued experience. Changes have now become more frequent, taking place within the decade, and the value of experience comes, therefore, to be called in question. Seniority may signify no more than being out of date and out of touch. It is the younger men who have been on the computer course and the present directors may not even know the language. It is doubtful, moreover, whether the present-day technologists will respond to any sort of leadership. They are absorbed in their own electronic world and unable to communicate with those who have not attended the same sort of polytechnic. There was a time for leadership, many believe, but that time has gone. There is no place for kingship, they claim, in the world of today.

6.   This argument may be plausible but it is based upon boom conditions and a seller's market. What when things go wrong? Shall we talk *then* about group decisions? One thing to remember is that authority brings, first and foremost, a sense of security. The sailor on board ship sleeps during his watch below in the knowledge that the officer on the bridge is both wakeful and competent. He would be more restless if he thought that the appearance of

another vessel, on a collision course, would be the occasion for calling a committee meeting and asking each member for his considered opinion. The soldier on active service can sleep as soundly on the assumption that the sentries have been posted and that an officer will be going the rounds. Nor is an industrial plant entirely different. It depends for its security on a whole series of safety precautions and the employer relies on the management to see that these are properly carried out. Without a measure of authority a railway line or coalpit can be heading for real disaster. Other establishments are less subject to risk, their potential hazards being more financial than physical, but this is not to say that risk is absent or that it may not sharply increase. But how can we supply then, in an instant, what we have for long dismissed as valueless?

7. Some people believe that leadership is a quality which you have at birth or not at all. This theory is false, for the art of leadership can be acquired and can indeed be taught. This discovery is made in time of war and the results achieved can surprise even the instructors. Faced with the alternatives of going left or right, every soldier soon grasps that a prompt decision either way is better than an endless discussion. A firm choice of direction has an even chance of being right while to do nothing will be almost certainly wrong. Starting with this premise the potential leader soon learns to make up his mind. It then remains to ensure that his action is based on common sense. Having reached that point, the future officer must make his authority persuasive and acceptable. There is a technique to be applied and it is one we can describe with confidence. The secrets of leadership have to be rediscovered by each generation but they are simple enough in themselves. There are six basic elements and all of them may be acquired or improved by study and practice.

8. The first element is imagination. If anything is to be created, constructed, moved or reorganized, the man responsible must have a clear picture in his mind of what the final result is to be. Such a picture, formed in the mind's eye, is a compound of things we have actually seen elsewhere and on other occasions but now re-arranged in a different context. Taking command of a new ship, as yet unmanned, an officer will imagine the end result he desires to see in terms of efficiency. Remembering all that was best in his past experience he combines all together in a mental image. The reality may be utterly different but he has begun at least with an

idea of what he is trying to do. Imagination is essential, and it comes first, for without imagination we are aimless.

9.   The second element is knowledge. This is obviously needed to plan the route by which the goal is to be reached. But it is knowledge again which gives the leader the necessary confidence; the feeling that he knows what he is talking about. The world is full of people in positions of responsibility who are ignorant of their own business, possibly as a result of a too swift promotion, possibly from mere lack of brain. It is difficult for them to command the respect of the technically competent. They tend to feel vulnerable and insecure. To compensate themselves for their weakness they tend to indulge in fault-finding, bad temper, shouting and abuse. All this may be attributed by others to a poor digestion or a nagging wife. The fact is, however, that the bully has his own unconscious motive. He knows that there will be frequent mistakes in his office—as there have always been in every office in which he has appeared—and he wants to prove in advance that the fault lies in others and not in him. All those junior to him are disloyal, careless, idle and dense. His equals are incompetent, jealous, interfering and blind. Those senior to him are incapable, alas, of recognizing merit when they see it. Can anyone wonder that documents should be lost, that letters should be unposted, that dates should be forgotten and notices ignored? Heaven knows that he has done his best but he cannot be everywhere and there is no one else he can trust. Incompetence of this kind is often (not always) due to the man's basic ignorance. He literally does not know what he is trying to do.

10.   So knowledge is important. The same can be said of the third element, ability. It is a word we need to define, making a sharp distinction between ability and skill. The skillful person is one who can do with relative ease what others will find difficult. He can play the cello, or score a century at cricket. When we go beyond skill, organizing the work of others—as in conducting the orchestra, or captaining a team—we need to display ability. Our own skill (which should be outstanding) is now less important than our capability to direct others. The man of ability is one who has the whole situation under control. Under him each man has been assigned to the task for which he is best suited and each knows exactly what his task is to be. There is a tidiness about the factory and office and a strong sense of economy in time, money and ef-

fort. But what, above all, distinguishes the man of ability is the hall-mark of artistry or style. Good organization is, finally, an aesthetic exercise; the fitting together of material and effort in such a way that no one is overworked and no one is idle. At the very center of the organization's daily activity is an area of calm, where the ablest man of all is totally free from irritation or panic.

11. Very occasionally there appears in the world a person of exceptional skill or ability with the added quality of vision. This is genius and there is very little of it in the world. The more we can breed and train people of ability, however, the more certain it is that some will be exceptional; and the greater number of these men, the outstandingly able, the greater is the likelihood that one of them may possess vision as well. For all ordinary purposes, ability is enough but the world offers occasional scope for genius. It is too often lacking, however, at the time and place where it is needed. What we need, perhaps, is a system for deploying what little genius there is available; such a system as only a genius could devise.

12. The next quality needed (for leadership) is determination. This means more than being grimly resolved to succeed. It is a quality which can be broken down into three elements. First of these and basic to the rest is the knowledge that the task to be accomplished is humanly possible. The general who has equipped and trained a sufficient number of troops and brought them, properly supplied, to the right place at the right time, knows that victory is within his grasp. To that knowledge he adds, if he is sufficiently determined, the belief that what can be done will be done. He has finally to reveal a capacity for conveying his confidence to everyone else. He must so describe the object to be gained that it seems worthwhile. In the light of his description the sacrifices must seem nothing, the probable losses trivial. From his attitude of calm certainty the rest of the team will draw their inspiration. For enemies in war or for rivals in business alike his supporters will feel something like pity. Could their opponents but know it, their opposition is futile, their doom already pronounced. Nothing can save them now from being outmaneuvred, outflanked, and outfought, disorganized, disrupted and dispersed.

13. The next factor is one that people today will not readily accept: ruthlessness, which many would like to replace by a diploma in industrial psychology. All experience goes to prove that the effective leader must be pitiless toward the disloyal, the careless and

the idle. If he is not, the work falls too heavily on the willing men. The sense of belonging to a picked team is soon lost in an organization where the useless are still included. The element of fear is vital to authority and enters largely into the atmosphere of leadership. There are leaders who are loved as well as admired but that does not mean that they have never been ruthless. As their authority comes to be firmly established they may have less need to inspire fear but it was usually, perhaps always, an element in their previous career. To say that it is unnecessary would be totally wrong.

14. The last factor is that of attraction. This does not mean attractiveness in the ordinary sense, for that is a quality beyond our control. The leader has, nevertheless, to be a magnet; a central figure towards whom people are drawn. Magnetism in that sense depends, first of all, on being seen. There is (as we have seen) a type of authority which can be exerted from behind closed doors, but that is not leadership. Where there is movement and action, the true leader is in the forefront and may seem, indeed, to be everywhere at once. He has to become a legend; the subject for anecdotes, whether true or false; a *character*. One of the simplest devices is to be absent on the occasion when the leader might be expected to be there, enough in itself to start a rumor about the vital business which has detained him. To make up for this, he can appear when least expected, giving rise to another story about the interest he can display in things which other folk might regard as trivial. With this gift for inspiring curiosity the leader always combines a reluctance to talk about himself. His interest is plainly in other people: he questions them and encourages them to talk and then remembers all that is relevant. He never leaves a party until he has mentally filed a minimum dossier on everyone present, ensuring that he knows what to say when he meets them again. He is not artificially extrovert but he would usually rather listen than talk. Others realize gradually that his importance needs no proof.

15. But if it is true that leadership is an art which can be learnt, it is probable that it needs to be learnt fairly soon in life. The eternal difficulty in human affairs is to combine experience with youth, giving the future leader a chance to develop his gift. Our danger today is that we tend to lengthen our years of instruction, demanding ever more technical qualifications, until the man who qualifies is approaching middle age. And after twenty years of routine subordination the chance has gone for ever.

QUESTIONS

1. What is the principle by which monarchy is divided in paragraph 2? What does this discussion of monarchy contribute to the thesis of the essay? Where is the thesis stated?
2. To what cause, or causes, does Parkinson trace the behavior of modern children?
3. Is Parkinson saying that women are by their nature submissive, and that their dominance today is biologically unnatural? Or is he making no judgments about the nature of men and women?
4. What illustrative analogies do you find in paragraph 6, and what purpose do you serve?
5. In what order are the six elements of leadership presented? Could imagination have been discussed after knowledge or determination?
6. Why is it necessary to distinguish between ability and skill?
7. In general, how is the discussion of changing patterns of authority in the family related to the discussion of leadership? How does the final paragraph join these two concerns of the essay?
8. Do you agree with Parkinson that men and women should play defined roles in the family? How many of the qualities enumerated do you believe essential in a good father? What about the President of the United States?
9. Is the essay an exposition of changing patterns of authority and the qualities of leadership, or is it argumentative—seeking to change the mind of the reader on a number of points?

WRITING ASSIGNMENTS

Use Parkinson's discussion of leadership to define the ideal teacher. You might discuss how many of the qualities he enumerates are essential to such a teacher.

Compare male and female teachers in your life to determine whether their success or failure as teachers had anything to do with their gender. Use your discussion to evaluate Parkinson's views on men and women.

Illustrate the difference between ability and skill from your own experience and observation.

GENE WELTFISH

The Pawnee Person

1.   There is no simple formula for describing the intricate logic of
the Pawnee people's lives. One thing is clear—that no one is
caught within the social code. Against the backdrop of his natural
environment, each individual stands as his own person. The Old
World design for the human personality does not apply to this New
World Man. The Pawnee child was born into a community from
the beginning, and he never acquired the notion that he was
closed in "within four walls." He was literally trained to feel that
the world around him was his home—*kahuraru,* the universe,
meaning literally the inside land, and that his house was a small
model of it. The infinite cosmos was his constant source of strength
and his ultimate progenitor, and there was no reason why he
should hesitate to set out alone and explore the wide world, even
though years should pass before he returned. Not only was he not
confined within four walls but he was not closed in with a permanent group of people. The special concern of his mother did not
mean that he was so closely embedded with her emotionally that
he was not able to move about.

2.   Other people also were clearly concerned with him in a variety
of ways. There was no mistaking the constant concern of Old Bull
for the boy, Otter, in the earth lodge. And as for his grandmother,
this was of course patently clear. There was no mistaking the affection felt for him by Horse Rider. Even from the earliest time the
Pawnee knew there were differences in kinds of affection. He
knew he should go to his grandmother for intimate care but he
also looked up to his mother as his provider and protector. His father he regarded in the same way wherever he might be, and his
mother had pointed out to him that he should emulate his father.
Otter's Uncle War Cry and his other uncles came to the house and
again showed affectionate concern, and one winter when he broke
his leg his uncle stayed home and nursed and protected him. He
knew very early that he "had a home" in the house of Eagle Chief
which had been literally demonstrated to him in special feasts and
visits. His older half-brother Fox Chief was there for him even

THE PAWNEE PERSON: In *The Lost Universe* by Gene Weltfish. Reprinted by permission of University of Nebraska Press. Copyright © 1965 by Basic Books, Inc.

though not in the house. The breakup of the household and travel on the hunt did not dismay him, even when his grandmother stayed behind one winter, for his community traveled with him. This bringing of the community's concern to the child's attention from an early age was deliberately carried out.

3.   The wide application of the kin terms gave the family relationships a much wider reference. It made him realize that there were shades of closeness with his immediate kin and that many varying factors determined this just as they did in his outside attachments. The case of his mother's half-brothers was a graphic example. He found out that, in the last analysis, one made one's own relationships with people and that none was absolutely given.

4.   The intensified family togetherness of our present society stands in sharp contrast to these arrangements. The very physical plant of our family household fosters this intensity. Within this century, the apartment or family dwelling has become more and more isolated. In the past ten years, the isolation has become absolute and we have become the loneliest people that ever existed. Mechanical elevators, mechanical shopping, mechanical transportation, and other mechanical devices preclude almost all casual social contacts. At the same time, within the apartment or household the sexes are thrown together in an incest-breeding welter of physical familiarity. Simultaneously a demand is made for personal detachment, so that we require intensive psychological reorganization to heal us from the ordeal of our childhood. This emotional turmoil is implanted so early that we are convinced it is inevitable. In the outside world a further kind of isolation has been set up. We have developed a series of age shelves so that each age becomes a segregated universe of its own. We must desegregate the ages and remingle as persons. There can be no complementarity of experience in such a plan. Retirement is now a shelf for social discard, while the younger age levels are left to their conformities and magnified rivalries. Individuality can be too costly if it does not have a flexible society within which to operate. It is our task to design such a society.

5.   It is not easy for us to perceive the wide gap in kind between Pawnee society and our own, and yet in the face of all the terrible events of the past and the pressure to destroy his personality, surely it must mean something that the American Indian has maintained his identity among us. It was 20,000 years ago in the

latter part of the Ice Age that the buffalo hunters of the Old and New Worlds parted company. What communication they might have maintained over the Bering Strait or even the wide Pacific could have been only a trickle compared with the maximum cultural osmosis of Old World peoples. Thus unwittingly the American Indian has furnished us with our major control case in the study of human society and the processes of its growth.

6.   Historically, the control of masses of people has been an important element in the building of Old World civilization. For millennia, people have been grouped into ruling classes and ruled masses. Setting aside the practice of applauding this approach to human affairs as an advance in history and therefore a human benefit, the emergence of mechanization in its most refined form, i.e., automation, has made this social device obsolescent. But we cannot readily free ourselves of this habitual approach to the human being. It is therefore important for us to find a model of a human being who has never been pressed into a mass mold, no matter how different his physical setting may have been from ours. The Pawnee Indian is such a person. For our present and future society, we will need to develop a society composed entirely of creative individual personalities, and for this it is important that we look carefully into the detailed circumstances of the life of a Pawnee individual and study his actions and reactions within them.

7.   The fact that Old World civilization for several millennia has been based on masses of people reflects itself in our view of the individual as a function of the statistical average. The process of statistical generalization involves a disregarding of the very characteristics that make a man an individual, i.e., his uniqueness. Therefore, no matter how objectively the statistical average is compiled, it becomes impossible to rederive the individual from the statistical norm, even when some distribution of the selected traits is given. The Amerindian who has never been subject to mass organization in the North American setting preserved an understanding of the individual personality as the keystone of society rather than as a function of it. His society is therefore fluid and creative, albeit within limited technical resources, rather than inhibiting of the person as an integral entity. He does not require doctrine in order to develop formal social structures, and the structures he does develop are currently functional rather than frozen.

8.   It does not matter what sort of empires the North American Indians would or would not have developed had the European not disrupted his society. What does matter is that in examining his society as a total functioning social organism we have a contrast situation through which we can throw into relief our most stubbornly held social biases.

9.   Although the Pawnee home is at opposite poles to our own, there are suggestions to be drived from it that can be applied concretely to our own mode of living. Within the home, the Pawnee has personal and social mobility and a diverse circle of contacts; within his kindred he has a wide latitude of personal interrelationships. His aspirations are his own. He sets his own goal, which is his personal secret. His aspiration is not to surpass someone else, but to go beyond his own past achievements. He gives himself a name to serve social notice on people that he is on his way. Love and friendship, though less stable than kin, are also honored.

10.   I think I have given enough detail of Pawnee life to show that it was in no sense a Utopia. The struggle for survival and for the maintenance of personal dignity was great. Leaving aside the survival question, the challenge to the individual to develop himself was much greater than our own, for it was not only an avowed, but a literal purpose in life. For those individuals who are concerned that the transition from a mercantilist to a humanist society which we are now perforce making will leave the human being without incentives and challenges, Pawnee life should serve to dispel his doubts. A society built on the basis of the objective personal fulfillment will not be a lazy or an insipid society. It will be full of strength and dynamic movement. Today for the most part the intellectual and the artist carries this mode. For the future it will belong to us all, for everyone has something to contribute to such a society by the very fact that individuals are different. We need no prima donnas—only people as they are.

QUESTIONS

1. How is the Pawnee way of life different from the non-Indian way in the United States, according to Weltfish?
2. How does she illustrate the point that "no one is caught within the social code"?
3. What is the point of her analysis—to inform her readers about the

Pawnee way of life, to change her readers' minds about the American Indian, or to change her readers' thinking about themselves?
4. What methods of analysis does Weltfish employ in the essay? How are these methods fitted to her purpose in writing?

WRITING ASSIGNMENTS

Contrast the Pawnee way of life with details of your own, giving particular attention to the impact of the "social code" in your own life.

Discuss whether in your opinion Americans can learn from the Pawnee way of life. Comment on particular features of non-Indian life in America.

ORDER OF IDEAS

WILLIAM O. DOUGLAS

The Right to Defy
an Unconstitutional Statute

1. There are circumstances where the otherwise absolute obligation of the law is tempered by exceptions for individual conscience. As in the case of the conscientious objector to military service, the exception may be recognized by statute or, as in the case of the flag salute for school children, it may be required by the First Amendment. But in countless other situations the fact that conscience counsels violation of the law can be no defense. Those are the situations in which the citizen is placed in the dilemma of being forced to choose between violating the dictates of his conscience or violating the command of positive law.
2. The problem is age-old. In Sophocles' play, Antigone had this

choice to make. She chose to follow the dictates of her conscience, attempting to bury the body of her brother, Polynices, rather than conform to the edict of the tyrant, Creon, that the corpse remain unburied. Socrates, convicted of corrupting the youth of Athens, refused to "hold his tongue," preferring to face death. Even Hobbes, who wrote that civil obedience is the highest duty of a citizen, recognized that a point could be reached where conscience would demand that the command of the leviathan state must be disobeyed. But for Hobbes, civil disobedience was not justified unless to obey would be to lose the right to eternal salvation after death.

3.   The moral right to defy an unjust law was certainly not unknown in the American colonies. The Puritans fled England after they had defied the English sovereigns by adhering to their forms of worship. John Locke, an intellectual father of the American Revolution, wrote that, if the sovereign should require anything which appears unlawful to the private person, he is not obliged to obey that law against his conscience. Locke's philosophy found expression in the Declaration of Independence.

4.   Emerson wrote that "no greater American existed than Thoreau." Thoreau's insistence on his right to lead his own life and to resist the encroachment of government was typically American. In 1846, he refused to pay the town tax because he disapproved of the purposes for which the money was to be spent. For this, he spent a night in jail. He was released only after a friend had "interfered" and paid the tax. His short imprisonment resulted in Thoreau's dramatic essay on civil disobedience, where he insisted that he had the right to disobey an unjust law. "Under a government which imprisons any unjustly," he wrote, "the true place for a just man is also a prison."

5.   Thoreau's writings had a great impact on Gandhi. Gandhi's concept of *satyagraha* was one which championed the moral right to disregard an unjust law and undergo the penalty for its breach. He wrote:

> The law-breaker breaks the law surreptitiously and tries to avoid the penalty; not so the civil resister. He ever obeys the laws of the state to which he belongs, not out of fear of the sanctions, but because he considers them to be good for the welfare of society. But there come occasions, generally rare, when he considers certain laws to be so unjust as

to render obedience to them a dishonour. He then openly and civilly breaks them and quietly suffers the penalty of their breach. And in order to register his protest against the action of the law-givers, it is open to him to withdraw his co-operation from the state by disobeying such other laws whose breach does not involve moral turpitude.

6.   Unless the law applies with equal force to those who dissent from it, there can be no ordered society. The choice given the individual is not to obey the law or to violate it with impunity, but to obey the law or incur the punishment for disobedience. Socrates recognized the obligation of the law which had unjustly sentenced him to die, when he explained to Crito that he would not flee from his punishment. He recognized that his choice was to incur the punishment of the law rather than conform to it, but did not contend that he was above the law. Locke, too, observed that the "private judgement of any person concerning a law enacted in public matters, for the public good, does not take away the obligation of that law, nor deserve a dispensation." Rousseau, who had defended the right to resist unjust law, still observed that no individual in a democracy should have the right to be above the law. Both Thoreau and Gandhi recognized that disobedience of the law may be punished.

7.   These two values, the right of the individual to follow his own conscience and the right of society to promulgate rules for the orderly conduct of its affairs, are sometimes antagonistic. American democracy is not the leviathan state which Hobbes pictured. Our society is built upon the premise that is exists only to aid the fullest individual achievement of which each of its members is capable. Our starting point has always been the individual, not the state. Nevertheless, democracy is built upon the rule of the majority, and a civilized society requires orderly rules, applicable to all alike. If a statute is otherwise valid, the law does not consider the moral values which led to its disobedience.

8.   But the Puritan tradition of the citizen's right to shake his fist at the legislature has found its place in American law in the right to defy an unconstitutional statute. An unconstitutional statute is a lawless act by the legislature. The humblest citizen, confronted by all the forces of the state which insist that he must obey the law, may take matters into his own hands, defy an unconstitutional

statute, and risk the outcome on the ultimate decision of the courts. He may forsake the orderly processes of society and proceed as if the statute does not exist. That was Jefferson's attitude toward the Alien and Sedition Laws. On July 22, 1804, he wrote:

> . . . I discharged every person under punishment or prosecution under the sedition law, because I considered, and now consider, that law to be a nullity, as absolute and as palpable as if Congress had ordered us to fall down and worship a golden image; and that it was as much my duty to arrest its execution at every stage, as it would have been to have rescued from the fiery furnace those who should have been cast into it for refusing to worship the image. It was accordingly done in every instance, without asking what the offenders had done, or against whom they had offended, but whether the pains they were suffering were inflicted under the pretended sedition law.

9.   The clearest example of an individual's right to ignore an unconstitutional ordinance is in the area of prior restraint upon First Amendment freedoms, which I have discussed in the first lecture. *Thomas* v. *Collins*, 323 U.S. 516, involved a statute which required a labor organizer to obtain a license before he could address an assembly of laborers. He ignored that statute and spoke. His conviction for speaking without a license was overturned because the statute constituted an infringement of his right to speak. He was not required to submit to the invalid ordinance, apply for the license, and be refused the right to speak, before he was allowed to challenge the validity of the statute. Under the principle of *Thomas* v. *Collins,* a minister who is required to get a license to address his flock could not be convicted for preaching without a license.

10. Of course, if an individual violates a statute under the mistaken view that is is unconstitutional, he may be punished. As Chief Justice Stone once said, "There is no freedom to conspire to violate a statute with impunity merely because its constitutionality is doubted. The prohibition of the statute is infringed by the intended act in any case, and the law imposes its sanctions unless the doubt proves to be well founded." *Keegan* v. *United States*, 325 U.S. 478, 505. The citizen who defies the statute takes the risk

that he is mistaken. But if his views of the Constitution are accepted, he goes free.

11. A striking analogy may be found in the Articles of the Uniform Code of Military Justice. In the Armed Forces, discipline and obedience to orders are of primary importance. Under military discipline, respect for authority is the prime virtue. But, under Articles 90 through 92 of the Uniform Code, an American serviceman has the absolute right to disobey any unlawful order of a superior officer, for he is punished only for disobedience of a *lawful* order. A recent decision of the United States Court of Military Appeals demonstrates that this right has real value. An airman stationed in Japan, suspected of using narcotics, had been ordered by his squadron commander to furnish a urine specimen for chemical analysis. Although the airman was warned of the possibility of court-martial for failure to comply, he refused to do so. He was court-martialed for willful disobedience of the command of a superior officer. The United States Court of Military Appeals set aside the conviction, holding that the order was unlawful because it compelled the airman to furnish evidence against himself. *United States* v. *Jordan,* 7 U.S.C.M.A. 452. This was an order from a superior officer, with all the force of military discipline behind it; yet, under the Uniform Code of Military Justice, it could be disobeyed with impunity because the order itself was not legal.

12. There will be specific instances where most people will agree that the individual's right to defy even an unconstitutional statute may be denied because of the interest of society in the continued conduct of the processes of government. For example, a taxpayer can be required to pay an unconstitutional tax and sue for its return. If he prevails, he has only been temporarily deprived of the use of his money. For this he can be compensated. On the other hand, if every taxpayer refused to pay his taxes, the business of government would grind to a halt.

13. There has developed, however, in recent years a tendency to require the citizen to obey an extreme ordinance or statute, even though it is unconstitutional. The rights of the individual are then sacrificed to the interests of orderly conduct of the processes of government. The Court has gone far in requiring that sacrifice. The most striking example is *Poulos* v. *New Hampshire,* 345 U.S. 395. Jehovah's Witnesses had been arbitrarily denied a license to speak in a public park. The Court, in affirming their convictions for holding a religious meeting without the required license, held

that their remedy for violation of their right to speak was to proceed as required by state law to compel issuance of the license.

14. The *Poulos* decision is a significant departure from prior decisions which have allowed the individual the right to resist the unconstitutional demands of government. The right to speak, guaranteed by the First Amendment, was sacrificed to the delays, the expense, and the necessities of pursuing the processes of an "orderly society." *Id.*, p. 409.

15. The risk—the great and agonizing danger—in situations of this kind is that the citizen will be caught in the treadmill of an elusive administrative remedy. While he pursues it, his constitutional rights are denied. And it may take so much time to go through the intricate adminstrative system with all of its hearings and appeals that any relief will come too late and the great occasion, when the right to speak, to worship, or to assemble might have been enjoyed, will be lost.

16. The right to defy an unconstitutional statute has its roots in our traditions of individualism and in our mistrust of the uncontrolled power of the state. That mistrust was written into numerous limitations on governmental power contained in the Constitution. The right to ignore a statute that is unconstitutional is a reflection of those limitations. Like them, it says—so far government may go and no farther.

17. I have said enough to indicate that the right to be let alone, though greatly impaired in recent years, still clamors for recognition. It is a sturdy part of our heritage, more American than European, more Western than Eastern. It cannot be easily stamped out on this continent, for it is a part of all of us. It can be eroded and depreciated. But it will always be one of our great rallying points.

DISCUSSION: ORDER OF IDEAS

As in the paragraph, the order of ideas in the whole essay may be determined by the writer's audience. Thus, if the audience is able to understand the thesis without explanation, it may be stated toward the beginning. But if explanation is required, writers may build to the thesis. It may also appear later if writers assume their audience will be hostile to it or easier to convince, once the evidence has been considered.

Certain patterns of organization have become traditional in the essay, mainly because they reflect the natural processes of explanation and argument. The formal essay has been strongly influenced by the oration of the law courts and legislature of ancient Greece and Rome. The parts of this oration correspond to the formal essay as written today and can be summarized as follows:

> *exordium, or introduction,* which shapes the mood of the audience, appeals to their interest and good will, and states the subject of the oration or essay
>
> *division of proofs,* which summarizes the kinds of evidence to be presented, and states the thesis partially or fully
>
> *narration, or background,* which states the facts of the case
>
> *confirmation, or proof,* which argues the thesis
>
> *refutation,* which answers opponents
>
> *peroration, or conclusion,* which reinforces the original appeal to the audience, makes new appeals, and perhaps summarizes the proofs of the argument

The formal essay may omit one or several of these parts; for example, the confirmation, or proof, may consist merely of a presentation of details in support of the main point or thesis. The parts may also be arranged in a different way, the refutation perhaps coming before the confirmation or combined with it. This procedure has the advantage of unifying the argument in accord with traditional approaches to the audience. In other words, the writer is able to exploit a familiar ordering of ideas.

The ideas of the informal essay may be as carefully organized as those of the formal essay, but the division of parts usually is less rigorous. For example, Orwell's "Shooting an Elephant" makes important comments on the relationship between imperialist ruler and those ruled through an episode that defines their relationship. These same comments could be made in a formal discussion of the problem, without illustration.

The ordering of ideas may reveal a characteristic way of thinking—one that we find in other essays by the same writer. We sometimes use the word *style* to describe this feature. In the larger sense of the word, *style* is the sum of choices we make—in diction and sentence construction as well as organization. One writer may favor long, heavily coordinated sentences, as in the speech of a non-stop talker. Another writer, used to speaking in short clipped sentences, may write in the same way. The preference for short or long paragraphs may reflect this same personal characteristic.

If choice is essential to style in writing, we might assume that only writing reflects style, since we usually do not plan how we talk. But we clearly do make choices in speaking—if only in our choice of vocabulary. In writing, our choices may be more deliberate—and usually *are* deliberate when we have a particular audience in mind. Choice and habit are hard to distinguish. The sentences we write depend on the shape and rhythm of the sentences we speak: we speak before we write. In the course of growing up, the influence of conventional usage affects our ways of expressing ourselves. Gradually we learn to fit these ways to various situations. Most of the time we depend on familiar phrases, and we usually do not depart from familiar sentence patterns. In formal situations our choices are increasingly selective: we are more sensitive to the appropriateness of words, and we may take care with our sentences and diction in ways we do not in ordinary conversation. Ultimately personal style is shaped not only by acquired habits of thought and feeling but by personality. Thought and expression in the literate person are inseparable processes. The order of ideas in our writing reflects how we think and also how we feel.

QUESTIONS

1. Douglas's essay is one of a series of lectures on civil rights and the law. In this particular essay he is not arguing a proposition, but explaining an antagonism arising from "two values," the rights of the individual and the rights of society. The essay omits, then, a refutation, and since Douglas had introduced his subject in previous lectures, he briefly states it in his opening paragraph: those situations where the individual must choose between the dictates of conscience and "the command of positive law." Here, briefly, is a paragraph outline of the essay:

1	Introduction, stating the subject of the essay
2–6	Narration, or background of the dilemma—from Antigone and Socrates in ancient Greece, to Thoreau and Gandhi; various views of the dilemma, from Socrates to Locke and Rousseau
7	Division of proofs, here a statement of the thesis: "These two values, the right of the individual to follow his own conscience and the right of society to promulgate rules for the orderly conduct of its affairs, are sometimes antagonistic."
8	Further explanation of the dilemma, through the Puritans and Jefferson on the Alien and Sedition Laws

9–10 A specific example: "prior restraint upon First Amendment freedoms"

11 A second example: military law

12–14 Recent examples of the antagonists between private conscience and positive law

15–17 Conclusions, chiefly an opinion on the current situation in law bearing on the dilemma

Does Douglas say in the concluding paragraphs how the dilemma might be resolved? Or does he say or imply that it is unavoidable and irresolvable? How do the concluding paragraphs raise questions to be taken up in succeeding lectures?

2. Douglas begins with a division of laws. What is the principle of division?

3. In paragraphs 9 and 10 Douglas distinguishes kinds of disobedience. What is the principle of his division?

4. What criterion differentiates the legitimate "interest of society in the continued conduct of the processes of government" from the illegitimate (paragraphs 12–15)?

5. In addition to division, in what other ways does Douglas develop his ideas?

WRITING ASSIGNMENT

Discuss the extent to which Martin Luther King, Jr. was in agreement with Douglas in his analysis of nonviolent resistance.

RALPH ELLISON
Living with Music

1. In those days it was either live with music or die with noise, and we chose rather desperately to live. In the process our apartment—what with its booby-trappings of audio equipment, wires, discs and tapes—came to resemble the Collier mansion, but that was later. First there was the neighborhood, assorted drunks and a singer.

LIVING WITH MUSIC: In *High Fidelity*, December, 1955. Reprinted by permission of *High Fidelity*.

2. We were living at the time in a tiny ground-floor-rear apartment in which I was also trying to write. I say "trying" advisedly. To our right, separated by a thin wall, was a small restaurant with a juke box the size of the Roxy. To our left, a night-employed swing enthusiast who took his lullaby music so loud that every morning promptly at nine Basie's brasses started blasting my typewriter off its stand. Our living room looked out across a small back yard to a rough stone wall to an apartment building which, towering above, caught every passing thoroughfare sound and rifled it straight down to me. There were also howling cats and barking dogs, none capable of music worth living with, so we'll pass them by.

3. But the court behind the wall, which on the far side came knee-high to a short Iroquois, was a forum for various singing and/or preaching drunks who wandered back from the corner bar. From these you sometimes heard a fair barbershop style "Bill Bailey," free-wheeling versions of "The Bastard King of England," the saga of Uncle Bud, or a deeply felt rendition of Leroy Carr's "How Long Blues." The preaching drunks took on any topic that came to mind: current events, the fate of the long-sunk *Titanic* or the relative merits of the Giants and the Dodgers. Naturally there was great argument and occasional fighting—none of it fatal but all of it loud.

4. I shouldn't complain, however, for these were rather entertaining drunks, who like the birds appeared in the spring and left with the first fall cold. A more dedicated fellow was there all the time, day and night, come rain, come shine. Up on the corner lived a drunk of legend, a true phenomenon, who could surely have qualified as the king of all the world's winos—not excluding the French. He was neither poetic like the others nor ambitious like the singer (to whom we'll presently come) but his drinking bouts were truly awe-inspiring and he was not without his sensitivity, In the throes of his passion he would shout to the whole wide world one concise command, "Shut up!" Which was disconcerting enough to all who heard (except, perhaps, the singer), but such were the labyrinthine acoustics of courtyards and areaways that he seemed to direct his command at me. The writer's block which this produced is indescribable. On one heroic occasion he yelled his obsessive command without one interruption longer than necessary to take another drink (and with no appreciable loss of volume, penetration or authority) for three long summer days and

nights, and shortly afterwards he died. Just how many lines of agitated prose he cost me I'll never know, but in all that chaos of
sound I sympathized with his obsession, for I, too, hungered and
thirsted for quiet. Nor did he inspire me to a painful identification,
and for that I was thankful. Identification, after all, involves feelings of guilt and responsibility, and since I could hardly hear my
own typewriter keys I felt in no way accountable for his condition.
We were simply fellow victims of the madding crowd. May he rest
in peace.

5.   No, these more involved feelings were aroused by a more intimate source of noise, one that got beneath the skin and worked
into the very structure of one's consciousness—like the "fate"
motif in Beethoven's Fifth or the knocking-at-the-gates scene in
Macbeth. For at the top of our pyramid of noise there was a singer
who lived directly above us; you might say we had a singer on our
ceiling.

6.   Now, I had learned from the jazz musicians I had known as a
boy in Oklahoma City something of the discipline and devotion to
his art required of the artist. Hence I knew something of what the
singer faced. These jazzmen, many of them now world-famous,
lived for and with music intensely. Their driving motivation was
neither money nor fame, but the will to achieve the most eloquent
expression of idea-emotions through the technical mastery of their
instruments (which, incidentally, some of them wore as a priest
wears the cross) and the give and take, the subtle rhythmical
shaping and blending of idea, tone and imagination demanded of
group improvisation. The delicate balance struck between strong
individual personality and the group during those early jam sessions was a marvel of social organization. I had learned too that the
end of all this discipline and technical mastery was the desire to
express an affirmative way of life through its musical tradition and
that this tradition insisted that each artist achieve his creativity
within its frame. He must learn the best of the past, and add to it
his personal vision. Life could be harsh, loud and wrong if it
wished, but they lived it fully, and when they expressed their attitude toward the world it was with a fluid style that reduced the
chaos of living to form.

7.   The objectives of these jazzmen were not at all those of the
singer on our ceiling, but though a purist committed to the mastery of the *bel canto* style, German *lieder,* modern French art songs

and a few American slave songs sung as if *bel canto*, she was intensely devoted to her art. From morning to night she vocalized, regardless of the condition of her voice, the weather or my screaming nerves. There were times when her notes, sifting through her floor and my ceiling, bouncing down the walls and ricocheting off the building in the rear, whistled like tenpenny nails, buzzed like a saw, wheezed like the asthma of a Hercules, trumpeted like an enraged African elephant—and the squeaky pedal of her piano rested plumb center above my typing chair. After a year of non-co-operation from the neighbor on my left I became desperate enough to cool down the hot blast of his phonograph by calling the cops, but the singer presented a serious ethical problem: Could I, an aspiring artist, complain against the hard work and devotion to craft of another aspiring artist?

8.   Then there was my sense of guilt. Each time I prepared to shatter the ceiling in protest I was restrained by the knowledge that I, too, during my boyhood, had tried to master a musical instrument and to the great distress of my neighbors—perhaps even greater than that which I now suffered. For while our singer was concerned basically with a single tradition and style, I had been caught actively between two: that of the Negro folk music, both sacred and profane, slave song and jazz, and that of Western classical music. It was most confusing; the folk tradition demanded that I play what I heard and felt around me, while those who were seeking to teach the classical tradition in the schools insisted that I play strictly according to the book and express that which I was *supposed* to feel. This sometimes led to heated clashes of wills. Once during a third-grade music appreciation class a friend of mine insisted that it was a large green snake he saw swimming down a quiet brook instead of the snowy bird the teacher felt that Saint-Saëns' *Carnival of the Animals* should evoke. The rest of us sat there and lied like little black, brown and yellow Trojans about that swan, but our stalwart classmate held firm to his snake. In the end he got himself spanked and reduced the teacher to tears, but truth, reality and our environment were redeemed. For we were all familiar with snakes, while a swan was simply something the Ugly Duckling of the story grew up to be. Fortunately some of us grew up with a genuine appreciation of classical music *despite* such teaching methods. But as an aspiring trumpeter I was to wallow in sin for years before being awakened to guilt by our singer.

9. Caught mid-range between my two traditions, where one attitude often clashed with the other and one technique of playing was by the other opposed, I caused whole blocks of people to suffer.

10. Indeed, I terrorized a good part of an entire city section. During summer vacation I blew sustained tones out of the window for hours, usually starting—especially on Sunday mornings—before breakfast. I sputtered whole days through M. Arban's (he's the great authority on the instrument) double- and triple-tonguing exercises—with an effect like that of a jackass hiccupping off a big meal of briars. During school-term mornings I practiced a truly exhibitionist "Reveille" before leaving for school, and in the evening I generously gave the ever-listening world a long, slow version of "Taps," ineptly played but throbbing with what I in my adolescent vagueness felt was a romantic sadness. For it was farewell to day and a love song to life and a peace-be-with-you to all the dead and dying.

11. On hot summer afternoons I tormented the ears of all not blessedly deaf with imitations of the latest hot solos of Hot Lips Paige (then a local hero), the leaping right hand of Earl "Fatha" Hines, or the rowdy poetic flights of Louis Armstrong. Naturally I rehearsed also such school-band standbys as the *Light Cavalry* Overture, Sousa's "Stars and Stripes Forever," the *William Tell* Overture, and "Tiger Rag." (Not even an after-school job as office boy to a dentist could stop my efforts. Frequently, by way of encouraging my development in the proper cultural direction, the dentist asked me proudly to render Schubert's *Serenade* for some poor devil with his jaw propped open in the dental chair. When the drill got going, or the forceps bit deep, I blew real strong.)

12. Sometimes, inspired by the even then considerable virtuosity of the late Charlie Christian (who during our school days played marvelous riffs on a cigar box banjo), I'd give whole summer afternoons and the evening hours after heavy suppers of black-eyed peas and turnip greens, cracklin' bread and buttermilk, lemonade and sweet potato cobbler, to practicing hard-driving blues. Such food oversupplied me with bursting energy, and from listening to Ma Rainey, Ida Cox and Clara Smith, who made regular appearances in our town, I knew exactly how I wanted my horn to sound. But in the effort to make it do so (I was no embryo Joe Smith or Tricky Sam Nanton) I sustained the curses of both Christian and

infidel—along with the encouragement of those more sympathetic citizens who understood the profound satisfaction to be found in expressing oneself in the blues.

13. Despite those who complained and cried to heaven for Gabriel to blow a chorus so heavenly sweet and so hellishly hot that I'd forever put down my horn, there were more tolerant ones who were willing to pay in present pain for future pride.

14. For who knew what skinny kid with his chops wrapped around a trumpet mouthpiece and a faraway look in his eyes might become the next Armstrong? Yes, and send you, at some big dance a few years hence, into an ecstasy of rhythm and memory and brassy affirmation of the goodness of being alive and part of the community? Someone had to; for it was part of the group tradition—though that was not how they said it.

15. "Let that boy blow," they'd say to the protesting ones. "He's got to talk baby talk on that thing before he can preach on it. Next thing you know he's liable to be up there with Duke Ellington. Sure, plenty Oklahoma boys are up there with the big bands. Son, let's hear you try those 'Trouble in Mind Blues.' Now try and make it sound like old Ida Cox sings it."

16. And I'd draw in my breath and do Miss Cox great violence.

17. Thus the crimes and aspirations of my youth. It had been years since I had played the trumpet or irritated a single ear with other than the spoken or written word, but as far as my singing neighbor was concerned I had to hold my peace. I was forced to listen, and in listening I soon became involved to the point of identification. If she sang badly I'd hear my own futility in the windy sound; if well, I'd stare at my typewriter and despair that I should ever make my prose so sing. She left me neither night nor day, this singer on our ceiling, and as my writing languished I became more and more upset. Thus one desperate morning I decided that since I seemed doomed to live within a shrieking chaos I might as well contribute my share; perhaps if I fought noise with noise I'd attain some small peace. Then a miracle: I turned on my radio (an old Philco AM set connected to a small Pilot FM tuner) and I heard the words

> *Art thou troubled?*
> *Music will calm thee . . .*

I stopped as though struck by the voice of an angel. It was Kathleen Ferrier, that loveliest of singers, giving voice to the aria from

Handel's *Rodelinda*. The voice was so completely expressive of words and music that I accepted it without question—what lover of the vocal art could resist her?

18. Yet it was ironic, for after giving up my trumpet for the typewriter I had avoided too close a contact with the very art which she recommended as balm. For I had started music early and lived with it daily, and when I broke I tried to break clean. Now in this magical moment all the old love, the old fascination with music superbly rendered, flooded back. When she finished I realized that with such music in my own apartment, the chaotic sounds from without and above had sunk, if not into silence, then well below the level where they mattered. Here was a way out. If I was to live and write in that apartment, it would be only through the grace of music. I had tuned in a Ferrier recital, and when it ended I rushed out for several of her records, certain that now deliverance was mine.

19. But not yet. Between the hi-fi record and the ear, I learned, there was a new electronic world. In that realization our apartment was well on its way toward becoming an audio booby trap. It was 1949 and I rushed to the Audio Fair. I have, I confess, as much gadget-resistance as the next American of my age, weight and slight income; but little did I dream of the test to which it would be put. I had hardly entered the fair before I heard David Sarser's and Mel Sprinkle's Musician's Amplifier, took a look at its schematic and, recalling a boyhood acquaintance with such matters, decided that I could build one. I did, several times before it measured within specifications. And still our system was lacking. Fortunately my wife shared my passion for music, so we went on to buy, piece by piece, a fine speaker system, a first-rate AM-FM tuner, a transcription turntable and a speaker cabinet. I built half a dozen or more preamplifiers and record compensators before finding a commercial one that satisfied my ear, and, finally, we acquired an arm, a magnetic cartridge and—glory of the house—a tape recorder. All this plunge into electronics, mind you, had as its simple end the enjoyment of recorded music as it was intended to be heard. I was obsessed with the idea of reproducing sound with such fidelity that even when using music as a defense behind which I could write, it would reach the unconscious levels of the mind with the least distortion. And it didn't come easily. There were wires and pieces of equipment all over the tiny apartment (I became a compulsive experimenter) and it was worth your life to move about without first

taking careful bearings. Once we were almost crushed in our sleep by the tape machine, for which there was space only on a shelf at the head of our bed. But it was worth it.

20. For now when we played a recording on our system even the drunks on the wall could recognize its quality. I'm ashamed to admit, however, that I did not always restrict its use to the demands of pleasure or defense. Indeed, with such marvels of science at my control I lost my humility. My ethical consideration for the singer up above shriveled like a plant in too much sunlight. For instead of soothing, music seemed to release the beast in me. Now when jarred from my writer's reveries by some especially enthusiastic flourish of our singer, I'd rush to my music system with blood in my eyes and burst a few decibels in her direction. If she defied me with a few more pounds of pressure against her diaphragm, then a war of decibels was declared.

21. If, let us say, she were singing *"Depuis le Jour"* from *Louise,* I'd put on a tape of Bidu Sayão performing the same aria, and let the rafters ring. If it was some song by Mahler, I'd match her spitefully with Marian Anderson or Kathleen Ferrier; if she offended with something from *Der Rosenkavalier,* I'd attack her flank with Lotte Lehmann. If she brought me up from my desk with art songs by Ravel or Rachmaninoff, I'd defend myself with Maggie Teyte or Jennie Tourel. If she polished a spiritual to a meaningless artiness I'd play Bessie Smith to remind her of the earth out of which we came. Once in a while I'd forget completely that I was supposed to be a gentleman and blast her with Strauss' *Zarathustra,* Bartók's *Concerto for Orchestra,* Ellington's "Flaming Sword," the famous crescendo from *The Pines of Rome,* or Satchmo scatting, "I'll be Glad When You're Dead" (you rascal you!). Oh, I was living with music with a sweet vengeance.

22. One might think that all this would have made me her most hated enemy, but not at all. When I met her on the stoop a few weeks after my rebellion, expecting her fully to slap my face, she astonished me by complimenting our music system. She even questioned me concerning the artists I had used against her. After that, on days when the acoustics were right, she'd stop singing until the piece was finished and then applaud—not always, I guessed, without a justifiable touch of sarcasm. And although I was now getting on with my writing, the unfairness of this business bore in upon me. Aware that I could not have withstood a similar comparison with literary artists of like caliber, I grew remorseful. I

also came to admire the singer's courage and control, for she was neither intimidated into silence nor goaded into undisciplined screaming; she persevered, she marked the phrasing of the great singers I sent her way, she improved her style.

23. Better still, she vocalized more softly, and I, in turn, used music less and less as a weapon and more for its magic with mood and memory. After a while a simple twirl of the volume control up a few decibels and down again would bring a live-and-let-live reduction of her volume. We have long since moved from that apartment and that most interesting neighborhood and now the floors and walls of our present apartment are adequately thick and there is even a closet large enough to house the audio system; the only wire visible is that leading from the closet to the corner speaker system. Still we are indebted to the singer and the old environment for forcing us to discover one of the most deeply satisfying aspects of our living. Perhaps the enjoyment of music is always suffused with past experience; for me, at least, this is true.

24. It seems a long way and a long time from the glorious days of Oklahoma jazz dances, the jam sessions at Halley Richardson's place on Deep Second, from the phonographs shouting the blues in the back alleys I knew as a delivery boy, and from the days when watermelon men with voices like mellow bugles shouted their wares in time with the rhythm of their horses' hoofs and farther still from the washerwomen singing slave songs as they stirred sooty tubs in sunny yards; and a long time, too, from those intense, conflicting days when the school music program of Oklahoma City was tuning our earthy young ears to classical accents— with music appreciation classes and free musical instruments and basic instruction for any child who cared to learn and uniforms for all who made the band. There was a mistaken notion on the part of some of the teachers that classical music had nothing to do with the rhythms, relaxed or hectic, of daily living, and that one should crook the little finger when listening to such refined strains. And the blues and the spirituals—jazz—? they would have destroyed them and scattered the pieces. Nevertheless, we learned some of it all, for in the United States when traditions are juxtaposed they tend, regardless of what we do to prevent it, irresistibly to merge. Thus musically at least each child in our town was an heir of all the ages. One learns by moving from the familiar to the unfamiliar, and while it might sound incongruous at first, the step from the spirituality of the spirituals to that of the Beethoven of the sym-

phonies or the Bach of the chorales is not as vast as it seems. Nor is the romanticism of a Brahms or Chopin completely unrelated to that of Louis Armstrong. Those who know their native culture and love it unchauvinistically are never lost when encountering the unfamiliar.

25. Living with music today we find Mozart and Ellington, Kirsten Flagstad and Chippie Hill, William L. Dawson and Carl Orff all forming part of our regular fare. For all exalt life in rhythm and melody; all add to its significance. Perhaps in the swift change of American society in which the meanings of one's origin are so quickly lost, one of the chief values of living with music lies in its power to give us an orientation in time. In doing so, it gives significance to all those indefinable aspects of experience which nevertheless help to make us what we are. In the swift whirl of time music is a constant, reminding us of what we were and of that toward which we aspired. Art thou troubled? Music will not only calm, it will ennoble thee.

QUESTIONS

1. How do the opening four paragraphs establish a tone and suggest a theme or line of thought to be pursued in the whole essay? How do these paragraphs prepare the reader for the more serious consideration of "a more intimate source of noise" in paragraph 5 and the paragraphs that follow, in particular the reference to "the chaos of living" at the end of paragraph 6?
2. What do the details of the opening seven paragraphs reveal about the background and character of the writer?
3. Ellison states an important idea in paragraph 8: "For while our singer was concerned basically with a single tradition and style, I had been caught actively between two: that of the Negro folk music, both sacred and profane, slave song and jazz, and that of Western classical music." Have paragraphs 1–7 anticipated this theme in any way? Is the conflict they deal with of the same kind?
4. How do the two kinds of music represent two cultural ideals and worlds in the whole essay? How does Ellison use his personal experience to keep the focus of the essay on these differences?
5. Ellison builds to a series of statements about music and about life in the United States. Could one of these be considered the thesis of the essay—a statement that explains the organization and accounts for the various details and considerations? Or are paragraphs 24 and 25 afterthoughts or reflections? Might the essay have ended with paragraph 23 without seeming incomplete?

WRITING ASSIGNMENTS

Characterize the author of the essay on the basis of the details he provides about himself and his interests. Build your characterization to a statement of the quality you believe stands out most in the essay.

First describe your musical preferences, distinguishing them carefully. Then account for them and indicate the extent to which they have produced a conflict in your life comparable to the conflict Ellison portrays in paragraph 8.

L. E. SISSMAN

"Into the Air, Junior Birdmen!"

1.   Detroit, summer, 1938. A spun-gold Sunday morning. In my small, north-facing bedroom, I wake slowly to the Sunday sounds. Big yellow Detroit Street Railway trolleys trundle infrequently by, a high, electric hum above the fierce metallic screech of the wheels upon the rails. A few early cars shift and start off from the Warren Avenue lights. Over on the polyglot East Side, a hundred various Catholic churches, Slavic churches, Scandinavian churches flung up by homesick immigrants begin their solemn monody of calling the faithful—and the habituated—to Mass or service. And then, faint but clear above the choirs of bells, comes the unignorable whine of a single-engined airplane. I slip out of bed, whip on my spectacles, and, after some drawing and quartering of the sky, descry a plane high over the Hotel Palmetto, Residential Rates. It is a Stinson monoplane, and the pilot, perhaps purely for his pleasure, is executing a series of shallow, lazy dives and zooms.

2.   Later in the day, if I can prevail upon my modestly machine-minded father, we will climb into our beetle-green 1935 Studebaker President sedan and make for the city airport, where we will stand behind a sawhorse barrier and watch the American Airlines DC-3s—described as "huge airliners" by the press of the day—arrive from or return to such exotic ports of call as Pittsburgh and

"INTO THE AIR, JUNIOR BIRDMEN!": Reprinted by permission of Peter Davison.

Chicago, joined in the pattern by a handful of light pleasure craft like the Stinson.

3.   Still later, I will steal out of the house and walk several blocks to the Cass-Warren Drug, where, surrounded by the apothecarial ambience of iodoform, lemonade, and chocolate soda-fountain syrup. I'll browse at length through the latest newsstand issues of *Flying Aces* and *Model Airplane News,* buying a 25¢ copy only if the pharmacist starts looking menacing and retaliatory.

4.   Why do—did—I spend so much of my early life as an observer of aircraft? Why did I linger, with sticky, cemented fingers, over several years' supply of balsa models? Why, between the ages of nine and fifteen, did I devote so much of my free time to aviation lore? Largely, I suspect, because my whole generation was brainwashed to think of flying as America's (and the world's) last frontier. To speed our escape into the empyrean, the times had provided the added spur of the Depression. Any self-respecting lad of twenty must have thought at some point about aviation as a career; even to us tads of ten or twelve, flying a plane for a living seemed both a suitable and an admirable lifework.

5.   Looking back from adulthood, it seems easy to see that my enthusiasm, like that of thousands of others my age, was based on the public-relations efforts of the aircraft industry and the complaisance of the media in feeding its trivia to readers (of all ages) like me. However, my passion seemed anything but artificially stimulated at the time. Let me tell you how it inveigled me into an abortive—and aborted—career of sorts in aviation.

6.   I had, as I've suggested, been interested almost from the cradle in man-made things that fly. My father, who had once been an automotive engineer, helped to awaken that interest; my fellows at school, subjected just as I was to the propaganda for air-mindedness, fanned it into something resembling an eternal flame. If I could take you back to the dim institutional corridors of Miss Newman's and Detroit Country Day School in the late thirties and early forties, you'd probably see nothing but a bunch of knickerbockered schoolboys; I, on the other hand, would see a corps of flying cadets like those so innocently apostrophized in the radio jingle (from the old Jack Armstrong children's show, I think) which I've appropriated for the title of this article.

7.   Soon—sometime in the late thirties—reading was not enough, and I began to test the accuracy of my eye and the efficacy of my unformed hand with a series of model airplanes. They started,

modestly enough, with "solid" models, carved from a block of balsa wood and hung, when completed, in the modeler's room for ornamentation. These rather static toys soon gave way to something more dynamic and exciting: flying models. Available then for as little as a quarter, fliers were rough replicas of famous planes—ranging from the Nieuports, Camels, and Spads of World War I to the Wacos and Bellancas of the thirties and even, by 1939, to the Messerschmitts and Spitfires of World War II. Assembly of these fliers was a tough test of the Junior Birdman's inner strengths. First you had to cut several score parts out of a printed (but unperforated) balsa sheet with an X-acto knife, a chore guaranteed to make strong boys weep and men—their fathers—despair in unison.

8.   Next came the assembling. To make the wings, the cut-out balsa wing ribs were cemented to thin balsa stringers with a cross section one sixteenth of an inch square. To make the body, you laced more thin (and maddeningly fragile) stringers along the cut-out pieces that gave the fuselage its shape. Then—after a few small side chores like the elevator and rudder—you covered the wings and fuselage with a flimsy Japanese paper called, appropriately, model-airplane tissue, and shrank the new covering tight with an application of dope, a banana-oil-like substance.

9.   But the proof of the modeler's prowess came in the flying. On a Saturday or Sunday—whenever your father was free—you'd pack the airplane in his car and he'd drive to some field on the outskirts where model airplanes were informally flown. You'd wind the rubber motor to within a literal inch of its life (I seem to remember 150 winds being *de rigueur* for smaller models of this kind) and hand-launch the craft into the wind. In most cases, the featherlight ship would be flung by the wind onto its nose at once, often breaking a wing and causing the modeler to repair to the drawing board; occasionally, the gods would permit a perfect hop of fifty or so feet and an uncruel landing, sparing the Fokker D-7 (or whatever it was) to fly another day. Most of my models followed the former course until, sometime around the beginning of the war, my old man kicked through with a big, tough, gasoline-powered model built to bounce off the great outdoors and come back for more abuse.

10. The gas model—though it wasn't used as often as I would have liked, owing to a reluctant father—represented some sort of coming of age for me, as did some experiments in the early forties with Jerzy, a Polish contemporary of mine from the East Side. If I

was far gone in air-mindedness, Jerzy was second only to the Brothers Wright in his pioneering enthusiasm; working from plans in adult aviation magazines, he had managed, when I appeared on the scene, to build several flyable miniature helicopters. Together we perfected the design—which looked a lot like your average traffic reporter's chopper today—and flew our prototypes in a number of model air meets, often winning our class when there *was* a helicopter class.

11. This conquest of the air, limited as it was, spurred me to make more of my avocational obsession. Since I was still in my lower teens, it was highly unlikely that I could learn to fly a real airplane, or, since I was myopic to the point of undraftability, that I could volunteer for the then Army Air Force and enjoy my training at Uncle Sam's expense. No, it was distressfully clear that I was not to take my seat at the controls of a genuine airplane for some time to come, if ever. (As it turned out, it was never to be; and I'm likely to die grounded unless I late and suddenly indulge the whim shared by my daring colleagues at the office.)

12. What could I, a mere schoolboy in numbing wartime, do instead? My mother, as usual, came up with A Plan. I was unfortunate in having a domineering mother who had all the answers to my future; by the same token, I was fortunate in having an aggressive mother who could open the most formidably locked doors for me. At any rate, my mother thought long and deeply, that winter of 1943 when I was just fifteen, and determined that I did possess one salable commodity in, or adjacent to, the field of aviation. To wit: an experienced, cement-fingered modeler myself, I could pass the gift of cutting balsa and stretching tissue along to even younger, but equally air-minded, boys and girls.

13. But how? I couldn't simply announce model-airplane-building seminars in my home; I had to have a base of operations. Very well, then: my mother, backed by my father, would set me up in a small hobby shop. They volunteered a round sum—I think $1000, a lot of money in those days—for the purchase of my stock in trade, plus $50 a month for rent. This latter amount was to be repaid from earnings, if any.

14. Obtaining stock was not a problem—even in mid-war, model-airplane kits and collateral items were available in quantity, presumably because they were morale-builders and propaganda-spreaders—but finding a suitable (i.e., cheap) storefront was. Since I could not afford to advertise, I required a high-traffic loca-

tion; my eyes fell on several untenanted stores on Woodward Avenue, the main drag of the city, which was only a two-minute walk from our home. Inquiries were unproductive: most landlords wanted $100 or more a month for these valuable spaces, and my (or my mother's) Plan seemed doomed. Until my father, heretofore a silent partner in the borning enterprise, noted that one of the stores for rent was owned by the New York *Times*. Why, he reasoned, wouldn't a high-minded enterprise like the *Times* want to help set up a worthy young man in an equally worthy—and virtually nonprofit—business? The trick, he reasoned, was to gather his family together—father, mother, and son—and make a personal pitch to the head of *Times* real-estate operations in Detroit.

15. He made inquiries; the said executive turned out to be a Mr. Sulzberger, a member of the *Times*'s ruling family, which my father felt augured well. He called for the appointment, which was duly granted. We met on a sunny morning in Mr. Sulzberger's modest office, high up in a downtown bank building that might well have been owned by the tentacular *Times*. It was my first business presentation, and, to my undying surprise, it went well. Mr. Sulzberger was chatty and avuncular, listening in grave and middle-aged courtesy to our shaky little scenario; when we finished our act, he quietly allowed as how something might be worked out; he'd be happy, he said, to assist such an ambitious young man. What it boiled down to was a reduced rent of $50 a month—right on target—but without a lease.

16. Model Airplanes Unlimited opened, with a new hand-lettered sign and the aforesaid $1000 in models and supplies, on April 1, 1943. School hours prevented my opening until two in the afternoon, but I made up for it by staying late in the evening. From the first, to my amazement, kids showed up in droves. Not just the middle-class kids from the immediate neighborhood, but dozens of blacks and poor whites from the slums of the East Side. And they brought money: war work had employed both of their parents in many cases, and their mothers were only too glad to spend a little cash on a place that would occupy and engross their kids while they were at work. So, at the early age of fifteen, I found myself running a kind of prototypical day-care center—and enjoying it immensely.

17. When school ended, in May, I extended my business hours with an assist from my parents, who often spelled me; as public schools also let out for the summer, the number of my customers

increased. It was busy, hectic, and even marginally profitable; despite the free tuition in modeling, I was clearing my rent and making a small and tidy profit on the sale of models. Best of all, my students and I had an enormously good time; as an only child, I had never worked closely with other children before, and the pleasure of teaching and teamwork was a revelation. And—in a city later to be famous for its racial tensions—black and white, hillbilly's son and sharecropper's son worked side by side with great goodwill.

18. But that was not to last. One hot day in that summer of 1943, there were rumors of riot, confirmed by a glance down Woodward Avenue: crowds of blacks and poor whites, advancing respectively from east and west, met in the middle of the street and did battle with fists and sticks, knives and blackjacks. Soon the National Guard was called in to restore peace, and olive-drab half-tracks patrolled the Avenue.

19. The riots continued sporadically for a few days, but my business, of course, came to a dead halt. Parents kept—and continued to keep—their kids at home. I might go through an entire day with half a dozen customers. Model Airplanes Unlimited was clearly moribund, and soon the time came to call once more on Mr. Sulzberger. As sympathetic as ever, he allowed us to shut down on short notice; we owed only that month's rent.

20. Now, as I write this, I hear the buzz of a light plane over in the west. In 1938, it was a wholly sweet sound, full of promise; now it is a bittersweet sound, reminding me with ever-increasing force that this is a life of choice and compromise; that I am no more a Junior Birdman; that the air and all its graces have escaped me. But grounded as I am, I still look up to see the light plane in the west.

QUESTIONS

1. Is Sissman merely describing an adolescent experience, or is he also using the experience to make a point?
2. How does he establish a point of view and state his subject before giving an account of his experience? How much background does he provide about boys' and girls' interest in aviation in the thirties? Is he concerned at all with the general interest in aviation in those years?
3. Why does he describe the process of building a model airplane? Does this detail help him to explain his business venture?

4. In general, what is the order of ideas in the essay? Do you see another way the ideas might have been organized?

WRITING ASSIGNMENTS

Walt Kelly and Sissman describe two different business ventures. Show how each author establishes a point of view and suggests the purpose of the essay. Then pinpoint the chief difference in their purpose in writing.

Describe an interest in your youth that led to a similar business venture or had unexpected consequences for your life. Provide sufficient background so that the reader understands your feelings and the general situation.

Argument and Persuasion

DEDUCTIVE REASONING

H. L. MENCKEN
Reflections on War

1.   The thing constantly overlooked by those hopefuls who talk of abolishing war is that it is by no means an evidence of decay but rather a proof of health and vigor. To fight seems to be as natural to man as to eat. Civilization limits and wars upon the impulse but it can never quite eliminate it. Whenever the effort seems to be most successful—that is, whenever man seems to be submitting most willingly to discipline, the spark is nearest to the powder barrel. Here repression achieves its inevitable work. The most warlike people under civilization are precisely those who submit most docilely to the rigid inhibitions of peace. Once they break through the bounds of their repressed but steadily accumulating pugnacity, their destructiveness runs to great lengths. Throwing off the chains of order, they leap into the air and kick their legs. Of all the nations engaged in the two World Wars the Germans, who were the most rigidly girded by conceptions of renunciation and duty, showed the most gusto for war for its own sake.

2.   The powerful emotional stimulus of war, its evocation of motives and ideals which, whatever their error, are at least more stim-

REFLECTIONS ON WAR: In *Minority Report—H. L. Mencken's Notebooks*, by H. L. Mencken. Copyright © 1956 by Alfred A. Knopf, Inc. Reprinted by permission of the publisher. Selection title by editor.

ulating than those which impel a man to get and keep a safe job—this is too obvious to need laboring. The effect on the individual soldier of its very horror, filling him with a sense of the heroic, increases enormously his self-respect. This increase in self-respect reacts upon the nation, and tends to save it from the deteriorating effects of industrial discipline. In the main, soldiers are men of humble position and talents—laborers, petty mechanics, young fellows without definite occupation. Yet no one can deny that the veteran shows a certain superiority in dignity to the average man of his age and experience. He has played his part in significant events; he has been a citizen in a far more profound sense than any mere workman can ever be. The effects of all this are plainly seen in his bearing and his whole attitude of mind. War may make a fool of man, but it by no means degrades him; on the contrary, it tends to exalt him, and its net effects are much like those of motherhood on women.

3.   That war is a natural revolt against the necessary but extremely irksome discipline of civilization is shown by the difficulty with which men on returning from it re-adapt themselves to a round of petty duties and responsibilities. This was notably apparent after the Civil War. It took three or four years for the young men engaged in that conflict to steel themselves to the depressing routine of everyday endeavor. Many of them, in fact, found it quite impossible. They could not go back to shovelling coal or tending a machine without intolerable pain. Such men flocked to the West, where adventure still awaited them and discipline was still slack. In the same way, after the Franco-Prussian War, thousands of young German veterans came to the United States, which seemed to them one vast Wild West. True enough, they soon found that discipline was necessary here as well as at home, but it was a slacker discipline and they themselves exaggerated its slackness in their imagination. At all events, it had the charm of the unaccustomed.

4.   We commonly look upon the discipline of war as vastly more rigid than any discipline necessary in time of peace, but this is an error. The strictest military discipline imaginable is still looser than that prevailing in the average assembly-line. The soldier, at worst, is still able to exercise the highest conceivable functions of freedom—that is, he is permitted to steal and to kill. No discipline prevailing in peace gives him anything even remotely resembling this. He is, in war, in the position of a free adult; in peace he is al-

most always in the position of a child. In war all things are ex-
cused by success, even violations of discipline. In peace, speaking
generally, success is inconceivable except as a function of discipline.

.   .   .

5.   The hope of abolishing war is largely based upon the fact that
men have long since abandoned the appeal to arms in their private
disputes and submitted themselves to the jurisdiction of courts.
Starting from this fact, it is contended that disputes between nations should be settled in the same manner, and that the adoption
of the reform would greatly promote the happiness of the world.
6.   Unluckily, there are three flaws in the argument. The first,
which is obvious, lies in the circumstance that a system of legal
remedies is of no value if it is not backed by sufficient force to impose its decisions upon even the most powerful litigants—a sheer
impossibility in international affairs, for even if one powerful litigant might be coerced, it would be plainly impossible to coerce a
combination, and it is precisely a combination of the powerful that
is most to be feared. The second lies in the fact that any legal system, to be worthy of credit, must be administered by judges who
have no personal interest in the litigation before them—another
impossibility, for all the judges in the international court, in the
case of disputes between first-class powers, would either be appointees of those powers, or appointees of inferior powers that
were under their direct influence, or obliged to consider the effects
of their enmity. The third objection lies in the fact, frequently
forgotten, that the courts of justice which now exist do not actually
dispense justice, but only law, and that this law is frequently in
direct conflict, not only with what one litigant honestly believes to
be his rights, but also with what he believes to be his honor. Practically every litigation, in truth, ends with either one litigant or the
other nursing what appears to him as an outrage upon him. For
both litigants to go away satisfied that justice has been done is almost unheard of.
7.   In disputes between man and man this dissatisfaction is not of
serious consequence. The aggrieved party has no feasible remedy;
if he doesn't like it, he must lump it. In particular, he has no feasible remedy against a judge or a juryman who, in his view, has
treated him ill; if he essayed vengeance, the whole strength of the
unbiased masses of men would be exerted to destroy him, and that
strength is so enormous, compared to his own puny might, that it

would swiftly and certainly overwhelm him. But in the case of first-class nations there would be no such overwhelming force in restraint. In a few cases the general opinion of the world might be so largely against them that it would force them to acquiesce in the judgment rendered, but in perhaps a majority of important cases there would be sharply divided sympathies, and it would constantly encourage resistance. Against that resistance there would be nothing save the counter-resistance of the opposition— *i.e.*, the judge against the aggrieved litigant, the twelve jurymen against the aggrieved litigant's friends, with no vast and impersonal force of neutral public opinion behind the former.

DISCUSSION: DEDUCTIVE REASONING

When the United Nations was formed in 1945, many people hoped that war could be abolished. But opinions differed. Hanson W. Baldwin wrote that we should not despair over war even if it took centuries to abolish it:

> The guiding star still shines; it cannot be attained in a century or two. But it is nevertheless worth struggling forward, pushing on; it would be worth the effort even if we knew the star was a mirage. *Death is an accepted part of life. Yet death is no cause for despair. The whole philosophy of man is keyed to the conception of the ultimate triumph of life over death.* Why, then, despair because war recurs?—*The New York Times*, May 21, 1945 [italics added—Ed.]

Notice the reasoning here. The italicized statements are presented as certain and well-established truths that provide decisive evidence for the conclusion: they are stated as if they were self-evident. One writer, Barrows Dunham, disagreed with Baldwin:

> Why despair? Because in war one's friends get killed, one's children get killed, and one gets killed oneself. Because everything one has built may be destroyed. Because it is idiocy to fight one war for the sake of fighting another later on. If human nature really does inevitably produce war, let us accept the fact without surrounding it with this comfortless nonsense.—*Man Against Myth*

Notice the difference in reasoning. Dunham moves from particular experiences to a generalization about them: the consequences of war are serious enough to make people despair. Dunham does not, however, assert that we *all* despair over war. His generalization is a probability only, not a certainty. Baldwin's reasoning is typical of deductive arguments; Dunham's, of inductive arguments.

Deductive reasoning concerning matters of fact begins with truths held to be certain—assumptions, beliefs, and suppositions about human beings and the world:

> We hold these truths to be self-evident; that all men are created equal; that they are endowed by their creator with certain unalienable rights; that among these are life, liberty, and the pursuit of happiness. . . .

Where do such "self-evident" truths come from? Some philosophers believe they are inborn in the human mind; others believe that they come from observation and experience. However derived, these assumptions or beliefs can be stated as propositions—statements that can be affirmed or denied, asserted as true or false. These propositions serve as the premises of deductive arguments, providing *decisive* evidence for the conclusion. In inductive arguments, by contrast, the premises provide *probable* evidence only for the conclusion.

Like the axioms of geometry, the premises of deductive arguments may be established by definition. The proposition that all squares have four sides is a premise of this kind: a body observed to contain *five* sides would not be called a square. Or people in a particular age may agree to consider a group of propositions as given: the propositions that open the Declaration of Independence are of this kind. For some philosophers a generalization based on repeated observation and experience (the process we call induction) may be regarded as so well established that it becomes a premise in a deductive argument: the statement that all human beings are mortal is such a generalization. For this generalization there must be no exceptions or counter-instances.

People in a later age may reject the deductive arguments of an earlier age, because they have come to reject the truth of the premises in light of new evidence. In Shakespeare's day people assumed that the body contained fluids or "humors" that governed health and personality. A "sanguine" personality—marked by rosy cheeks and a cheerful disposition—was attributed to an excess of blood, one of these humors. Indeed, heavenly bodies were thought to influence which of the humors dominated; a person born "under Jupiter" was sanguine or "jovial." And thinking was based on assumptions such as these. The scientific beliefs of yesterday are often the superstitions of today—at least to some of us.

The foremost characteristic of deductive arguments is that they may be valid or invalid—that is, correct or incorrect—in the process of reasoning from premises to conclusion:

major premise	Whatever increases self-understanding is useful.
minor premise	The study of literature increases self-understanding.
conclusion	The study of literature is useful.

Note that the conclusion of this deductive argument can serve as the major premise of another:

major premise	The study of literature is useful.
minor premise	Poetry is one kind of literature.
conclusion	The study of poetry is useful.

If all terms mentioned in the conclusion are mentioned in the premises, and if the terms are properly arranged, then whether or not the premises are true in fact, the argument is considered valid. The following argument is valid in form even though its premises are patently false:

All Americans speak French.
All waiters in French restaurants are Americans.
All waiters in French restaurants speak French.

It is clearly necessary not only that the process of reasoning be valid, but that the premises be true.

Invalid arguments are not easy to analyze, and logicians have rather complicated procedures for testing the validity of the many kinds of syllogism, the name given to the form of argument shown above. Here, we will note just a few of the common tests for validity and soundness:

First, the *middle term* of the syllogism may be undistributed. The middle term is the term that appears in the premises but not in the conclusion. The following syllogism is valid:

All *property owners* are taxpayers.
My neighbors are *property owners.*
My neighbors are taxpayers.

The middle term is *property owners.* It is "distributed" if it refers to *all* of the members of the class; it is "undistributed" if it refers only to

some of the members of the class. In the above syllogism a characteristic of all property owners is that they are taxpayers; this characteristic or fact is distributed among all members of the class; it is true of
all property owners, and therefore is true of all my neighbors. But if
the syllogism is written

> All property owners are *taxpayers*.
> My neighbors are *taxpayers*.
> My neighbors are property owners.

the middle term is *taxpayers* and is undistributed in relation to the
conclusion. Not all taxpayers are property owners, only *some* are;
therefore only *some* of my neighbors are property owners. Yet the
conclusion states all of my neighbors are. The syllogism is invalid.

A syllogism is defective if the middle term is ambiguous. In the
syllogism

> *Whoever thrusts a knife into a person* is a murderer.
> A surgeon is *someone who thrusts a knife into a person*.
> A surgeon is a murderer.

the middle term is incompletely defined and therefore ambiguous.

Finally, both premises must be affirmative if the conclusion is to
be affirmative; if one of the premises is negative, the conclusion must
be negative. The following syllogism is valid:

> No dogs are allowed in the grocery store.
> Rover is a dog.
> Rover is not allowed in the grocery store.

The following syllogism is invalid:

> No dogs are allowed in the store.
> Rover is not a dog.
> Rover is allowed in the store.

If the two premises are negative, no conclusion can be drawn, and the
argument is considered invalid.

To sum up, disagreement over deductive reasoning does not arise
only over the way conclusions are derived from premises: it may arise
over the premises themselves, as Dunham's criticism of Baldwin
shows. An argument may sound "logical" because the process of
reasoning is valid, but still be unsound because its premises are questionable or false.

QUESTIONS

1. In paragraphs 1–4, Mencken argues that war will not be easily abolished, and he states his major assumption explicitly: "To fight seems to be as natural to man as to eat." How does the wording of this statement and the wording of others in these paragraphs show that Mencken regards these assumptions as certain and decisive evidence for his conclusions? What conclusions does he reach, based on these assumptions?

2. Though he regards these assumptions as certain, Mencken explains and illustrates them. What examples does he present? Does he discuss one civilization, or instead generalize about "warlike people" on the basis of observations made over a period of time?

3. In testing the logic of an essay, the premises are sometimes restated according to the standard syllogism described above. Paragraph 1 of the Mencken contains the makings of several syllogisms; in the first of these, the major premise may be stated in these words: "The expression of a natural instinct is evidence of health and vigor." What are the minor premise and conclusion?

4. In paragraph 1 Mencken argues that repression of a natural instinct leads to increased destructiveness. What are the minor premise and conclusion?

5. L. A. White, in *Science of Culture,* argues that the need for military conscription refutes the assumption that people are naturally warlike. Given his assumptions and evidence, how might Mencken answer this objection? What do paragraphs 5–7 suggest?

6. In paragraphs 5–7 Mencken challenges "the hope of abolishing war," a hope based on the assumption that people have long since "submitted themselves to the jurisdiction of courts." What flaws does Mencken find in the argument, and what kind of evidence does he present in refutation? Does he deal with particular instances or instead generalize from observations made over a period of time?

7. Evaluate the following arguments. It may be necessary to reword the premises:

   a. Since all voters are citizens and I am a voter, I am a citizen.

   b. Since all voters are citizens and I am a citizen, I am a voter.

   c. Since the Irish are vegetarians and Bernard Shaw was Irish, Shaw was a vegetarian.

   d. Those who made 93 or better on the exam will receive an A in the course. Seven of us received an A in the course and therefore must have made 93 or better on the exam.

   e. Since beneficent acts are virtuous and losing at poker benefits others, losing at poker is virtuous.

8. An *enthymeme* is a condensed syllogism, one of whose premises is implied: Because I am a human being, I am mortal. In the following enthymemes, reconstruct the original syllogism by supplying the missing premise, and evaluate the argument. The premises and conclusion may need rewording:

   a. John F. Kennedy was a good President because he supported the space program and other kinds of scientific research.
   b. Capital punishment protects society from depraved individuals.
   c. I am a successful businessman because I had a paper route as a boy.
   d. I am an Independent voter, just as my father and grandfather were.

WRITING ASSIGNMENTS

Many thinkers have considered the problem of war: William James, in his essay "The Moral Equivalent of War"; Ruth Benedict, in *Patterns of Culture;* L. A. White, in *Science of Culture;* Sigmund Freud and Albert Einstein in their correspondence entitled . . . *Why War?* Compare the assumptions of two of these writers, or other writers who have dealt with the issue of war, and discuss how each seems to have arrived at them.

Write an argument for or against one of the following. In an additional paragraph identify one or more assumptions that underlie your argument, and explain why you hold these assumptions:

   a. nuclear power plants
   b. Aid to Dependent Children
   c. the 55 mile-per-hour speed limit
   d. periodic examination of licensed drivers
   e. required attendance in college classes
   f. compulsory gun registration

JACQUES MARITAIN

The Aims of Education

1.   Man is a person, who holds himself in hand by his intelligence and his will. He does not merely exist as a physical being. There is

THE AIMS OF EDUCATION: In *Education at the Crossroads.* Reprinted by permission of Yale University Press. Selection title by editor.

in him a richer and nobler existence; he has spiritual superexistence through knowledge and love. He is thus, in some way, a whole, not merely a part; he is a universe unto himself, a microcosm in which the great universe in its entirety can be encompassed through knowledge. And through love he can give himself freely to beings who are to him, as it were, other selves; and for this relationship no equivalent can be found in the physical world.

2.   If we seek the prime root of all this, we are led to the acknowledgment of the full philosophical reality of that concept of the soul, so variegated in its connotations, which Aristotle described as the first principle of life in any organism and viewed as endowed with supramaterial intellect in man, and which Christianity revealed as the dwelling place of God and as made for eternal life. In the flesh and bones of man there exists a soul which is a spirit and which has a greater value than the whole physical universe. Dependent though he may be upon the slightest accidents of matter, the human person exists by virtue of the existence of his soul, which dominates time and death. It is the spirit which is the root of personality.

3.   The notion of personality thus involves that of wholeness and independence. To say that a man is a person is to say that in the depth of his being he is more a whole than a part and more independent than servile. It is this mystery of our nature which religious thought designates when it says that the person is the image of God. A person possesses absolute dignity because he is in direct relationship with the realm of being, truth, goodness, and beauty, and with God, and it is only with these that he can arrive at his complete fulfillment. His spiritual fatherland consists of the entire order of things which have absolute value, and which reflect, in some manner, a divine Absolute superior to the world and which have a power of attraction toward this Absolute.

4.   Now it should be pointed out that personality is only one aspect or one pole of the human being. The other pole is—to speak the Aristotelian language—individuality, whose prime root is matter. The same man, the same entire man who is, in one sense, a person or a whole made independent by his spiritual soul, is also, in another sense, a material individual, a fragment of a species, a part of the physical universe, a single dot in the immense network of forces and influences, cosmic, ethnic, historic, whose laws we must obey. His very humanity is the humanity of an animal, living by sense and instinct as well as by reason. Thus man is "a horizon

in which two worlds meet." Here we face that classical distinction between the *ego* and the *self* which both Hindu and Christian philosophies have emphasized, though with quite diverse connotations.

5.   I should like to observe now that a kind of animal training, which deals with psychophysical habits, conditioned reflexes, sense-memorization, etc., undoubtedly plays its part in education: it refers to material individuality, or to what is not specifically human in man. But education is not animal training. The education of man is a human awakening.

6.   Thus what is of most importance in educators themselves is a respect for the soul as well as for the body of the child, the sense of his innermost essence and his internal resources, and a sort of sacred and loving attention to his mysterious identity, which is a hidden thing that no techniques can reach. And what matters most in the educational enterprise is a perpetual appeal to intelligence and free will in the young. Such an appeal, fittingly proportioned to age and circumstances, can and should begin with the first educational steps. Each field of training, each school activity—physical training as well as elementary reading or the rudiments of childhood etiquette and morals—can be intrinsically improved and can outstrip its own immediate practical value through being *humanized* in this way by understanding. Nothing should be required of the child without an explanation and without making sure that the child has understood.

7.   We may now define in a more precise manner the aim of education. It is to guide man in the evolving dynamism through which he shapes himself as a human person—armed with knowledge, strength of judgment, and moral virtues—while at the same time conveying to him the spiritual heritage of the nation and the civilization in which he is involved, and preserving in this way the century-old achievements of generations. The utilitarian aspect of education—which enables the youth to get a job and make a living—must surely not be disregarded, for the children of man are not made for aristocratic leisure. But this practical aim is best provided by the general human capacities developed. And the ulterior specialized training which may be required must never imperil the essential aim of education.

QUESTIONS

1. What are the sources of Maritain's assumptions about people, and how does he indicate these sources?
2. Does Maritain explain or illustrate these assumptions, or merely state them?
3. What conclusions does he derive from these assumptions relating to education?
4. What makes Maritain's argument a deductive one?

WRITING ASSIGNMENT

Show how your assumptions about yourself as a person shape your attitudes toward the courses you are now taking. Compare these attitudes with those you held in high school?

ROBERT A. GOLDWIN

Is It Enough
to Roll With the Times?

1. Many private institutions of higher education around the country are in danger. Not all will be saved, and perhaps not all deserve to be saved. There are low-quality schools just as there are low-quality businesses. We have no obligation to save them simply because they exist.

2. But many thriving institutions that deserve to continue are threatened. They are doing a fine job educationally, but they are caught in a financial squeeze, with no way to reduce rising costs or increase revenues significantly. Raising tuition doesn't bring in more revenue, for each time tuition goes up, the enrollment goes down, or the amount that must be given away in student aid goes up. Schools are bad businesses, whether public or private, not usually because of mismanagement but because of the nature of the enterprise. They lose money on every customer, and they can go bankrupt either from too few students or too many students.

IS IT ENOUGH TO ROLL WITH THE TIMES? In *Change* Magazine, vol. 7, no. 4, May 1975. Reprinted by permission of *Change* and of the author.

Even a very good college is a very bad business. That has always been true.

3.   It is such colleges, thriving but threatened, I worry about. Low enrollment is not their chief problem. Even with full enrollments, they may go under. Efforts to save them, and preferably to keep them private, are a national necessity. There is no basis for arguing that private schools are inherently better than public schools. Examples to the contrary abound. Anyone can name state universities and colleges that rank as the finest in the nation and the world. It is now inevitable that public institutions will be dominant, and therefore diversity is a national necessity. Diversity in the way we support schools tends to give us a healthy diversity in the forms of education. In an imperfect society such as ours, uniformity of education throughout the nation could be dangerous. In an imperfect society, diversity is a positive good. Ardent supporters of public higher education know the importance of sustaining private higher education.

4.   Diversity is a familiar argument, and a sound one, for sustaining a mixture of private and public educational institutions. But let me suggest another, perhaps less familiar argument: There are public elements and private elements in different kinds of education, striving toward different educational goals. Vocational or career education programs are designed to give the student salable skills and enable him to find a useful job. The public has an interest because skills are needed to keep our economy going, and so there is a public reason to provide such training. But the student's new skills are his exclusively, to sell as he chooses. This private aspect gives him a private reason to pay for the training. We get the benefit of his skills; he gets the income for himself.

5.   Another element of education might be called civic education. One important function of schools is development of an understanding of government and of the rights and duties of citizens. Especially in a democratic republic such as ours, citizens must be skilled in understanding the powers of government, and how those powers must be limited if our fundamental rights are to be secured. We are in danger if our many governments do too much or too little, and the only way to find the moderate middle ground is through education.

6.   The public has a very great stake in this task of civic education. If one is skilled in good citizenship, fellow citizens benefit at least as much. Is it the business of colleges to train good citizens?

I think it is, at a higher and more discerning level than in grade schools, which means a more questioning and challenging level. Undergraduates should inquire into the nature of the American government, its past, its present, its future—not as in graduate programs, from the detached viewpoint of the political scientist or the professional historian, but from the viewpoint of the concerned citizen who is part of a living community facing problems.

7.   There is a third element of education that is harder to name and that cannot easily be classified in terms of the benefits—who gets them or what they are. Some call these studies valueless. I call them invaluable. I mean those skills called the liberal arts. We don't often think of liberal studies as connected with skills, but in fact the liberal skills are the highest and hardest skills.

8.   There is a story that Euclid was giving a first geometry lesson to a young man, demonstrating the first theorem of geometry, the construction of an equilateral triangle. When he finished, the young man asked, "But Euclid, what shall I gain by learning such things?"

9.   Now consider how Euclid might have answered. He might have said, "Learn this and the theorems that follow, and when you get to the end of the first book of only 47 theorems, you will learn the Pythagorean theorem, which depends on this first theorem. And with that Pythagorean theorem you will have the basis of physics, and vectors of forces, and be able to design a bridge that will not fall down when the chariots cross. And with that theorem you will have the basis of trigonometry, which you can use to survey your next real estate purchase. That theorem also starts you on an understanding of irrational numbers, a great advance in number theory." Euclid might have said all of that—and more—to explain the practical benefits that could flow, and have flowed, from studying his first theorem.

10. Instead, Euclid turned to another in the group and said, "Give this man a coin since he must show a profit for everything he learns."

11. Why should he have given such a scornful response to that question? My guess is that Euclid was greatly disappointed in the young man because he did not see at once that mathematics is a liberal skill, in addition to being a powerful practical skill. Euclid hoped that the young man's heart would be gladdened, his spirit enlivened, his soul lifted, his mind expanded at the first experience of geometrical proof.

12. We call such studies "the humanities," because when we engage in them we discover something extraordinary about ourselves. We discover how exciting being human can be. We find we can develop very special skills that imitate the Creator himself, for we too can make new worlds, not out of nothing, but with nothing more than a pencil, a straight edge, and a mind. Such humanistic skills are also called liberal because they free us from the restraint of our material existence and let us soar as free men and women in the realm of the mind.

13. In a recent speech, Terrel H. Bell, U.S. Commissioner of Education, gave some advice to the leaders of small private colleges, from a different point of view than mine. He very properly said first that as U.S. Education Commissioner he had no right to tell anyone how to run his college. In fact, he said, there is a law against it. But he did feel that he had a personal responsibility to speak out candidly and exercise some leadership. I, of course, write on the same basis, expressing my own opinion, seeking to contribute to thinking on this vital question.

14. His message was that private colleges must "roll with the times" if they are to survive. The college that devotes itself "totally and unequivocally to the liberal arts today is just kidding itself." There is a "duty to provide our students also with salable skills. We are facing the worst economic situation that this country has seen since the end of World War II, with an unemployment rate of over 8 percent. To send young men and women into today's world armed only with Aristotle, Freud, and Hemingway is like sending a lamb into the lion's den. It is to delude them as well as ourselves. But if we give young men and women a useful skill, we give them not only the means to earn a good living, but also the opportunity to do something constructive and useful for society. Moreover, these graduates will experience some of those valuable qualities that come with meaningful work—self-respect, self-confidence, independence."

15. At first glance it would seem that Commissioner Bell means that the study of liberal arts is a useless luxury we cannot afford in hard times. But I don't think that is his meaning. I think he is criticizing those who send students into the world of work without skills. There are, unfortunately, schools in which students do not develop useful skills, especially skills of analytical thinking and experimenting and calculating. I agree that it is unfair to students,

and to all of us, just as Commissioner Bell says, to leave them to seek jobs in such an unprepared state.

16. But there is a problem in speaking of "salable skills." What skills are salable? Right now, skills for making automobiles are not highly salable, but they have been for decades and might be again. Skills in teaching are not now as salable as they were during the past 20 years, and the population charts indicate they may not be soon again. Home construction skills are another example of varying salability, as the job market fluctuates.

17. The first difficulty, then, is that if one wants to build a curriculum exclusively on what is salable, one will have to make the courses very short and change them very often, in order to keep up with the rapid changes in the job market. But will not the effort be in vain? In very few things can we be sure of future salability, and in a society where people are free to study what they want, and work where they want, and invest as they want, there is no way to keep supply and demand in labor in perfect accord.

18. A school that devotes itself totally and unequivocally to salable skills, especially in a time of high unemployment, sending young men and women into the world armed with only a narrow range of skills, is also sending lambs into the lion's den. If those people gain nothing more from their studies than supposedly salable skills, and can't make the sale because of changes in the job market, they have been cheated. But if those skills were more than salable, if study made them better citizens and made them happier to be human beings, they have not been cheated. They will find some kind of job soon enough. It might even turn out that those humanizing and liberating skills are salable. Flexibility, an ability to change and learn new things, is a valuable skill. People who have learned how to learn can learn outside of school. That is where most of us have learned to do what we do, not in school. Learning to learn is one of the highest liberal skills.

19. There is more to living than earning a living, but many earn good livings by the liberal skills of analyzing, experimenting, discussing, reading, and writing. Skills that are always in demand are those of a mind trained to think and imagine and express itself.

20. When the confidence of some is shaken, and many are confused about the direction the nation ought to follow in a new world situation, then civic education is more important than ever. And when the foundations of Western civilization are being challenged,

and resolution seems to falter because many people are not sure what we are defending and how we ought to defend it, then it seems to me we ought not to abandon liberal studies, but rather the reverse: We ought to redouble our commitment to that study, as if our lives depended on it.

21. Any college worthy of itself must set its sights higher than to "roll with the times." It must strive to make the times roll our way. And only if we understand our time and try to shape it and make it conform to what is right and best, are we doing what we are capable of doing. Perhaps that is the right way to deal with the times— with daring and class and style—as befits a truly great people.

22. We have always known that America made no sense as just another nation, as just one more power in the long historical parade. We have always known that we must stand for something special, or we don't stand at all. Without such a special commitment to liberty and justice for all, can America survive except perhaps under the most severe sort of dictatorship? What else can hold together such a vast and diverse territory and people? Liberal studies of human nature and the nature of things in general are not luxuries for us, but matters of life and death, and certainly a matter of our political liberty, which should be as dear to us as our lives.

QUESTIONS

1. Goldwin originally delivered this essay as a speech to the faculty and students of a small liberal-arts college in Florida. How does he address himself to the special concerns of this audience—the survival of the liberal arts college in face of the widespread demand for practical education?

2. Notice that Goldwin does not dismiss practical goals in education: he puts these goals into perspective. What is that perspective?

3. Goldwin builds to his thesis, stating it fully in paragraph 21: "Any college worthy of itself must set its sights higher than to 'roll with the times.'" How does he anticipate his thesis in earlier paragraphs, and how does he restate it later in the essay?

4. How does the story about Euclid prepare for the definition of liberal education?

5. Goldwin organizes his essay as a formal argument:

   introduction (paragraph 1, opening sentences of paragraph 2): general statement of subject

narration or background (paragraphs 2–7): review of the current situation in education
confirmation or main argument (paragraphs 8–12): definition and defense of liberal education
refutation (paragraphs 13–18): an answer to the idea that colleges must "roll with the times"
conclusion (paragraphs 19–22)

To what uses does Goldwin put the conclusion? How might the refutation have been combined with the confirmation?

WRITING ASSIGNMENT

Evaluate your education so far, focusing on some or all of the following questions:
  a. To what extent was your previous education "liberal" as Goldwin defines this word?
  b. Were the decisions about your studies—courses as well as general curriculum—yours or those of others or both?
  c. Should these decisions have been yours in high school? Should they be yours entirely in college?
  d. What personal needs has your education not met?

KENNETH B. CLARK
The Limits of Relevance

1. As one who began himself to use the term "relevant" and to insist on its primacy years ago, I feel an obligation to protest the limits of relevance or to propose a redefinition of it to embrace wider terms.
2. Definitions of education that depend on immediate relevance ignore a small but critical percentage of human beings, the individuals who for some perverse reason are in search of an education that is not dominated by the important, socially and economically required pragmatic needs of a capitalist or a communist or a socialist society. Such an individual is not certain what he wants to be;

THE LIMITS OF RELEVANCE: In *Pathos of Power* by Kenneth B. Clark. Copyright © 1974 by Kenneth B. Clark. Reprinted by permission of Harper & Row, Publishers, Inc.

he may not even be sure that he wants to be successful. He may be burdened with that perverse intelligence that finds the excitement of life in a continuous involvement with ideas.

3.   For this student, education may be a lonely and tortuous process not definable in terms of the limits of course requirements or of departmental boundaries, or the four- or six-year span of time required for the bachelor's or graduate degree. This student seems unable to seek or to define or to discuss relevance in terms of externals. He seems somehow trapped by the need to seek the dimensions of relevance in relation to an examination and re-examination of his own internal values. He may have no choice but to assume the burden of seeking to define the relevance of the human experience as a reflection of the validity of his own existence as a value-seeking, socially sensitive, and responsive human being. He is required to deny himself the protective, supporting crutch of accepting and clutching uncritically the prevailing dogmatisms, slogans, and intellectual fashions.

4. . If such a human being is to survive the inherent and probably inevitable aloneness of intellectual integrity, he must balance it by the courage to face and accept the risks of his individuality; by compassion and empathetic identification with the frailties of his fellow human beings as a reflection of his own; by an intellectual and personal discipline which prevents him from wallowing in introspective amorphousness and childlike self-indulgence. And, certainly, he must demonstrate the breadth of perspective and human sensitivity and depth of affirmation inherent in the sense of humor which does not laugh at others but laughs with man and with the God of Paradox who inflicted upon man the perpetual practical joke of the human predicament.

5.   American colleges, with few notable exceptions, provide little room for this type of student, just as American society provides little room for such citizens. Perhaps it is enough to see that institutions of higher education do not destroy such potential. One could hope wistfully that our colleges and even our multiuniversities could spare space and facilities to serve and to protect those students who want to experiment without being required to be practical, pragmatic, or even relevant.

6.   Is it still possible within the complexity and cacophony of our dynamic, power-related, and tentatively socially sensitive institutions for some few to have the opportunity to look within, to read, to think critically, to communicate, to make mistakes, to seek va-

lidity, and to accept and enjoy this process as valid in itself? Is there still some place where relevance can be defined in terms of the quest—where respect for self and others can be taken for granted as one admits not knowing and is therefore challenged to seek?

7. May one dare to hope for a definition of education which makes it possible for man to accept the totality of his humanity without embarrassment? This would be valuable for its own sake, but it might also paradoxically be the most pragmatic form of education—because it is from these perverse, alone-educated persons that a practical society receives antidotes to a terrifying sense of inner emptiness and despair. They are the font of the continued quest for meaning in the face of the mocking chorus of meaninglessness. They offer the saving reaffirmation of stabilizing values in place of the acceptance of the disintegration inherent in valuelessness. They provide the basis for faith in humanity and life rather than surrender to dehumanization and destruction. From these impracticals come our poets, our artists, our novelists, our satirists, our humorists. They are our models of the positives, the potentials, the awe and wonder of man. They make the life of the thinking human being more endurable and the thought of a future tolerable.

QUESTIONS

1. How does Clark explain the meanings of the term *relevant?* Why does he briefly review these meanings?
2. Do you think Clark would agree with Maritain's basic assumptions about people and education? Does he state the sources of his own assumptions, as Maritain does?
3. What conclusions does Clark derive from his assumptions? Is he in partial or full agreement with Goldwin on the issue of relevance?
4. Do you agree that American colleges have little room for the kind of student described in paragraph 4? What is your answer to the questions Clark asks in paragraph 6?
5. Does Clark seek to refute those who argue the "pragmatic needs" of education? Or does he present confirming arguments only?

WRITING ASSIGNMENT

Evaluate one of the following statements on the basis of your experience and observation:

a. "American colleges, with few notable exceptions, provide little room for this type of student, just as American society provides little room for such citizens."

b. ". . . it is from these perverse, alone-educated persons that a practical society receives antidotes to a terrifying sense of inner emptiness and despair."

ANDREW HACKER

The Illusion of Individuality

1.   Among the more widespread postwar preoccupations has been the growing impersonality of life in America. While the major causes will turn on each commentator's disposition, most agree that rootlessness, alienation, and a crisis of identity characterize the time. Confused over goals and values, and no longer capable of establishing meaningful relationships with one another, Americans find themselves powerless and frustrated appendages in an age of dehumanized institutions.

2.   My interest in this chapter will be to inquire why criticism of this sort has evoked such a strong response. One reason is that these commentaries depict much that is true about post-war America. Mass production, mass consumption, and the mass media; specialization, secularization, and suburbanization; the growth of government, of corporate capitalism, and of messianic militarism—these are all clear and present conditions having deep-seated effects on the attitudes of Americans. However, the social structure and economic development of any society leave a mark on the character of its citizens. What is different here is the intensity of concern over the status and predicament of "the individual."

3.   While philosophers have been locating "the individual" at the center of their systems for several centuries, it is only recently that this emphasis has entered the vernacular. When a society's population consists mainly of peasants or proletarians, only a small mi-

THE ILLUSION OF INDIVIDUALITY: In *The End of the American Era* by Andrew Hacker. Copyright (©) 1968, 1970 by Andrew Hacker. Reprinted by permission of Atheneum Publishers.

nority can voice the theory of individuality. However, most Americans, now liberated from the confines of rural bondage and industrial exploitation, have embraced an outlook that was once the property of an elite few. Thus, today virtually everyone looks upon himself as an "individual." For with new occupations, enhanced education, and liberation from constricting surroundings, people formulate new conceptions of themselves and their hitherto hidden potentialities. Not only do more Americans expect more out of life, but they are also more sensitive to forces pronounced harmful to their newly discovered capacities.

4. Assertions of individuality, while ideologically understandable, form the basic myth of American democracy. More Americans have attained new jobs, more schooling, and a greater exposure to the variety of what life has to offer. Nevertheless, in major attributes they remain essentially the same sort of people as were their peasant and proletarian forebears. This is to suggest not only that their new conceptions of self have no factual basis—for it would be difficult to show that the materials of which Americans are made have undergone a marked improvement—but also that the average person cannot be expected to live up to the standards he now sets for himself. Moreover, most of the sensations of injustice about which citizens complain arise from overinflated hopes concerning what an ordinary person may experience throughout his life.

5. But because assumptions are not examined, even the most sophisticated commentaries take the view that in more salutary circumstances American men and women would reveal capacity for outlooks and accomplishments they have not yet achieved. Current attitudes and behavior are seen as corrupted crudescences: for contemporary humanity has been distorted by institutions and imperatives resulting from either accidents of history or the intrigues of those who profit from a maldistribution of power. Were these constrictions to be removed, "the individual"—every man and woman—could ascend to a level of life where their potentialities for a creative existence would reach a full flowering.

6. But the problem with discussions of human "potentialities" is that no facts support the arguments. The historical record may be used to demonstrate man's inherent good nature, his tendency toward evil, or some mixture of these and other attributes. Equally authoritative evidence can be cited to demonstrate that he has the reason and intelligence to control his destiny, or that he has always drifted in a chartless sea. Indeed, the historical record is irrelevant:

for mankind's capabilities have hardly had an opportunity for realization in any society the world has known. Thus, the release of potentialities remains a hope for the future rather than an extrapolation from past performance.

7.   One can only speculate, therefore, about what may reasonably be expected from the people who comprise our present society. Here is an automobile salesman in New Jersey, there a television repairman in Alabama; here is a black teenager in Chicago, there a housewife in suburban San Diego. What capabilities lie dormant in them?

8.   Honest observation indicates that on the whole these Americans—and millions like them—are not extraordinarily intelligent, not terribly ambitious, and tend chiefly to be wrapped up in themselves. But suppose that they were somehow released from the thralldom of salesmanship and racial prejudice, from the destructive life of the slums and the dull domesticity of the suburbs—supposing all this, can it be conceived that such people as these, even given the most encouraging conditions, would display some inherent "individuality"? For it may be that assumptions about unfathomed potentialities are only a myth—an illusion that persists because any serious investigation of its premises may prove hazardous to a nation at a difficult stage in its history.

9.   Most people are ordinary. And ordinary people are ordinary, regardless of the time or society or setting in which they live. Moreover, ordinary people are relatively unintelligent, incapable of abstraction or imagination, lacking any special qualities of talent or creativity. They are for the most part without drive or perseverance; easily discouraged, they prefer the paths of security. Whether slave or serf or sweated worker, most people in the past have displayed these traits. And most who inhabit the present, whether scientist or suburbanite or sophisticate, continue to manifest these tendencies.

10. This is the human condition. One need not invoke theology, nor is it necessary to assert that man is a creature of evil and tainted with sin. I simply argue that in any society all save an exceptional few will lack the capacity for attainments that transcend the mediocre.

11. Quite obviously words such as these can carry unpleasant implications. However, allusions to differentials in human talents need not originate in pseudo-genetic doctrines or ideologies intended to flatter members of a particular class, race or nationality.

What I mean is that most people—white as well as black, rich no less than poor—are not terribly clever or creative or venturesome. Yet, despite these disclaimers, the mere mention of mediocrity raises problems for democratic rhetoric. Indeed, of all the world's peoples, Americans have the greatest difficulty in facing the fact that human beings can be subjected to qualitative judgments.

12. Hence the emphasis on "excellence"—a quality Americans are prepared to discover in more people and places than was ever thought possible. While competition often compels the ranking of individuals, this does not discourage the concept that the achievements and products of excellence may be attained by virtually everyone.* To inform an American that he has limited intelligence or a sinewless character can only be construed as an insult. Not only does the democratic spirit make it difficult for one person to pass judgment on another; an accompanying presumption is that everyone carries the capacity for excelling in at least several areas of life.

13. The ideology of individuality—and I purposely use this term—is of comparatively recent origin. Until the last generation or so, the emphasis was on "individualism," and the connotations were almost exclusively economic. Moreover, this doctrine was quite straightforward in its intentions: to exalt the entrepreneur and encourage the quest for profit. Hence the qualities it celebrated: a willingness to put aside current earnings and defer gratifications; a readiness to risk these savings in an enterprise of one's own creation; and the determination to make that enterprise succeed by hard work, native wit, and the seizing of opportunities. For all these requisites, those who succeeded were hardly exemplary figures by contemporary standards. Rough-hewn and self-centered, they displayed a bare minimum of moral awareness and eschewed any notions of social responsibility. Patronizing the arts and supporting civic causes earned esteem in certain circles, but such activities were by no means expected by the individualist ethic. One could achieve that status simply by building or enlarg-

---

* To be sure, many middle-class Americans enjoy dilating on the moral and intellectual shortcomings of whole categories of citizens they deem their inferiors. And by the same token not a few Caucasians find it difficult to discover potentialities in persons more darkly hued than themselves. Yet, despite the standards they set for others, such individuals attribute quite flattering qualities and accomplishments to members of their own race and class. Perhaps, then, it would be more accurate to say that it is *within* their own races and classes that Americans display their magnanimity toward one another's capacities.

ing an enterprise that surpassed and outlasted the efforts of others.
14. Current assumptions require that expressions of individuality
be more than economic. However, any attempt to extend an ideology of this sort to non-economic areas encounters serious difficulties. For, while success in entrepreneurial individualism lay solely
in how much money a self-made man might amass, no methods
have been devised for assessing or identifying qualities unsuscepti-
ble to monetary measurement. What one person will see as a genuine philosophical talent, another will perceive as exhibitionism or
eccentricity. Where some will detect a statesmanlike courage,
others will find opportunism and expediency. (Certainly not all
departures from convention can be construed as evidence of
praiseworthy qualities. Why else has the term "neurotic" become
so common?) Because of the impossibility of agreeing on its attributes, the democratic resolution has been to bestow candidacy for
individuality on everyone.
15. Clashes over definitions fail to impress middle-class Americans, who remain persuaded that with just a little more effort and
some added insight they may discover their true selves. Thus the
growing commitment to education, and the conviction that with
schooling can come not only worldly success but also an awareness of one's own potentialities. Yet the majority content themselves with unexamined assumptions: one is that what happens in
classrooms has an influence on subsequent behavior. Yet, on the
whole, the educational process has surprisingly little effect in determining how people will finally shape their lives. Apart from
technical training, what education imparts is chiefly a set of per-
ceptions through which the world may be seen, plus a vocabulary
for describing that vista. The process may occasionally instill values or induce feelings of guilt, although this is far rarer than most
would like to believe. And while there can be no denying that aug-
mented schooling can awaken both a consciousness of style and a
sophistication of manner, these are chiefly lessons in how to make
the most of prevailing conditions.
16. Certainly the overwhelming majority of college graduates—
presumably the class from which the most should be expected—
show little in their lives which can reasonably be called individuality. Despite their exposure to higher education and their heightened awareness of life's options, they nevertheless take paths of
least resistance when faced with critical decisions throughout their
lives. What their education gives them is the ability to rationalize

these choices: a series of verbal strategies for justifying their actions to others and for making peace with themselves.*

17. Neither the information in a person's head nor the values in his conscience have much to do with his behavior. The principal determinant of human action stems from the fact that most people lack the courage to take chances. Learning lessons of right conduct has become an academic exercise; but conversations of this sort are incapable of instilling the self-confidence needed to pursue even the most noble principles. Americans who have experienced higher education find themselves especially vulnerable because society offers them an array of ascending opportunities—on the condition that they conform to the codes set by those who bestow the material rewards and symbols of success. In short, the college graduate, more than others, has a great deal to gain by being the sort of person others want him to be. And in this situation all talk of inculcating individuality has little meaning.† The one trait America's educational institutions cannot teach is personal courage, and the one quality they cannot abscind is human weakness. Considering the prizes held out to those educated for future

---

* What about the liberal-arts curriculum, which a growing number of Americans elect to study? Quite clearly, most students still go to college to secure credentials for the status and occupations of middle-class careers. Even so, a rising proportion of undergraduates evidence genuine eagerness for a critical understanding of themselves and their world. During these years of suspended animation they can be a real pleasure to teach: their eyes are opened; they ask interesting and important questions; they begin to abandon the cautionary maxims that hitherto held their minds in check.

However, this is an interlude in their lives. For the years of liberal learning cannot extend into the time when careers must be chosen and bargains struck with the arbiters of promotion. This is one reason why professors show little enthusiasm for meeting those students later on. For minds that were once inquiring have now settled into place; and the verbal skills learned in the liberal arts are deployed to defend compromises and accommodations.

† It is, of course, easy enough to solve the problem simply by debasing the coinage of individuality. Anyone who wishes to discover uniqueness in every member of a community can achieve this end by inflating small talents and marginal distinctions: this woman has a unique recipe for angel cake, that housewife knits her husband's neckties; this man rides to work on a bicycle, that one collects old circus posters; he plays a fine game of golf, she set a shorthand speed record, and they vacationed on a barge canal. Perhaps something is gained in telling the orthodox that they are unconventional, by persuading the weak that they are creatures of courage. Such fictions may obviate the endemic envy of the average and impart a veneer of romance to lackluster lives. Certainly most of those choosing to congratulate everyman on his individuality understand that they tell gentle lies. Perhaps no great harm results from these exercises, except that they encourage the unexceptional to believe that all avocations are of equal quality.

success, it should not be surprising that so many strike the bargains they do.

18. Even if the United States could end poverty and bigotry, diffuse its pyramids of power, and suppress its imperial tendencies, there is no reason to believe that such a society would contain a greater quotient of talented people. For talent has always been, and will always be, a scarce commodity.

19. Recall for a moment the classical literature of Utopia: portrayals of a benign future where the authors have caused the pressures of contemporary life to disappear. But then take a closer look at the characters who inhabit these idyllic communities. While they are polite, sensible, and socially responsible, most also emerge as very ordinary and unprepossessing people. Even the creators of Utopia, free to devise any manner of population, avoided creating societies of philosophers, artists, and heroes. Perhaps they realized that even in Utopian circumstances the majority of citizens would remain unexceptional. (They may also have suspected that too many talents would strain the community structure.) And in so doing most Utopians have been eminently realistic: their aim has been to make men happy rather than to elevate their aptitudes.

20. In the past, ordinary people thought of themselves in unpretentious terms, acknowledging their limitations and accepting stations relatively consonant with their capacities. But the emergence of individuality has changed self-conceptions, creating discontents of a sort that were unlikely to occur to men and women of earlier eras. Once persuaded that he is an "individual" entitled to realize his assumed potentialities, a citizen will diagnose himself as suffering quite impressive afflictions.

21. The intensity with which Americans now explore their egos arises from the conviction that even an average personality is a deep and unparalleled mechanism. Whether psychoanalytic or existential in emphasis, people take pleasure in examining the quality of their "relationships" and achieving an "insight" into their own internal functioning. The heightened concern over sex derives in no small measure from a search for one's "real self" and attempts to find realization through close contact with another person. Hence also the stress on individual "powerlessness," and the constrictions that large institutions impose on self-discovery and self-development. While these terms of discourse are not of recent invention, their employment by so large a part of society is certainly new. Alienation, powerlessness, and crises of identity come

into being only if citizens decide to invest their personalities with potentialities ripe for liberation. As soon as people make such decisions about themselves, regulations once taken for granted appear as oppressive instruments of government and society.

22. Thus, most of those who describe themselves as "alienated" lack any credentials for so tragic a predicament. Given the unexceptional quality and character of the vast majority of Americans, it should be apparent that, however painful the problems they encounter, little is gained by inflating their troubles to traumatic proportions. The average college student—or factory worker or welfare recipient—may indeed feel pushed around, robbed of dignity, or consigned to a status incommensurate with his talents. But to call him "alienated" assumes that if he were liberated from constraints that now annoy him, he would emerge as a different person. To be sure, millions of Americans live at a subsistence level, while others face arbitrary and irrational discriminations throughout their lives. The grievance of such persons is that they have been deprived of experiences enjoyed by people really no different from themselves. To say that you wish to enjoy amenities now available to others ought to be a sufficient argument for eliminating inequality. Considering the behavior of those who have achieved such privileges, the claim that sharing these enjoyments will enhance one's humanity remains a most precarious proposition.

23. The notion that modern society thwarts self-discovery, compelling people to don masks and distort their true personalities, carries a series of parallel assumptions. However, the fact that so many Americans have become absorbed with asking "Who am I?" need not be construed as evidence of a nationwide "identity crisis." On the contrary, it shows that citizens now feel entitled to give their personal problems philosophical connotations. Self-indulgence of this sort merely indicates that Americans have expanded their vocabularies: it does not mean that these self-estimates have much to do with reality.

24. To ask "Who am I?" is really rather presumptuous. In actual fact, people may still be summed up largely by the roles they fill in society—housewife or husband, soldier or salesman, student or scientist—and by the qualities others ascribe to them: a person "is" black or blind, fat or feminine, indolent or efficient. No one likes being "identified" as simply a fat salesman or a black housewife, and of course the list of a person's roles and characteristics can be

extended, but it remains an inventory of attributes externally imposed. Quite clearly many Americans prefer to believe that beneath all the labels lies a unique and identifiable self. Unfortunately for them, the "Who am I?" question can never be answered except in inventoried terms. But the fact that people persist in asking it shows how a little learning can disrupt sensibilities and produce crises unknown in less literate days.

25. Nor should society be blamed for these problems, particularly those afflicting members of the middle class who complain about restrictions imposed by their communities and careers. It is quite disingenuous to maintain that society forces anyone to be or become anything at all. A person still has the freedom to decide whether or not he will compromise with the world of rewards. If he wishes the comfort and security available to those who join this game, then he will be required to follow certain rules. Those opting for "success" will of course have to adjust to occupational and organizational imperatives. But no one is compelled to enter this gamut. If an individual elects to live an anonymous and unexposed life, if he chooses to stand apart from competitive pressures, then his personality will be left alone. American society has plenty of such places; of course the jobs they offer tend to be uninteresting and poorly paid. Many people obviously want the best of both worlds: material and social success and the freedom to indulge their idiosyncrasies. But it is difficult to muster sympathy for those who complain about the costs of competition. A society that distributes the good things of life with an uneven hand should require some sacrifice of those who reap its rewards.*

26. Anxieties over problems such as "alienation" and "identity" will continue to preoccupy Americans, for each year more people

---

* If I may digress for a moment, I would like to apply this general observation to a quite different question: Who is to be held responsible for wartime atrocities? Every soldier can plead that he was simply following orders, in which case only a single national leader can ultimately be blamed. However, an alternative answer would divide any military force into those who apply for or accept promotions, and those who don't. Individuals who seek or accept elevation above the rank of conscript in effect give their consent to the regime and its works. In taking the rewards it offers, they become tacit participants and acquiesce in its acts. No one has to accept promotion; no private soldier is penalized for choosing to remain a private. Hence, guilt for war crimes should be ascribed to everyone, from corporal to field marshal, who elects to succeed under the regime. Having opted to do as well as they could in the system, such persons cannot complain if they are held as consenting members and hence answerable for its atrocities.

develop a heightened sense of their own importance. Feelings of isolation and injustice, of powerlessness and oppression, will become more exacerbated among all classes as people expand the enjoyments they consider their due. A people so impressed with their entitlements cannot be expected to revert to simpler settings, to codes and conventions that would prevent the ills they now say they suffer. Skeptical toward all authority and made restive by an encapsulated existence, Americans have divested themselves of the attitudes required for a more commonplace contentment.

27. The difficulty is that, for all their verbal facility, the great majority of Americans are basically no different from their forebears who lived with a minimum of self-created dilemmas. As contemporary citizens have no higher an endowment of quality or character than did their less literate predecessors, it remains only to say that pursuit of an ephemeral individuality will certainly increase their frustrations. It is a symptom of our age that people invest themselves with grand attributes, even though they lack the talent or perseverance to realize potentialities they have convinced themselves they have. Hence the need for the illusion of individuality. For this fragile myth is the only support that remains for uncertain spirits in their quest for self-respect.

QUESTIONS

1. Establishing the premises on which arguments are built is often more important than the conclusions reached—particularly when the argument is over that broad and elusive term "human nature." Arguments over the proper definition and role of education inevitably deal with statements like the following:

> A sound philosophy in general suggests that men are rational, moral, and spiritual beings and that the improvement of men means the fullest development of their rational, moral, and spiritual powers. All men have these powers, and all men should develop them to the fullest extent.—Robert Maynard Hutchins, "The Basis of Education"

> The modern secular way of life is not suited to the real nature of men. For it withholds from them that discipline of their own impulses which is indispensable to their health and their happiness.—Walter Lippmann, "An Image of Man for Liberal Democracy"

Notice that these statements make no qualification about *kinds* of people. Does Hacker make comparable assertions about *all* people?

2. What assumptions about human nature is Hacker attacking? Does he reject them because they contradict his observations of what people are like or because they contradict other self-evident assumptions?

3. What evidence or support does Hacker provide for his statements on "ordinary" people in the whole essay? To what extent would he agree with the statements of Hutchins and Lippmann quoted above?

4. Note these statements in paragraph 9:

> Most people are ordinary. And ordinary people are ordinary, regardless of the time or society or setting in which they live. Moreover, ordinary people are relatively unintelligent, incapable of abstraction or imagination, lacking any special qualities of talent or creativity.

How is this basic view related to middle-class Americans in paragraph 15?

5. Does Hacker defend or support "the fact"—discussed in paragraph 17—that "most people lack the courage to take chances"? Does he consider the statement self-evident?

6. Hacker grants that a number of definitions of individuality are possible. How does he seek to persuade his reader that the usual definition—discussed in the footnote to paragraph 17—is misleading or inadequate?

7. What is the principle of division in the footnote to paragraph 25? Are you persuaded by Hacker's reasoning?

8. Does Hacker assert or imply what the goals of education ought to be? Is his purpose in writing merely to analyze the current situation without making recommendations?

WRITING ASSIGNMENTS

Indicate the extent of your agreement with Hacker through a discussion of the "individuality" of your fellow students in high school or college.

Argue whether a soldier ought to be held responsible for "wartime atrocities" if he were ordered by a superior to perform them. Be careful to distinguish your assumptions from your conclusion.

Basing your reasoning on Hacker's statements, discuss how you think he would regard the admissions policy and aims of your college as stated in its catalog.

LEONARD GROSS

Is Less More?

1. The following superlative is offered after considerable thought: Americans are, or will shortly be, in the process of making the most fundamental adjustment they have ever had to make. If this adjustment concerned solely their standard of living, the superlative would not be valid. What makes it so is that this is the first time Americans have ever had to change the *assumptions* about the manner in which they live.

2. There have been times of sacrifice before, particularly during wars, but the assumption was that times would be "good" again when the emergency ended. Today, however, economic factors are such that the prudent American must adjust to the likelihood that material life may never be the same again.

3. This country is in the process of discovering that it can no longer afford the big life. That is the downstream meaning of our present economic turmoil. From whatever area you approach the problem, be it resources, inflation, population or politics, the prospect remains the same. Solutions will necessarily require permanent alterations in the size and scope of our activities, possessions and dreams.

4. Already, the broadly shared dream of upper-middle-class affluence has passed the average dreamer by. He figured that if he ever earned $20,000 a year, he'd have it made. Today, he's got the salary, but he's also got hobbling debts. Gains in real income for the middle class have been tiny; there's almost no upward mobility any longer. Aspirations to send children to college have been tempered by the immense cost and inability of degree holders to find employment.

5. Call it "middle-class discontent." It's demonstrably higher now than at any time in recent history. It will not lessen in our lifetime, not, at least, as a consequence of improved conditions. The cost of land will not diminish. The cost of money may diminish somewhat, but not to the levels that enabled millions of Americans to build their own homes in the years after the second world war. The value of the dollar will not increase. The cost of goods and services will not diminish, if only because the cost of fuel, a major production factor in every economic sector, will never return to previous levels. Populations will increase here and abroad, compounding problems of employment, education and maintenance.

6. It all sounds pretty bleak. And yet, and yet. Inherent in the problem is a stunning resolution—nothing less than a change in the values by which we measure life. Because there *is* one variable in all this picture: the individual. He can diminish his discontent by reordering his priorities.

7. What happens to a society when its members have less purchasing power is already beginning to be apparent. There will be practical changes in the way people live: smaller, less elaborate houses, fewer single-family dwellings, more cluster zoning, more condominiums, better use of land so as to provide more recreation near the home. Because travel will be so expensive, the environment near the home will receive greater attention.

8. With the price of food so high, discretionary income will be diverted to supplement food budgets. That means less money for entertainment and an increasing reliance on the home as the family entertainment center. Such vacations as will be possible will change their nature. Vacation clubs, little known in the United States but enormously successful in Europe, will come into vogue. The Club Méditerranée, originator of the concept and prototype for other clubs, has already developed an American market.

9. Railroads work in Europe because Europeans use railroads. And because they work, Europeans can board a train in the evening and be at their skiing station early the next morning after an inexpensive and acceptable night in a couchette. When Americans can no longer afford long trips in automobiles or airplanes, they will return to the railroads, the least expensive and the least environment-punishing form of mass transportation.

10. A subtle strain runs through these eventualities. Without neglecting the individual, we address ourselves to the common good. Everyone isn't vying for first cabin any longer; we're content to get

there more modestly—and happy in the knowledge that our arrival is assured. The new American dream will esteem "small" more than "big." The trend to smaller cars, recently made concrete by the General Motors announcement that its new models will be an average of 700 pounds lighter, is thus not simply a response to the fuel shortage. Eventually, it becomes an expression of taste.

11. "Less is more" is a phrase attributed to Mies van der Rohe, the German architect, a leader of the Bauhaus group and pivotal force in the field of modern design. That single statement crystallized the philosophy of contemporary architecture and design—to do away with frilly styles. Would a life-style that did away with unnecessary baggage achieve the same simplicity and purity? Every week, it seems, I hear of one more American who thinks so. All were successful. All had made it to the top and then decided that the prize hadn't been worth the trip. "Can you imagine spending your life getting to a place and then finding you didn't want to be there?" one of them asked rhetorically.

12. Economic necessity will do more to change styles of life than any previous factor. Moral imperatives don't embody an imperative for change. But when you can no longer afford the life you're living, or the life you can buy for what you earn becomes unacceptable, *then* you're motivated to change.

13. Since our inception, the American Premise has stated that happiness lay ahead, in the bigger job, the bigger home, the bigger life. The larger implication of our new economic reality is nothing less than a rejection of that premise, with profound consequences in terms of social objectives and how they're expressed commercially. That many Americans will continue to grab for the brass ring while others are letting go in no way invalidates the premise. Facts in apparent contradiction can be simultaneously true.

QUESTIONS

1. Gross organizes his essay in the argumentative form discussed earlier:

   introduction (paragraph 1)
   division of proofs: partial statement of thesis (paragraphs 2–3)
   narration (paragraphs 4–6)
   confirmation (paragraphs 7–11)
   refutation (paragraphs 12–13)
   conclusion (paragraph 13)

Where in the confirmation does Gross state his thesis fully? How does he restate his thesis in the concluding paragraph?

2. What information does he provide in the narration, and for what purpose? Is he writing to a special or a general audience, and how do you know?

3. Gross is writing a special kind of essay that refutes assumptions held by a large number of Americans. What are these assumptions, and how does Gross challenge them? What assumptions of his own does he make explicitly and implicitly?

4. Gross supports his own ideas from experience: he is thus showing that new assumptions can and do find support in the world today. What are these experiences?

WRITING ASSIGNMENTS

Discuss how an experience like the gas shortage of 1974 forced you to change your standard of living and perhaps your thinking. Use this discussion to support or challenge one of Gross's ideas.

Challenge an assumption held by people your age, or perhaps your teachers or parents. Do so by showing how this assumption is contradicted by your experiences and observations. Follow the pattern of the argumentative essay shown above. Vary this pattern as you find necessary.

INDUCTIVE REASONING

ROGER ROSENBLATT
Growing Up on Television

1.   Adulthood on American television is represented most often and most clearly on family shows. These continuing stories about the adventures of families became popular in the fifties and have grown more so since (I can count thirty-five). Most have been light comedies (*The Stu Erwin Show*, *The Life of Reilly*, *Life with Fa-*

GROWING UP ON TELEVISION: Reprinted by permission of *Daedalus*, Journal of the American Academy of Arts and Sciences, Boston, Massachusetts. Fall, 1976, *American Civilization: New Perspectives*.

ther, Make Room for Daddy, Father Knows Best, Ozzie and Har-riet) or farces (*The Munsters, The Addams Family*). A few have been gentle melodramas (*One Man's Family, The Waltons, Little House on the Prairie*). Fewer still, such as *All in the Family* and *The Jeffersons*—comedies essentially—have reached for a deeper nature by dealing with real conflicts. The titles of these shows have generally shifted from a father-centered conception of the family to a community operation, but that, I think, represents so-cial appeasement more than genuine change. In fact, the televi-sion family has been an unusually consistent institution, far more stable than its real-life counterpart.

2.   One reason for this stability is that families on television are not families with special coherences; they consist of interchangea-ble parts. Family members share the same surnames, live in the same house or apartment, or, more specifically, the same combina-tion living room and kitchen, and they hang around together and recognize each other. Ordinarily families consist of one father, one mother, and some children who confront problems of the magni-tude of surprise parties, garbled telegrams, overcooked chickens, high-school proms, and driving lessons. We could trade the mother of the Andersons on *Father Knows Best* for the mother of the Wal-tons without ruffling the chickens.

3.   Since the family arrangement is so basic to television we could even exchange certain family members with characters on non-family shows. The relationships among the detectives on *Hawaii Five-O* or the paramedics on *Emergency* are no less familial than those among the *Partridge Family* members or those in *Family Af-fair*. If Kojak were to marry Mary Tyler Moore and raise the Brady Bunch, we would still get the same conception of problems and solutions as each holds alone: every week Kojak, Mary, and the children would rid Minneapolis of ethnic abuses.

4.   That conception of problems and solutions follows the same formula for all family shows: a problem is made evident within the first three minutes, usually as a result of some new direction or decision of the family (a picnic, a new car); one by one, the family becomes aware of the problem so that each member can adopt the characteristic stance which he or she adopts for all occasions; the problem then serves as a catalyst for the individual performances that occupy the rest of the show; the problem is "solved," gotten rid of, at the wire by means of a telephone call or some other *deus ex machina*. The show ends with everybody laughing. (Detective

shows use much the same formula, incidentally, substituting murders for picnics and stool pigeons for the *deus*.)

5.   In so standardized a situation it would be hard to pick out the grown-ups were it not for certain allegorical assignments. When a problem strikes *Father Knows Best,* for example, the family arranges itself around it, responding as humors: Jim is Recalcitrant Wisdom, sought only (yet always sought eventually) as a last resort; his wife Margaret is Anxiety; elder daughter Betty is Panic or Extreme Emotion; her brother Bud, Dullness; and little Cathy is Childlike Sensitivity, providing an unspoiled account and "special" perception of the problem as it develops. On *All in the Family* the Bunkers' childishness and panic reside in the father; therefore, when a problem (abortion, death, racism) hits the Bunkers, the mental process of dealing with it begins out of control in the one member of the family who is supposed to represent order and authority. Thanks to Edith, whose constitutional bewilderment serves as Right Instinct, things eventually calm down on *All in the Family,* but are rarely resolved or set straight. A bunker is a bulwark, a fortification; problems attack the Bunkers at a terrific rate, but ricochet just as quickly, denting nothing.

6.   Jim Anderson and Archie Bunker seem very different kinds of adults, and in more than stylistic ways they are. It is better to dwell in the palace of wisdom than panic, and so better to see Anderson as a model of adulthood than Bunker. Curiously, however, neither father is necessarily identifiable as an adult. In fact nobody in the allegorical arrangements of TV families is identifiable as a child or adult except by physical size, dress, and age. Experience, one thing that might effect such identification is not called upon. Anderson's wisdom usually does not derive from experience but from in-born perspicacity. Bunker's terrors rarely result from experience, but burst upon a problem as if one like it had never been seen before. There are more wise than panicky grown-ups on family shows, but they simply function as the wisest minds in groups of contemporaries. Their wisdom is separable from their adulthood, and so says nothing for adulthood generally, suggests no particular advantage to growing up.

7.   This, I believe, is one of the ideas that television has about adulthood—that adulthood is, may be, perhaps should be, unconnected to experience, and exists as an admirable state of mind (when shown as admirable) insofar as it exhibits the most general

virtues. Experience is not evil, merely unnecessary for growing up, and thus memory, the medium of experience, is unusable. If this proves true, then what appears to be an expression of approval or encouragement on television's part, in usually assigning wisdom to grown-ups, may in fact be the opposite; because to praise something in terms applied to many things is to exaggerate the possibility that those same terms fit other things more appropriately, leaving the original object peculiarly vulnerable by comparison. The question ought to be raised here, however, as to whether there *are* such things as ideas in television; or are the notions we pick out merely ephemera tied to commerical interests, which vary with those interests?

8.   Because it emerges from a single history, because nearly all its parts, at least on commercial television, operate on the same standards of success (sponsors, ratings), because its technical methods are the same for all stations and what variety exists within broadcast companies is still the same variety for all such companies; because it appeals to and reaches the same audience in relatively similar situations, and because its opinion of that audience is continuous and stable, television must, I think, be regarded as a world *in toto*. That is, whatever differences in tone or invention there are among situation comedies, mysteries, quiz shows, talk shows, et al., none of these "genres" is basically separable from the others. Among all are the samenesses of the medium fed by every show's active awareness of every other show. They function alertly in William James's systemic universe: cooperate, reinforce themselves, create, sustain, and eventually proselytize for a single vision of most things.

9.   Adulthood, then, as one of the ideas set forth by television, is not presented solely in one type of show, but in all types, even—perhaps particularly—in shows that have nothing to say about grown-ups, but simply show them in action. Quiz shows, for example, usually have grown-ups playing what appear to be the simplest kinds of children's games, which range from pie-tossing (*People are Funny*) and bedroom olympics (*Beat the Clock*) to versions of spelling and math bees on shows that test contestants on information. (*It Pays to Be Ignorant,* both a radio and TV show, was an interesting perversion of these information quizzes.) Yet adults are not, in fact, behaving as children on these shows, nor are the shows trying to bring out the child in them. The quiz show

takes grown-ups as they are, and takes them seriously. Having detected certain weaknesses in our conception of adulthood, which sometimes means our self-esteem, it goes to work on them.

10. *Let's Make A Deal* is the most popular American quiz show, and probably the most sinister. Its audience is divided into two sections. There is the regular audience, and in front of it, in a roped off portion, is the participating audience, would-be contestants who have come dressed as animals or in other outlandish costumes and who forcefully vie for the attention of the master of ceremonies. The master of ceremonies patrols the aisle, choosing players at random. Only a few can participate, so every person in costume continually screams and flails his arms in order to attract the emcee as he makes his selections. Those whom he chooses to "deal" with can barely contain their excitement and have to be forcibly quieted before the show can continue.

11. What the master of ceremonies offers these people is a choice between unknowns. He tells somebody dressed as Mother Goose, for instance, that he may have whatever is in this box (which a professionally delighted assistant produces) or whatever is behind that curtain (to be drawn apart by a long-legged girl). The contestant is baffled, but he chooses the box. Before he has a chance to open it, however, the master of ceremonies says, I'll give you five hundred dollars for whatever is in that box. The contestant hesitates. Six hundred. The regular audience shouts, "keep it!," "sell!" Seven-fifty. The contestant decides to keep the box. When the lid is lifted there may be jewelry on display worth two thousand dollars, and the contestant howls and whoops. If the contestant is a woman, she flings her arms around the emcee's neck and kisses him powerfully. A man usually jumps up and down like a great cartoon frog. Or, there may be a sandwich in the box, whereupon everybody guffaws and the contestant collapses in disappointment. Sometimes there is a live animal behind one of the curtains, and, as the audience roars, a look of genuine terror comes into the contestant's eyes as he or she not only deals with the despair of losing, but with the possibility of taking home a pig or a mule.

12. The excitement of the show derives not from the price or size of the prizes available, but from the act of depriving people of their ability to make informed decisions, in other words, to reason. To deprive them of their sanity at the outset, the show's producers insist that the contestants disguise their actual appearances in order to qualify for losing their reason. When the "deals" are presented,

there is nothing for these people to go on but bare intuition, tortured and prodded by the rest of the audience shouting "the curtain," "the box," "the money." In the center of the mayhem, controlling it, is the master of ceremonies, offering people money for things which they cannot know the value of, things which they cannot see, distributing punishments and rewards as capriciously as the devil he is.

13. What *Let's Make A Deal* does for, or to, the reasoning process, a new quiz show, *The Neighbors,* does for civility. *The Neighbors* enlists five participants, all women, who live in the same neighborhood and know each other very well. These women are seated in rows, three over two. The two are the principal contestants, but all five get into the act. They are positioned on a white fake-filigreed porch. The floor is green, to suggest a village sward, and hedges and potted geraniums are placed about to suggest a quiet suburban neighborhood.

14. As with *Let's Make A Deal,* the audience is in constant frenzy, here not goaded by the emcee who affects the studied quiet of a sermonette preacher (and in fact plays the role of a trouble-making parson), but by the questions he puts. We asked your neighbors, he tells the two principals, which one of you wears short shorts in the neighborhood to attract other women's husbands? A collective gasp and false hilarity are followed by each of the pair guessing that the majority of the three neighbors picked herself or the other one, justifying her guesses either in terms of the character deficiencies of the other principal or the maliciousness of the three neighbors. If a woman guesses herself and is right, she "wins" and is mortified. In the process, at least one of the principals will insult at least one of the three in the upper row. The game continues.

15. In the second stage of the show, the emcee tells the two principals that one of their neighbors has said something vicious about them, and they must try to guess who. Each of the three neighbors now competes to convince first one and then the other of the principals that it was *she* who made the slur. They do this by revealing secrets or confidences which until that moment on national television were shared only with the contestant in question. Each neighbor is encouraged by the fifty dollars she will receive if one of the principals picks her incorrectly. At various intervals in the program, prizes have been mentioned—such as large supplies of La Choy Chinese food and four gallons of paint—that will go to all the contestants. But what the emcee calls "the fantastic grand prize"

will not be revealed until the end. As in the first stage of the show, the principals justify their guesses of one of the three neighbors by emphasizing that particular one's unsavoriness, but they will also cover their bets by generalizing unfavorably on the trio as a whole.

16. Stage three of the show has the emcee tell the principals that all three of the neighbors are unanimous in the opinion that they are . . . and here the comments incorporate vanity, spite, noseyness, selfishness, ungratefulness, corpulence, snobbery, and so forth. Here finally is the full weight of their neighbors' judgments. The two principals guess themselves or each other as the insults are enumerated, the prize money increasing with each question. Eventually one wins the grand prize—a kitchen—and the five neighbors, having destroyed their neighborhood, meet for a good hard hug as the show ends.

17. Civility, which is a grown-up attribute, is deliberately undermined on *The Neighbors,* as indeed it is on other quiz shows and other shows generally on television. Reason is undermined on *Let's Make A Deal* and elsewhere. Memory and experience are undermined on family shows. And the total effect of all such underminings is the undermining of authority, which may be the central adult attribute. Oddly, the only voices of authority undisputed within television are the newsmen—oddly, because they are often the voices least trusted by us. Yet even on the news there is a certain undermining of adulthood, not by overt derision, but by the general cultural theater in which almost all news programs participate.

18. There are no more grown-up-looking or -sounding people on television than newscasters. John Chancellor, David Brinkley, Walter Cronkite, Howard K. Smith, Harry Reasoner—all are about as adult, in the theatrical sense, as one can get: clear and forceful in presentation; well barbered and tailored in appearance; deliberate and settled in manner; non-panicky in tone; emotionally stable almost, but not quite, to a fault. In these terms, if Eric Sevareid were any more grown-up, he would have to deliver his speculations from Shangri-la, and he may yet. These people have nothing quite so much in common with anything as with each other. Differences among them are detectable, to be sure, but television does not seek to point out their differences, certainly not to elaborate on them, because it has decided that we do not simply expect the news of the news, but the world of news as well, a nightly *Front Page.*

19. We have two distinct yet cooperative images of newsmen in our culture, images established and reinforced in the movies more than anywhere else. One is the adventurous reporter—hatted, trench-coated, either hard-drinking and -loving (to be played by James Cagney) or belligerently innocent, awkward yet cocky, seeking only the whole truth (to be played by Joel McCrea—or now is it Robert Redford?); contemptuous of money, pure of motive, defender of underdogs—the discoverer, a man who dares to go where no one else has been permitted, or has thought, to go before. His editor is the other image: snorting, stomping, wild yet established, the authority (hirer and firer) on which the reporter depends, at once romantic, envisioning scoops and stopping the presses, and suspicious or afraid of the truth as well—unlike his colleagues, he has come to believe in City Hall and political realities. In the end, nevertheless, he is as one with his reporter-antagonist as they collaborate to set history right for a moment. Afterwards, we trust, they revert to their separate barkings and ravings.

20. In television these two images combine into a single character—both Perry White and Superman—who is a sort of polished version of each of his contributive actors. Often he is positioned in a simulated newsroom lined with desks at which simulated reporters sit, busy with simulated copy. As he talks, people walk on and off the set carrying messages and bulletins. Typewriters clatter in the background. The newscaster appears to have just looked up from his desk in order to tell the latest story. Or, as with Chancellor, one only senses the background activity. The newscaster is trusted by his reporter-colleagues—they report in before our eyes, courteous and efficient. We feel that they feel that the newscaster is one of them, the grounded former ace. He is also the editor, directing the sequence of presentations. No antagonism here; no hysterics or passion either. The newscaster has been neutralized into a model of both decorum and sensibility (to be played by Frederic March).

21. The effect of this deliberate theatricality is to separate the news from the character who speaks it. Whatever we may think of the content or order of the newscaster's presentations, he remains in the clear, which of course allows him longevity in his position. Yet the clear in which he remains, bright and mellow as it is, is not adulthood in real or ideal terms, because adulthood is not a form of play-acting in which a man is dissociated from his words—quite the opposite. So even here, with newscasters looking and sounding

as grown up as can be, adulthood is misrepresented as a pose, a set of trappings through which information may be conveyed without concern for integrity or emotional and intellectual responsibility. (This is not to say that Chancellor, Cronkite, et al., are without thoughts or feelings about the news; only that the mold they fill makes their minds impertinent.) The result, curiously, is that television newsmen have come to represent not a celebration of stature, another adult attribute, but a mockery of it.

22. More curiously, the only place on television where some of the attributes of adulthood, or ideal adulthood, are realized—helpfulness, guidance, gentleness, self-sacrifice—are on children's shows. Saturday-morning cartoons generally recreate the old chase-and-miss mayhem of movie cartoons; even today Tweety-Bird and Road Runner still watch their pursuers rolled like dough under boulders. And there are other "adventure" cartoons that merely make cartoons of the real shows on television (a gratuitous art). But *Sesame Street, Captain Kangaroo,* and *Mr. Rogers* do in fact show adults behaving thoughtfully and compassionately, often creatively. The trouble, of course, is that the adults on these shows are depicted either as wise oversized children or as those living their lives solely *for* children, or both. No child measures his parents by the adults on these programs because no parent spends his day as Mr. Rogers does, except Mr. Rogers.

23. Where television invents its characters and situations, adulthood is chided, scoffed at, ignored, by-passed, and occasionally obliterated. What could be the purpose (assuming there is one) of these underminings? Not satire, certainly—the destruction is too scattergun, and there is no moral position or corrective imagination behind it. In many ways the depiction of adulthood seems merely the revenge of a peevish child, albeit a Gargantuan one: a free-wheeling diminution of adult stature for a laugh or for the hell of it. If there is a scheme here, it need not be intentional. As one instrument of popular culture, television contains the properties of popular culture as a whole, and its collective attitude toward anything may be grounded in the general ways in which popular culture works.

24. Conventional wisdom has it that contemporary life changes so rapidly that we are unable both to see its shapes and to apply standards of value to the whole or its parts. Since popular culture carries the signs of the times, people who exclaim over the transitoriness or shakiness of modern man ordinarily use elements

of popular culture as referents. Look closely, however, and the signs read differently. Rather than disowning the past (history and traditions), popular culture persistently resurrects and reinforces it. But it works by sleight of hand. It operates on two levels of tradition simultaneously, and it uses one to cover the other and, in many ways and for some important reasons, to disguise its existence.

25. The more obvious level of tradition in popular culture is the one it creates for itself. This is tradition born of mounting conventions. In television, for example, it takes shape by building program upon program, format upon format, character role upon character role, situation upon situation down to things as small as lines of dialogue and gestures—all continually repeating themselves as soon as a certain receptivity on our part has been perceived. All forms of "newness" and "change" rely upon these conventions both as the standard against which their apparent novelty may be measured and as the future repository for our quick assimilations. The "new" becomes the "old" in a flash, as it also becomes part of, and strengthens, this level of tradition.

26. This process of assimilation, seen by some observers as genuine change, is like fast-falling rain which creates its own water surface on the ground. It is *not* the ground but a *surface on* the ground. We, in turn, move like cars in a rainstorm on that surface, at a high speed often determined by the rain itself. The surface tradition built by popular culture, because it is ephemeral in its parts, only exists as a total body by means of the rapidity of additional elements, reinforcements, to it. This tradition is formed not necessarily by merit on objective standards of excellence (although it may be so), but by repetition.

27. Advertising on television uses this sort of repetition not only to sell products, but also to sell people selling products. Actors who perform in commercials very often perform in regular programs as well, and in similar roles—the know-it-all mother on the situation comedy *Rhoda* pushes Bounty paper towels; the authoritative "professional dishwasher" who advocates Ajax liquid once had his own detective series. The effect of these interchanges is to turn the actor himself into a product that becomes as familiar as the thing he hawks. The mere sight of him in any context elicits visions of clean counters and shiny dishes and, naturally, sustains a terrifyingly smooth transition between advertising and programming.

28. While this is happening, we are told that it is not. Instead, we

are assured that everything presented to us by various media is new and startling, to which announcements we willingly suspend disbelief. The reason we are told that everything is new is simple: those formats or character roles of which we recently grew tired may easily be refurbished, and we, seeing them again and again, may have our powers of discrimination worn down accordingly. Why we suspend disbelief, however, is a much deeper problem. Part of the answer, I believe, lies in the fact that popular culture makes us just as happy as we wish to be, no more, no less. The other part is our abhorrence, perhaps fear, of making connections generally, which allows us to go along with, and in some instances to become, those who tell us "there's a new you coming every day."

29. This abhorrence or, at the least, avoidance is at the heart of the second and darker level at which popular culture operates. This level of tradition is real tradition—those elements of American factual and intellectual history that encouraged and permitted our start as a nation and that have both dogged and inspired us since. Our history—the significant part of it—resides in popular culture, often confused and jumbled, often hiding like the purloined letter, nevertheless coming through with the inevitability of fate in the classics. It comes through with particular clarity on television and with particularly particular clarity on the subject of adulthood.

30. I believe the belittling of adulthood on television is no different at base from Emerson's decision to shuck the courtly muses of Europe. It derives from a wish for improbable freedom in the name of some higher, if indeterminable, virtue. "Abstract liberty, like other mere abstractions, is not to be found," said Burke. But Burke did not imagine a world so dominated by the expression of abstractions that the abstractions could develop their own symbolic logic, and rapidly become the definitions of themselves.

31. To be without memory, reason, civility, stature, and authority sounds like a wish for savagery. In fact, it may turn out to be so, though it is unlikely that television consciously promotes such a wish. There is, however, a state of mind that falls short of savagery, which simulates a dream state, where all freedoms associated with savagery flourish without histrionics. We have no name for this state, for it did not exist before television and still does not exist outside it. But, whatever its name, it is a state of freedom—apolitical, though it admits politics, asocial, though it depends on social life—a celebration of pure irresponsibility.

32. In many ways, television is the medium of irresponsibility, which is why the idea of adulthood within television is a contradiction in terms. The medium itself allows freedoms that no other medium will; it doesn't hold us like the theater or movies: we can place it where we choose, we can eat, do push-ups, answer the door. We are free to spin the channels, free to take or leave it. In turn, it shows us freedoms never won before—tapes and repeats that play havoc with time and sequential actions, with order and the idea of order. Of course these freedoms are illusory, but that doesn't seem to lessen our interest in them. Television is so far the only medium to take us out of history, making paltry such nuisances as original sin.

33. "Grow up!" as an imperative means "behave and control yourself": understand your limitations and be reasonable and civil accordingly. One does not grow up on television. It is not in television's commercial interests to have one do so, because a free-floating mind is more apt to buy large quantities of La Choy Chinese food. But we are complicit in this as well, having found and tacitly urged on television a strange answer to our wildest dream. The question, how free can you be?, which bestrides the democracy as does no other, is in television rhetorical.

34. You *can* yell fire in a crowded television set. You can do anything you please. Adults are interchangeable and lack the virtues of adulthood, and soap operas rely on perpetually changing characters and circumstances. New series every season, new logos for networks. All this for us, as we sit alone in our separate houses dazzled by the freedoms within the medium and the ferocious self-reliance *of* the medium. Our memories go, too, for the experience of television is itself unmemorable.

35. As for the ever-recurrent question of influence, it is hard to tell what these images do. I seriously doubt that watching panicky or wise adults on television will make children grow one way or the other, or that seeing adults forfeit sense and manners will cause children to do likewise. But what of these fierce freedoms: the message continually sent, dot by dot, that a person needs no one but himself in this world and no other person needs him? What of the message of the box? Every night in America the doors lock, the screens glow bright, and man sits down to see how free he can be. Nothing will disturb him, if he can help it. He is a grown-up, after all, and has earned his independence.

DISCUSSION: INDUCTIVE REASONING

Induction means deriving generalizations from particular instances—for example, parents and teenagers seldom like the same kind of music. Inductive arguments are neither valid nor invalid; they are characterized as more or less *probable* depending on the strength of the evidence in relation to the conclusion. The more parents and teenagers I survey in a random sample of families representing a cross section of backgrounds, incomes, and education, the stronger my conclusion will be.

Perfect inductions or generalizations are possible when the group surveyed is small: the teenagers in my family like the same kind of music. But most inductions deal with groups or classes containing a very large number of members—a number much too great to survey. It would be impossible to find out whether all teenagers past and present have liked the same kind of music; it would be hard to find out whether all living teenagers do. The problem in induction is to choose particular instances that we can say are truly representative of the group or class about which the generalization is made.

We often make statements in the form of generalizations that do not seem preposterous to us, though they may to other people, as James Thurber humorously shows (see page 267). Some people assume without question that small towns are safer to live in than cities; that Irishmen have short tempers; that New Yorkers are rude; that children who watch television more than two hours a day are fast (or slow) learners. To establish these generalizations we must show that the small towns we have lived in or the New Yorkers we have encountered are typical of all small towns or all New Yorkers—that there are no special circumstances that would account for the quality cited. The New Yorkers who prompted the generalization about rudeness may have been observed on a crowded, stalled bus on the hottest day of the year. Showing that these particular instances are indeed representative is exceedingly difficult: this is why generalizations must be carefully limited and qualified.

An inductive argument is considered probable only—never certain—because of the difficulty of guaranteeing a representative sample. A special kind of inductive argument—argument by analogy, in which similar objects or situations are taken to imply other similarities—is probable for other reasons. If identical twins are both English majors, wear the same clothes, enjoy the same films and music, play the same sports, and have the same hobbies, it may be argued that their respective friends will have a lot in common. As a rule, the greater the number of points of similarity, the stronger the probability of this conclusion. But these points of similarity—particulars in the process of generalization—must be relevant to the conclusion and lend strength to it. They do not, for example, establish that the twins have the same friends or always will have the same kind.

The points of dissimilarity must not weaken the conclusion. If, in seeking a job as a shoe salesman, I argue that my three years as an army drill sergeant fit me for the job, I will have to show that certain indispensable skills are common to both jobs and that certain differences in situation or dissimilarities are relatively insignificant. It is significant, for example, that customers can walk out of the store, but recruits cannot walk off the parade ground. Dissimilarities may increase the strength of an argument, too. If I argue that fifty former army drill sergeants are now successful shoe salesmen and that I should be hired for this reason, my argument will be strengthened if the sergeants *differ* in age, background, experience in selling, and any other relevant characteristics.

In general a limited conclusion may be drawn from a limited analogy if the points of similarity are clearly specified (or at least agreed on), if there is agreement on the relevance of the points considered, and if inferences are drawn from these points only. If these limits are not observed, the analogy may be considered false. Many people will accept the notion that "anything goes" in advertising because, they are told, the world of buying and selling is a jungle in which only the "fit" survive. The shoe salesman who thinks of himself as a "tiger" may discover that deceived buyers (unlike the tiger's dinner) are permitted to learn from their mistakes.

Cause-and-effect reasoning, on which analogy often depends, is also capable of reaching probable—sometimes highly probable—but not absolutely certain conclusions. We may think (on the basis of repeated efforts) that we know the conditions sufficient to produce a perfect soufflé—until we try to make one in a city at a high elevation, and the soufflé fails to rise. This limitation on cause-and-effect reasoning applies to the various kinds considered earlier (see pages 86–87).

Here, briefly described, are a few common errors in reasoning:

Post hoc, ergo propter hoc ("after this, therefore because of this"): the mistaken assumption that one event is the cause of a second merely because it precedes it. If nuclear explosions precede a sudden increase in tornado activity, they cannot be blamed for the increase in tornados unless a direct relationship can be established. One way to do this is to show that *every* such increase in tornado activity since 1945 was preceded by one or more nuclear explosions. However, that would establish a probable causal relationship only; further investigation might disclose the why of this relationship.

Begging the question: If I argue that "the useless custom of tipping should be abolished because it no longer has a purpose," I have assumed that the custom is useless before I have shown it to be. A close relative is

Arguing in a circle: "Nice girls don't chew gum because that is something no nice girl would do." I have not given a reason; I have merely restated my opening assertion.

Non sequitur ("it does not follow"): If I assert that I am against capital punishment because my father is, I am assuming without saying so that fathers know best. Since this premise has not been made explicit, the second part of the statement "does not follow" from the first part. The hidden premise may have been suppressed because, once stated, it shows the statement to be questionable or absurd.

Irrelevant conclusion: If the point-at-issue is whether private insurance companies or the federal government should operate a national health insurance plan, the argument that national health insurance is needed *now* is an irrelevant argument.

Argumentum ad hominem: an attack on the individual rather than the issue—for example, arguing that a proposal for national health insurance is unsound because its proponents are in the pay of special-interest groups. In other circumstances (as in an election campaign), the individual may be the specific issue.

Argumentum ad populum: an appeal to such things as popular prejudice and patriotic feeling to gain support for or to attack an issue—Abraham Lincoln would have favored (or opposed) national health insurance; therefore, national health insurance is good (or bad).

Either-or hypothesis: the setting up of two alternatives—for example, national health insurance *or* private insurance plans—and not allowing for other plans or other solutions to the problem. Such reasoning may be highly emotional, even threatening: either we disarm completely *or* we face nuclear annihilation.

Hasty generalization: a judgment on the basis of insufficient evidence or special cases—arguing that people over seventy should be denied licenses to drive because an extraordinary number of old people were involved in traffic accidents during a particular winter. The argument might be worth considering if the behavior of the old people involved in accidents could be shown to be typical. But other relevant evidence must be considered: an extraordinary number of drivers of *all* ages might have been involved in accidents that winter. Judgments and generalizations should be tested by exceptions that we can think of or that are brought to our attention; the statement "the exception proves the rule" means the generalization must explain *all* apparent exceptions to it, not that the rule must have an exception.

QUESTIONS

1. Rosenblatt begins with television families like the Waltons and extends the discussion to family-like relationships. What particular relationships does he discuss, and what additional points is he able to make about television through them?
2. Rosenblatt's subject is, in fact, adulthood as represented on television. What other images of adulthood does he discuss?
3. What point is he making about the use of tradition in popular culture? What does he mean by "tradition born of mounting conventions" (paragraph 24), and what point is he making through this idea?
4. Do *Let's Make a Deal* and *The Neighbors* illustrate the same point, or does Rosenblatt need both examples to make different points?
5. Rosenblatt works from details to probable conclusions based on these details. What is the chief conclusion he reaches, and where does he state it? What related conclusions does he also reach?
6. How does he anticipate and even partially state his conclusions early in the essay?
7. How does the wording of the concluding paragraphs show that Rosenblatt considers his argument probable rather than certain?

WRITING ASSIGNMENTS

Examine advertisements that depict family life and analyze the attitudes they convey implicitly about the meaning of adulthood. Use your analysis to evaluate Rosenblatt's conclusions about television family shows.

Analyze two or three episodes of a television show to illustrate the use of "tradition born of mounting conventions." Discuss whether your analysis supports Rosenblatt's conclusions in paragraphs 24–26.

Discuss the extent of your agreement with Rosenblatt's statement that television is "the medium of irresponsibility." Base your discussion on your own examples.

Write your own definition of adulthood, and illustrate it with examples of public figures.

EDWARD JAY EPSTEIN

Network News: The Mirror Analogy

1.   David Brinkley, in an N.B.C. News special entitled "From Here to the Seventies," reiterated a description of television news that is frequently offered by television newsmen:

> What television did in the sixties was to show the American people to the American people. . . . It did show the people places and things they had not seen before. Some they liked, and some they did not. It was not that television produced or created any of it.

In this view, television news does no more than mirror reality. Thus, Leonard Goldenson, the chairman of the board of A.B.C., testified before the National Commission on the Causes and Prevention of Violence that complaints of news distortion were brought about by the fact that "Americans are reluctant to accept the images reflected by the mirror we have held up to our society." Robert D. Kasmire, a vice-president of N.B.C., told the commission, "There is no doubt that television is, to a large degree, a mirror of our society. It is also a mirror of public attitudes and preferences." The president of N.B.C., Julian Goodman, told the commission, "In short, the medium is blamed for the message." Dr. Frank Stanton, vice-chairman and former president of C.B.S., testifying before a House committee, said, "What the media do is to hold a mirror up to society and try to report it as faithfully as possible." Elmer Lower, the president of A.B.C. News, has described television news as "the television mirror that reflects . . . across oceans and mountains," and added, "Let us open the doors of the parliaments everywhere to the electronic mirrors." The imagery has been picked up by critics of television, too. Jack Gould, formerly of the *Times,* wrote of television's coverage of racial riots, "Congress, one would hope, would not conduct an examination of a mirror because of the disquieting images that it beholds."

NETWORK NEWS: THE MIRROR ANALOGY: In *News from Nowhere: Television and the News,* by Edward Jay Epstein. Copyright © 1973 by Edward Jay Epstein. Reprinted by permission of Random House, Inc. Most of the material appeared in *The New Yorker.* Selection title by editor.

2.   The mirror analogy has considerable descriptive power, but it also leads to a number of serious misconceptions about the medium. The notion of a "mirror of society" implies that everything of significance that happens will be reflected on television news. Network news organizations, however, far from being ubiquitous and all-seeing, are limited newsgathering operations, which depend on camera crews based in only a few major cities for most of their national stories. Some network executives have advanced the idea that network news is the product of coverage by hundreds of affiliated stations, but the affiliates' contribution to the network news programs actually is very small. Most network news stories are assigned in advance to network news crews and correspondents, and in many cases whether or not an event is covered depends on where it occurs and the availability of network crews.

3.   The mirror analogy also suggests immediacy: events are reflected instantaneously, as in a mirror. This notion of immediate reporting is reinforced by the way people in television news depict the process to the public. News executives sometimes say that, given the immediacy of television, the network organization has little opportunity to intervene in news decisions. Reuven Frank once declared, on a television program about television, "News coverage generally happens too fast for anything like that to take place." But does it? Though it is true that elements of certain events, such as space exploration and political conventions, are broadcast live, virtually all of the regular newscasts, except for the commentator's "lead-ins" and "tags" to the news stories, are prerecorded on videotape or else on film, which must be transported, processed, edited, and projected before it can be seen. Some film stories are delayed from one day to two weeks, because of certain organizational needs and policies. Reuven Frank more or less outlined these policies on "prepared," or delayed, news in a memorandum he wrote when he was executive producer of N.B.C.'s nightly news program. "Except for those rare days when other material becomes available," he wrote, "the gap will be filled by planned and prepared film stories, and we are assuming the availability of two each night." These "longer pieces," he continued, were to be "planned, executed over a longer period of time than spot news, usable and relevant any time within, say, two weeks rather than that day, receptive to the more sophisticated techniques of production and editing, but journalism withal." The reason for delaying filmed stories, a network vice-president has explained, is that "it

gives the producer more control over his program." First, it gives the producer control of the budget, since shipping the film by plane, though it might mean a delay of a day or two, is considerably less expensive than transmitting the film electronically by satellite or A.T. & T. lines. Second, and perhaps more important, it gives the producer control over the content of the individual stories, since it affords him an opportunity to screen the film and, if necessary, re-edit it. Eliminating the delay, the same vice-president suggested, could have the effect of reducing network news to a mere "chronicler of events" and forcing it "out of the business of making meaningful comment." Moreover, the delay provides a reserve of stories that can be used to give the program "variety" and "pacing."

4.   In filming delayed stories, newsmen are expected to eliminate any elements of the unexpected, so as not to destroy the illusion of immediacy. This becomes especially important when it is likely that the unusual developments will be reported in other media and thus date the story. A case in point is an N.B.C. News story about the inauguration of a high-speed train service between Montreal and Toronto. While the N.B.C. crew was filming the turbotrain during its inaugural run to Toronto, it collided with—and "sliced in half," as one newspaper put it—a meat trailer-truck, and then suffered a complete mechanical breakdown on the return trip. Persistent "performance flaws" and subsequent breakdowns eventually led to a temporary suspension of the service. None of these accidents and aberrations were included in the filmed story broadcast two weeks later on the N.B.C. evening news. David Brinkley, keeping to the original story, written before the event, introduced the film by saying, "The only high-speed train now running in North America has just begun in Canada." Four and a half minutes of shots of the streamlined train followed, and the narration suggested that this foreshadowed the future of transportation, since Canada's "new turbo just might shake [American] lethargy" in developing such trains. (The announcement of the suspension of the service, almost two weeks later, was not carried on the program.) This practice of "preparing" stories also has affected the coverage of more serious subjects—for instance, many of the filmed stories about the Vietnam war were delayed for several days. It was possible to transmit war films to the United States in one day by using the satellite relay; but the cost was considerable at the height of the war—more than three thousand dollars for a

ten minute transmission, as opposed to twenty or thirty dollars for shipping the same film by plane. And, with the exception of momentous battles, such as the Tet offensive, virtually all of the network film was sent by plane. To avoid the possibility of having the delayed footage dated by newspaper accounts, network correspondents were instructed to report on the routine and continuous aspects of the war rather than unexpected developments, according to a former N.B.C. Saigon bureau manager.

5.   The mirror analogy, in addition, obscures the component of "will"—of initiative in producing feature stories and of decisions made in advance to cover or not to cover certain types of events. A mirror makes no decisions; it simply reflects what takes place in front of it. But considerable initiative was displayed in the feature story with which David Brinkley closed N.B.C.'s evening news program on the same night he told the public that news was not "produced or created." Brinkley reported:

> A vastly popular hit song through most of the summer and fall is called "Ruby, Don't Take Your Love to Town." It's been high on the best-seller list, sung by Kenny Rogers and the First Edition. But it's more than a pop song; it's a social document, a comment on our times, and on the war. It is the lament of a Vietnam veteran, returned home gravely wounded, confined to his bed, lying there listening as his wife goes out at night leaving him, because the war has left him unable to move. Well, what the song says, and its wide popularity in this country, may tell more about the ordinary American's view of the Vietnam war than all the Gallup Polls combined, and here is the song, set to film.

6.   A three-minute film followed, supposedly illustrating the song. It showed the room of a crippled veteran, complete with pills, medicines, photographs, and "Ruby's" belongings. Interspersed with scenes of the room were scenes having to do with the Vietnam war—flamethrowers, helicopters, tanks, and casualties, and Presidents Eisenhower, Kennedy, Johnson, and Nixon—all combined in a montage. The illustration of the pop song was, of course, pure invention. The "veteran's room" was a set in Los Angeles, rented for the occasion. All the props were selected, the field producer explained to me later, "to create an atmosphere of futility and absurdity." A few seconds of battle scenes, intercut into the story "to

show what the veteran was thinking as his wife left him," were culled from ten years of stock film footage, according to the producer. And, of course, the song itself was a work of the imagination. In its total effect, such a feature story may, as Brinkley claimed, have accurately captured "the ordinary American's view of the Vietnam war," but this one obviously required a number of decisions on the part of the producer and commentator. First, a song had to be selected from literally hundreds of popular ballads that could be identified as "a comment on our times." Second, the song, once selected, could have been used to illuminate the news in a number of entirely different ways, and not only as an index of public opinion on Vietnam. Third, a decision had to be made on what type of film would be used in the montage to show the veteran's thoughts; scenes of enemy atrocities would have fit the lyrics just as easily as the scenes of American bombing attacks that were actually used. Finally, the selection of props to "create an atmosphere" also offered a great deal of leeway.

7.   When the question of their responsibility is raised, the networks freely acknowledge that their coverage of events can be controlled by advance decisions, or policy. For example, an N.B.C. staff lawyer informed the Federal Communications Commission that during the Democratic National Convention in Chicago in 1968 "special directives" were issued to N.B.C. news personnel that "no demonstrations were to be telecast live, no mobile units were to be dispatched until an event had actually occurred, and demonstrations or violent confrontations were not to be telecast until properly evaluated." Reuven Frank, explaining why few of the early demonstrations or "provocations" in Chicago were broadcast, wrote, in *Television Quarterly,* "Up until the serious violence, it was our conscious policy to avoid covering too much of the activities of demonstrators lest we fall into the trap of doing their advertising for them." C.B.S. had a similar policy during the Convention. Richard Salant, the president of C.B.S. News, told the National Commission on the Causes and Prevention of Violence, "We have a policy about live coverage of disorders and potential disorders. . . . The policy is that we will not provide such live coverage except in extraordinary circumstances."

8.   Policy can determine not only whether or not a subject is shown on television but also, if it is shown, how it is depicted. At a time when American ground troops were still involved in the Vietnam war, Av Westin, executive producer of the A.B.C. Evening

News, wrote to correspondents. "I have asked our Vietnam staff to alter the focus of their coverage from combat pieces to interpretive ones, pegged to the eventual pull-out of the American forces. This point should be stressed for all hands." In a Telex to A.B.C. News's Saigon bureau, Westin informed news personnel of the kind of specific stories he expected that altered focus to produce:

> I think the time has come to shift some of our focus from the battlefield, or more specifically American military involvement with the enemy, to themes and stories which can be grouped under the general heading: We Are On Our Way Out of Vietnam. . . . To be more specific, a series of story ideas suggest themselves.

9.   The list of suggested stories included such topics as black marketeering ("Find us that Oriental Sidney Greenstreet, the export-import entrepreneur," the Telex suggested), a replaced province chief ("Is the new man doing any better than his corrupt and inefficient predecessor?"), political opposition ("Could you single out a representative opposition leader . . . and do a story centered about him? Preferably we would like to know about the most active opposition leader"), medical care for civilians "(Does the granddaughter sleep under the old man's hospital bed, scrounge food for him, etc?"), and the treatment of ex-Vietcong. After Westin made these suggestions, a radical change from combat stories to "We Are On Our Way Out" stories ensued in A.B.C.'s coverage of the Vietnam war.

10.   A somewhat similar decision was reached at N.B.C. after President Johnson announced a halt in the bombing of North Vietnam. The executive producer of the nightly news program told the news staff that the "story" now was the negotiations, not the fighting, and although combat footage was sent to New York from Saigon virtually every day for two months following the decision, almost none of it was used. Yet, as it turned out, the end of United States participation in the war was actually more than four years off.

11.   Policy decisions of this kind can also affect the depiction of domestic events in important ways. During the riots that followed the assassination of Martin Luther King, N.B.C. News apparently decided to minimize the extent of the violence—which was considerable—in New York City. An N.B.C. memorandum on riot coverage says that "Robert Northshield, executive producer of the

Huntley-Brinkley Report, told us that he made an effort to use the minimum amount of riot footage following the assassination of King." The correspondent who narrated the story told me subsequently that he was aware of the "rioting" and the "tense situation" in the black community but that the producer had decided before he edited the story that it should emphasize the restoration of peace rather than continued violence (and the correspondent agreed). The producer later said that it was his responsibility to "evaluate all the information, including the social context" of a news event and then "decide how it should be presented." In evaluating such a story, he said, it must be decided whether the violence is "isolated incidents" or a "general trend." The point here is not the journalistic soundness or the social value of such policy decisions but simply that they exist, and that television news is something more than a mirror.

12. Some television executives, while admitting the weakness of the mirror analogy, maintain that decisions in network news are shaped less by organizational needs and expectations than by the independent judgment of "professionals." They argue that television newsmen, as professionals, are in some ways analogous to doctors and scientists, who take their values from the standards and code of their profession rather than from any organization employing them. Doctors and scientists are given a good deal of latitude, if not complete autonomy, by their administrators, because the presumption is that they have a virtual monopoly of knowledge in their special fields. Television journalists, however, have no such claim to a monopoly of knowledge in their work. Consequently, interventions by the producer or by assistant producers in decisions on how to play the news are the rule rather than the exception. Television newsmen sometimes explain these interventions by saying that all the members of news organizations, whether they are executives, producers, or correspondents, share certain concepts of what constitutes news and will conform to these concepts rather than simply serving the interests of the organization that employs them. The trouble with applying this formulation of "professionalism" to television newsmen is that the various members of news organizations necessarily have different responsibilities and values. Executives are responsible for seeing to it that the product of the news division meets its budget and the expectations of the network; producers are responsible for seeing to it that their programs conform to budget, quality, and policy

guidelines; correspondents and other newsmen are responsible only for their own work on individual stories. These different sets of responsibilities necessarily create tensions between the correspondents, with their basic news values, and the executives, whose values are predominantly organization values.

13. Network news operations do provide opportunities for initiative and idiosyncratic judgments on the part of correspondents, editors, and producers. But over the long run such an organization must rely heavily on a set of internal rules and stable expectations. Although operating rules may not predetermine any particular stories, they do define general characteristics of network news, such as the length of film reports (whether three minutes or thirty minutes long, say), the amount of time and money available for individual film reports (which, in turn, may define the "depth" of news coverage), the areas that are covered most heavily (which might be said to delineate the geography of news), the models for dealing with controversy (whether the "dialectical" model, in which two sides are presented together with a synthesis, or the "thesis" model, which tries to prove that one side is correct), the ratio of "prepared" or delayed news to immediate news, and the general categories that are given preference by producers. And it is these general characteristics, proceeding from the structure and the needs of the organization—not the choice of one story rather than another—that give network news an over-all consistency.

QUESTIONS

1. In how many ways do executives view television news as a mirror? How are these ways stated?
2. What is Epstein's objection to the mirror analogy? Does he accept any point of similarity between the mirror and the news show?
3. How does Epstein employ the mirror analogy not only to tell us about the conception of television news but also to criticize that conception? Is his criticism implicit throughout the discussion?
4. Does he reject the analogy between television news commentators and doctors and scientists?
5. Does he attribute motives to the television news executives or merely analyze what they do?

WRITING ASSIGNMENTS

Take notes on the order of news stories in a single half-hour evening news program and consider whether a pattern emerges. For example, are the less serious stories saved for the middle or the end, or are they interspersed with the more serious ones? Does the news commentator express an attitude toward the story being reported?

Discuss whether, in your opinion, commentators should take stands on the news and the issues they report.

BARRY COMMONER
Nature Knows Best

1.   In my experience this principle is likely to encounter consider-able resistance, for it appears to contradict a deeply held idea about the unique competence of human beings. One of the most per-vasive features of modern technology is the notion that it is in-tended to "improve on nature"—to provide food, clothing, shelter, and means of communication and expression which are superior to those available to man in nature. Stated baldly, the third law of ecology holds that any major man-made change in a natural sys-tem is likely to be *detrimental* to that system. This is a rather ex-treme claim; nevertheless I believe it has a good deal of merit if understood in a properly defined context.

2.   I have found it useful to explain this principle by means of an analogy. Suppose you were to open the back of your watch, close your eyes, and poke a pencil into the exposed works. The almost certain result would be damage to the watch. Nevertheless, this result is not *absolutely* certain. There is some finite possibility that the watch was out of adjustment and that the random thrust of the pencil happened to make the precise change needed to improve it. However, this outcome is exceedingly improbable. The question at issue is: why? The answer is self-evident: there is a very consider-able amount of what technologists now call "research and develop-

NATURE KNOWS BEST: In *The Closing Circle: Nature, Man and Technology,* by Barry Commoner. Copyright © 1971 by Barry Commoner. Portions of the book originally appeared in *The New Yorker.* Reprinted by permission of Alfred A. Knopf, Inc.

ment" (or, more familiarly, "R & D") behind the watch. This means that over the years numerous watchmakers, each taught by a predecessor, have tried out a huge variety of detailed arrangements of watch works, have discarded those that are not compatible with the over-all operation of the system and retained the better features. In effect, the watch mechanism, as it now exists, represents a very restricted selection, from among an enormous variety of possible arrangements of component parts, of a singular organization of the watch works. Any random change made in the watch is likely to fall into the very large class of inconsistent, or harmful, arrangements which have been tried out in past watchmaking experience and discarded. One might say, as a law of watches, that "the watchmaker knows best."

3.   There is a close, and very meaningful, analogy in biological systems. It is possible to induce a certain range of random, inherited changes in a living thing by treating it with an agent, such as x-irradiation, that increases the frequency of mutations. Generally, exposure to x-rays increases the frequency of all mutations which have been observed, albeit very infrequently, in nature and can therefore be regarded as *possible* changes. What is significant, for our purpose, is the universal observation that when mutation frequency is enhanced by x-rays or other means, nearly all the mutations are harmful to the organisms and the great majority so damaging as to kill the organism before it is fully formed.

4.   In other words, like the watch, a living organism that is forced to sustain a random change in its organization is almost certain to be damaged rather than improved. And in both cases, the explanation is the same—a great deal of "R & D." In effect there are some two to three billion years of "R & D" behind every living thing. In that time, a staggering number of new individual living things have been produced, affording in each case the opportunity to try out the suitability of some random genetic change. If the change damages the viability of the organism, it is likely to kill it before the change can be passed on to future generations. In this way, living things accumulate a complex organization of compatible parts; those possible arrangements that are not compatible with the whole are screened out over the long course of evolution. Thus, the structure of a present living thing or the organization of a current natural ecosystem is likely to be "best" in the sense that it has been so heavily screened for disadvantageous components that any new one is very likely to be worse than the present ones.

5.   This principle is particularly relevant to the field of organic chemistry. Living things are composed of many thousands of different organic compounds, and it is sometimes imagined that at least some of these might be improved upon if they were replaced by some man-made variant of the natural substance. The third law of ecology suggests that the artificial introduction of an organic compound that does not occur in nature, but is man-made and is nevertheless active in a living system, is very likely to be harmful.
6.   This is due to the fact that the varieties of chemical substances actually found in living things are vastly more restricted than the *possible* varieties. A striking illustration is that if one molecule each of all the possible types of proteins were made, they would together weigh more than the observable universe. Obviously there are a fantastically large number of protein types that are *not* made by living cells. And on the basis of the foregoing, one would reason that many of these possible protein types were once formed in some particular living things, found to be harmful, and rejected through the death of the experiment. In the same way, living cells synthesize fatty acids (a type of organic molecule that contains carbon chains of various lengths) with even-numbered carbon chain lengths (i.e., 4, 6, 8, etc., carbons), but no fatty acids with odd-numbered carbon chain lengths. This suggests that the latter have once been tried out and found wanting. Similarly, organic compounds that contain attached nitrogen and oxygen atoms are singularly rare in living things. This should warn us that the artificial introduction of substances of this type would be dangerous. This is indeed the case, for such substances are usually toxic and frequently carcinogenic. And, I would suppose from the fact that DDT is nowhere found in nature, that somewhere, at some time in the past, some unfortunate cell synthesized this molecule—and died.
7.   One of the striking facts about the chemistry of living systems is that for every organic substance produced by a living organism, there exists, somewhere in nature, an enzyme capable of breaking that substance down. In effect, no organic substance is synthesized unless there is provision for its degradation; recycling is thus enforced. Thus, when a new man-made organic substance is synthesized with a molecular structure that departs significantly from the types which occur in nature, it is probable that no degradative enzyme exists, and the material tends to accumulate.
8.   Given these considerations, it would be prudent, I believe, to

regard every man-made organic chemical *not* found in nature which has a strong action on any one organism as potentially dangerous to other forms of life. Operationally, this view means that all man-made organic compounds that are at all active biologically ought to be treated as we do drugs, or rather as we *should* treat them—prudently, cautiously. Such caution or prudence is, of course, impossible when billions of pounds of the substance are produced and broadly disseminated into the ecosystem where it can reach and affect numerous organisms not under our observation. Yet this is precisely what we have done with detergents, insecticides, and herbicides. The often catastrophic results lend considerable force to the view that "Nature knows best."

QUESTIONS

1. What are the points of similarity between poking a pencil into the back of the watch and introducing man-made changes into nature? Does the fact that the watch is man-made, unlike nature, weaken the analogy?
2. What other analogy might Commoner have chosen? What would have been gained or lost had he employed this analogy?
3. What knowledge and assumptions does Commoner assume in his audience, and how do you know?

WRITING ASSIGNMENT

Explain a phenomenon you are familiar with—stereophonic or quadriphonic sound, or condensation, or the "knuckler" or "spitball" in baseball—through a familiar analogy. Write to a general audience that needs an explanation of basic terms.

BROOKS ATKINSON

The Warfare in the Forest
Is Not Wanton

1.   After thirty-five years the forest in Spruce Notch is tall and
sturdy. It began during the Depression when work gangs planted
thousands of tiny seedlings in abandoned pastures on Richmond
Peak in the northern Catskills. Nothing spectacular has happened
there since; the forest has been left undisturbed.
2.   But now we have a large spread of Norway spruces a foot
thick at the butt and 40 or 50 feet high. Their crowns look like
thousands of dark crosses reaching into the sky.
3.   The forest is a good place in which to prowl in search of
wildlife. But also in search of ideas. For the inescapable fact is that
the world of civilized America does not have such a clean record.
Since the seedlings were planted the nation has fought three catastrophic wars, in one of which the killing of combatants and the
innocent continues. During the lifetime of the forest 350,000
Americans have died on foreign battlefields.
4.   Inside America civilized life is no finer. A President, a Senator,
a man of God have been assassinated. Citizens are murdered in
the streets. Riots, armed assaults, looting, burning, outbursts of
hatred have increased to the point where they have become commonplace.
5.   Life in civilized America is out of control. Nothing is out of
control in the forest. Everything complies with the instinct for survival—which is the law and order of the woods.
6.   Although the forest looks peaceful it supports incessant warfare, most of which is hidden and silent. For thirty-five years the
strong have been subduing the weak. The blueberries that once
flourished on the mountain have been destroyed. All the trees are
individuals, as all human beings are individuals; and every tree
poses a threat to every other tree. The competition is so fierce that
you can hardly penetrate some of the thickets where the lower
branches of neighboring trees are interlocked in a blind competition for survival.

7.   Nor is the wildlife benign. A red-tailed hawk lived there last summer—slowly circling in the sky and occasionally drawing attention to himself by screaming. He survived on mice, squirrels, chipmunks and small birds. A barred owl lives somewhere in the depth of the woods. He hoots in midmorning as well as at sunrise to register his authority. He also is a killer. Killing is a fundamental part of the process. The nuthatches kill insects in the bark. The woodpeckers dig insects out. The thrushes eat beetles and caterpillars.

8.   But in the forest, killing is not wanton or malicious. It is for survival. Among birds of equal size most of the warfare consists of sham battles in which they go through the motions of warfare until one withdraws. Usually neither bird gets hurt.

9.   Nor is the warfare between trees vindictive. Although the spruces predominate they do not practice segregation. On both sides of Lost Lane, which used to be a dirt road, maples, beeches, ashes, aspens and a few red oaks live, and green curtains of wild grapes cover the wild cherry trees. In the depths of the forest there are a few glades where the spruces stand aside and birches stretch and grow. The forest is a web of intangible tensions. But they are never out of control. Although they are wild they are not savage as they are in civilized life.

10. For the tensions are absorbed in the process of growth, and the clusters of large cones on the Norway spruces are certificates to a good future. The forest gives an external impression of discipline and pleasure. Occasionally the pleasure is rapturously stated. Soon after sunrise one morning last summer when the period of bird song was nearly over, a solitary rose-breasted grosbeak sat on the top of a tall spruce and sang with great resonance and beauty. He flew a few rods to another tree and continued singing: then to another tree where he poured out his matin again, and so on for a half hour. There was no practical motive that I was aware of.

11. After thirty-five uneventful years the spruces have created an environment in which a grosbeak is content, and this one said so gloriously. It was a better sound than the explosion of bombs, the scream of the wounded, the crash of broken glass, the crackle of burning buildings, the shriek of the police siren.

12. The forest conducts its affairs with less rancor and malevolence than civilized America.

QUESTIONS

1. One sometimes hears the argument that violence is natural to man, since man is a part of a warring natural world. How does Atkinson implicitly reject this analogy? More specifically, what are the points of dissimilarity between the world of the forest and the world of man?
2. How might the world of the forest be used to argue that competition in the world of man need not be destructive of some of those competing—as the argument that only the "fit" survive in the world of business implies?
3. How does Atkinson increase the probability of his argument through the details he marshals in support of it?

WRITING ASSIGNMENT

Each of the following statements suggests an analogy. Write on one of them, discussing points of similarity and dissimilarity and using this discussion to argue a thesis.
   a. The family is a small nation.
   b. The nation is a large family.
   c. College examinations are sporting events.

NORMAN COUSINS

Who Killed Benny Paret?

1.   Sometime about 1935 or 1936 I had an interview with Mike Jacobs, the prize-fight promoter. I was a fledgling newspaper reporter at that time; my beat was education, but during the vacation season I found myself on varied assignments, all the way from ship news to sports reporting. In this way I found myself sitting opposite the most powerful figure in the boxing world.
2.   There was nothing spectacular in Mr. Jacobs's manner or appearance; but when he spoke about prize fights, he was no longer a bland little man but a colossus who sounded the way Napoleon must have sounded when he reviewed a battle. You knew you

WHO KILLED BENNY PARET?: In *Present Tense* by Norman Cousins. Copyright ©
1967 by Norman Cousins. Used with permission of McGraw-Hill Book Company.

were listening to Number One. His saying something made it true.
3.   We discussed what to him was the only important element in successful promoting—how to please the crowd. So far as he was concerned, there was no mystery to it. You put killers in the ring and the people filled your arena. You hire boxing artists—men who are adroit at feinting, parrying, weaving, jabbing, and dancing, but who don't pack dynamite in their fists—and you wind up counting your empty seats. So you searched for the killers and sluggers and maulers—fellows who could hit with the force of a baseball bat.
4.   I asked Mr. Jacobs if he was speaking literally when he said people came out to see the killer.
5.   "They don't come out to see a tea party," he said evenly. "They come out to see the knockout. They come out to see a man hurt. If they think anything else, they're kidding themselves."
6.   Recently a young man by the name of Benny Paret was killed in the ring. The killing was seen by millions; it was on television. In the twelfth round he was hit hard in the head several times, went down, was counted out, and never came out of the coma.
7.   The Paret fight produced a flurry of investigations. Governor Rockefeller was shocked by what happened and appointed a committee to assess the responsibility. The New York State Boxing Commission decided to find out what was wrong. The District Attorney's office expressed its concern. One question that was solemnly studied in all three probes concerned the action of the referee. Did he act in time to stop the fight? Another question had to do with the role of the examining doctors who certified the physical fitness of the fighters before the bout. Still another question involved Mr. Paret's manager; did he rush his boy into the fight without adequate time to recuperate from the previous one?
8.   In short, the investigators looked into every possible cause except the real one. Benny Paret was killed because the human fist delivers enough impact, when directed against the head, to produce a massive hemorrhage in the brain. The human brain is the most delicate and complex mechanism in all creation. It has a lacework of millions of highly fragile nerve connections. Nature attempts to protect this exquisitely intricate machinery by encasing it in a hard shell. Fortunately, the shell is thick enough to withstand a great deal of pounding. Nature, however, can protect man against everything except man himself. Not every blow to the head will kill a man—but there is always the risk of concussion and damage to the brain. A prize fighter may be able to survive even

repeated brain concussions and go on fighting, but the damage to his brain may be permanent.

9. In any event, it is futile to investigate the referee's role and seek to determine whether he should have intervened to stop the fight earlier. This is not where the primary responsibility lies. The primary responsibility lies with the people who pay to see a man hurt. The referee who stops a fight too soon from the crowd's viewpoint can expect to be booed. The crowd wants the knockout; it wants to see a man stretched out on the canvas. This is the supreme moment in boxing. It is nonsense to talk about prize fighting as a test of boxing skills. No crowd was ever brought to its feet screaming and cheering at the sight of two men beautifully dodging and weaving out of each other's jabs. The time the crowd comes alive is when a man is hit hard over the heart or the head, when his mouthpiece flies out, when blood squirts out of his nose or eyes, when he wobbles under the attack and his pursuer continues to smash at him with poleax impact.

10. Don't blame it on the referee. Don't even blame it on the fight managers. Put the blame where it belongs—on the prevailing mores that regard prize fighting as a perfectly proper enterprise and vehicle of entertainment. No one doubts that many people enjoy prize fighting and will miss it if it should be thrown out. And that is precisely the point.

QUESTIONS

1. Cousins distinguishes between the immediate and the remote causes of Paret's death. What does he show to be the immediate cause, and why can this cause be stated with virtual certainty?
2. Cousins is concerned chiefly with the remote cause of Paret's death. How is this concern basic to his purpose in writing the essay? What are the chief indications of that purpose?
3. How would a different purpose have required Cousins to focus instead on the immediate cause?
4. How does Cousins establish the remote cause? Is his evidence statistical—based on a sample of statements of boxing fans? Is it theoretical—based on a discussion of "human nature"? Is he concerned with the psychology of the crowd or the sociology of boxing? Is his analysis of the event intended to offer a complete explanation?

WRITING ASSIGNMENTS

Analyze the appeals of a mass sport like pro football or hockey to determine the extent of the appeal to violent emotions.

Contrast Cousins' view of the causes of Paret's death with Mailer's view in "The Death of Benny Paret."

HERBERT HENDIN

Students and Drugs

1.   No more dramatic expression of the dissatisfaction students feel with themselves can be found than students abusing drugs. Students often become drug abusers, that is, heavy and habitual users, in an attempt to alter their emotional lives, to transform themselves into the people they wish they could be, but feel they never could be without drugs. What they crave is to restructure their own emotions, not to be themselves, but to live as some "other." What this "other" is like and how it can be achieved cut to the center of the changing American psyche.

2.   The turmoil over performance, achievement, and success, the increasing terror of becoming "too" involved with anyone; the attempt to find in fragmentation the means of effecting a pervasive change in one's total relation to life—all these are everywhere prevalent on campus. Students abusing drugs are often attempting to cure themselves of the malaise they see everywhere around them and in themselves.

3.   Why do some students take LSD or heroin while others take marijuana or amphetamines? Why do still others take anything and everything? Students who are intrigued by drugs can learn through trial and error and from other students to find and favor the drugs which most satisfy their particular emotional needs. They rapidly become expert psychopharmacologists, able to locate the specific drug cure for what disturbs them. One student who by seventeen had tried just about everything and had become a daily,

STUDENTS AND DRUGS: In *The Age of Sensation* by Herbert Hendin. Reprinted by permission of W. W. Norton & Company, Inc. Copyright © 1975 by Herbert Hendin. Selection title by editor.

intravenous heroin user, had rejected LSD early in his drug career, explaining, "I can't see what anyone gets out of it. It just sort of makes you schizy—quiet one minute and freaked out the next."
4.   Some students were initially drawn to the "cops-and-robbers" quality of drug abuse. While they were clearly out to defy their parents and the whole structure of authority, they were often unaware that their abuse had anything to do with their families, so profoundly had they pushed their rage at them out of their consciousness. Such students were invariably unable to deal with their parents directly and were bound in a need to defy them and a simultaneous need to punish themselves for their rebellion.
5.   Drugs provided these students with both crime and punishment, while removing their defiance out of the direct presence of their parents. One student would "let his mind float away" and concentrate on music he liked whenever his father berated him. Afterward he went out and took whatever drugs he could buy. While he never connected his drug abuse with his anger toward his father, he often dreamed of it as a crime for which he would be punished. He had a dream in which a riot was going on in another part of town while he was shooting heroin. He was afraid that somehow he would be arrested along with the rioters. Drugs were clearly his way of rioting, of diverting the crime of rebellion to the crime of drug abuse and focusing his destructive potential on himself. The expectation this student had that he would be arrested was typical, and revelatory of the appeal of drugs for him. Jail signified to such students a concrete way of locking up their rage. Drugs permitted them to both contain their rage and to express it in a way that gave them a sense of defiance, however self-damaging that defiance may be. Often, students who are most in trouble with the police over drugs are those for whom the need for crime and punishment was more significant than the need for drugs.
6.   For most of the students who abused them, drugs also provided the illusion of pleasurable connection to other people while serving to detach them from the emotions real involvement would arouse. Drugs were, for these students, the best available means of social relations. Heroin abusers found in the junkie underworld a sense of security, belonging, and acceptance derived from the acknowledgment and the shared need for heroin. LSD abusers felt their most intimate experiences involved tripping with another person. Marijuana abusers felt that drugs "took the edge off their personality" enough to permit them to be gentle and to empathize

with other people. Amphetamine abusers were pushed into the social round on amphetamine energy, often being enabled to go through sexual experience they would otherwise have found unendurable.

7.   For many students drug abuse is the means to a life without drugs. Such students take drugs to support the adaptation they are struggling to make. Once it is established, they are often able to maintain it without drugs. The period of heavy drug abuse often marks the crisis in their lives when they are trying to establish a tolerable relation to the world and themselves. Appealing, tumultuous, sometimes frighteningly empty, the lives of students who turn to drugs are an intense, dramatic revelation of the way students feel today, what they are forced to grapple with not only in the culture, but in themselves.

QUESTIONS

1. Does Hendin single out a cause of drug use among students, or instead identify a number of related (or unrelated) causes?
2. Does he distinguish psychological from social causes, or does he assume these are one and the same?
3. Is Hendin generalizing about all students today—even those who do not use drugs—or is he commenting merely on student drug users?
4. How does drug use foster "fragmentation" in the drug user? How can "fragmentation" provide a solution to the problems Hendin identifies in paragraph 2?
5. What does Hendin mean by the statement, "For many students drug abuse is the means to a life without drugs"?

WRITING ASSIGNMENT

Describe the tensions you have observed in yourself or in fellow students, and discuss the extent to which these tensions resemble those that Hendin identifies. Suggest some of the causes for those you have experienced or observed.

CONTROVERSY

BERNARD SHAW
Capital Punishment and Imprisonment

1.   Some of the popular objections to [capital punishment] may be
considered for a moment. Death, it is said, is irrevocable; and after
all, they may turn out to be innocent. But really you cannot handle
criminals on the assumption that they may be innocent. You are
not supposed to handle them at all until you have convinced yourself by an elaborate trial that they are guilty. Besides, imprisonment is as irrevocable as hanging. Each is a method of taking a
criminal's life; and when he prefers hanging or suicide to imprisonment for life, as he sometimes does, he says, in effect, that he
had rather you took his life all at once painlessly, than minute by
minute in long-drawn-out torture. You can give a prisoner a pardon; but you cannot give him back a moment of his imprisonment.
He may accept a reprieve willingly in the hope of a pardon or an
escape or a revolution or an earthquake or what not; but as you do
not mean him to evade his sentence in any way whatever, it is not
for you to take such clutchings at straws into account.
2.   Another argument against the death penalty for anything
short of murder is the practical one of the policeman and the
householder, who plead that if you hang burglars they will shoot to
avoid capture on the ground that they may as well be hanged for a
sheep as for a lamb. But this can be disposed of by pointing out,
first, that even under existing circumstances the burglar occasionally shoots, and, second, that acquittals, recommendations to
mercy, verdicts of manslaughter, successful pleas of insanity and
so forth, already make the death penalty so uncertain that even
red-handed murderers shoot no oftener than burglars—less often,
in fact. This uncertainty would be actually increased if the death
sentence were, as it should be, made applicable to other criminals
than those convicted of wilful murder, and no longer made compulsory in any case.

CAPITAL PUNISHMENT AND IMPRISONMENT: In *Crude Criminology* in *The Selected
Prose of Bernard Shaw*. Reprinted by permission of The Society of Authors, as
Agent for the Bernard Shaw Estate. Selection title by editor.

3.   Then comes the plea for the sacredness of human life. The State should not set the example of killing, or of clubbing a rioter with a policeman's baton, or of dropping bombs on a sleeping city, or of doing many things that States nevertheless have to do. But let us take the plea on its own ground, which is, fundamentally, that life is the most precious of all things, and its waste the worst of crimes. We have already seen that imprisonment does not spare the life of the criminal: it takes it and wastes it in the most cruel way. But there are others to be considered beside the criminal and the citizens who fear him so much that they cannot sleep in peace unless he is locked up. There are the people who have to lock him up, and fetch him his food, and watch him. Why are their lives to be wasted? Warders, and especially wardresses, are almost as much tied to the prison by their occupation, and by their pensions, which they dare not forfeit by seeking other employment, as the criminals are. If I had to choose between a spell under preventive detention among hardened criminals in Camp Hill and one as warder in an ordinary prison, I think I should vote for Camp Hill. Warders suffer in body and mind from their employment; and if it be true, as our examination seems to prove, that they are doing no good to society, but very active harm, their lives are wasted more completely than those of the criminals; for most criminals are discharged after a few weeks or months; but the warder never escapes until he is superannuated, by which time he is an older gaolbird than any Lifer in the cells.

4.   How then does the case stand with your incurable pathological case of crime? If you treat the life of the criminal as sacred, you find yourself not only taking his life but sacrificing the lives of innocent men and women to keep him locked up. There is no sort of sense or humanity in such a course. The moment we face it frankly we are driven to the conclusion that the community has a right to put a price on the right to live in it. That price must be sufficient self-control to live without wasting and destroying the lives of others, whether by direct attack like a tiger, parasitic exploitation like a leech, or having to be held in a leash with another person at the end of it. Persons lacking such self-control have been thrust out into the sage-brush to wander there until they die of thirst, a cruel and cowardly way of killing them. The dread of clean and wilful killing often leads to evasions of the commandment "Thou shalt not kill" which are far more cruel than its frank violation. [. . .]

5.   Modern imprisonment: that is, imprisonment practised as a punishment as well as a means of detention, is extremely cruel and mischievous, and therefore extremely wicked. The word extremely is used advisedly because the system has been pushed to a degree at which prison mortality and prison insanity forced it back to the point at which it is barely endurable, which point may therefore be regarded as the practicable extreme.

6.   Although public vindictiveness and public dread are largely responsible for this wickedness, some of the most cruel features of the prison system are not understood by the public, and have not been deliberately invented and contrived for the purpose of increasing the prisoner's torment. The worst of these are (a) unsuccessful attempts at reform, (b) successful attempts to make the working of the prison cheaper for the State and easier for the officials, and (c) accidents of the evolution of the old privately owned detention prison into the new punitive State prison.

7.   The prison authorities profess three objects (a) Retribution (a euphemism for vengeance), (b) Deterrence (a euphemism for Terrorism), and (c) Reform of the prisoner. They achieve the first by simple atrocity. They fail in the second through lack of the necessary certainty of detection, prosecution, and conviction; partly because their methods are too cruel and mischievous to secure the co-operation of the public; partly because the prosecutor is put to serious inconvenience and loss of time; partly because most people desire to avoid an unquestionable family disgrace much more than to secure a very questionable justice; and partly because the proportion of avowedly undetected crimes is high enough to hold out reasonable hopes to the criminal that he will never be called to account. The third (Reform) is irreconcilable with the first (Retribution); for the figures of recidivism, and the discovery that the so-called Criminal Type is really a prison type, prove that the retributive process is one of uncompensated deterioration.

8.   The cardinal vice of the system is the anti-Christian vice of vengeance, or the intentional duplication of malicious injuries partly in pure spite, partly in compliance with the expiatory superstition that two blacks make a white. The criminal accepts this, but claims that punishment absolves him if the injuries are equivalent, and still more if he has the worse of the bargain, as he almost always has. Consequently, when absolution on his release is necessarily denied him, and he is forced back into crime by the refusal to employ him, he feels that he is entitled to revenge this in-

justice by becoming an enemy of Society. No beneficial reform of our treatment of criminals is possible unless and until this superstition of expiation and this essentially sentimental vice of vengeance are unconditionally eradicated.

9.   Society has a right of self-defence, extending to the destruction or restraint of lawbreakers. This right is separable from the right to revenge or punish: it need have no more to do with punishment or revenge than the caging or shooting of a man-eating tiger. It arises from the existence of (A) intolerably mischievous human beings, and (B) persons defective in the self-control needed for free life in modern society, but well behaved and at their ease under tutelage and discipline. Class A can be painlessly killed or permanently restrained. The requisite tutelage and discipline can be provided for Class B without rancor or insult. The rest can be treated not as criminals but as civil defendants, and made to pay for their depredations in the same manner. At present many persons guilty of conduct much viler than that for which poor men are sent to prison suffer nothing worse than civil actions for damages when they do not (unhappily) enjoy complete immunity.

10.   The principle to be kept before the minds of all citizens is that as civilized society is a very costly arrangement necessary to their subsistence and security they must justify their enjoyment of it by contributing their share to its cost, and giving no more than their share of trouble, subject to every possible provision by insurance against innocent disability. This is a condition precedent to freedom, and justifies us in removing cases of incurable noxious disability by simply putting an end to their existence.

11.   An unconquerable repugnance to judicial killing having led to the abolition of capital punishment in several countries, and to its reservation for specially dangerous or abhorrent crimes in all the others, it is possible that the right to kill may be renounced by all civilized States. This repugnance may be intensified as we cease to distinguish between sin and infirmity, or, in prison language, between crime and disease, because of our fear of being led to the extirpation of the incurable invalid who is excessively troublesome as well as to that of the incurable criminal.

12.   On the other hand, the opposite temperament, which is not squeamish about making short work of hard cases, and which is revolted by the daily sacrifice of the lives of prison officials, and of relatives and nurses, to incurable criminals and invalids, may be

reinforced by the abandonment of ethical pretentiousness, vengeance, malice, and all uncharitableness in the matter, and may become less scrupulous than at present in advocating euthanasia for all incurables.

13. Whichever party may prevail, punishment as such is likely to disappear, and with it the ear-marking of certain offences as calling for specially deterrent severities. But it does not follow that lethal treatment of extreme cases will be barred. On the contrary, it may be extended from murder to social incompatibility of all sorts. If it be absolutely barred, sufficient restraint must be effected, not as a punishment but as a necessity for public safety. But there will be no excuse for making it more unpleasant than it need be.

14. When detention and restraint are necessary, the criminal's right to contact with all the spiritual influences of his day should be respected, and its exercise encouraged and facilitated. Conversation, access to books and pictures and music, unfettered scientific, philosophic, and religious activity, change of scene and occupation, the free formation of friendships and acquaintances, marriage and parentage: in short, all the normal methods of creation and recreation, must be available for criminals as for other persons, partly because deprivation of these things is severely punitive, and partly because it is destructive to the victim, and produces what we call the criminal type, making a cure impossible. Any specific liberty which the criminal's specific defects lead him to abuse will, no doubt, be taken from him; but if his life is spared his right to live must be accepted in the fullest sense, and not, as at present, merely as a right to breathe and circulate his blood. In short, a criminal should be treated, not as a man who has forfeited all normal rights and liberties by the breaking of a single law, but as one who, through some specific weakness or weaknesses, is incapable of exercising some specific liberty or liberties.

15. The main difficulty in applying this concept of individual freedom to the criminal arises from the fact that the concept itself is as yet unformed. We do not apply it to children, at home or at school, nor to employees, nor to persons of any class or age who are in the power of other persons. Like Queen Victoria, we conceive Man as being either in authority or subject to authority, each person doing only what he is expressly permitted to do, or what the example of the rest of his class encourages him to consider as tacitly permitted. The concept of the evolving free man in an evolving soci-

ety, making all sorts of experiments in conduct, and therefore doing everything he likes as far as he can unless there are express prohibitions to which he is politically a consenting party, is still unusual, and consequently terrifying, in spite of all the individualist pamphlets of the eighteenth and nineteenth centuries. It will be found that those who are most scandalized by the liberties I am claiming for the convict would be equally scandalized if I claimed them for their own sons, or even for themselves.

16. The conclusion is that imprisonment cannot be fully understood by those who do not understand freedom. But it can be understood quite well enough to have it made a much less horrible, wicked, and wasteful thing than it is at present.

DISCUSSION: CONTROVERSY

A single argument may involve both inductive and deductive reasoning, though one kind usually dominates. In debates over current issues like capital punishment and nuclear power, the kind of reasoning employed depends on what is taken to be the *point-at-issue*. The proponents of nuclear power plants may insist that the economic welfare of a particular region is the point-at-issue in locating a nuclear plant in the vicinity. Opponents may argue that the relative safety of these plants (compared to coal-fueled power plants) or the difficulty of disposing of nuclear wastes is the point-at-issue. Much of the debate may be devoted to establishing this point.

The arguments employed in such a debate probably will be inductive: statistical information on productivity and electrical fuels, eyewitness accounts of nuclear operations, scientific reports on waste disposal, accident reports, and the like. The parties to the dispute may agree on certain assumptions: that a high standard of living is a desirable goal for Americans; that the rights of society must be compatible with the rights of the individual citizen; that world peace depends on continuing high productivity in industrial nations like the United States. From these assumptions certain conclusions may be drawn directly, but used to different advantage by each party in the debate. Or these assumptions may underlie—and determine the outcome of—the debate without being identified and argued. Each party may direct the argument to specific opponents, or may direct it to the general public. The kind of evidence chosen will depend in part on the audience and in part on the needs of the argument.

QUESTIONS

1. The Shaw passages are taken from his *Crude Criminology*, written in 1921–22. The second passage (paragraphs 5–16) is the concluding summary of the main argument in the whole book. In an earlier passage Shaw argues that some criminals cannot be changed and when released from prison continue to torture and murder people:

> Now you cannot get rid of these nuisances and monsters by simply cataloguing them as subthyroidics and superadrenals or the like. At present you torment them for a fixed period, at the end of which they are set free to resume their operations with a savage grudge against the community which has tormented them. That is stupid. Nothing is gained by punishing people who cannot help themselves and on whom deterrence is thrown away. Releasing them is like releasing the tigers from the Zoo to find their next meal in the nearest children's playing ground.

   In the passages printed here, what other arguments does Shaw present in favor of capital punishment? What assumptions is he making about society and the individual in these arguments?

2. How does Shaw answer the objections to capital punishment he presents?

3. Why does he reject life imprisonment as an alternative to capital punishment? What does he believe the purpose of imprisonment should be?

WRITING ASSIGNMENT

Shaw distinguishes three attitudes toward imprisonment. Discuss which of these attitudes represents your own, and defend your reasons for holding one of them and rejecting another. Compare your assumptions about society and the individual with Shaw's.

GEORGE F. WILL
In Cold Blood

1.   Much opposition to capital punishment is, like mine, a strong emotion searching uneasily for satisfactory reasons to justify it. Such reasons cannot be found in the Constitution.

2.   The founders did not consider capital punishment "cruel and unusual" and neither does today's nation: since 1972, 35 states have enacted death penalties. The Supreme Court says the ban on "cruel and unusual" punishment must draw its meaning from "evolving standards of decency." Those standards do evolve: the First Congress passed a statute prescribing 39 lashes for larceny, and one hour in the pillory for perjury. And one prescient congressman opposed the "cruel and unusual" clause because it might someday be construed to ban such "necessary" punishments as ear-cropping. Someday capital punishment may offend the evolving consensus.

3.   But, then, someday mutilation may again be acceptable. Mutilation (castration of sex offenders; removal of brain segments from the unmanageably deranged) is still practiced in some Western societies. Aggressive "behavior modification" techniques result from the "progressive" theory that sin is sickness, so crime ("deviant behavior") is disease. That theory prescribes therapy instead of punishment, and assigns the "curing" of criminals to persons C. S. Lewis called "official straighteners."

4.   Today "progressives" oppose capital punishment, but it is not invariably a conservative policy. It was used aggressively in the U.S., Britain and France when these liberal societies were in their most rationalist phases. They then had extravagant confidence in carefully calibrated punishments as means of social control. On the other hand, one can imagine a conservative like Dostoevski (who knew something about crime and punishment) disdaining capital punishment as a deterrent. Such a conservative would argue that people in this fallen world cannot transcend the impulse to sin; and it is impious to believe that even savage punishment can overcome that impulse, and thus do the work of God's grace. Dostoevski did say

. . . that evil is buried more deeply in humanity than the cure-all socialists think, that evil cannot be avoided in any organization of society, that a man's soul will remain the same, that it is from a man's soul alone that abnormality and sin arise, and that the laws that govern man's spirit are still so unknown, so uncertain and so mysterious that there cannot be any physicians, or even judges, to give a definitive cure or decision.

5.   Today, "cure-all progressives" oppose capital punishment on the ground that crime is a product of individual or social pathology and therefore rehabilitation is the only just purpose of punishment. The logic of this theory also discounts the deterrent value of punishment: no sickness—crime no more than the common cold—can be deterred by threats. But as Robert Bork, Solicitor General of the U.S., says, "The assertion that punishment does not deter runs contrary to the common sense of the community and is, perhaps for that reason, a tenet fiercely held by a number of social scientists."

6.   In fact, there is ample evidence that the rates of many specific crimes are related negatively to the likelihood of punishment, and its severity. Capital punishment surely would deter double parking. And one elaborate statistical study suggests that capital punishment deters murder, that each execution may save as many as eight lives. But because such studies must grapple with many variables, and because murder is frequently a crime of passion, not calculation, the most that can be said confidently is that it is not clear that capital punishment does not deter murder.

7.   The silliest argument against capital punishment is that, deterrent or not, it is wrong because it is "retributive." *All* punishment is retribution. The Marquis of Halifax was delightfully quotable but wrong when he said: "Men are not hanged for stealing horses, but that horses may not be stolen." The point to be made against Halifax is a logical, not an ideological, point. It is that the word "punishment" is only properly used to describe suffering inflicted by authority in response to an offense. Punishment is always (to use the archaic verb) "to retribute," to "pay back for" guilt.

8.   Although concern for rehabilitation or deterrence *may* influence how a crime is punished, punishment *must* have a retributive

dimension. Thus "the object so sublime . . . is to make the punishment fit the crime." And a "fit" is a rough proportionality between what the criminal suffers and what his victim suffered.

9. The complaint that capital punishment is "retributive" is a muddled way of charging that it is disproportionate. It occasionally has been grotesquely so: a British law prescribed death for damaging Westminster Bridge or impersonating a Chelsea pensioner. But the nub of the matter still is: Is death a disproportionate response to murder?

10. Many thoughtful persons argue that categorical opposition to capital punishment even for murder depreciates life. They say, rightly, that one function of law is to affirm and thereby reinforce values, and that one way law should do this is by making punishments "fit" crimes, not criminals. They say, rightly, that society's justified anger should be tamed and shaped by law into just retribution. And they also insist that to punish the taking of life with less than death reinforces the modern devaluing of life. Society, they say, must take lives to demonstrate that it properly reveres life.

11. These people understand the problem, if not necessarily the solution. The problem is the cheapening of life in our time. But other persons of sobriety reasonably regard capital punishment as part of the problem, not of the solution.

12. These are interesting times. The nation's security rests on its ability to deter aggression by treating its principal enemy's civil population as hostages; that is, national security rests on the credible threat of a form of warfare universally condemned since the Dark Ages, the wholesale slaughter of noncombatants. The nation's capital has just become the nation's first city in which abortions exceed births. The growing torrent of violence and other pornography in popular entertainment is both cause and effect of the desensitization of the nation.

13. Now a Texas convict is demanding prompt execution and asking that his death be televised. He says the spectacle would shatter support for capital punishment. Perhaps. But I detect no evident standards that would prevent, say, NBC from making an execution part of "The Big Event" and finding ample sponsors from among the companies subsidizing today's television violence.

14. Pending more powerful evidence that capital punishment is a powerful deterrent saving innocent lives, the burden of proof is

still on those who say that today the valuation of life can be enhanced by violent deaths inflicted by the state, in private, in cold
blood.

QUESTIONS

1. What use does Will make of the brief narration of the origins of capital punishment in America, in paragraphs 2–3?
2. Will builds the arguments for and against capital punishment to a
   statement of the point-at-issue, in paragraph 9. Does he order these
   arguments chronologically—that is, according to their history—or
   are the arguments pro and con roughly contemporaneous?
3. Is Will merely reviewing the arguments, or is he taking sides in the
   debate?
4. What point is he making in paragraphs 12–13, and how are these
   paragraphs related to the rest of the essay?
5. What use does he make of etymological and other kinds of definition? Is he stipulating a particular use of words, offering a theory,
   or seeking to make words more precise in their application?

WRITING ASSIGNMENT

Discuss your own attitude toward capital punishment, through the
arguments Will presents for and against it. Explain which arguments
you disagree with, before turning to those you agree with. Finish with
arguments of your own.

ANTHONY LEWIS
Let's Do It

1. In the early morning of Nov. 13, 1849, Charles Dickens came
upon a crowd outside Horsemonger Lane Jail in London. People
were waiting to see a Mr. and Mrs. Manning hanged for the
murder of their lodger. Dickens watched through the hours until
sunrise, as the crowd screamed and laughed and sang "Oh Mrs.
Manning" to the tune of "Oh Susannah." Later that day he wrote a
letter to The Times of London.

2.   "A sight so inconceivably awful as the wickedness and levity of the immense crowd collected at that execution could be imagined by no man . . ." he wrote. "I am solemnly convinced that nothing that ingenuity could devise to be done in this city, in the same compass of time, could work such ruin as one public execution."

3.   Three days later, after some other comment, Dickens wrote a second letter to the editor. He said executions attracted as spectators "the lowest, the most depraved, the most abandoned of mankind." And he said steps should be taken to limit titillation of the public by stories about a condemned person.

4.   "I would allow no curious visitors to hold any communication with him," Dickens said. "I would place every obstacle in the way of his sayings and doings being served up in print on Sunday mornings for the perusal of families."

5.   Not even Dickens, with his sense of the grotesque, could have imagined the spectacle enacted last week in the United States. The last sayings and doings of a murderer were retailed by the press. His picture graced the weekly journals. And the grossest details of his execution were reproduced on television, to be savored by millions of families in their homes.

6.   Most people I know who have been physically present when the state killed a human being—prison wardens, priests, newspaper reporters—have thereafter been opposed to capital punishment. Twenty years ago, on assignment as a reporter, I watched an electrocution in the District of Columbia jail. When it was over, the room smelled of roasted flesh.

7.   But to experience such scenes vicariously removes, for many, the nausea factor. Television drama has made blood and violence as acceptable as cherry pie. It was only a small additional step to restage an actual execution. And so we had the scene of Gary Gilmore's death on the evening news programs, and sketches of his last moment in sober newspapers.

8.   Some press agencies wanted to hire helicopters to circle over the prison yard, but the Federal Aviation Agency vetoed that idea. Reporters were forced to rely on hourly bulletins from the prison authorities, which some complained were dull.

9.   The great innovation in the Gilmore case was an execution literary agent. A movie producer named Lawrence Schiller signed the condemned man and his relatives to an exclusive contract for a film to be shown on television. Schiller was allowed to interview

Gilmore for many hours in prison, and then to attend the execution.

10. The agent gave the press the juicy details of the end. When the execution order was read out by an official, Schiller said, "Gary looked at him, holding his own, not quivering." It was Schiller who said he "believed" Gilmore's last words were "Let's do it"—a phrase that the press flashed across the land.

11. Later, the press learned that Gilmore in his last days had had an intense correspondence with an 11-year-old girl named Amber Hunt. Miss Hunt was interviewed, and a week later her voice was still being heard on the radio.

12. The slaughter of gladiators and Christians in the Circus Maximus is generally regarded as a symptom of the decadence of Rome. What does it say about a country when punishment for crime becomes a circus, to be reenacted in every home? Can a society savor such spectacles without being coarsened?

13. Murderers do not usually deserve sympathy. But the objection to having the state kill them in turn is not sentimental. Using the apparatus of official power to extinguish a life has corrupting consequences—the more so when capital punishment is, as it has become in this country, a spectacular occasion: an event cruel and unusual.

14. In the absence of convincing evidence that executions deter murderers, there must be a suspicion that the practice goes on to satisfy an atavistic public desire for dramatized vengeance. Revival of the death penalty in the United States may in fact encourage murder by persons such as Gary Gilmore—a man with suicidal impulses, who could have seen a way to assure his own spectacular death.

15. Dickens saw that point. In 1845, in a letter to a friend, he argued among other grounds for opposing capital punishment: "I believe it to have a horrible fascination for many of those persons who render themselves liable to it, impelling them onward to the acquisition of a frightful notoriety."

QUESTIONS

1. What is Lewis's purpose in writing—to show what Americans have become, or to warn them about what they may become? Does he generalize about all Americans?
2. How strong is the argument of deterrence for Lewis?

3. How do you think Lewis would answer Shaw's defense of capital punishment?

WRITING ASSIGNMENT

Analyze the reports of the Gary Gilmore legal proceedings in November and December, 1976 or those of his execution on January 17, 1977. Discuss the prominence given certain features of the case—for example, Gilmore's statements concerning the proceedings and his behavior, and his "last words." Or analyze the reporting of a similar event.

PERSUASION

BARBARA WARD
"Triage"

1.   Now that the House of Representatives has bravely passed its resolution on the "right to food"—the basic human right without which, indeed, all other rights are meaningless—it is perhaps a good moment to try to clear up one or two points of confusion that appear to have been troubling the American mind on the question of food supplies, hunger, and America's moral obligation, particularly to those who are not America's own citizens.

2.   The United States, with Canada and marginal help from Australia, are the only producers of surplus grain. It follows that if any part of the world comes up short or approaches starvation, there is at present only one remedy and it is in Americans' hands. Either they do the emergency feeding or people starve.

2.   It is a heavy moral responsibility. Is it one that has to be accepted?

4.   This is where the moral confusions begin. A strong school of thought argues that it is the flood tide of babies, irresponsibly produced in Asia, Africa and Latin America, that is creating the certainty of malnutrition and risk of famine. If these countries in-

sist on having babies, they must feed them themselves. If hard times set in, food aid from North America—if any—must go strictly to those who can prove they are reducing the baby flood. Otherwise, the responsible suffer. The poor go on increasing.

5.   This is a distinctly Victorian replay of Malthus.* He first suggested that population would go on rising to absorb all available supplies and that the poor must be left to starve if they would be incontinent. The British Poor Law was based on this principle. It has now been given a new descriptive analogy in America. The planet is compared to a battlefield. There are not enough medical skills and supplies to go round. So what must the doctors do? Obviously, concentrate on those who can hope to recover. The rest must die. This is the meaning of "triage."

6.   Abandon the unsavable and by so doing concentrate the supplies—in the battlefield, medical skills; in the world at large, surplus food—on those who still have a chance to survive.

7.   Thus the people with stable or stabilizing populations will be able to hold on. The human experiment will continue.

8.   It is a very simple argument. It has been persuasively supported by noted business leaders, trade-unionists, academics and presumed Presidential advisers. But "triage" is, in fact, so shot through with half truths as to be almost a lie, and so irrelevant to real world issues as to be not much more than an aberration.

9.   Take the half truths first. In the last ten years, at least one-third of the increased world demand for food has come from North Americans, Europeans and Russians eating steadily more high-protein food. Grain is fed to animals and poultry, and eaten as steak and eggs.

10. In real energy terms, this is about five times more wasteful than eating grain itself. The result is an average American diet of nearly 2,000 pounds of grain a year—and epidemics of cardiac trouble—and 400 pounds for the average Indian.

11. It follows that for those worrying about available supplies on the "battlefield," one American equals five Indians in the claims on basic food. And this figure masks the fact that much of the North American eating—and drinking—is pure waste. For instance, the

---

*Thomas Malthus (1766–1834), in his *Essay on the Principle of Population* (1798), argued that population growth would have to be controlled, because population increases faster than the food supply. He opposed relief for the poor and higher wages on the ground that these encouraged idleness and early marriage. G.L.

American Medical Association would like to see meat-eating cut by a third to produce a healthier nation.

12. The second distortion is to suggest that direct food aid is what the world is chiefly seeking from the United States. True, if there were a failed monsoon and the normal Soviet agricultural muddle next year, the need for an actual transfer of grain would have to be faced.

13. That is why the world food plan, worked out at Secretary of State Henry A. Kissinger's earlier prompting, asks for a modest reserve of grain to be set aside—on the old biblical plan of Joseph's "fat years" being used to prepare for the "lean."

14. But no conceivable American surplus could deal with the third world's food needs of the 1980's and 1990's. They can be met only by a sustained advance in food production where productivity is still so low that quadrupling and quintupling of crops is possible, provided investments begin now.

15. A recent Japanese study has shown that rice responds with copybook reliability to higher irrigation and improved seed. This is why the same world food plan is stressing a steady capital input of $30 billion a year in third-world farms, with perhaps $5 billion contributed by the old rich and the "oil" rich.

16. (What irony that this figure is barely a third of what West Germany has to spend each year to offset the health effects of overeating and overdrinking.)

17. To exclaim and complain about the impossibility of giving away enough American surplus grain (which could not be rice anyway), when the real issue is a sustained effort by all the nations in long-term agricultural investment, simply takes the citizens' minds off the real issue—where they can be of certain assistance— and impresses on them a nonissue that confuses them and helps nobody else.

18. Happily, the House's food resolution puts long-term international investment in food production firmly back into the center of the picture.

19. And this investment in the long run is the true answer to the stabilizing of family size. People do not learn restraint from "giveaways." (The arms industry's bribes are proof enough of that.) But the whole experience of the last century is that if parents are given work, responsibility, enough food and safe water, they have the sense to see they do not need endless children as insurance against calamity.

20. Because of food from the Great Plains and the reform of sanitation, Malthusian fears vanished as an issue in Europe and North America in the 1880's. China is below 2 percent population growth today on the basis of intensive agriculture and popular health measures.

21. Go to the root of the matter—investment in people, in food, in water—and the Malthus myth will fade in the third world as it has done already in many parts of it and entirely in the so-called first and second worlds.

22. It may be that this positive strategy of stabilizing population by sustained, skilled and well-directed investment in food production and in clean water suggests less drama than the hair-raising images of inexorably rising tides of children eating like locusts the core out of the whole world's food supplies.

23. But perhaps we should be wise to prefer relevance to drama. In "triage," there is, after all, a suggestion of the battlefield. If this is how we see the world, are we absolutely certain who deserves to win—the minority of guzzlers who eat 2,000 pounds of grain, or the majority of despairing men of hunger who eat 400 pounds?

24. History gives uncomfortable answers. No doubt as they left their hot baths and massage parlors for the joys of dining, vomiting and redining, Roman senators must have muttered and complained about the "awkwardness of the barbarians." But the barbarians won. Is this the battlefield we want? And who will "triage" whom?

DISCUSSION: PERSUASION

How we choose to present our ideas depends on our purpose in writing or speaking. The demands of exposition and persuasion are not the same. In exposition, we are guided by the need to make our ideas clear to the audience we have in mind. In persuasion, we are guided not only by the need for clarity but also by the need to present our ideas in the most convincing way. There are occasions when the need to persuade an audience quickly makes a brief but clear statement of assumptions imperative. An address to a jury allows a more leisured or extended statement of assumptions as well as an account of pertinent experiences. Socrates, in his "apology" to the jury that sentenced him to death, dealt at length with the charges against him in light of the principles by which he had lived.

Classical orators were concerned with defining the occasion of their speeches as a preliminary to organizing them. The rhetoric of the law courts (forensic rhetoric) usually required an extended narration or review of the facts of the case and an extended confirmation and refutation, since the defendant would want to establish the facts of his presumed innocence and to attack the charges made. In eulogies and funeral orations (ceremonial rhetoric) the narration, or account of a great man's deeds, might be the center of the oration and the refutation dispensed with altogether (it would be inappropriate in a funeral oration to defend the virtues of the dead man or to refute charges against him). Mark Antony's funeral oration, in Shakespeare's *Julius Caesar,* begins as a ceremonial oration and ends as an indictment of Brutus and his fellow conspirators. Antony is concerned ostensibly with praising the dead Caesar; actually, he turns this praise into an accusation of Caesar's murderers. The ironic repetition of "But Brutus is an honorable man" implies that the real issue is the character of Caesar's assailant—the very point-at-issue on which Brutus had defended himself in his previous statement to the assembled Romans. In the rhetoric of law-making bodies (deliberative rhetoric) narration, confirmation, and refutation are employed for other purposes: the narration may constitute a review of grievances that require a remedy in legislation; the confirmation, a defense of proposed legislation; refutation, an answer to objections raised against the legislation.

These points suggest this reminder: writers can make no choices in paragraph development, sentence structure, diction, and the general ordering of ideas until they have defined their purpose and decided what audience they wish to reach. And the act of writing has this advantage: new choices can be made if the original ones prove to be ineffective. Revision means something more than catching spelling and grammatical errors: it involves thinking and rethinking an essay in light of what writers discover they want to say—and in the most effective way.

QUESTIONS

1. The general issue of Ward's essay is the feeding of the poor throughout the world: the point-at-issue is stated in paragraph 3: "It is a heavy responsibility. Is it one that has to be accepted?" What are the real issues that Ward identifies later, in dealing with the point-at-issue?
2. What background or narration does Ward provide? How does she use this narration to state the assumptions of those who argue for triage?
3. What assumptions does she present, in opposition to those she is criticizing? How does she explain these assumptions?
4. Notice that Ward has put a deductive argument to the use of per-

suasion: this is why she must explain and defend her own assumptions. In doing so, what appeal to experience does she make, particularly in the concluding paragraph?
5. In the course of the essay, Ward poses a dilemma: either we select certain people to feed, or we all eventually starve and die. How does she deal with this dilemma?

WRITING ASSIGNMENT

Discuss the extent of your agreement with Ward's assumptions and conclusions. If you agree with her conclusion for different reasons, explain what these are, and defend them.

JONATHAN SWIFT

A Modest Proposal

For Preventing the Children of Poor People in Ireland from Being a Burden to Their Parents or Country, and for Making Them Beneficial to the Public

1. It is a melancholy object to those who walk through this great town, or travel in the country, when they see the streets, the roads, and cabin-doors crowded with beggars of the female sex, followed by three, four, or six children, all in rags, and importuning every passenger for an alms. These mothers, instead of being able to work for their honest livelihood, are forced to employ all their time in strolling to beg sustenance for their helpless infants: who, as they grow up, either turn thieves for want of work, or leave their dear native country to fight for the Pretender in Spain, or sell themselves to the Barbadoes.
2. I think it is agreed by all parties, that this prodigious number of children in the arms, or on the backs, or at the heels of their mothers, and frequently of their fathers, is, in the present deplorable state of the kingdom, a very great additional grievance; and, therefore, whoever could find out a fair, cheap, and easy method of making these children sound and useful members of the commonwealth, would deserve so well of the public, as to have his statue set up for a preserver of the nation.
3. But my intention is very far from being confined to provide

only for the children of professed beggars; it is of a much greater
extent, and shall take in the whole number of infants at a certain
age, who are born of parents in effect as little able to support them
as those who demand our charity in the streets.

4.   As to my own part, having turned my thoughts for many years
upon this important subject, and maturely weighed the several
schemes of other projectors, I have always found them grossly
mistaken in their computation. It is true, a child, just dropped
from its dam, may be supported by her milk for a solar year with
little other nourishment; at most, not above the value of two shillings, which the mother may certainly get, or the value in scraps,
by her lawful occupation of begging; and it is exactly at one year
old that I propose to provide for them in such a manner, as, instead
of being a charge upon their parents or the parish, or wanting food
and raiment for the rest of their lives, they shall, on the contrary,
contribute to the feeding, and partly to the clothing, of many thousands.

5.   There is likewise another great advantage in my scheme, that
it will prevent those voluntary abortions, and that horrid practice of
women murdering their bastard children, alas, too frequent among
us, sacrificing the poor innocent babes, I doubt more to avoid the
expense than the shame, which would move tears and pity in the
most savage and inhuman breast.

6.   The number of souls in this kingdom being usually reckoned
one million and a half, of these I calculate there may be about two
hundred thousand couple whose wives are breeders; from which
number I subtract thirty thousand couple, who are able to maintain their own children (although I apprehend there cannot be so
many, under the present distresses of the kingdom); but this being
granted, there will remain an hundred and seventy thousand
breeders. I again subtract fifty thousand for those women who
miscarry, or whose children die by accident or disease within the
year. There only remain a hundred and twenty thousand children
of poor parents annually born. The question therefore is how this
number shall be reared and provided for? which, as I have already
said, under the present situation of affairs, is utterly impossible by
all the methods hitherto proposed. For we can neither employ
them in handicraft or agriculture; we neither build houses (I mean
in the country) nor cultivate land: they can very seldom pick up a
livelihood by stealing until they arrive at six years old, except
where they are of towardly parts; although I confess they learn the

rudiments much earlier; during which time they can, however, be properly looked upon only as probationers; as I have been informed by a principal gentleman in the county of Cavan, who protested to me, that he never knew above one or two instances under the age of six, even in a part of the kingdom so renowned for the quickest proficiency in that art.

7. I am assured by our merchants that a boy or a girl before twelve years old is no salable commodity; and even when they come to this age they will not yield above three pounds or three pounds and half-a-crown at most, on the exchange; which cannot turn to account either to the parents or kingdom, the charge of nutriment and rags having been at least four times that value.

8. I shall now, therefore, humbly propose my own thoughts, which I hope will not be liable to the least objection.

9. I have been assured by a very knowing American of my acquaintance in London, that a young healthy child, well nursed, is, at a year old, a most delicious, nourishing, and wholesome food, whether stewed, roasted, baked, or boiled; and I make no doubt that it will equally serve in a fricassee or a ragout.

10. I do therefore humbly offer it to public consideration, that of the hundred and twenty thousand children already computed, twenty thousand may be reserved for breed, whereof only one-fourth part to be males; which is more than we allow to sheep, black cattle, or swine; and my reason is, that these children are seldom the fruits of marriage, a circumstance not much regarded by our savages, therefore one male will be sufficient to serve four females. That the remaining hundred thousand may, at a year old, be offered in sale to the persons of quality and fortune through the kingdom; always advising the mother to let them suck plentifully in the last month, so as to render them plump and fat for a good table. A child will make two dishes at an entertainment for friends; and when the family dines alone, the fore or hind quarter will make a reasonable dish, and, seasoned with a little pepper or salt, will be very good boiled on the fourth day, especially in winter.

11. I have reckoned, upon a medium, that a child just born will weigh twelve pounds, and in a solar year, if tolerably nursed, increaseth to twenty-eight pounds.

12. I grant this food will be somewhat dear, and therefore very proper for landlords, who, as they have already devoured most of the parents, seem to have the best title to the children.

13. Infants' flesh will be in season throughout the year, but more plentifully in March, and a little before and after: for we are told by a grave author, an eminent French physician, that fish being a prolific diet, there are more children born in Roman Catholic countries about nine months after Lent than at any other season; therefore, reckoning a year after Lent, the markets will be more glutted than usual, because the number of popish infants is at least three to one in this kingdom; and therefore it will have one other collateral advantage, by lessening the number of papists among us.

14. I have already computed the charge of nursing a beggar's child (in which list I reckon all cottagers, labourers, and four-fifths of the farmers) to be about two shillings per annum, rags included; and I believe no gentleman would repine to give ten shillings for the carcass of a good fat child, which, as I have said, will make four dishes of excellent nutritive meat, when he has only some particular friend, or his own family, to dine with him. Thus the squire will learn to be a good landlord, and grow popular among his tenants; the mother will have eight shillings net profit, and be fit for work till she produces another child.

15. Those who are more thrifty (as I must confess the times require) may flay the carcass; the skin of which, artificially dressed, will make admirable gloves for ladies, and summer-boots for fine gentlemen.

16. As to our city of Dublin, shambles[1] may be appointed for this purpose in the most convenient parts of it, and butchers we may be assured will not be wanting; although I rather recommend buying the children alive, and dressing them hot from the knife, as we do roasting pigs.

17. A very worthy person, a true lover of his country, and whose virtues I highly esteem, was lately pleased, in discoursing on this matter, to offer a refinement upon my scheme. He said, that many gentlemen of this kingdom, having of late destroyed their deer, he conceived that the want of venison might be well supplied by the bodies of young lads and maidens, not exceeding fourteen years of age, nor under twelve; so great a number of both sexes in every country being now ready to starve for want of work and service; and these to be disposed of by their parents, if alive, or otherwise by their nearest relations. But, with due deference to so excellent a

---

[1] Butcher shops. (All notes in this selection are the editor's.)

friend, and so deserving a patriot, I cannot be altogether in his sentiments; for as to the males, my American acquaintance assured me from frequent experience, that their flesh was generally tough and lean, like that of our schoolboys, by continual exercise, and their taste disagreeable; and to fatten them would not answer the charge. Then as to the females, it would, I think, with humble submission, be a loss to the public, because they soon would become breeders themselves: and besides, it is not improbable that some scrupulous people might be apt to censure such a practice (although indeed very unjustly) as a little bordering upon cruelty; which, I confess hath always been with me the strongest objection against any project, how well soever intended.

18. But in order to justify my friend, he confessed that this expedient was put into his head by the famous Psalmanazar,[2] a native of the island Formosa, who came from thence to London above twenty years ago; and in conversation told my friend, that in his country, when any young person happened to be put to death, the executioner sold the carcass to persons of quality as a prime dainty; and that in his time the body of a plump girl of fifteen, who was crucified for an attempt to poison the emperor, was sold to his Imperial Majesty's prime minister of state, and other great mandarins of the court, in joints from the gibbet, at four hundred crowns. Neither indeed can I deny, that if the same use were made of several plump young girls in this town, who, without one single groat to their fortunes, cannot stir abroad without a chair, and appear at playhouse and assemblies in foreign fineries which they never will pay for, the kingdom would not be the worse.

19. Some persons of a desponding spirit are in great concern about that vast number of poor people who are aged, diseased, or maimed; and I have been desired to employ my thoughts what course may be taken to ease the nation of so grievous an encumbrance. But I am not in the least pain upon that matter, because it is very well known, that they are every day dying, and rotting, by cold and famine, and filth and vermin, as fast as can be reasonably expected. And as to the younger labourers, they are now in almost as hopeful a condition: they cannot get work, and consequently pine away for want of nourishment, to a degree, that if at any time they are accidentally hired to common labour, they

---

[2] A French writer, George Psalmanazar, who posed as a native of Formosa in a fake book he published about that country in 1704, in England.

have not strength to perform it; and thus the country and themselves are happily delivered from the evils to come.

20. I have too long digressed, and therefore shall return to my subject. I think the advantages by the proposal which I have made are obvious and many, as well as of the highest importance.

21. For first, as I have already observed, it would greatly lessen the number of papists, with whom we are yearly overrun, being the principal breeders of the nation as well as our most dangerous enemies; and who stay at home on purpose with a design to deliver the kingdom to the Pretender, hoping to take their advantage by the absence of so many good Protestants, who have chosen rather to leave their country than stay at home and pay tithes against their conscience to an idolatrous Episcopal curate.[3]

22. Secondly, the poorer tenants will have something valuable of their own, which by law may be made liable to distress, and help to pay their landlord's rent; their corn and cattle being already seized, and money a thing unknown.

23. Thirdly, whereas the maintenance of an hundred thousand children, from two years old and upwards, cannot be computed at less than ten shillings a piece per annum, the nation's stock will be thereby increased fifty thousand pounds per annum; besides the profit of a new dish introduced to the tables of all gentlemen of fortune in the kingdom who have any refinement in taste. And the money will circulate among ourselves, the goods being entirely of our own growth and manufacture.

24. Fourthly, the constant breeders, besides the gain of eight shillings sterling per annum by the sale of their children, will be rid of the charge of maintaining them after the first year.

25. Fifthly, this food would likewise bring great custom to taverns; where the vintners will certainly be so prudent as to procure the best receipts for dressing it to perfection, and, consequently, have their houses frequented by all the fine gentlemen, who justly value themselves upon their knowledge in good eating: and a skilful cook, who understands how to oblige his guests, will contrive to make it as expensive as they please.

26. Sixthly, this would be a great inducement to marriage, which all wise nations have either encouraged by rewards, or enforced by laws and penalties. It would increase the care and tenderness of

---

[3] Swift is attacking the prejudice against Irish Catholics in his time, and also the motives of a number of Protestant dissenters from the Church of England.

mothers towards their children, when they were sure of a settlement for life to the poor babes, provided in some sort by the public,
to their annual profit instead of expense. We should soon see an
honest emulation among the married women, which of them could
bring the fattest child to the market. Men would become as fond of
their wives during the time of their pregnancy, as they are now of
their mares in foal, their cows in calf, or sows when they are ready
to farrow; nor offer to beat or kick them (as is too frequent a practice) for fear of a miscarriage.

27. Many other advantages might be enumerated. For instance,
the addition of some thousand carcasses in our exportation of bar-
relled beef; the propagation of swine's flesh, and improvement in
the art of making good bacon, so much wanted among us by the
great destruction of pigs, too frequent at our tables, which are no
way comparable in taste or magnificence to a well-grown, fat yearl-
ing child, which, roasted whole, will make a considerable figure at
a Lord Mayor's feast, or any other public entertainment. But this,
and many others, I omit, being studious of brevity.

28. Supposing that one thousand families in this city would be
constant customers for infants' flesh, besides others who might
have it at merry meetings, particularly weddings and christenings, I compute that Dublin would take off annually about twenty
thousand carcasses; and the rest of the kingdom (where probably
they will be sold somewhat cheaper) the remaining eighty thousand.

29. I can think of no one objection that will possibly be raised
against this proposal, unless it should be urged, that the number of
people will be thereby much lessened in the kingdom. This I freely
own, and it was indeed one principal design in offering it to the
world. I desire the reader will observe that I calculate my remedy
for this one individual kingdom of Ireland, and for no other that
ever was, is, or I think ever can be, upon earth. Therefore let no
man talk to me of other expedients: of taxing our absentees at five
shillings a pound: of using neither clothes nor household-furniture
except what is of our own growth and manufacture: of utterly
rejecting the materials and instruments that promote foreign luxury: of curing the expensiveness of pride, vanity, idleness, and
gaming in our women; of introducing a vein of parsimony, prudence, and temperance: of learning to love our country, wherein
we differ even from Laplanders, and the inhabitants of Topinam-

boo:[4] of quitting our animosities and factions, nor act any longer like the Jews, who were murdering one another at the very moment their city was taken:[5] of being a little cautious not to sell our country and consciences for nothing: of teaching landlords to have at least one degree of mercy towards their tenants: lastly, of putting a spirit of honesty, industry, and skill into our shopkeepers; who, if a resolution could now be taken to buy only our native goods, would immediately unite to cheat and exact upon us in the price, the measure, and the goodness, nor could ever yet be brought to make one fair proposal of just dealing, though often and earnestly invited to it.

30. Therefore I repeat, let no man talk to me of these and the like expedients, till he hath at least some glimpse of hope that there will ever be some hearty and sincere attempt to put them in practice.

31. But, as to myself, having been wearied out for many years with offering vain, idle, visionary thoughts, and at length utterly despairing of success, I fortunately fell upon this proposal; which, as it is wholly new, so it hath something solid and real, of no expense and little trouble, full in our own power, and whereby we can incur no danger in disobliging England. For this kind of commodity will not bear exportation, the flesh being of too tender a consistence to admit a long continuance in salt, although perhaps I could name a country which would be glad to eat up our whole nation without it.

32. After all, I am not so violently bent upon my own opinion as to reject any offer proposed by wise men which shall be found equally innocent, cheap, easy, and effectual. But before something of that kind shall be advanced in contradiction to my scheme, and offering a better, I desire the author, or authors, will be pleased maturely to consider two points. First, as things now stand, how they will be able to find food and raiment for a hundred thousand useless mouths and backs? And, secondly, there being a round million of creatures in human figure throughout this kingdom, whose whole subsistence put into a common stock would leave them in debt two millions of pounds sterling, adding those who are beggars by profession, to the bulk of farmers, cottagers, and labourers, with the wives and children who are beggars in effect; I

[4] A district of Brazil notorious for its barbarism and ignorance.
[5] Swift is referring to the fall of Jerusalem to the Babylonians.

desire those politicians who dislike my overture, and may perhaps be so bold as to attempt an answer, that they will first ask the parents of these mortals, whether they would not at this day think it a great happiness to have been sold for food at a year old, in the manner I prescribe, and thereby have avoided such a perpetual scene of misfortunes as they have since gone through, by the oppression of landlords, the impossibility of paying rent without money or trade, the want of common sustenance, with neither house nor clothes to cover them from the inclemencies of weather, and the most inevitable prospect of entailing the like, or greater miseries, upon their breed for ever.

33. I profess, in the sincerity of my heart, that I have not the least personal interest in endeavouring to promote this necessary work, having no other motive than the public good of my country, by advancing our trade, providing for infants, relieving the poor, and giving some pleasure to the rich. I have no children by which I can propose to get a single penny; the youngest being nine years old, and my wife past child-bearing.

QUESTIONS

1. Jonathan Swift (1667–1745), the son of English Protestant parents, was born and educated in Ireland. He therefore witnessed early in his life the sufferings of the Irish poor, most of whom were Catholic. Swift left Ireland in 1688 to make a career for himself in England; he returned to Ireland permanently in 1714, as Dean of St. Patrick's Cathedral in Dublin. In the succeeding years Swift wrote widely on various questions bearing on Ireland and England; for Ireland was an occupied country, impoverished and incapable of remedies for evils created by English policies. The Irish, for example, were restricted in selling their goods and could not produce enough food for themselves. In 1729 Swift, writing as a disinterested observer, proposed a "modest" solution to the poverty of the Irish. How does he establish the basic character and motives of this observer in the opening paragraphs of the proposal?

2. How does Swift reveal his attitude toward the writer of the proposal? Is he in accord with his general views of English motives? Are those motives stated directly or instead implied?

3. Is the proposer—and perhaps Swift himself—critical of the Irish poor, or does he exonerate them entirely?

4. Short of adopting the actual "modest proposal," is there another way of remedying the evils exposed in the course of the essay? In

other words, does Swift suggest other policies that would reduce poverty and starvation in Ireland?

5. In general, what strategy does Swift employ to deal with English policies and motives and perhaps Irish attitudes too?

6. How persuasive do you find the essay? Is it an essay of historical interest or literary interest only, or does it have something to say to people today?

WRITING ASSIGNMENTS

Write your own "modest proposal" for dealing with a current social or political evil. You may wish to write as yourself or, like Swift, impersonate someone who wishes to make a modest proposal. Maintain a consistent tone throughout your essay, or at least make any shifts in tone consistent with the character of your speaker and his or her motives in writing.

Contrast Swift's attack on the English with Ward's attack on the idea of "triage." Distinguish the various persuasive means that they employ.

BAYARD RUSTIN

The Premise of the Stereotype

1.   The resort to stereotype is the first refuge and chief strategy of the bigot. Though this is a matter that ought to concern everyone, it should be of particular concern to Negroes. For their lives, as far back as we can remember, have been made nightmares by one kind of bigotry or another.

2.   This urge to stereotype groups and deal with them accordingly is an evil urge. Its birthplace is in that sinister back room of the mind where plots and schemes are hatched for the persecution and oppression of other human beings.

3.   It comes out of many things, but chiefly out of a failure or refusal to do the kind of tough, patient thinking that is required of

THE PREMISE OF THE STEREOTYPE: In *Down the Line* by Bayard Rustin. Copyright © 1971 by Bayard Rustin. Originally appeared in the *New York Amsterdam News*, April 8, 1967. Reprinted by permission of Quadrangle/The New York Times Book Co.

difficult problems of relationship. It comes, as well, out of a desire
to establish one's own sense of humanity and worth upon the ruins
of someone else's. Nobody knows this, or should know it, better
than Negroes and Jews.

4.   Bigots have, for almost every day we have spent out of Africa
or out of Palestine, invented a whole catalogue of Negro and Jewish characteristics, invested these characteristics with inferior or
undesirable values, and, on the basis of these fantasies, have
engaged in the most brutal and systematic persecution.

5.   It seems to me, therefore, that it would be one of the great
tragedies of Negro and Jewish experience in a hostile civilization if
the time should come when either group begins using against the
other the same weapon which the white majorities of the West
used for centuries to crush and deny them their sense of humanity.

6.   All of which is to say that we ought all to be disturbed by a
climate of mutual hostility that is building up among certain segments of the Negro and Jewish communities in the ghettos.

7.   Jewish leaders know this and are speaking to the Jewish conscience about it. So far as Negroes are concerned, let me say that
one of the more unprofitable strategies we could ever adopt is now
to join in history's oldest and most shameful witch hunt, anti-
Semitism. This attitude, though not typical of most Negro communities, is gaining considerable strength in the ghetto. It sees the
Jew as the chief and only exploiter of the ghetto, blames the ghetto
on him, and seems to suggest that anything Jews do is inherent in
the idea of their Jewishness.

8.   I believe, though, that this attitude has two aspects—one entirely innocent of anti-Semitic animus. The first is that the Negro,
in responding justifiably to bitterness and frustration, blames the
plight of the ghetto on any visible reminder or representative of
white America. . . .

9.   Since in Harlem Jews happen to be the most immediate re-
minders of white American oppression, they naturally inherit the
wrath of black frustration. And I don't believe that the Negroes
who attack out of this attitude are interested in the subtleties of
ethnic, cultural, and religious distinction, or that they would find
any such distinction emotionally or intellectually useful.

10.   It is the other aspect of the attitude that is more dangerous,
that is consciously anti-Semitic, and that mischievously separates
Jews from other white Americans and uses against them the old

stereotypes of anti-Semitic slander and persecution. It is outrageous to blame Harlem on Jewishness. Harlem is no more the product of Jewishness than was American slavery and the subsequent century of Negro oppression in this country.

11. In the ghetto everybody gets a piece of the action: those who are Jews and those who are Christians; those who are white and those who are black; those who run the numbers and those who operate the churches; those—black and white—who own tenements and those—black and white—who own businesses.

12. Harlem is exploited by American greed. Even those who are now stirring up militant anti-Semitic resentments are exploiting the ghetto—the ghetto's mentality, its frustration, and its need to believe anything that brings it a degree of psychological comfort.

13. The Jews are no more angels than we are—there are some real grounds for conflict and contention between us as minority groups—but it is nonsense to divert attention from who it is that really oppresses Negroes in the ghetto. Ultimately the real oppressor is white American immorality and indifference, and we will be letting off the real oppressor too easily if we now concentrate our fulminations against a few Jews in the ghetto.

14. The premise of the stereotype is that everything that a man does defines his particular racial and ethnic morality. The people who say that about Jews are the same people who say it about Negroes. If we are now willing to believe what that doctrine says about Jews, then are we not obligated to endorse what it says about us?

15. I agree with James Baldwin entirely. I agree with him that we should "do something unprecedented: to create ourselves without finding it necessary to create an enemy . . . the nature of the enemy is history; the nature of the enemy is power; and what every black man, boy, woman, girl is struggling to achieve is some sense of himself or herself which this history and this power have done everything conceivable to destroy."

16. To engage in anti-Semitism is to engage in self-destruction—man's most tragic state.

QUESTIONS

1. Rustin deals with a specific point-at-issue—the attitude of the Harlem black to the Jewish businessman and landlord—but he addresses certain larger issues also. What are these issues?

2. These larger issues are a means—a strategy—of persuasion. Rustin
   might have appealed to the sense of fair play—another strategy—
   but he does not. Is the strategy he adopts more effective, in your
   opinion, and would an appeal to fair play have been ineffective?
3. Has Rustin sought to shame his reader? Is his tone accusing or
   conciliatory? Could the issue be treated in a satirical manner?

WRITING ASSIGNMENT

Rustin states: "The premise of the stereotype is that everything that a
man does defines his particular racial and ethnic morality." Show how
the "premise of the stereotype" can be used to deal unfairly with
another minority, social or ethnic: women in public life, women in
business, college students, the Irish, the Italians, the Poles, and so
forth.

ELIZABETH JANEWAY
Women and Change

1.   I have been wondering lately whether there is not a useful
and revealing analogy to be drawn between the position of women
today and that of the middle classes at the beginning of modern
times. It was the bourgeoisie which embodied the expansive forces
that ended the limitations laid on society by the feudal structure of
the Middle Ages. There have been arguments aplenty among his-
torians as to whether the bourgeoisie really represented a "progressive" force in this period or not. But if we leave aside the value
judgment implied by the word "progressive" we can surely agree
that the new class of merchants and traders and makers of goods
for sale and heapers-up of capital for future investment did function as the instrument which smashed hierarchical feudal society
at a time when feudal order, once sustaining, had become crip-
pling. Of course the rise of this class was a response to social and
economic trends already in being: to a growing population which,
by the twelfth century, had accumulated enough wealth and en-

WOMEN AND CHANGE: In *Between Myth and Morning* by Elizabeth Janeway. Reprinted by permission of William Morrow & Company, Inc. Copyright © 1972,
1973, 1974 by Elizabeth Janeway. Selection title by editor.

joyed enough time off from necessary labor to build the cathedrals and to set powerful minds considering physical relationships in the actual world in a way that would, in time, produce true science. It was a response to existing, continuing technological advance. If we take only the three inventions which Lynn White cites in his *Medieval Technology and Social Change,* namely, the stirrup, the crank which improved wind- and watermills and fathered the lathe, and the harness for draft animals, which allowed them to pull ploughs heavy enough to turn wet bottomlands into fertile fields, we see that a revolutionary reprogramming of work had already begun. No longer was its motive force to be that of human muscles. In the period of peace which followed the end of the Viking raids, trade flourished and traders with it. And so on.

2.   The strength of this new social force can be judged by the fact that it survived the disasters of the fourteenth century and, having done so, began to build an internal organization and to find a name of its own. A vitality of its own, too. Huizinga, in *The Waning of the Middle Ages,* has told unforgettably the tale of the decline and growing despair of the aristocracy of the fifteenth century. Against this dying fall, the vulgar, shoving rise of the bourgeoisie displayed a rough and not very attractive vigor. Chekhov wrote it all out for us, in terms we can understand, at a time when nineteenth-century Russia was still straddling the divide between a feudal society and modern times. Those charming, ineffectual aristocrats whose cherry orchard grew a crop of dreams but not of fruit confronted Lopakhin, the bourgeois climber, and went down before him. We sympathize, we regret their fate—but should the world grow nothing but dreams? As Firs, the old servant knew, the fruit had once been sold profitably; the orchard had once fed its product into the real world. When it ceased to do so, other forces in the real world rose to reclaim the dream orchard and return it to use. A new use, be it noted, for Lopakhin had no intention of marketing cherries. He was planning a housing development.

3.   The middle class, that is, not only took over power from the aristocracy of the feudal world as the centuries passed, but it invented new ways to do things, new ways to live, new connections among human beings—not simply new knowledge, but new kinds of knowledge. This didn't happen because of a sudden mutation in the human species though, if we believed the neo-Darwinians, we'd have to think so. It happened because a whole order of society was given an opportunity for the first time to use the minds

and energies and imaginations of its members. If they smashed the old order, it was done in a fit of absent-mindedness for the most part, just because it got in the way. They were building a new order in a new place. Trade. Money. Towns. Capitalism. Exploration; ruthless, inhuman, this nascent force discovered the unknown New World, exploited it, grew rich on it and founded new societies there, one of which, at least, imagined new human values. Indeed, new human values and ideals rose like weeds in the footsteps of the bourgeois revolution. We owe it the Renaissance and the Reformation and the Enlightenment and the ideas of democracy, science, the factory system, the modern world. It created a society that was unimaginable in the world that gave it birth.

4.　One of the things it has created is a female sex that is ceasing to be second and subordinate, and that is beginning to come together. Around us a world seems fading toward a dying fall as its hope and its imagination fail. That is the world the bourgeois revolution made. So perhaps it is time for a new force to venture out. A female revolution? Not exclusively, by any means. But because women are the repository of the largest store of unused abilities they will surely be a primary source and resource of ideas and energy. We have been taught to be pleasing, yes, polite and deferential in public, properly reverent before the great male structure of ideas that governs the world. But in fact we have never been all that reverential inside our own heads. Good, devoted, loyal wives may see men's hierarchies as games. And when you tell a woman that her proper role is that of mother, its centrality will affect the way she looks at the world. "They're all like little boys, aren't they?" say those good wives to each other.

5.　I think it very possible that the fundamental irreverence with which women regard men's world will, in time, provide the answer to those who deplore the tendency of women who are moving out into men's world to move also into men's roles. At the beginning, acting a male role is a learning process; but even today, women are modifying masculine ways of doing things within the business structure. It is extremely difficult for men, even men of great good will, to conceive of interpersonal relationships which do not incorporate an element of dominance. Someone, they assume, has to be top dog. Women find it much easier to imagine, to create and to work within relationships of shifting power and initiative; you're better at this, I'm better at that, but it won't hurt for each of us to know how to do all that we're responsible for doing. These attitudes come out of old, normative experience. We expect to be able to ask for help. The "best-friendships" we grew up with were more often flexible rather than one-way dominant. And, to a considerable degree, we are less hung up on issues of "face." We have never had much "face" to worry about.

6.   In the end I suspect that we are not simply going to modify man's world, as the bourgeoisie modified the feudal world; we are also going to amplify it, as they did. Man's world, the power world, is impoverished and in need of emotional values which will restore to it true human significance. They can't be thought up and pumped in like a transfusion of idealism. They will grow with new activities and processes not yet conceived, but which will deal with areas of life now empty. "The Lonely Crowd" desperately needs new, functioning communities. There is an enormous amount of work for such communities to do, linking individuals together and supporting isolated families. These communities will coalesce to meet felt needs which are now unsatisfied and unsatisfiable. They will involve themselves in political action at all levels. They will begin to shape new structures of living and new connections between people. They will turn up rewards and pleasures we have no way of picturing. And they can begin anywhere, come together at any level to achieve any sort of goal, great or small. Perhaps some will start with a few women who decide to introduce neighbors to each other, either for a purpose or simply for social interaction; some of these have already started. Perhaps some denizens of the residential ghettos we call housing developments will set up meeting places within them for discussions or learning or gripe sessions—or who knows what? Energy shortages promote car-pooling, and car-pooling involves organization. High food prices and other consumer issues join housewives together for talk and protest. They get gardens started, and gardeners exchange advice, and produce too. Any aggregate can grow, under the right circumstances, into a snowballing movement.

7.   Such a world of ordinary daylight, one that lies not only beyond old myths but beyond the rosy light of dawn too, is where women are going; not easily, not simply, not without making mistakes, some of which will be grievous, not without sacrifices and losses. We face struggle and setback and boredom. We will find our hopes overblown, our efforts ineffective often and often. But

we have no choice, for this is reality and we can't live in fantasyland any more. "For the time being, here we all are," wrote Auden,

> Back in the moderate Aristotelian city
> Of darning and the Eight-Fifteen, where Euclid's geometry
> And Newton's mechanics would account for our experience,
> And the kitchen table exists because I scrub it . . .
> There are bills to be paid, machines to keep in repair,
> Irregular verbs to learn, the Time Being to redeem
> From insignificance. The happy morning is over,
> The night of agony still to come; the time is noon.*

8.   It is not Utopia and never will be, but it is the world we have been given and can learn to change. And will change, according to human capacities and for common ends.

QUESTIONS

1. Do you think Janeway is writing to women only, or to a general audience including men and women?
2. What are the points of analogy between the middle class at the end of the feudal period and women today? Which of these points does Janeway stress most?
3. What persuasive devices does she employ, in addition to a carefully developed argument? Does she make an appeal to the reader's emotions?

WRITING ASSIGNMENT

Compare Janeway's view of women with Parkinson's, in his essay "Imperative Tense." Give attention to implicit assumptions.

---

* From "For the Time Being," in *The Collected Poetry of W. H. Auden*. Copyright, 1945, by W. H. Auden. By permission of Random House, Inc.

INTERPRETATION
OF EVIDENCE

WALTER HOUGHTON
The Victorian Woman

1.   Of the three conceptions of woman current in the Victorian period, the best known is that of the submissive wife whose whole excuse for being was to love, honor, obey—and amuse—her lord and master, and to manage his household and bring up his children. In that role her character and her life were completely distinct from his:

> Man for the field and woman for the hearth;
> Man for the sword, and for the needle she;
> Man with the head, and woman with the heart;
> Man to command, and women to obey;
> All else confusion.

Against that conservative view, spoken by the Prince's father in Tennyson's poem,[1] the Princess Ida represents the most advanced thought. She is the "new woman," in revolt against her legal and social bondage (and against the boredom of life in homes where servants and nurses now do all the household chores), and demanding equal rights with men: the same education, the same suffrage, the same opportunity for professional and political careers. Ida's passionate oration closes with a prophecy which Tennyson hardly imagined would come true:

> Everywhere
> Two heads in council, two beside the hearth,
> Two in the tangled business of the world,

[1] *The Princess* (1847), Pt. V, lines 437–41. See John Killham, *Tennyson and "The Princess": Reflections of an Age* (London, 1958) for an illuminating account of the whole question.

THE VICTORIAN WOMAN: In *The Victorian Frame of Mind, 1830–1870* (Yale University Press, 1957). Reprinted by permission of the publisher. Selection title by editor.

> Two in the liberal offices of life,
> Two plummets dropt for one to sound the abyss
> Of science and the secrets of the mind;
> Musician, painter, sculptor, critic, more.[2]

Between these two poles there was a middle position entirely characteristic of the time in its mediation between conservative and radical thinking. By all means let us remove the legal disabilities and give "more breadth of culture"; but higher education is unwise, the vote is dubious, and professional careers are dangerous. For after all woman is *not* man; she has her own nature and function in life, not inferior to his but entirely different; and the only test to apply to the "woman question" is simply, "Does this study or this activity help or injure her womanhood?" That is Tennyson's stand, expounded by the Prince and Ida at the close of the poem. Together they

> Will clear away the parasitic forms
> That seem to keep her up but drag her down—
> Will leave her space to burgeon out of all
> Within her—let her make herself her own
> To give or keep, to live and learn and be
> All that not harms distinctive womanhood.
> For woman is not undevelopt man,
> But diverse.

Let be with the proud watchword of "equal,"

>   seeing either sex alone
> Is half itself, and in true marriage lies
> Nor equal, nor unequal. Each fulfils
> Defect in each.[3]

2.   What is meant by "distinctive womanhood" and what defect in man the woman should fulfill are only implied by Tennyson. The answers are spelled out in Ruskin's important lecture "Of Queens'

---

[2] Ibid., Pt. II, lines 155–61. Amy Cruse, *The Victorians and Their Reading*, chap. 16, gives a good sketch of "The New Woman," with many illustrations from contemporary literature.
[3] *The Princess*, Pt. VII, lines 253–60, 283–6.

Gardens" in 1865. There he begins by rejecting the notion both that woman is "the shadow and attendant image of her lord, owing him a thoughtless and servile obedience," and that she has a feminine mission and feminine rights that entitle her to a career in the world like man's. Her true function is to guide and uplift her more worldly and intellectual mate: "His intellect is for speculation and invention; his energy for adventure, for war, and for conquest, wherever war is just, wherever conquest necessary. But the woman's power is for rule, not for battle,—and her intellect is not for invention or creation, but for sweet ordering, arrangement, and decision." Although this lofty theory had been gaining ground through the 1850's, Ruskin is aware that he is challenging the ordinary assumptions of male superiority and command. He marshals his evidence. In Shakespeare and Scott, in Dante and Homer, women are "infallibly faithful and wise counsellors"; and by their virtue and wisdom men are redeemed from weakness or vice. Then, with their role defined, he proceeds at once to his description of the home, since it is women so conceived who make it a temple and a school of virtue. The more reason, therefore, to keep it a walled garden. While the man in his rough work must encounter all peril and trial, and often be subdued or misled, and always hardened, "he guards the woman from all this; within his house, as ruled by her, unless she herself has sought it, need enter no danger, no temptation, no cause of error or offence."[4]

3. This woman worship, as it came to be called in the sixties, was as much indebted to the need for fresh sources of moral inspiration as it was to Romanticism in general. In a sketch by Lancelot Smith, the hero of Kingsley's *Yeast* (made, it should be noted, when his only bible was Bacon), Woman was portrayed walking across a desert, the half-risen sun at her back and a cross in her right hand, "emblem of self-sacrifice." In the foreground were scattered groups of men. As they caught sight of this "new and divine ideal of her sex,"

[4] "Of Queens' Gardens," sec. 68 in *Works*, 18, 111–22. With the last remark cf. George Eliot in "Amos Barton," *Scenes of Clerical Life, 1,* chap. 7, p. 85: "A loving woman's world lies within the four walls of her own home; and it is only through her husband that she is in any electric communication with the world beyond." In *Silas Marner* the bad habits of Godfrey and Dunstan Cass are attributed mainly to their growing up in a home without a mother (chap. 3, pp. 30–1), and Godfrey longs to marry Nancy Lammeter because she "would make home lovely" and help him conquer his weakness of will (chap. 3, pp. 39–41)—which is exactly what she does effect after the marriage (chap. 17, pp. 207–8).

the scholar dropt his book, the miser his gold, the savage his weapons; even in the visage of the half-slumbering sot some nobler recollection seemed wistfully to struggle into life. . . . The sage . . . watched with a thoughtful smile that preacher more mighty than himself. A youth, decked out in the most fantastic fopperies of the middle age, stood with clasped hands and brimming eyes, as remorse and pleasure struggled in his face; and as he looked, the fierce sensual features seemed to melt, and his flesh came again to him like the flesh of a little child.

The drawing is entitled "Triumph of Woman."[5] Other writers emphasized a more specific mission in more mundane terms: to counteract the debasing influence on religion as well as morals of a masculine life preoccupied with worldly goods and worldly ambitions. Mrs. Sara Ellis, whose *Daughters of England, Wives of England,* and *Women of England* were standard manuals, brought that argument to bear directly on the "Behaviour to Husbands." Since the life of men, especially businessmen, is tending, she said, to lower and degrade the mind, to make its aims purely material, and to encourage a selfish concern for one's own interests, a wife should be supremely solicitous for the advancement of her husband's intellectual, moral, and spiritual nature. She should be "a companion who will raise the tone of his mind from . . . low anxieties, and vulgar cares" and will "lead his thoughts to expatiate or repose on those subjects which convey a feeling of identity with a higher state of existence beyond this present life."[6] Indeed, the moral elevation of man became so closely identified with this femi-

---

[5] Chap. 10, pp. 148–50. Kingsley was one of the leading exponents (along with Ruskin, Tennyson, Patmore, and—more moderately—George Eliot) of this view of woman. See his statement in 1870 (*Letters and Memories,* 2, 283: unabridged ed., 2, 330): He will continue, he says, "to set forth in every book I write (as I have done for twenty-five years) woman as the teacher, the natural and therefore divine guide, purifier, inspirer of the man."

This woman worship was not, of course, universal. It is less likely to be found among "earnest" Victorians than "enthusiastic" Victorians. It is conspicuously absent from Macaulay, Carlyle, Trollope, and both the Arnolds, and from Mill as a general principle (Mrs. Taylor is a very special case!). In "Emancipation—Black and White," (1865), *Science and Education,* pp. 68–9, Huxley protested against "the new woman-worship which so many sentimentalists and some philosophers are desirous of setting up."

[6] *The Wives of England. Their Relative Duties, Domestic Influence, and Social Obligations* (London, 1843), pp. 99–100.

nine duty that a moralist like Baldwin Brown in his sermons called *The Home Life* was ready to blame women for the deterioration of men under the hardening influence of business. They have themselves succumbed to mean desires for money and family position; or they have been seduced by the ridiculous phantom of woman's rights when their true power, the birthright they would sell for a mess of pottage, is the "power to love, to serve, to save." But many, thank God, are still faithful to their trust: "I know women whose hearts are an unfailing fountain of courage and inspiration to the hard-pressed man, who but for them must be worsted in life's battle . . . and who send forth husband or brother each morning with new strength for his conflict, armed, as the lady armed her knight of old, with a shield which he may not stain in any unseemly conflicts, and a sword which he dares only use against the enemies of truth, righteousness and God." Like the hero, the angel in the house serves, or should serve, to preserve and quicken the moral idealism so badly needed in an age of selfish greed and fierce competition.[7]

4.   This accounts (as Brown's remark would suggest) for the wide hostility to her emancipation. Feminist claims to intellectual equality with man and to the same education and professional opportunity were attacked by liberals—let alone conservatives; partly, no doubt, to forestall competition, but much more to prevent what they honestly believed would mean the irreparable loss of a vital moral influence. Lancelot Smith is the more eager to assert his mental superiority over Argemone, the heroine of *Yeast* (who imagined there was no intellectual difference between the sexes), and at the same time to look up to her "as infallible and inspired" on all "questions of morality, of taste, of feeling," because he longs to teach her "where her true kingdom lay,—that the heart, and not the brain, enshrines the priceless pearl of womanhood."[8] Even a perfectly commonplace writer like Edwin Hood calls a chapter of *The Age and Its Architects* "Woman the Reformer" and begins by announcing: "The hope of society is in woman! The hope of the age is in woman! On her depends mainly the righting of wrongs, the correcting of sins, and the success of all missions," and goes on, therefore, to condemn the utterly mistaken tendency now growing up to encourage women to enter professional and political

[7] Brown, pp. 23–5.
[8] Chap. 10, pp. 143–5.

careers.[9] All this is touched with melodramatic and sentimental exaggeration, but many intelligent women—George Eliot, Mrs. Humphry Ward, Mrs. Lynn Linton, Beatrice Potter Webb, for example—viewed with uneasiness or apprehension any emancipation of their sex which would weaken its moral influence by distracting attention to the outside world or by coarsening the feminine nature itself.[10]

5. However conceived, the Victorian woman was not Venus, nor was meant to be. If it was only the feminists who rejected love—and often dressed accordingly—their more conservative sisters were not exactly objects of desire. Their sexual attraction was kept under wraps, many and voluminous. To employ it, except obliquely, was to run the risk of being considered "fast." Victorian ideas about sex were—very Victorian.

BIBLIOGRAPHY

Brown, James Baldwin. *The Home Life: in the Light of Its Divine Idea* (1866). New York, 1967.

Cross, J. W. *George Eliot's Life as Related in Her Letters and Journals.* 3 vols. New York, 1885. Vols. 22–24 of her *Works.*

Cruse, Amy. *The Victorians and Their Reading.* Boston and New York, 1935.

Eliot, George. *Works,* Illustrated Cabinet Edition, 24 vols. New York, n.d.

Ellis, Sara. *The Wives of England, Their Relative Duties, Domestic Influence, and Social Obligations.* London, 1843.

Hood, Edwin P. *The Age and Its Architects. Ten Chapters on the English People, in Relation to the Times* (1850). London, 1852.

Huxley, Thomas Henry. *Science and Education. Essays* (1893). New York, 1898.

Killham, John. *Tennyson and "The Princess": Reflections of an Age.* London, 1958.

Kingsley, Charles. *His Letters, and Memories of His Life,* ed. by his wife (1879), 2 vols. New York, 1900 ["abridged edition"]

——. *Works,* 28 vols. London, 1880–85.

——. *Yeast. A Problem* (1851), in *Works,* Vol. 2.

Ruskin, John. *Works,* 39 vols. ed. E. T. Cook and A. D. O. Wedderburn. London, 1902–12.

Tennyson, Alfred Lord. *The Poetic and Dramatic Works,* ed. W. J. Rolfe. Boston and New York, 1898.

Beatrice Webb. *My Apprenticeship* (1926). London and New York, 1950.

[9] Pages 393, 400. The particular sins woman is to correct (pp. 393–4)—revolution, prostitution, and atheism—are major anxieties of the period.

[10] The main document is "An Appeal against Female Suffrage," *The Nineteenth Century,* 25 (1889), 781–8, signed by about 100 women, including Mrs. T. H. Huxley, Mrs. Leslie Stephen, Mrs. Matthew Arnold, Mrs. Walter Bagehot, and Mrs. Arnold Toynbee, as well as all of those cited in the text except George Eliot. For her, see Cross' *Life, 3,* 346, in his summary of her character and ideas. There is an account of this "Appeal" by Beatrice Webb, *My Apprenticeship,* pp. 302–4.

DISCUSSION: INTERPRETATION OF EVIDENCE

The kind of evidence writers present depends on whether their approach in an essay is chiefly inductive or deductive. If they assume that their major ideas will be accepted, they will select explanatory and illustrative material to remind readers of what they already know and to provide a background of ideas. If writers intend to establish the probability of their ideas, they will present explanations and arguments to clarify and support them. Whether their reasoning is chiefly inductive or deductive, the writers' evidence will represent their own point of view. However, they will also select a variety of examples to show that other people in different circumstances could arrive at the same conclusion.

The effective presentation of evidence depends on its organization: if it is disordered, the most convincing evidence will persuade few people. The principle of order will depend on the nature of the subject and the thesis—some points and examples must be presented in chronological order—as well as on the audience.

In choosing evidence it is important to distinguish between primary and secondary sources—between first-hand accounts by participants or observers, and later reports and interpretations. Primary evidence must be sifted for differing versions of an event and for distinctive viewpoints that color the reporting. More than ten years after the assassination of President Kennedy, authorities disagree on what to consider evidence and on what alleged eyewitnesses heard or saw. Determining the reliability of certain eyewitness accounts is one of the writer's major difficulties; the motives of witnesses can obviously affect the reports of events and their interpretation. A German general's account of the Normandy invasion, in a dispatch to Hitler, is certain to be different from the account of an American general witnessing the same events. Secondary sources may help the writer determine what is factual and accurate in interpreting primary sources, but these secondary sources also must be used with caution since later writers often shape evidence to fit a particular view of man or history. Primary and secondary sources supplement each other as means to arriving at the truth about a subject. As in all inductive investigations, the truth can be probable and never certain, but a careful sifting and comparison of evidence can increase that probability considerably.

QUESTIONS

1. What kinds of primary evidence does Houghton draw on?
2. What would have been lost if Houghton had drawn his evidence

solely from poems and novels of the Victorian age? Could an accurate portrayal of the American woman be drawn from contemporary films or magazine fiction?

3. What information is reserved for the footnotes? Is it of less weight or significance than the information of the text?

4. Why does Houghton believe that the desire to preserve "the angel in the house" is a sufficient explanation for widespread hostility toward emancipation? Why is it important to cite the views of women like George Eliot and Beatrice Potter Webb?

5. How does the concluding comment on sexual attraction (developed in the succeeding section of Houghton's book) support the thesis of this section?

WRITING ASSIGNMENTS

Use magazine advertisements to draw a conclusion about qualities generally taken to be ideal in housewives. Be careful to note differences that suggest divergent views.

Compare the fathers, teenagers, or high-school or college students in various television advertisements or shows to determine whether they are stereotyped.

Use primary and secondary sources to determine how closely the fictional character in one of the works listed below corresponds to the historical person:

a. Stalin, in Solzhenitsyn's *The First Circle*
b. Hitler, in Richard Hughes' *The Fox in the Attic*
c. Franklin or Eleanor Roosevelt, in Dore Schary's *Sunrise at Campobello*
d. Winston Churchill, in Rolf Hochhuth's *Soldiers*

THEMATIC TABLE OF CONTENTS

INDEX OF AUTHORS AND TOPICS